CON

D0119995

1994

DIRECTIONS IN
MANAGING CONSTRUCTION

CONSTRUCTION MANAGEMENT AND ENGINEERING
Edited by John F. Peel Brahtz

DIRECTIONS IN MANAGING CONSTRUCTION

A CRITICAL LOOK AT PRESENT AND FUTURE INDUSTRY PRACTICES, PROBLEMS, AND POLICIES

DONALD S. BARRIE
Vice President
Kaiser Engineers, Inc.

CITY OF BIRMINGHAM
LIBRARY
POLYTECHNIC

A Wiley-Interscience Publication
JOHN WILEY & SONS, New York • Chichester • Brisbane • Toronto

CITY OF BIRMINGHAM
POLYTECHNIC LIBRARY

BOOK
No. 05205778

SUBJECT
No. 690·068 | Bar

Copyright © 1981 by John Wiley & Sons, Inc.

All rights reserved. Published simultaneously in Canada.

Reproduction or translation of any part of this work
beyond that permitted by Sections 107 or 108 of the
1976 United States Copyright Act without the permission
of the copyright owner is unlawful. Requests for
permission or further information should be addressed to
the Permissions Department, John Wiley & Sons, Inc.

Library of Congress Cataloging in Publication Data:

Barrie, Donald S
   Directions in managing construction.

   (Construction management and engineering ISSN 0193-
9750)
   "A Wiley-Interscience publication."
   Bibliography: p.
   Includes indexes.
   1. Construction industry—United States—Management.
I. Title.

HD9715.U52B37   624′.068   80-20001
ISBN 0-471-04642-6

Printed in the United States of America

10 9 8 7 6 5 4 3 2 1

To those men and women who have helped themselves, their associates, their company, and the industry through demonstrated performance, leadership, and integrity.

CONTRIBUTORS

Audrey Barrie, Free Lance Writer
Diablo, California

John D. Borcherding, Associate Professor,
University of Texas at Austin, Austin, Texas

D. M. Bridges, Partner, Thelen, Marrin, Johnson and
Bridges, San Francisco, California

Paul P. Burke, General Manager National Accounts,
Ingersoll-Rand Company, San Leandro, California

Gerald L. Challenger, Manager, Equal Employment Opportunity
Kaiser Engineers, Inc., Oakland, California

Keith Crandall, Professor
University of California, Berkeley, California

Joel B. Leighton, Executive Director, Associated General
Contractors of Massachusetts, Chestnut Hill, Massachusetts

Raymond L. Levitt, Associate Professor
Massachusetts Institute of Technology, Cambridge, Massachusetts

Franklin T. Matthias, Consulting Professional Engineer,
Danville, California

George T. McCoy, President
Guy F. Atkinson Company, South San Francisco, California

S. R. McDonald, Division Construction Manager,
Kaiser Engineers, Inc., Oakland, California

Dennis F. Murphy, Senior Project Engineer
Exxon Company, U.S.A., Los Angeles, California

Boyd C. Paulson, Jr., Associate Professor,
Stanford University, Palo Alto, California

B. F. Thompson, Manager, Sales and Marketing Administration
Kaiser Cement Corp., Oakland, California

R. H. Verdier, Project Manager,
Kaiser Engineers, Inc., Oakland, California

Rolland M. Wilkening, President
Barton-Mallow Company, Detroit, Michigan

SERIES PREFACE

Industry observers agree that most construction practitioners do not fully exploit the state of the art. We concur in this general observation. Further, we have acted by directing this series of works on Construction Management and Engineering to the continuing education and reference needs of today's practitioners.

Our design is inspired by the burgeoning technologies of systems engineering, modern management, information systems, and industrial engineering. We believe that the latest developments in these areas will serve to close the state of the art gap if they are astutely considered by management and knowledgeably applied in operations with personnel, equipment, and materials.

When considering the pressures and constraints of the world economic environment, we recognize an increasing trend toward large-scale operations and greater complexity in the construction product. To improve productivity and maintain acceptable performance standards, today's construction practitioner must broaden his concept of innovation and seek to achieve excellence through knowledgeable utilization of the resources. Therefore our focus is on skills and disciplines that support productivity, quality, and optimization in all aspects of the total facility acquisition process and at all levels of the management hierarchy.

We distinctly believe our perspective to be aligned with current trends and changes that portend the future of the construction industry. The books in this series should serve particularly well as textbooks at the graduate and senior undergraduate levels in a university construction curriculum or continuing education program.

JOHN F. PEEL BRAHTZ

La Jolla, California
February 1977

PREFACE

Construction projects are becoming increasingly complex, and full exploitation of the existing state of the art is becoming increasingly difficult. In keeping with the objectives of the Wiley-Interscience Series on Construction Management and Engineering, this book focuses on overall policy level considerations regarding the existing state of the art, current and emerging major industry problems, potential solutions, and guidance for future evolution.

One of the major problems of the entire construction industry is its fragmentation and consequent lack of overall industry spokesmen. This book represents an effort to outline the overall industry position as seen by a number of policy level spokesmen representing each of the major industry divisions including residential, building, industrial, and heavy construction along with special interest groups whose interaction will affect the continued evolution of the industry.

This book is intended to provide policy level guidance and to stimulate thought to concerned construction managers, superintendents, engineers, craftsmen, functional specialists, and other special interest groups at all organizational levels. It recognizes that material and equipment suppliers, organized labor, employee and owner associations, lawyers, educators, government regulators, minorities, and others form an integral part of the industry and that construction managers and leaders of the future must effectively bring together all segments of the industry and its special interest groups if improved performance is to be achieved in the ever changing climate foreseen for the future.

As a college text, this volume can serve as an overall guide to the state of the art of the entire construction industry as seen by recognized industry leaders. It can also be a valuable reference to the underlying problems of the industry that must be overcome if the construction industry in the United States is to continue in a position of leadership in domestic and world evolution. While the preponderance of material is based on functional and managerial concepts, all of the industry spokesmen recognize that performance in today's and tomorrow's climate requires that managers and leaders at every organizational level must understand and help to achieve the humanistic and social needs of the individual, which must also be attained along with technical excellence if the goals of productivity improvement and industry success are to be achieved.

DONALD S. BARRIE

Diablo, California
November 1980

CONTENTS

CHAPTER 9   MATERIAL AND EQUIPMENT SUPPLIERS   203

PART III   SPECIAL INTEREST GROUPS AND OTHER FACTORS

CHAPTER 10   CONSTRUCTION LABOR UNIONS IN THE
                  UNITED STATES   231

CHAPTER 11   EMPLOYER AND OWNER ASSOCIATIONS   253

CHAPTER 12   OPEN SHOP MOVEMENT   279

CHAPTER 13   LEGAL AND CONTRACTUAL
                  CONSIDERATIONS   301

DIRECTIONS IN
MANAGING CONSTRUCTION

PART 1

CHANGE AND THE CONSTRUCTION INDUSTRY

CHAPTER 1

INTRODUCTION TO THE MANAGEMENT OF CONSTRUCTION PRODUCTS

Donald S. Barrie

"The management boom is over. The time for management performance has come." These words of Peter Drucker,* while referring to the broad spectrum of American business, are especially appropriate in the construction industry. From the end of World War II to the end of the 1960s heavy construction projects became larger and more challenging with each passing year. Industrial projects grew at an unprecedented rate, culminating in billion dollar nuclear power plants. Housing and commercial construction grew fully with the growth of our economy. In the construction industry the growth of electronic data processing (EDP) resulted in widespread use of several new management tools including Program Evaluation and Review Technique (PERT), Critical Path Method scheduling (CPM), Management Information Systems (MIS), Project Management System (PMS), and many other computer-based interrelated programs based on a common data bank and heralding a new era in construction efficiency and performance. The sharp growth of the economy and the unprecedented demand for construction of all types may be moderating in the United States, while continuing at an even greater rate in other parts of the world such as the Middle East, Canada and South America. Federal regulation and the emergence of the environmental or consumer group intervenor have placed new complications on construction projects in the United States affecting the single-family home as well as nuclear power plants.

*Management, Harper & Row, New York, 1974.

Everywhere we are told that we are in an age of the optimization of planning, scheduling, and controlling construction projects. The CPM precedence diagram has finally brought logic to the industry and multipage computer reports purport to track performance against the plan down to the smallest details. Yet increasingly many of our projects are out of control. Costs are exceeding estimates. completion times are exceeding schedules, and owners are becoming increasingly dissatisfied with the status quo. Some blame organized labor for the inability to achieve forecast costs and completion dates on major projects, including almost every nuclear power plant and the Alaska Pipeline. Yet similar dissatisfaction takes place on many open shop projects. Others blame the designers who continue to revise plans and specifications throughout the program. Still others blame the increasing governmental regulation and question whether we have passed the point of reasonableness. Contractor management blames labor and the design engineer. Labor blames management. And the owner blames them all. Industrial owners have listened to the promises of the management salesman and have increasingly overlapped the traditional design, procurement, and construction cycle through the use of phased construction, fast tracking, and other revolutionary new techniques. Yet the performance has not always lived up to the billing. Some of the largest and most financially sound owners are now beginning to take over the overall management process on their major projects. On one of the biggest projects of all time, the Alaska pipeline, the owner took over the management responsibility for the construction program prior to job completion. A growing number of major utilities have appointed an entire first line cadre of managers for major power projects using construction managers, general contractors, subcontractors, and individual prime contractors to perform assigned component portions of the project but not the overall top management direction necessary for a successful project. Other owners in the industrial field are setting up similar management organizations on essentially all of their new programs. See Figure 1-1 for the challenges of construction.

Truly the management boom is over. The time for management performance has come. This book represents an effort to review the management concepts in the construction industry, to assess the strengths and weaknesses in the present state of the art, and hopefully to indicate some suggestions for achieving some of the many as yet unfulfilled promises still possible from the management boom.

AN OVERVIEW OF THE CONSTRUCTION INDUSTRY

What is the construction industry? Each of the members of the industry will have different ideas about the industry's makeup. In fact, many maintain that construction is not an industry at all because of the fragmented

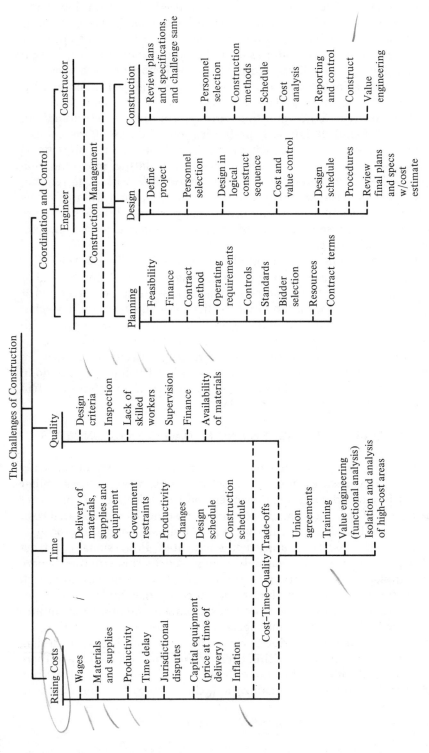

Figure 1-1 The challenges of construction. From Donald S. Barrie and Boyd C. Paulson, Jr., *Professional Construction Management*, McGraw-Hill, New York, 1978. Boyd C. Paulson, Jr., Technical Report No. 202, Stanford University, Department of Civil Engineering, Stanford, Calif., July 1975.

5

and loosely aligned relationships. Some might restrict the definition to the builders themselves. This restrictive viewpoint would, however, include contractors of many descriptions, ranging from the individual entrepreneur who builds one speculative house at a time to a multinational corporation whose operations are global in nature. Component portions of a construction job are increasingly being performed in an integrated manner, with design, manufacture, and installation being performed by a single entity. A major design-construction corporation can perform process determination, conceptual and detail design, and prefabrication of many of the components and be responsible for the construction, installation, and start-up as well. On most individual houses the heating, ventilating, and plumbing contractor will design the entire system in accordance with code requirements, will prefabricate major components in the shop, and will install the overall systems at the jobsite. Other projects or portions of projects feature a traditional designer, separate material suppliers, and a general contractor or a construction manager.

The objectives, applicability, profitability, and performance of the active industry participants are becoming increasingly affected by the labor unions, the governmental regulators, groups such as consumer advocates or environmental organizations, and many others. For this book we have chosen to define the construction industry in its broadest sense, and through the use of individual chapter authors of considerable experience we attempt to review the state of the art in managing construction, assess its strengths and weaknesses, and attempt to see what the industry can do in an effort to reverse many of the management shortcomings that have had their effect on all aspects of the industry.

ORGANIZATIONAL APPROACHES AND MANAGEMENT CONCEPTS

Organizational approaches and general management concepts for construction projects are varied. Each of the major divisions, however, uses similar contractual forms and concepts, dependent on the objectives of the owner and the degree of risk each party may care to assume. The negotiated cost, plus a fee general contract or the turnkey or design-construct approach, is often used when a fast track approach is indicated. Professional construction management is also increasingly being used in this situation where earliest completion is important to the owner. The traditional approach represents the lowest risk to the owner, since he has the option of not proceeding with the work if the fixed price is outside the budgetary limitations. Owner-builders, owner-managers, and a wide range of developers who supply a completed product, while arranging for their own design, round out the major options. Within each major conceptual approach there is a wide range of individual company approaches to organizing construction projects. The functional organization, the military line and staff concept, the task force favored by design-constructors, and the emerging matrix organization offer a wide range of choices to industry participants.

MANAGEMENT TOOLS IN THE CONSTRUCTION INDUSTRY

Management planning and control tools have always been important implements used by successful construction companies in any industry division. Before the introduction of the computer, management was always forced to restrict planning and controlling to significant items only. Planning and controlling every detail was obviously impossible in a manually operated system. With the advent of the computer many companies elected to plan to very detailed levels from the home office. Some visionaries planned to the detail levels but controlled to more manageable summary levels consistent with the precomputer practice. Other organizations, principally operating in a cost reimbursable climate elected to plan and control to minute detail with a large number of fully integrated programs, all dependent on a single data bank. In precomputer days management control systems viewed from home office management level were intended to isolate deviations from milestone level schedules and broad cost parameters.

When the control indicated a problem, management went to the job and reviewed the details with the job manager or superintendent. From this meeting came the current facts that either justified a removal of the job management or a replanning of the job based on the changed conditions which were different from the assumptions made in the original plan. The sophisticated computer programs, which too often are understood by neither the management or the front line supervision, attempted to develop a new dimension in operational control. This control was dependent on detailed computer printouts, running to hundreds of pages on a moderate-sized job. It was theoretically correct. Yet the implementation has never lived up to the promises, and the firms that make their living in a competitively bid, fixed price environment have tended to simplify the management control system to summary levels understood by both home office and field management in spite of the computer capability to provide inexhaustible detail to all management levels. In the final appraisal, control is helpful only to detail levels that fit that facts and permit action. On many design-construction projects where the baseline is established prior to completion of detail drawings, control to anything except broad major cost objectives and individual milestones is of no value to management at any level. Yet integrated management control systems continue to be operated in great detail on assumed baseline information when the actual baseline for individual efforts identifiable to jobsite management may have quantity, cost, or price variations of over 100%. The computer is a fantastic tool for the workwise construction man or woman. Yet like any tool if it is dull or not used by journeymen it cannot help to produce an economical or timely finished product.

THE GROWING INDUSTRY MANAGEMENT PROBLEM

The construction industry methods are slow to change. Yet they must adapt to larger and larger projects of great technical requirements. The management principles that were successful in building the industry are no longer as effective in the ever-changing construction environment. Productivity continues to be very good on many small and medium-sized projects where management continues to identify personally with the work force in both the unionized and non-unionized projects. Where management has lost touch with the work force, in either union or nonunion operations, productivity has deteriorated to an alarming degree. Some major projects have had four or five or even more project managers and general superintendents as deteriorating performance forces clients or contractor management to make a change. People are assigned to supervise staffs based on resumés that the client will accept on many of the largest projects without an understanding of how the people will work together. The current manager of a major project seldom has the responsibility to staff the project with favored superintendents, managers, and engineers who have worked together as a team as did his counterpart of 20 years ago. Governmental regulation is presenting almost insurmountable problems to the major construction project with red tape and documentation efforts often requiring more personnel than are actually used in performing or supervising the work.

The constant battles between local unions at the job level, the disorganization of contractor groups at the local and national level, and the increasing effect of other self-interest groups promote a climate of internal strife that is manageable on the smaller projects (individual pride of every party is still evident), and unmanageable on almost all our large jobs. At the superproject level it is clearly evidenced in the numerous studies showing that the typical craftsman is fully effective only 30% of the time.

MAJOR INDUSTRY DIVISIONS

The construction industry is made up of several major divisions that while broadly applicable overlap in many areas so that classifying them becomes difficult. The traditional breakdown might divide major divisions as follows:

- Housing and residential construction.
- Building, institutional, and commercial construction.
- Industrial construction.

- Heavy engineering construction.

Material and equipment suppliers often act as installation contractors and are a major factor affecting contractor performance and owner satisfaction. This book would not be complete without a substantial discussion about the major industry suppliers. The significant designer influence on the construction process is covered under the individual division discussion.

HOUSING AND RESIDENTIAL CONSTRUCTION

Residential construction includes single-family homes, duplex homes, garden apartments, high-rise apartments, town houses and condominiums. Residential construction is subject to wide fluctuations in volume due to many factors and is one of the largest and most sensitive divisions, accounting for about 30 to 35% of construction expenditures in an average year. The supply and demand for residential construction is heavily weighted by the business cycle, governmental regulation and fiscal policy, and the attitudes and preferences of the individual homeowners. There are several very large firms, but by far the major volume is handled by a large number of very small firms and individuals. During periods of rising demand, accompanied by rising selling prices, large numbers of new firms enter the market, survive or prosper with the boom times, and fail or barely survive with the inevitable contraction of the business cycle. Traditional construction in the United States has been field labor intensive, although in many areas factory precutting and prefabrication is increasingly being used. The low capital and technology requirements foster both easy entry into the business and a high failure rate among the home building firms.

Home designs are performed by traditional architects, by registered building designers, and in many cases by the builders themselves, and while individual aesthetic treatments may vary basic structural, mechanical, and electrical features are relatively standard as set forth in the applicable building code. The preponderance of construction is performed either nonunion or open shop, although some sections of the country continue to be heavily unionized. Perhaps the use of both union and nonunion subcontractors is highest in the home building sector with minimal difficulties. Major industry achievements are the ability to react to increasing demand at a rapid rate and in the increasingly built-in conveniences to assist in leading the good life. Major problems will include the financial instability of a large section of the contractors, the widely fluctuating demand, the fluctuating interest rates, and the increasing direct and indirect costs associated with the construction of the individual home.

BUILDING, INSTITUTIONAL, AND COMMERCIAL CONSTRUCTION

Building construction and its allied categories range from the construction of small retail stores to large shopping centers. The range is from grade schools to large universities, from small medical buildings to multistory hospitals, and for a wide range of buildings, hotels, churches, high-rise buildings, recreation and sports complexes, light manufacturing plants, distribution centers, and warehouses. The main function of this seqment of the industry is to build structures for the housing of people or goods. Much of the industry uses methods and codes similar to the residential work and is therefore also very heavily labor intensive. Considerable innovation has been developed over the years with the evolution of tilt-up walls, lift slab construction, slip forming, systems construction for mechanical and electrical components, use of tower cranes, and other innovations. This type of construction may account for 35 to 40% of the construction market. Most of the structures are built for and financed by the private sector of the economy, and the projects are very sensitive to the business cycle and interest rates. Prices, while accelerating rapidly in an expansion cycle, tend to more closely follow the actual inflation rate over the intermediate term, possibly because of the greater technological and monetary qualifications necessary to enter the industry as compared to homebuilding. However, many homebuilders alternate between housing and building and commercial work as does a sizable segment of the skilled labor supply who perform the actual work. Construction is usually managed by general contractors or construction managers who coordinate the overall project, but most of the work is performed by specialty subcontractors. An increasing amount of work is being performed by developers who build for their own account and either lease or sell the completed facility. Design is typically performed by architects ranging from one man or woman firms to large multidiscipline organizations that may include the engineering disciplines as well. Other architects typically use independent engineering firms for the structural, mechanical, and electrical designs. In the southern regions the preponderance of the work is performed on a nonunion or open shop basis. In the middle areas many of the larger projects are performed union, while the smaller projects are not organized. Certain heavily unionized sections of the country are almost fully unionized. However, each year shows an increasingly larger amount of this class of construction going to nonunion or open shop contractors as the accelerating cost of unionized construction continues. Major problems of the industry include the heavy on-site labor demands, with much of the cost of the typical building spent in material handling operations. Building codes in many areas inhibit or preclude innovative solutions to hold down the cost.

INDUSTRIAL CONSTRUCTION

Industrial construction encompasses a wide range of projects. A light manufacturing plant may involve companies and craftsmen from the home building segment, from the building and commercial area, as well as from heavy industrial work, dependent on the type of project, the business cycle, the availability of men and materials, individual skills or preferences and other factors peculiar to the project locale. A nuclear power plant may involve craftsmen from every industry division, including "travelers" from outside the state and even from Canada, dependent on economic conditions. Contractors, subcontractors, design engineers and others will join the program from other industry areas where they have developed the particular skills they bring to the project. In the past the preponderence of projects have been constructed by the major design-constructors generally affiliated with the National Constructors Association (NCA). Starting in the South, but increasingly spreading northward, major open shop firms continue to experience sharp growth at the expense of the unionized segment of the industry. Major problems of the industry include the difficulties involved in the overlapping of design and construction, the cost plus atmosphere found on many major projects, owner interference in the management process and the effect of the intervenors and regulators both before construction can commence and continually throughout the program. The impersonal relations and declining productivity associated with the very biggest projects have been cause for substantial concern. It is in this area that the management boom showed the greatest promise but may have produced the least results.

HEAVY ENGINEERING CONSTRUCTION

Heavy construction includes dam and tunnel projects, highways and canals, heavy marine structures, rapid transit systems, and portions of heavy industrial projects such as power plants. The industry has been very labor intensive on certain operations but has shown a remarkable ability to improve productivity through the use of increasingly larger and more efficient earthmoving machinery, tunnel boring machines, concrete and gravel plants, and other massive machinery. The industry requires highly skilled craftsmen to operate the heavy equipment as well as skilled miners, teamsters, carpenters, and others in addition to the mechanical and electrical crafts. Some of the jobs take place in remote areas such as the Alaska Pipeline, where all craftsmen are recruited from outside the project area. Others such as a major metropolitan rapid transit program take place in the heart of the central city. A feature of major projects has been the use of the joint venture to minimize the risk and to pool skills for the execution of the project. Heavy construction in the United States will inevitably continue shifting its interests as the major hydroelectric, flood control, and interstate highway programs decline. Heavy construction firms are increasingly entering the mining business, and their application of heavy construction equipment and techniques has been mutually beneficial. Most of the major projects in the past have been constructed on a union basis, although many major projects have been handled by a few very large open shop contractors. As mining applications become increasingly important, the traditional building trades portion of the work will inevitably continue to decline. The Alaska Pipeline has illustrated that in terms of physical performance in a short time period, the industry response was unparalleled. However, in terms of controlling costs to predetermined limits, the financial overrun was equally unprecedented.

MATERIAL AND EQUIPMENT SUPPLIERS

Material and equipment suppliers play a major role in a construction project. They set the price and the delivery commitment for all the permanent materials and equipment items the contractor must install. The suppliers' reliability and actual delivery dates have a major effect on the performance and profitability of the contractor, the reputation of the designer, and on the ultimate satisfaction and utility of the owner. Many of the major suppliers such as structural steel fabricators, generator and turbine manufacturers, boiler manufacturers, pipe manufacturers, and others also maintain construction divisions or subsidiaries to handle the on-site installation as well as the manufacturing. Other manufacturers supply factor representatives to oversee the erection of a complicated piece of equipment such as a large walking dragline that may take several years to erect. As nonstandard, specialized equipment requirements on major projects have increased, so have the reliability and delivery problems become more prevalent. Some manufacturers have let short-term economic factors introduce equipment that has not been fully proved. In other instances engineers and owners have competitively bid complicated equipment on performance type specifications and then insisted on particular materials or subsystems after contract award. As in other parts of the industry the once personal relationships between key managers are becoming impersonal with mixed results. Certainly, the major suppliers must be included in the broadly defined construction industry.

SPECIAL INTEREST GROUPS AND OTHER CONSIDERATIONS

Special interest groups are having an increasingly important effect on all facets of the industry. Special interests or movements that play a vital role in the construction will include the following:

- Organized labor.
- Employer and owner associations.
- Open shop movement.
- Legal and contractual considerations.
- Education and training.
- Federal financing and governmental regulation.

- Women and minorities.
- Research and development.

ORGANIZED LABOR

Some projects are constructed nonunion in which no individual is a member of a labor union. Others are done open shop in which both union and nonunion craftsmen may work together. Other projects are built using the closed shop where all craftsmen are members of affiliated labor organizations. Labor unions can provide significant benefit to the industry in providing hiring halls staffed with skilled journeymen, in developing and overseeing apprentice programs for the training of new craftsmen, in negotiating wage, health, and welfare benefits for the individual craftsman, in demanding and obtaining safe and reasonable working conditions, and in maintaining a pool of skilled manpower that is sufficiently mobile to flow to areas of need with minimum difficulty. The detrimental aspects of compulsary unionism are, however, extremely harmful in certain areas of the country and on certain projects. The continual jurisdictional disputes that plague the industry have defied solution on many projects yet have been able to be solved reasonably well on others. Who is to blame for the many labor problems? Management certainly has a major responsibility that must be shared with big labor. Who is responsible for the results of studies that show that on a major nuclear power plant only about 30% of a craftsman's time is spent on productive work? Much of the problem can be attributed to management at the contractor, engineer, and owner level. Yet certainly the unions must face up to affirmatively assisting in the improvement of on-site productivity or face inevitable extinction.

EMPLOYER AND OWNER ASSOCIATIONS

In an effort to combat the increasing power of organized labor, several contractor and user organizations have been formed over many years. Labor unions may battle among themselves on craft jurisdiction and other internal matters. However, in Washington, D.C., they remain united in a way no contractor or user spokesmen have ever achieved.

AGC and NCA have been engaged in a continual dispute for many years that in spite of several abortive attempts at unification on major issues has allowed labor to increase its power at both the local and national level. The National Electrical Contractors Association (NECA) and NCA engaged in a massive lawsuit contesting the applicability of an industry promotion fund in labor contracts. The owners, principally on major cost plus industrial and utility projects, have affected the division of the employer groups by first demanding crash programs working too many craftsmen for long hours six and seven days per week until the point of counterproductivity was clearly reached. Many owners began to see that they must take steps to improve conditions if things were to be improved at all, and they have formed several high-level user organizations such as the Business Round Table and other regional and local groups. AGC has begun to actively support both open shop and union contractors, while the other major organizations such as NCA, NECA, Mechanical Contractors Association of America (MCA), and other regional groups have remained supportive of the union shop. The employers associated with the overall construction industry have slipped in their ability to achieve industry spokesmen and negotiators comparable to the achievements of the American federation of Labor and Congress of Industrial Organizations (AFL-CIO) at the local level and have proved far behind the unification and lobbying successes achieved by the labor unions at the Washington scene. The National Construction Employers Council (NCEC) is the newest attempt to supply unification to the employer groups.

THE OPEN SHOP MOVEMENT

The laws of economics and survival of the fittest will continue to apply in the construction industry even though their effects on individual projects may be questioned. Each year a significantly larger amount of construction is performed on an open shop basis. While construction in the southern states has traditionally been performed without compulsory unionism, each year sees more penetration of open shop into northern, central and western areas of the country. One of the problems of open shop on medium to large projects was that in the absence of a large number of specialty craft contractors and subcontractors, it took very large companies such as Brown and Root, H. B. Zachary, or Daniels Construction to be able to maintain a large and skilled work force that could be dispatched to the project area while using and training local help for the semiskilled requirements of the work force. The elimination of the jurisdictional dispute and the ability to use craftsmen on any work they are skilled enough to perform is a major economic advantage even if the same fringe benefits and wage rates are paid, which is usually not the case. In recent years a new organization has begun to bring to the open shop movement many of the advantages of skilled trade subcontractors previously enjoyed only in the unionized sector. The Associated Builders and Contractors (ABC), proponents of the Merit Shop (an open shop that is not necessarily nonunion), has grown into a truly national organization with local chapters in major areas throughout the country. In these areas several merit shop contractors can band together to handle sizable projects heretofore only able to be constructed by the very large open shop firms. The sharp growth of these contractors has been carved from previously unionized projects. Even the traditional advantage of the union hiring hall is beginning to be challenged by a craftsman registration program for providing skilled manpower availability to Merit Shop contractors as well as portable health and welfare benefits to the individual craftsman.

LEGAL AND CONTRACTUAL CONSIDERATIONS

As projects become more complex the number of interfaces between individual participants increases. As major projects increasingly suffer cost and schedule overruns and individual firms and owners suffer financial reverses, legal costs are accounting for an increasing share of the construction dollar. Not only is the legal profession engaging in redress activity, but also in many organizations lawyers are determining the business direction of the company. This increasingly legalistic approach has accounted for many changes within the industry, some good, some detrimental. Yet to ignore the legal implications and liabilities in any construction program is a luxury that few successful firms can afford today. In the formative years of the construction industry there was considerable individual trust between contractor and subcontractor, between owner and contractor, between equipment dealer and contractor, and between other members of the industry. Some violated this trust; others recognized that personal relationships were disappearing and must be replaced with more formal approaches. An especially dangerous trend is emerging in which owners, contractors, or engineers request fixed price quotations on drawings that are said to be substantially complete but which will require considerable more development by the engineer. These documents may or may not be legally sound, but when a contractor is forced to bid a fixed price when the work is not fully defined, the inevitable result is increasing litigation, dissatisfaction, and fragmentation on the part of all industry members. A similar situation exists when contractors are required to underwrite underground conditions on fixed or unit price heavy construction bids. The law was originally conceived as a means of granting reasonable equity to all parties. In the construction industry we need to find equitable and reasonable ways to assign the risk and combine soundly conceived projects with businesslike methods, including a sound preventative law program in order to eliminate the potential for dispute in advance of costly arbitration and/or litigation.

EDUCATION AND TRAINING

Management, education, and training in the construction industry are undergoing an interesting acceleration, along with the management boom. Thirty years ago there were no graduate-level construction courses given at a major university in the United States and few undergraduate course pertaining to other than the civil engineering or trade school aspects of construction. Today, many of the brightest undergraduates are working summers at construction and are returning for masters degrees in construction at major universities such as the Berkeley Campus of the University of

California or Stanford University that feature the programs. Seminars in value enegineering, estimating, construction management, critical path scheduling, and many of the other construction disciplines are being promoted by a large number of entrepreneurs, professional societies, and universities as well as by many others. Yet much of the promise of academia has failed to produce at the jobsite. The bright young graduate who appreciates the overall relationships on a project is assigned to work for a supervisor of a functional department who is in no way interested in the overall program. In other instances he or she is not given operational responsibility. Top management blames the university when the promising young manager leaves for a position of more responsibility. The construction industry has all the technical skills necessary to construct anything that engineers and architects can design. Yet the industry needs managers at every level to be able to put the projects together in an efficient and timely manner which many now believe requires that all involves parties must achieve job satisfaction and pride in their performance if reasonable productivity is to be achieved. Possibly, we need management training, not necessarily at the undergraduate level, but among industry practitioners themselves. Possibly, we should try to find some way to take the most promising middle managers who have survived and achieved major accomplishments and give them management training at the university level. Possibly, this would work better than early identification of future management prospects at the new hire level and then trying to teach them the business through programs and structured work assignments.

FEDERAL FINANCING AND GOVERNMENTAL REGULATION

The effect of bureaucratic regulations on the cost and duration of construction projects has been monumental. Projects that 15 years ago were fully completed in three years now take five or six, with a consequent impact on the cost far outweighing simple inflation. On some major high-priority government programs it takes a selection board one year to follow the procedures required by law in the selection of a construction contractor. Add a similar time schedule for the selection of an engineer, and the resulting effects are almost unbelievable. Starting in a new project in many areas of the country requires obtaining permits from 30 or 40 governmental agencies in addition to the overall environmental impact statement approval. On government projects the documentation requirements are almost unbelievable to persons familiar with the traditional private industry approach, and many of the best-qualified contractors no longer wish to pursue government work because of the increasing red tape. The Department of Energy (DOE), and the Department of Defense (DOD), Nuclear Regulatory Commission (NRC), the Occupational Safety and Health Administration (OSHA), the Federal Mine Safety and Health Administration (MSHA), and many other local, state, and federal agencies may control the source of major funding, and/or may have a substantial say in the way that the project is performed. Mandatory use of minority firms, while beneficial in humanitarian ways, can be detrimental when controlling escalating costs is necessary for industry survival. The use of women in the craft work force based on arbitrary standards will have a similar effect. Like it or not, the regulators' effect on most projects is substantial and is escalating every year. Who will regulate the regulators before the building process becomes secondary to the documentation and compliance with regulatory requirements?

WOMEN AND MINORITIES

Women and monorities are becoming increasingly important factors in the construction industry. Women are increasingly being used at all levels from craftsman to engineer and manager as well as in secretarial and clerical positions. Affirmative action plans have resulted in increasingly sizable minority participation in almost every section of the country. Progress for both women and ethnic minorities has been greater in some areas of the industry than in others. Increasing the participation of these groups, while preserving or improving the skill levels, will continue to be a future challenge. Contractor groups and others are increasingly challenging the quota system in the courts, and reverse discrimination is increasingly being alleged.

RESEARCH AND DEVELOPMENT

Research and development accomplishment in the construction industry has included the development of PERT, CPM, and numerous overall management systems featuring the digital computer as well as increasingly efficient excavation and hauling equipment for massive heavy construction projects. Lifting equipment has undergone similar changes. Manufacturing equipment of all kinds coantinues to show yearly improvement that help to offset the increasing cost of construction on all projects. Yet in the traditional construction process little is being accomplished. There has been little difference in the skills required of a carpenter in forming walls for a major project in the last 20 years. Today, with the computerized cost control system, some managers know the cost of form hardware per square foot and per yard of concrete. Yet the man-hours per square foot of contact area may be running twice what a comparable operation would require on past projects. The foreman may be tolerating practices his predecessor would not allow because of his pride in the result. We still have this pride on many of our projects, but deterioration of pride in workmanship seems to be directly proportional to the size of the project. All the management systems have found heaviest use on the cost plus superprojects. When the contractor's own money is at stake, a return to giving more responsibility to the foreman and superintendent is clearly evident with management reporting on a control rather than detail level. The development of managers who are sufficiently knowledgeable about the building process to help motivate the craftsmen who do the work and to implement sound planning in an increasingly complex environment is the greatest single need of the construction industry. We have achieved in the management boom the theoretical, technological, or management solution to any individual problem that can be defined. However, we have not achieved a management level on major projects that can be responsive to the available facts and achieve performance from all levels of workers in a fashion comparable to performance levels achieved on comparative major projects in the past.

WHERE ARE WE NOW, AND WHERE ARE WE GOING?

The authors of the various chapters are successful, knowledgeable industry professionals. Each has been subject to the short-term pressures of the maketplace for the achievement of short-term objectives to the detriment of long-range objectives that benefit the overall industry. However, each of the chapter authors is aware of this conflict. In this book each author has tried to assess the present state of the art in the management of construction projects from an overall viewpoint irrespective of day to day pressures. Each of the industry spokesmen has endeavored to present his point of view in an honest appraisal of the state of the art in current management knowledge, to initiate a frank discussion of problems that if not resolved have the potential to destroy or drastically curtail the industry, as we know it, and to set forth ideas and possible solutions which the emerging generation of construction men and women may find useful in the future. Every author in this book has had the courage to sometimes disagree with his colleagues throughout his career. Yet each is united in the belief that the future of the construction industry in the United States and our participation elsewhere in the world will be largely determined by the performance of the next generation of managers and craftsmen. Some of the old hands are aware that they have helped keep the industry conscience. Passing it on to the next generation of managers may not be the best of legacies. However, if a bit of the pride of performance that grew up in the construction industry as the authors knew it is willed to the emerging top managers, middle managers, engineers, technicians, superintendents, foremen, and most of all craftsmen of the future, possibly, the time for management performance will arrive. The solution will not be found in newer and more sophisticated computerized management control systems. If it is to be achieved, it will be found in the restoration of pride and performance at the worker level. Management performance and the promise of the management boom will then become a reality.

CHAPTER 2

ORGANIZATIONAL APPPROACHES AND GENERAL MANAGEMENT CONCEPTS IN CONSTRUCTION

Donald S. Barrie

The principal industry divisions as set forth in Chapter 1 include housing and residential, building, institutional and commercial, industrial, and heavy engineering construction. Each of the industry branches has developed favored organizational approaches and management concepts that may be best suited to individual company or owner needs. However, in practice it is believed that all the fundamental organizational and management approaches find varying degrees of use in each of the industry branches.

ALTERNATIVE ORGANIZATIONAL APPROACHES

There are several alternative contractual and organizational approaches to a new construction program. The principal categories will include traditional general contracting, design-construct or turnkey (including design-build or design-manage), professional construction management, and the owner-builder. Each approach has its own advantages and disadvantages for a particular application and viewpoint. In addition, each has developed a large degree of flexibility so that in reality many of the methods overlap one another, and it may be difficult to categorize an individual project. Figure 2-1 *Alternative Conceptual and Contractual Approaches* sets forth in chart form a simplified version of the major alternative approaches. Each of the major alternate approaches is designed to be competitive with

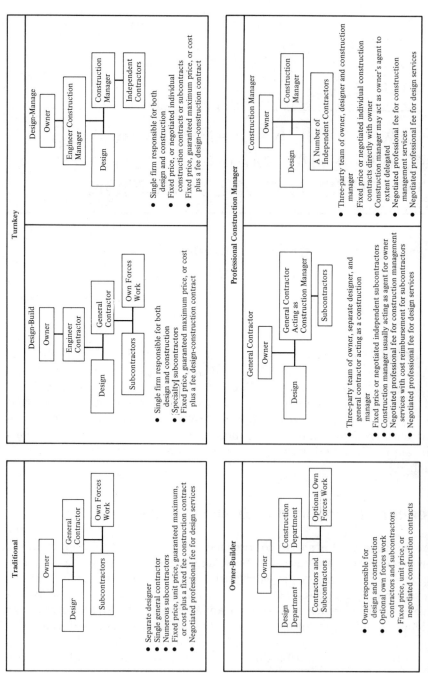

Figure 2-1 Project management concepts. From Donald S. Barrie and Boyd C. Paulson, Jr., *Professional Construction Management*, McGraw-Hill, New York, 1978.

Traditional

Owner
Design
General Contractor
Own Forces Work
Subcontractors

- Separate designer
- Single general contractor
- Numerous subcontractors
- Fixed price, unit price, guaranteed maximum, or cost plus a fixed fee construction contract
- Negotiated professional fee for design services

Turnkey

Design-Build

Owner
Engineer Contractor
Design
General Contractor
Own Forces Work
Subcontractors

- Single firm responsible for both design and construction
- Specialty subcontractors
- Fixed price, guaranteed maximum price, or cost plus a fee design-construction contract

Design-Manage

Owner
Engineer Construction Manager
Design
Construction Manager
Independent Contractors

- Single firm responsible for both design and construction
- Fixed price, or negotiated individual construction contracts or subcontracts
- Fixed price, guaranteed maximum price, or cost plus a fee design-construction contract

Owner-Builder

Owner
Design Department
Construction Department
Optional Own Forces Work
Contractors and Subcontractors

- Owner responsible for design and construction
- Optional own forces work
- Contractors and subcontractors
- Fixed price, unit price, or negotiated construction contracts

Professional Construction Manager

General Contractor

Owner
Design
General Contractor Acting as Construction Manager
Subcontractors

- Three-party team of owner, separate designer, and general contractor acting as a construction manager
- Fixed price or negotiated independent subcontractors
- Construction manager usually acting as agent for owner
- Negotiated professional fee for construction management services with cost reimbursement for subcontractors
- Negotiated professional fee for design services

Construction Manager

Owner
Design
Construction Manager
A Number of Independent Contractors

- Three-party team of owner, designer and construction manager
- Fixed price or negotiated individual construction contracts directly with owner
- Construction manager may act as owner's agent to extent delegated
- Negotiated professional fee for construction management services
- Negotiated professional fee for design services

each of the other alternates, and it takes considerable skill to anticipate which approach may prove most rewarding for a particular project.

THE TRADITIONAL APPROACH

The traditional approach has been historically advocated by the Associated General Contractors of America (AGC) and other similar builders' exchanges or affiliated organizations. In this approach the owner will engage a designer (architect, architect-engineer, or engineer) to prepare plans and specifications and to exercise some degree of inspection, monitoring, or control during the construction phase. The construction responsibility is usually assigned to a single general contractor who is under contract to the owner. Much of the work may be performed by specialty trade contractors who are under a subcontract to the general contractor. The subcontractors are normally responsible for certain portions of the plans and specifications to the general contractor who is responsible to the owner for all work, including that which may be performed with his own forces as well as that which was subcontracted. Variations of the traditional approach may include separate mechanical, electrical, or sitework contracts directly with the owner, with coordination responsibilities assigned to the general contractor or to a resident engineer who represents the owner at the jobsite.

Types of Contracts

The traditional approach can be implemented using a single fixed price or lump sum contract, a unit price contract, a cost plus a fixed or variable fee contract, a guaranteed maximum price contract, or several other variations or combinations.

The traditional method historically has developed several contractual alternates that have generally followed the extent and accuracy of the information available to the contractor during the bid or negotiating period.

FIXED AND UNIT PRICE GENERAL CONTRACTS. This type of contract was for many years the principal contracting form and continues to be heavily used by owners in all the principal industry divisions. Essentially all major public works and heavy engineering construction projects are performed through some combination of competitively bid, unit price, and/or lump sum bid items. Many individual homes and apartments continue to be built using this form of contract. The concept can be successfully applied to industrial construction, although many industrial owners prefer a phased schedule to minimize overall design-construct duration. In the building, institutional, and commercial sectors, public and private, clients rely heavily on the single fixed price general contractor concept. Advantages of this form of contract from the owner's standpoint include the following:

1. This method is generally accepted and is historically supported with well-established legal and contractual precedents.
2. The lump sum type permits overall cost to the owner to be determined before the contract is awarded.
3. The unit price type permits variable amounts of work to be paid for in a fair and equitable manner.
4. Minimum owner involvement is required in the construction process.
5. The owner benefits from price competition to achieve a fair price for the project.

Advantages from the contractor's standpoint include the following:

1. The contractor can name his own price for the work as well as his profit objective in his bid.
2. There is minimum involvement of the owner and/or engineer in the details of the building process other than for quality control.
3. The innovative contractor may obtain an opportunity to maximize his profits through his innovation.
4. Administrative requirements are based on the applicable law and the contractor's own determination.
5. the contractor may pass on much of the risk to lower-tier specialty contractors when feasible.

Disadvantages from the owner's position include the following:

1. Design usually does not benefit from construction expertise through value engineering or constructability analysis prior to contact award.
2. Overall design-construct time is generally the longest of any method.
3. The owner, architect/engineer, and contractor are often in an adversary position.
4. Changes to the work, the encountering of unforeseen ground conditions, or other changed conditions can increase cost, negating the fixed price concept and often results in substantial arbitration and/or litigation expenses, delays, and dissatisfaction.

Disadvantages from the contractor position may include the following:

1. To be competitive the builder must often use marginal subcontractors who may have problems performing the work.
2. On many contracts too many bidders may make it difficult to obtain the work for a fair price and in weak markets the cumulative cost of preparing the proposal by all builders may exceed the profit potential to the successful bidder.

3. The owner controls the funding on disputed extra work or changed conditions, and the contractor must often resort to expensive arbitration on litigation with no assurance that he will, in fact, recover for the additional costs.

4. The contractor usually bears the economic risk of unusual weather conditions, strikes, or other external factors that influence a contractor's cost but which may not be directly under his control.

NEGOTIATED COST REIMBURSEMENT TYPE CONTRACTS. Negotiated contracts for purpose of this discussion include cost plus a percentage fee, cost plus a fixed fee, cost plus a variable fee, guaranteed maximum cost, and target price with a share of overruns or savings to be divided.

Cost plus percentage fee contacts are generally not favored except in special circumstances covering extra or minor work. Where the variable nature of the work makes it difficult to obtain reasonable cost estimates, use of a multiplier on basic wage rates or of percentage allowances for overhead and profit may prove fair for all parties.

With the standard cost plus a fixed fee type contract the owner agrees to pay all of a contractor's cost plus a predetermined profit. The owner removes the economic risk from the contractor who normally settles for a much smaller fee than he would for a more risky fixed price contract. This form of contract is used throughout the construction industry where an owner wishes to use the traditional method of a single general contractor but generally wishes to minimize overall design-construct duration by using a phased construction program. During the height of a housing boom, many individual builders will only perform on a cost plus a fee basis, since they are not forced to take the usual business risks in periods of very high demand. Most local and state agencies are prohibited by law from engaging in a cost plus a fee type contract. However, the federal government has used the negotiated contract with a fixed fee, award fee, or other variation on many if not most of the critical projects associated with the defense and energy programs. With a few exceptions such as tunnels or dams associated with major industrial or power projects for private or utility owners, most heavy engineering construction projects fall in the public or semipublic sector where cost plus construction is not normally used.

Modified forms of the cost plus a fee contract attempt to reward the contractor for superior performance or to penalize him when performance is substandard. When intelligently determined such alternate concepts as the cost plus an award fee, guaranteed maximum price with a share of the savings, or a target price with a share of over runs and underruns provide an incentive to all parties to achieve predetermined objectives while minimizing contractor risk.

Advantages from the owner position include the following:

1. The contract principals are equally accepted and historically supported.

2. Overall design-construct time is minimized by overlapping design and construction.

3. This approach enables the contractor to react quickly to major design changes or to changed conditions and may help minimize adversary relationships.

4. The owner pays for the actual cost of the work that may represent a savings in periods of high demand for construction work.

5. The owner and the general contractor can still subcontract a sizable portion of the work to prequalified subcontractors, thus achieving the advantage of eliminating marginal subcontractors as well as achieving fixed prices for specialty work.

6. The owner may participate fully in the management and control of the project to the extent that he has qualified personnel and may exercise control of expenditures in advance, participate in major decisions to the extent desired, or actually supply certain services to the contractor.

Advantages from the contractor's standpoint include the following:

1. The contractor has eliminated most of the risk inherent in fixed price contracting.

2. The contractor is generally paid for the preparation of his initial planning, including development of cost estimates, schedules, and other work plan items he must absorb in the preparation of a fixed price bid.

3. The contractor has an opportunity to obtain future work from the owner with minimal competition if the objectives of the program can be achieved in a harmonious climate.

4. The jobsite can generally be staffed to provide most of the required services on a reimbursable basis, thus minimizing the contractor's home office overhead.

Disadvantages from the owner's standpoint include the following:

1. Cost plus a fee (or other variation) may not be the most economical alternative in a competitive market.

2. Disreputable, unskilled, or unknowledgeable contractors can abuse the arrangement, resulting in substantial cost overruns.

3. The guaranteed maximum price, target price, or other incentive may not stand up in the event of substantial changed conditions or major design changes.

4. Definition of reimbursable items of cost, particularly those for contractor furnished tools and equipment, contractor home office expenses, and other items that directly affect contractor profit, may be the subject of overruns, disputes, and foster adversary relationships.

5. Owner involvement is substantially increased over the lump sum method in view of the necessity for procedures, controls on expenditures, audits, approvals, and other administrative checks and balances that are considered to be good practice or cost reimbursement type contracts.

6. Contractor top management may defer to the owner's field representatives regarding differences of opinion, methods, or resource requirements that may add substantially to the cost of performance when compared to the contractor's normal practice in fixed price work. Crash programs involving excessive manpower and overtime at the client's direction have been counterproductive on many projects.

Disadvantages from the contractor's point of view include the following:

1. Fees may be minimal in comparison to profit potential in areas of known performance with a favorable risk/reward ratio.

2. Contractor supervision and management may resent major decisions being made or questioned by the client in areas where they would normally have full responsibility on fixed price work.

3. Planning and control functions and assignment of personnel are made increasingly difficult because of the simultaneous nature of construction and design. Numerous changes may foster a hip-shooting response that may not be the best training ground for growing young managers.

4. The contractor's reputation may be hurt in the event of significant delays, cost overruns, or compatibility or personality clashes with owner supervision.

5. Contractor personnel assigned to the project may be difficult to release because of owner approval requirements when a promotional opportunity arises on another project.

6. The contractor must share the overall management and control of the project with the owner who is paying the bills.

DESIGN-CONSTRUCT

The design-construct approach generally uses one organization to handle all phases of a project from concept through design and construction. This form of building has been used for the majority of process-oriented heavy industrial projects constructed in the United States in the past few decades. Reference to the *Engineering News-Record's* annual list of the 400 largest contractors shows that the design-constructors affiliated with the NCA are heavily represented in the top 20. However, many building, commercial, and light industrial projects also utilize design-construct. The major design-constructors occasionally obtain projects from the private sector in heavy construction applications, but the overall effect in this area domestically is small. On the other hand foreign applications in the Mideast,

South America, and elsewhere are broadening the design-construct opportunities in high-growth areas. Many individual entrepreneurs construct individual houses on a design-build or design-manage program, and most of the major developers in the residential field could fall in this category whether they perform the design themselves or obtain it from outside their own organization.

In the design-build subdivision, the design-constructor (engineer-contractor) acts as a general contractor as well as the designer. In the design-manage alternate the design-construct firm acts as a construction manager with the actual work being performed by several independent contractors who may be subcontractors in the traditional sense or multiple prime contractors under individual contract to the owner. In either variation the design-constructor generally acts as the agent for the owner and supplies on-site direction to the independent contractors.

Type of Contract

The design-construct or design-manage approach can be performed using just about any form of contract as discussed in the traditional approach. However, most of the turnkey work performed in recent years has been using some form for the negotiated cost reimbursement type contract. Performance incentives, however, in recent years are becoming increasingly used by price-conscious owners. The major objective of the turnkey approach is to minimize the overall design-construct schedule by use of a phased construction program with overlapping design and construction. The importance of the industrial process, individual equipment selection, and the integration of several subsystems simultaneously throughout the building process requires a number of process, engineering, construction, and administrative skills for successful execution that are not normally found in individual construction or design engineering organizations.

Since turnkey contracts can take the form of all the traditional methods, with minor exceptions, the individual advantages and disadvantages to the parties will be basically similar.

The advantages or the turnkey approach to the owner when compared to other methods in a highly industrialized process-sensitive atmosphere may include the following:

1. There is usually only one overall contact for the owner; design, construction, and often process knowledge are furnished by a single organization, usually under the direction of a project manager who reports directly to the owner.

2. Minimal or no owner coordination is required between construction, design, and other project elements.

3. Design-construct duration can be reduced through a phased construction program.

4. There is considerable opportunity for construction expertise to be used during the design period.

5. Implementation of changes is simplified at any state of the construction program.

Advantages to the design-constructor may include the following:

1. The ability to develop a specialized organization with particular expertise in several specialized fields where knowledgeable competition is minimal.

2. The ability to offer a wide range of diversified services in addition to design-construct projects, including feasibility studies, design engineering, construction, construction managment, consulting engineering studies, and several other specialies in order to achieve diversification and to minimize the effect of the business cycle on particular industries.

3. An opportunity to develop managers under varying technical and managerial assignments within a single company.

4. Minimal risk so long as some form of cost reimbursement type contract is used. Opportunity to control the facility within broad guidelines in the event of fixed price contracts.

Disadvantages to the owner may include the following:

1. On most projects no firm project cost is established until construction is well underway. If performed on a fixed price or guaranteed maximum type contract overall utility may be subordinated to insure profitable performance for the design-constructor.

2. There are few checks and balances. The owner is often not aware of potential design, construction, or integration problems that may greatly affect costs or schedules.

3. Because of minimal owner involvement, the final result may not fully live up to expectations. Over owner involvement may result in delays to the work, high administrative cost burden, or abdication of responsibility by the design-constructor.

4. Insistence by owner personnel in making major decisions regarding equipment specifications, process, or construction resource allocation (overtime or too many men) where consequences are not fully defined or understood can prejudice the overall program results.

Disadvantages to the design-constructor include the following:

1. A very large multidisciplinary organization is required. This large supply of talent will result in heavy overhead requirements in periods of reduced capital spending.

2. Owners are increasingly expecting the design-constructor to assume

sizeable performance and price risks that he generally was able to avoid during the rapid expansion years in the recent past.

3. A large sales force is required to turn up continuing new opportunities. Promises and programs developed by sales or marketing personnel that cannot be achieved by operating personnel reflect in reduced repeat business and customer dissatisfaction.

4. The task force, a favorite method of operation, may not have full access to the corporate memory of lessons learned or outstanding achievements developed on similar projects.

5. The heavy individual burden that must be assumed by the project manager and the construction and design managers and the subordinates of these managers can produce considerable internal tension and stress that may make economical coordination of design, construction, and process equipment selection difficult.

6. The projects are becoming so large and the interfaces so many that acknowledging and rewarding personal accomplishment and assigning finite responsibilities is becoming increasingly difficult and relationships are becoming increasingly impersonal.

PROFESSIONAL CONSTRUCTION MANAGEMENT

Professional construction management unites a three-party team consisting of owner, designer, and construction manager in a nonadversary relationship while providing the owner the opportunity to participate fully in the construction process. It is competitive in overall design-construct time with both the turnkey and traditional approaches. It normally features several fixed price or unit price contracts that are generally fully competitive with other methods. The construction manager under one concept called "professional construction management" does not normally perform design or construction work directly with his own forces, nor does he guarantee the overall cost of the work. Under the AGC concept, the construction manager may perform portions of the work with his own forces and may guarantee the overall cost of the work if required by the owner. Both methods contemplate that the construction manager works closely with the owner and the design organization from the beginning of the design through the completion of construction. The construction manager proposes construction and design alternatives to be studied by the project team during the planning phase and analyzes the effects of various alternatives on the project cost and schedule. Once the project budget, schedule, and quality requirements are established, the construction manager closely monitors subsequent developments in order to assist in achieving the project objectives. Throughout the construction program, the manager advises on and coordinates or performs the procurement of long lead material, equipment, and the selection and performance of all construction contractors. The firm will usually monitor payments to contractors, changes, and

claims and may perform inspection for conformance to design requirements and in general monitors actual cost, schedule, and quality accomplishments compared to the project plan. Construction management featuring the three-party team of owner, designer, and construction manager
is relatively new as a major factor on the construction scene. In the past 10
years, however, it has grown to become a viable alternative to more traditional methods as its increasing use is proving. It is interesting to note that
a construction manager was initially chosen to head up the Alaska Pipeline
Project, one of the major heavy construction efforts of its time. A construction management firm was also chosen to take the lead in the management
of a major trade school and university program in Saudi, Arabia, which
must rank among the largest most complex building projects of all time.
Construction management has been increasingly competitive on large and
small industrial work, building work, and commercial construction and
could emerge as a factor in residential and heavy construction as well.

Types of Contracts

The AGC and the American Institute of Architects have developed model
contrats along the line of a negatiated construction contract. The principal
difference is that the AGC document includes a guaranteed maximum price
alternate.

Construction management contracts or agreementswill normally provide
for full reimbursement by the owner of all out-of-pocket costs, including
contracts, subcontracts, materials, equipment, and the manager's own
forces. A fixed fee is normally added to cover home office costs, general
overhead, and profit. These arrangements can include a guaranteed maximum cost for the manager's own costs or for the overall project as negotiated between the parties.

Advantages to the owner include the following:

1. Special construction skills may be used for the economic benefit of the
project at all stages, including conceptual and detail design with no conflict
of interest.

2. Independent evaluation of costs, schedules, and overall construction
performance, including similar evaluation for changes, helps assure a decision in the best interest of the owner in a nonadversary relationship.

3. Full-time coordination between design and construction contracts is performed in a manner fully visible to the owner.

4. Phased construction can minimize overall design-construct time.

5. The use of several lump sum contracts obtained through competitive
bidding in a manner similar to the traditional method.

6. Significant opportunities for reducing total cost through the use of value
engineering are available in the design, building, award, and construction
phases.

Advantages to the construction manager include the following:

1. The ability to perform on a professional assignment for a fixed fee without the necessity of appraising the short-term effects of job-related decisions on his own economic profit or loss.

2. Minimum or no risk under the professional construction management approach and minimum risk under the guaranteed maximum price alternate concept.

3. An excellent opportunity to obtain repeat projects from satisfied clients based on prior successful performance with minimum or no competition.

4. Minimum capital requirements when compared to an ordinary construction company.

Disadvantages to the owner include the following:

1. Under a phased construction program the owner begins a project before the total price is established. Early completion may not provide a sufficient trade-off for this risk. Under the AGC guaranteed maximum price option, the owner may be able to obtain partial protection against this risk.

2. If the owner has only a fixed amount to spend and will not build the project if costs would exceed this amount, the traditional fixed price contract would probably be preferable in a go-no-go situation.

3. The owner must fulfill his obligations in a timely and efficient manner.

4. Success of the program depends greatly on the planning, scheduling, estimating, and management skills of the construction management firm and of the individuals actually assigned to the project.

5. With the exception of the AGC alternate, the professional construction manager does not usually guarantee the overall price or quality of the work as does the general contractor in the traditional lump sum single contract approach.

Disadvantages to the construction manager include the following:

1. If he is solely in the construction management business his personnel may not be fully knowledgeable about current industry conditions, methods, prices, and other considerations in an ever-changing and evolving construction environment.

2. If he establishes a guaranteed maximum price as contemplated by the AGC alternate, he may be gambling on the willingness of the designer and owner to compromise their initial program if costs prove to be greater than budgeted funds.

3. Opportunities for no risk engagements may be minimal in a deteriorating economy.

THE OWNER-BUILDER

Theoretically, many city, county, and state public works departments have performed some or all of their minor design and construction work with their own forces. The Tennessee Valley Authority and several private companies have performed both design and construction work with their own forces on major projects. Other owner (or owners' representatives) such as the Army Corps of Engineers, the Bureau of Reclamation, the Public Building Service of the General Services Administration, and Proctor and Gamble in the private sector have retained many of the management and conceptual responsibilities while using construction contractors for the actual hiring and supervision of the labor force.

In part because of the failure of the other alternatives to cope with the special problems of the utility industry, many utilities are assuming overall project management responsibility for both nuclear and fossil-power plants. Many of these organizations feature a first line of utility management supplemented by a design firm, a construction management or construction firm, or individuals from a management or engineering consulting firm to supply the personnel necessary to carry out the overall management responsibilities.

Some have called this emerging concept the "integrated organization" in which client and consultant personnel share duties in an integrated organization established under overall client management for the execution of a major construction project. Other examples of the integrated organization are those from many of the third world and developing countries where a management cadre of advisers are employed to give advice and counsel to the third world counterparts who hold the ultimate responsibility, and in the reorganization applicable to the final stages of the Alaska Pipeline.

In the apartment, condominium, commercial, and tract housing areas, many successful construction companies have entered the developer field as a sideline to their basic business. In many instances their success as owner-builder and developer has minimized or replaced the general contrating or design-construct parent company.

The owner-builder can use all the techniques and contractual approaches of the traditional general contractor, design constructor, and the professional construction manager. Since the emergence of the owner-builder as direct competition to other methods on major utility programs, on massive third world programs, and on other applications is relatively new, it is premature to assess whether the owner's assumption of the overall management responsibilities using hired hands from industry practitioners is a viable emerging concept. Tabulation of the advantages and disadvantages to the participating parties for this type of operation must await the performance evaluation on several projects.

GENERAL MANAGEMENT CONCEPTS

Within each of the alternative conceptual and contractual approaches shown on Figure 2-1, several different internal organization structures can be used, depending on several variables. There is the traditional functional organization, the task force, the line and functional staff concept, and the relatively new matrix organization. Figure 2-2, illustrates the four organizational approaches to a design-construct project. Similar organizational differences can be applied to straight construction and construction management projects and companies.

FUNCTIONAL ORGANIZATIONS

Functional approaches have traditionally been used in the construction industry. The strengths of these approaches will include high stability; high professional standards, incorporating the latest technology; and an excellent corporate memory.

Everybody knows where he stands compared to others, understands his or her task, and has a permanent home base. Weaknesses of functional organizations can include low adaptability, minimum appreciation of overall project objectives, overly rigid operating rules, resistance to change, and difficulty in developing overall well-rounded project managers. Many individual managers may tend to over optimize their particular specialty to the possible detriment of the overall project.

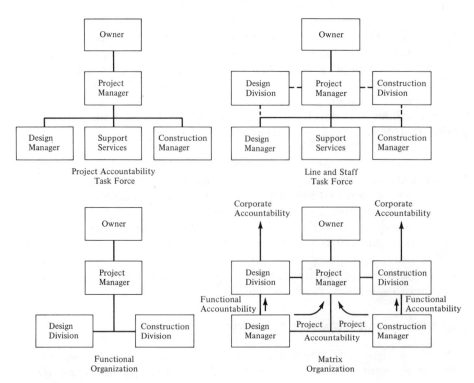

Figure 2-2 Organizational concepts. From Donald S. Barrie and Boyd C. Paulson, Jr., *Professional Construction Management*, McGraw-Hill, New York, 1978.

Notable success has been achieved by functional organizations when design and construction do not fully overlap, thus minimizing intereaction. In this case the overall project management plan can be said to be on a functional basis, using a separate designer and a separate contractor or construction manager. Most fixed or unit price type construction contracts fall in this category. An overall functional organization can be helpful when the owner acts as project manager with a minimum staff, depending on others for the functional expertise. Functional organizations work best when overall managers are skillful and people oriented and can help avoid internal conflict. The functional organization permits the tightest discipline control of any organizational concept. Figure 2-3 shows a functional organization for a construction management project.

THE AUTONOMOUS TASK FORCE

The task force has been notably successful when a fully self-sufficient organization is required. The strengths of the task force include high adapt-

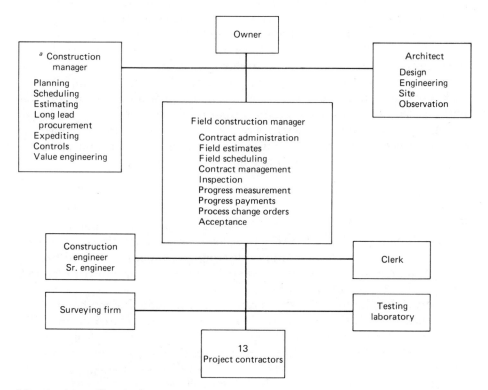

[a] Part-time home office planning, control, estimating and support.

Figure 2-3 Functional organization construction management. From Donald S. Barrie and Boyd C. Paulson, Jr., *Professional Construction Management*, McGraw-Hill, New York, 1978.

ability and high understanding of the overall task and can foster an excellent team spirit if given the proper leadership. The task force features close personal relationships and can be receptive to new ideas and methods.

The weaknesses of a task force feature poor stability. Everyone may not have a corporate home base for encouragement and for between assignment periods. The task force by itself has no corporate memory, the "memory" being that of the individuals assigned to the project. Everyone may not understand his own task, and there are no functional checks and balances to preserve workmanship quality and accepted standards. The task force may be preoccupied in inventing the wheel because of the unavailability of the corporate memory.

Automous task forces are increasingly being set up by utility clients and others (sometimes called integrated organizations, as mentioned earlier), where task force members are made up by both owner, manager, and individuals hired from outside firms.

Task forces work best when all team members can be physically located in the same area to foster closer personal relationships. The task force seems to work best when attempting something new without recognized standards and when the team is made up of very experienced members. Large remote overseas construction projects are generally organized on a task force basis as are numurous large projects in the United States and Canada. Figure 2-4 shows a task force for a remote construction management project in an overseas or relatively inaccessible location.

Some very successful construction companies have been organized on a task force basis, taking one project at a time while devoting essentially the entire corporate resources to an individual project accomplishment. Interestingly enough when financial success has permitted branching out into several projects constructed simultaneously, profit margins and performance have often shown considerable erosion.

LINE AND STAFF ORGANIZATIONS

The military line and central staff organizations and the General Motors organization as developed by Alfred P. Sloan form outstanding examples of this method of organization. Many construction companies evolved from a functional organization to a line and staff organization as growth required additional managment strengths.

Strengths of the line and staff organization include the combination of functional strengths and expertise with the project-oriented team. This form or organization strikes a balance between overall control of both craftsmanship and project objectives. The functional staff provides a high corporate memory and, if managers are given diversified assignments, offers an excellent climate for developing project managers.

Weaknesses are sometimes evident in the conflict between the operating organization and the functional staff. Organizational structures tend to be

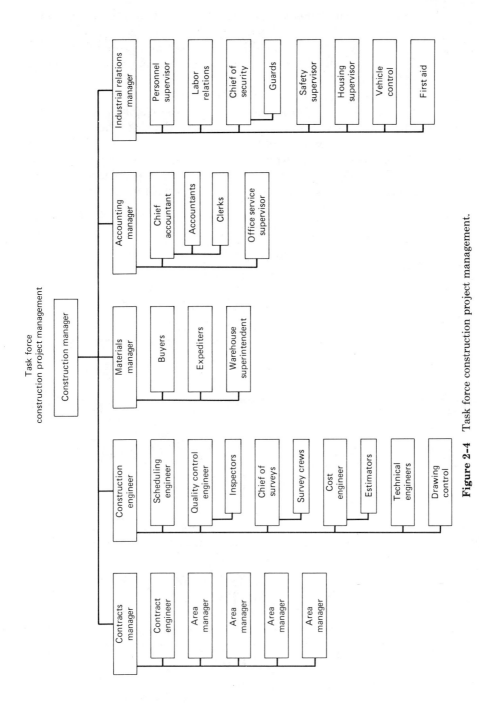

Figure 2-4 Task force construction project management.

somewhat top-heavy, and overall costs may exceed more simplified operating concepts. Individuals may be troubled by dual accountability to both a project and functional boss.

The line and staff organization has worked well in the manufacturing industries. It can be successfully used when both team spirit and functional expertise are required for best performance. It works best when both functional and project management authority can be explicity defined and divided. The concept requires experienced and capable managers and can offer a high degree of both project and functional control. Figure 2-5 shows a line and functional staff organization for a construction company.

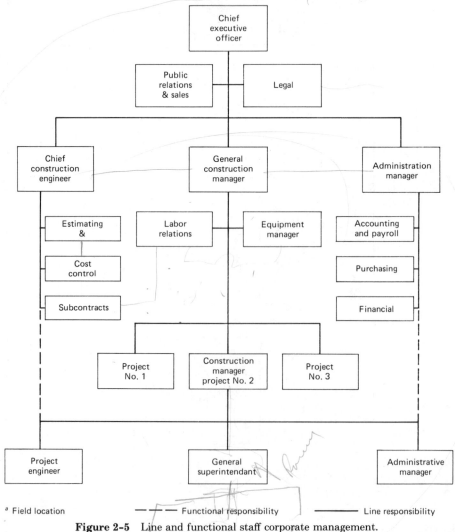

ᵃ Field location   — — — Functional responsibility   ———— Line responsibility

Figure 2-5   Line and functional staff corporate management.

THE MATRIX ORGANIZATION

Matrix organizations have become fashionable. The matrix organization purportedly solves the conflict between the operating line organizations and the functional staff by opening up lines of communication at all levels and gives people dual responsibilities. Figure 2-6 shows schematically the lines of communication and dual responsibilities inherent in a matrix organization. The matrix organization is generally credited to be effective with knowledgeable workers in a productive environment. The effectiveness of the matrix organization in the construction industry has yet to be effectively demonstrated, possibly because of widespread misunderstanding. However, some authorities believe the adaptations of this form or organization could, if used in the right situation, help to improve productivity at the craft as well as the management level through increased communication and responsibilities.

PROJECT SIZE AND ORGANIZATIONAL SELECTION

The construction industry has had great difficulty adjusting to the increasing size and complexity of major construction projects. Superproject construction management organizations continue to grow substantially larger and more complex. Some major projects may be eight to ten or years, or more, from ground breaking to operation. Theoretically, these projects should benefit from continuity and economies of scale as do comparable-sized manufacturing concerns. Productivity and efficiency should benefit

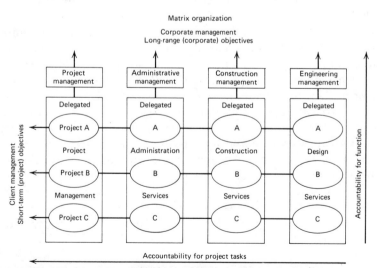

Figure 2-6 Matrix organization. Courtesy American Society of Civil Engineers, Keener, Donald F., *Effective Product Management Techniques*, San Francisco, April 1973.

from the increased ability to improve operations in much the same way as a comparable manufacturing operation would over a similar time period. However, productivity is in reality far lower on the major industrial projects than it is on the smaller- or median-level jobs irrestive of the individual manager's qualifications. Individual performance expressed in manhours per unit of production may range from a scale of 1.0 on the best-managed smaller- and median-sized projects to 2.5 or 3.0 on comparable superprojects; yet the task of the individual workman may be quite similar or even identical.

Many successful small- and median-sized projects seem to have a common attribute. The management group on which the success of the project is based is still small and cohesive enough that all the members (including craft foremen) continue to be in personal contact with one another. In many cases, this personal contact extends to the craft labor force.

On the superproject, however, the top management group no longer works with the work force directly. There may be many levels of managers, administrators, and others whose time is increasingly spent in interacting with one another rather than with the craft work force. Problems that would be solved at the foreman level on a moderate-sized project many require weeks and months of effort by a number of nonmanual personnel affiliated with several different organizations.

PUTTING IT ALL TOGETHER

The management boom has developed several managerial approaches to the control and management of the superproject. However, few or none have achieved the production efficiencies and learning curve improvements that would be obtained by any similar-sized manufacturing organization. Increasingly, we are creating an army of specialists who are experts in their individual fields. Yet the overall whole has not gained efficiency through the optimization of the component parts. It is in the area of management of large projects where the management boom offered the greatest promise but has shown the least result. Major projects are often comparable to service institutions where managerial performance is rewarded for programs and good intentions and for pleasing important client personalities rather than marketplace or bottom line performance. As initial budgets and schedules prove unrealistic, the base for performance evaluation approximates the service organization where each department uses its skills to obtain as large a budget as can be justified by increasingly complex programs designed to improve overall performance but that prove difficult to achieve in reality.

CHAPTER 3

MANAGEMENT TOOLS IN THE CONSTRUCTION INDUSTRY

Donald S. Barrie

Management planning and control tools are important yardsticks for use by contractors, managers, and supervisors. With the advent of the computer a considerably more sophisticated approach to planning and control has evolved. Yet in the opinion of many knowledgeable construction men, overall management and control of projects has not improved. Planning, scheduling, estimating, and cost control have in many organizations become separate and distinct disciplines, with only the integrated computer program to tie them all together. On many projects fully computerized reports generate hundreds of pages of detail. Yet in many cases these reports are of little value for either schedule or cost control to the line managers actually in charge of and in positions to influence the conduct of the actual construction work. Many of the managers, superintendents, and foremen have returned to fundamentals and continue to rely on their own rules of thumb, common sense, or individual methods in an effort to understand and directly influence the performance of the work.

The emergence of the cost plus a fee approach as well as governmental regulation on most projects has increasingly resulted in larger engineering, supervisory, technical, and clerical forces. On a typical nuclear power plant the ratio between hourly craft personnel to salaried or hourly noncraft personnel is approaching 4 : 1. On the other hand, on competitively bid heavy construction projects, with design fully complete before construction begins, the ratio may still be as high as 25 : 1.

On medium-sized industrial projects the number of salaried and clerical personnel continues to be substantially higher on cost plus negotiated and turnkey jobs than it is on competitively bid work even on essentially similar projects. The use of very detailed sophisticated computerized cost and schedule planning and control systems appears to be widespread on the cost plus projects. Yet when the contractors' own monies are at stake on the lump sum work, a less elaborate, somewhat more simplified system is generally chosen. The application of the central data file or data bank for a management information system using a large number of integrated individual programs may have proved to be effective in the manufacturing industries. However, the the effective use of such in the construction industry has yet to be consistently demonstrated. In too many cases such an integrated system results in up to seven or eight levels of detail in all individual programs even though the usefulness of the mass of data to the superintendent of foreman has not been demonstrated at the jobsite. Individual managers and superintendents must be able to use the results of the planning and control reports to achieve at least sufficient savings in dollars and time to justify the cost of the increased personnel and the voluminous reports if the system is to be cost effective.

A successful construction manager must be familiar with the requirements of the project. He must develop a successful organization. He must also take advantage of all the available tools if he is to survive in today's changing and increasingly complex construction climate. Managers at every level must understand the fundamentals of planning and control if only so that they will question the output of the computer when common sense questions the answer. This chapter discusses the basic planning and control tools that have proved to be fundamentally sound and simple enough to be of actual use in planning and directing the work. Many of the tools can and are expanded to additional levels of detail using the computer. Yet in the final analysis it is the construction engineer, superintendent, foreman, and craftsman who must act if the management tools are to have any effect on the progress or cost of the work. If the tools do not promote improvement in productivity or accomplishment, the entire management control system degenerates to an expensive recording system that can document events long past but which is of little use in assisting front line supervision to introduce or maintain improved practices in a timely manner at any organizational level.

PLANNING AND CONTROL CONSIDERATIONS

Planning tools can be subdivided into at least two distinct levels of effort. There is the conceptual or broad level that occurs early in the project performance, based on general drawings and criterias usually before any work is performed at the site, using parameters to determine the extent of the work. Then there is the detail level of planning that is based on detailed drawings and specifications and accompanied by a quantity takeoff to determine the work requirements. On a conventional fixed price bid on completed drawings and specifications the contractor is able to plan the work in detail before submitting his bid. On the other hand under the phased construction or fast track approach, initial packages are planned in detail and work begins at the site when most of the work has been planned only to the conceptual level. The government refers to the conceptual or preliminary planning stage as Title I, with the detailed development stage being referred to as Title II. The accuracy of the planning in the Title I stage has a greater tolerance for error than does the detail or Title II stage that is based on completed drawings. Carrying out Title I planning to details that cannot be firmed up until Title II is equally unproductive as is oversimplifying Title II planning when nearly all the information is available. In many organizational concepts conceptual and detail construction planning are prepared by different organizations as in the fixed price single general contract approach.

SETTING PERFORMANCE STANDARDS

The function of the plan is to enable management to assess the overall resource requirements for initiating the work and to then set a number of performance standards that must be equaled or bettered if the project is to achieve a successful conclusion. The performance standards can be called "budgets regarding cost aspects" and "milestones regarding schedule requirements." Based on the initial planning management is able to develop initial requirements for men, women, money, equipment, materials, and other resources necessary to carry out the program. As the program develops the actual resources required are compared against the standards. By observing the deviation in cost and time, management is able to reassess the requirements and to add or subtract resources or to modify the plan or the performance standards as may be required to meet project objectives or to meet revised objectives if initial planning was inadequate. Obviously, if conceptual or Title I planning is used to set performance standards in detail for Title II work performance, the standards and the performance units may vary so significantly that the standard serves no useful purpose because of its incompatability with conditions not apparent from the assumptions and general nature of the conceptual planning. Therefore, detail performance standards must be set with great care and must be reasonably achievable when compared to the actual conditions if they are to be effective as a management tool. The classic example is the conflict between the estimator and the job superintendent on a money-losing job. In most cases the job superintendent maintains that the estimate was far too low. The estimator maintains equally authoritatively that the estimate was competitive but the job superintendent did not follow the plan and was responsible for the increased costs. Many times it is a difficult problem for top management to determine which party was most accurate in his analysis.

When conceptual planning is used to develop detail standards for jobsite performance measurement little real control is achieved, although the multipage computer printouts are equally bulky and appear authoritative to managers who do not understand what is behind the numbers.

CONCEPTUAL AND DETAIL PLANNING

Conceptual and detail planning are used in all the branches of the industry and in all the organizational concepts, including single competitively bid contracts on completed drawings, turnkey design-construction contracts, owner-developer projects, and professional construction management. Most successful conventional general contractors will prepare job abstracts that contain a digest of the pertinent terms and conditions of the contract, a conceptual level schedule, and a "doorknob" or "green sheet" cursory estimate of probable cost. This initial appraisal of the project is used to determine approximate magnitude and whether the project is desirable from a risk-reward ratio when compared to other possible projects that the firm may bid. A design-constructor or professional construction manager using a phased construction program will have prepared a complete job program, based on a conceptual estimate, schedule, and scope. The owner's appropriation budget is often obtained from this level. In many projects it becomes important to compare actual results to both a more detailed set of standards to monitor job performance and productivity as well as to the original conceptual budget so that funding requirements can be monitored and controlled. Skilled developers or custom home builders doing repetitive work in a given location may find that the conceptual approach, based on data from prior projects, may be more accurate than detailed estimates in many applications as well as being considerably cheaper.

In many projects conceptual planning is performed by one organization and subsequent detail planning is performed by another party later in the overall project life cycle. Consider an individual who wishes to construct a new home. By visiting dwellings for sale in the area or by consulting with an architect or builder, the prospective homeowner can develop a very preliminary idea of the size and cost of the new home by multiplying the required square feet by the approximate going price per square foot for similar homes in the area. The plan designer or architect may come up with a somewhat more detailed conceptual estimate, based on several parameters found to be useful in the area. When the home is put out for complete bids a number of contractors will make detailed estimates of cost. During periods of high demand and prosperity in the housing cycle the new speculator-builder may never make a detailed estimate of cost and may price his home based on actual cost determined just before final completion.

In the heavy construction field the owner or his engineer will make the conceptual level estimates and schedules that are used to obtain required funds, form the engineer's fair cost estimate, and fix the anticipated project schedule duration.

In the industrial construction or building areas a design-constructor may make both conceptual and detail level estimates and schedules on turnkey projects. On other projects the engineer may make conceptual estimates only, relying on the contractor bids to develop the detail level planning in order to accomplish objectives set by the conceptual plan.

Each of the branches of the construction industry has developed its own planning tools. However, while the individual formats may differ, the broad principles of planning are consistent throughout the industry, although detailed implementation may take many forms. Planning tools that can be helpful to the building industry as well as to heavy industrial construction can be broadly grouped into planning, scheduling, and estimating subdivisions. Each of these tools may be used at the summary or detailed level, depending on the information level available to the planner or estimator. Each must be fully consistent with one another if best results are to be obtained.

Paralleling the planning and scheduling tools are the control tools. The plan takes into account the information level available and develops a logical program for achieving a desired result. The plan sets forth quantitative or qualitative project objectives. The schedule takes into account the required resources for achieving the planning goals. The control tools are designed to measure actual results compared to planned results so that various management levels are informed at all times about the actual status of the job compared to the planned status. Broad control tools that follow the planning tools include progress compared to schedule reports, cost compared to estimate reports, and a large number of other reports which are intended to measure actual accomplishment compared to the plan. Each of these broad range of control tools may be used to control either the conceptual or detail level of planning, or both, as determined by individual objectives, economic consideration, and management preference.

SEQUENTIAL OR PHASED CONSTRUCTION

The typical construction project life cycle is made up of a design phase, a procurement phase, and a construction phase. On the traditional project, each phase follows the other in a sequential manner. On a fast track or phased construction program some or all of the phases may overlap. The overall advantage of the sequential program is that the level of facts available for planning and control are significantly more accurate when on site work begins than are the initial concepts available at work commencement using the phased approach. The obvious advantage of the phased construction program is to minize the overall design-construct duration. Such a timesaving approach compared to the traditional sequential approach may have different utility value to the principals, dependent on project economic considerations. Figure 3-1 shows a traditional sequential program compared to a phased construction program applicable to essentially any branch of the industry.

CONCEPTUAL PLANNING TOOLS

In the following discussion of planning, estimating, and control tools examples will generally be chosen from the conceptual or summary level only since broad, conceptual tools are generally equally applicable to all branches of the industry. The individual chapter authors discuss more detail tools applicable to a particular industry division where appropriate.

Planning tools have proliferated with the management boom. Network-based critical path methods (PERT and CPM) have swept the industry and, in fact, have created a sizable subindustry of planners and hardware purveyors who have developed proprietary programs and substitute equipment that is available to attack any known industry problem. The network diagram has many advantages to the conceptual planner. The logical interrelationship between activities is much more easily shown on a precedent

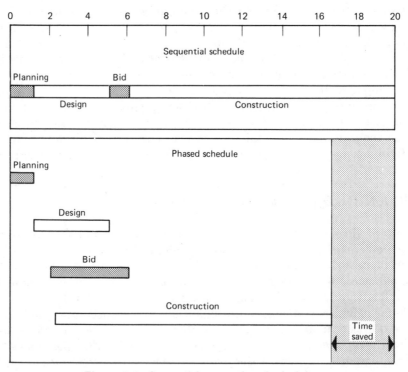

Figure 3-1   Sequential versus phased schedule.

diagram or an arrow diagram. Figure 3-2 shows a CPM arrow diagram for a simple project, while Figure 3-3 shows a CPM precedence diagram for the same project. Each of the methods has its own advocates, but both essentially produce similar results. CPM probably has reached its peak with the management boom. The time for performance has come, and in this area some practitioners have obtained much more benefit than have others.

Bar charts date back at least to the Gantt charts developed by Henry L. Gantt early in the twentieth century. The bar chart represents the simplest and most widely used scheduling tool in the construction industry and finds application in every branch of the industry. Figure 3-4 shows a bar chart schedule for an example project. In an integrated management planning system, estimates and schedules are fully consistent with one another. Figure 3-5 shows a conceptual estimate summary for a selected project. Figure 3-6 shows six levels of estimates, with informational requirements and probable contingencies. By listing man-hours of effort on the estimate and assuming a linear or other distribution of the bar chart, we can come up with a summary manpower forecast for the project. Figure 3-7 shows both the early and late start manpower requirements and overall progress curves, also called "S" curves, showing cumulative progress on the vertical axis against time on the horizontal axis. Cash flow can be plotted in a similar manner as shown in Figure 3-8.

Matrix schedules have become fairly common in repetitive operations such as a high-rise building where each floor has essentially a similar plan. Figure 3-9 shows such an example. Operations such as a rapid transit project or a major hydroelectric project have often used "Horse Blanket" schedules. Figure 3-10 gives an example chosen from a rapid transit project.

Linear balance charts have application where sequential operations are normally significant. Figure 3-11 shows an example for a pipeline.

CONCEPTUAL CONTROL TOOLS

Control tools consist of measuring actual accomplishment and comparing it to planned accomplishment or resource use so that the manager may be aware of the critical items requiring management attention. Figure 3-12 illustrates the concepts of control.

Figure 3-13 shows actual progress compared to planned progress for a sample project. Figure 3-14 shows a summary cost and comparison to an estimate report that gives a similar comparison for project costs. Similarly, Figure 3-15 shows actual manpower requirements compared to an early start manpower curve. Figure 3-16 shows a progress report based on the principles of PMS and mini-PMS earned value reports.

Planning and control are clearly closely related. Refer again to Figure 3-6 that shows six levels of estimates and the information required for each. A project can be planned to any or all the listed levels, first to level one and subsequently replanned to levels two, three, four, five, and six. A funda-

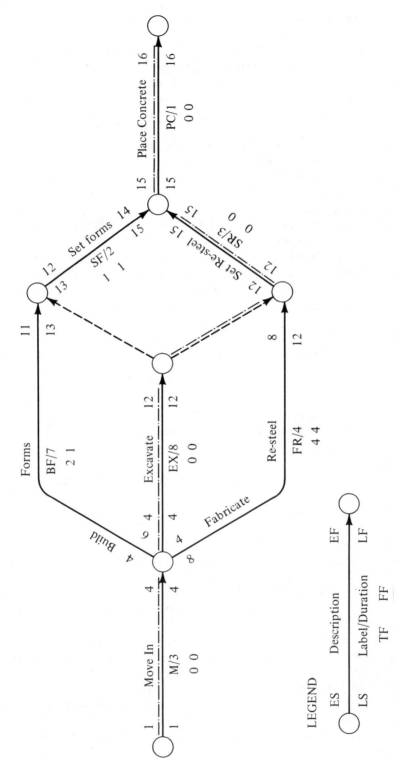

Figure 3-2 CPM arrow diagram. From Donald S. Barrie and Boyd C. Paulson, Jr., *Professional Construction Management*, McGraw-Hill, New York, 1978.

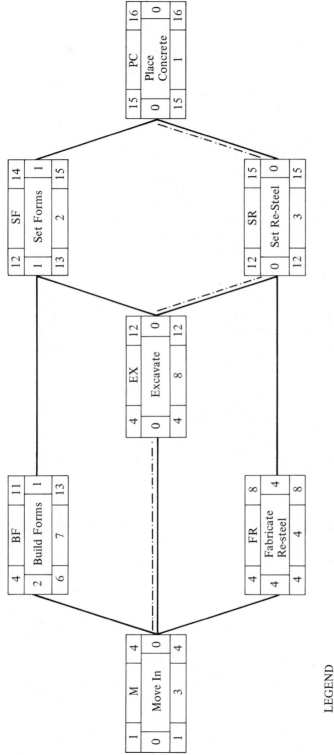

LEGEND

ES	Label	EF
TF	Description	FF
LS	Duration	LF

Figure 3-3 CPM precedence diagram. From Donald S. Barrie and Boyd C. Paulson, Jr., *Professional Construction Management*, McGraw-Hill, New York, 1978.

Item No.	Description	First Year												Second Year											
		J	F	M	A	M	J	J	A	S	O	N	D	J	F	M	A	M	J	J	A	S	O	N	D
M-10	Mobilization																							
E-10	Foundation excavation																							
D-10	Diversion stage — 1																							
D-20	Diversion stage — 2																							
G-40	Foundation grouting																							
C-10	Dam concrete																							
I-20	Install outlet gates																							
I-30	Install trash racks																							
P-10	Prestress																							
R-80	Radial gates																							
S-50	Spillway bridge																							
G-60	Curtain grout																							
L-90	Dismantle plant, clean up																							

Figure 3-4 Preliminary schedule. From Donald S. Barrie and Boyd C. Paulson, Jr., *Professional Construction Management*, McGraw-Hill, New York, 1978.

DETAILS OF ESTIMATE OF COST

COST ACCOUNT NO	DESCRIPTION	QUANTITY	TOTAL UNIT $	LABOR 00	BURDEN 10	EQUIP USAGE 20	MATERIAL 30	SUBCON 40	50	ENGRD EQUIP 60	TOTAL
:: 2000.0000	BUILDINGS AND STRUCTURES										
.: 2100.0000	CONCENTRATOR PLANT										
: 2101.0000	PRIMARY CRUSHING BUILDING										
2101.1400	EARTHWORK										
-	ENGINEERED BACKFILL	9000CY	2.50					22500			22500
2101.2100	BUILDING FOUNDATIONS										
-	FORMS	2900SF	1.69	3100	900	100	800				4900
-	REBAR	17600LB	0.18	1200	400	200	1400				3200
-	EMBEDDED	2900LB	0.86	700	200	100	1500				2500
-	CONCRETE	135CY	27.41	900	200	200	2400				3700
2101.2300	SLAB-ON-GRADE										
-	FORMS	900SF	3.56	2200	600		400				3200
-	REBAR	21000LB	0.18	1500	400	200	1700				3800
-	EMBEDDED	1400LB	0.86	350	150		700				1200
-	CONCRETE	170CY	24.71	700	200	200	3100				4200
2101.3100	STRUCTURAL STEEL	205TN	629.27	22400	6600	6100	93900				129000
2101.3200	MISCELLANEOUS STEEL	15TN		5500	1600	400	10500				18000
2101.4300	ROOFING										
-	METAL ROOF DECK	7600SF	0.91					6900			6900
-	BUILT UP ROOFING	7600SF	1.11					8400			8400
-	METAL SIDING	17300SF	2.25					38900			38900
2101.4400	VERTICAL LIFT DOORS	4EA						96000			96000
2101.4800	GENERAL CONSTRUCTION							10000			10000
2101.6100	HEATING AND VENTILATION							15800		5000	20800
2101.8100	INTERIOR BUILDINGS										
-	CONTROL ROOM	140SF	20.00					2800			2800
-	ELECTRICAL ROOM	588SF	20.07					11800			11800
-	TOOL ROOM										
-	OIL AND PUMP ROOM	308SF	20.13					6200			6200
-	WASH ROOM	150SF	20.00					3000			3000
: 2101.0000	TOTAL			38550	11250	7500	116400	222300		5000	401000
.: 2100.0000				38550	11250	7500	116400	222300		5000	401000

Budget Estimate

The budget estimate establishes the basic targets for monitoring and analyzing cost. The computer printout includes: account number, account description, quantity and unit, manhours, estimated cost by elements and total.

Figure 3-5 Preliminary cost estimate.

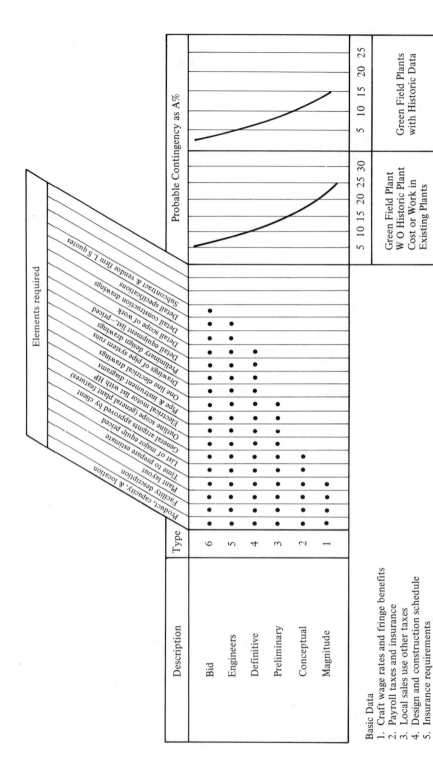

Figure 3-6 Estimate types. From Donald S. Barrie and Boyd C. Paulson, Jr., *Professional Construction Management*, McGraw-Hill, New York, 1978. Adapted from E. D. Lowell chapter, Building Construction Handbook, second edition, 1975, McGraw-Hill, New York, 1975.

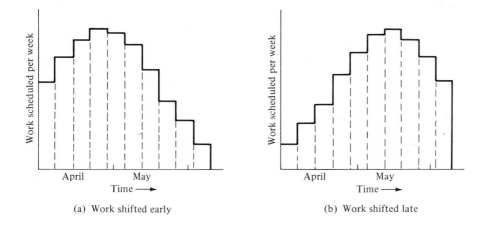

(a) Work shifted early

(b) Work shifted late

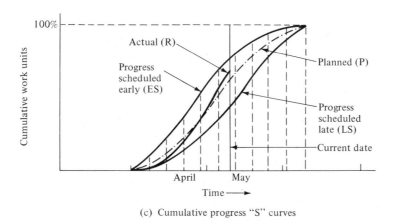

(c) Cumulative progress "S" curves

Figure 3-7 Early, late, and actual progress. From Donald S. Barrie and Boyd C. Paulson, Jr., *Professional Construction Management*, McGraw-Hill, New York, 1978. Adapted from Boyd C. Paulson, Jr., *Concepts of Project Planning and Control, Journal of the Construction Division*, ASCE Vol. 102, No. CO1, March 1976.

mental control principle is that controlling to levels of information that are more detailed than the plan is not economically sound. Many nuclear power plants have been built using conceptual estimates with cost recording to detail levels down to the smallest component of the smallest subsystem. In this case there was no control beyond the conceptual level. Complex computerized management control systems have developed thousands of informational bits, few of which are of an aid to the foreman or superintendent in trying to keep the project proceeding according to the plan. On the other hand, initial feasibility estimates can be developed to a chosen

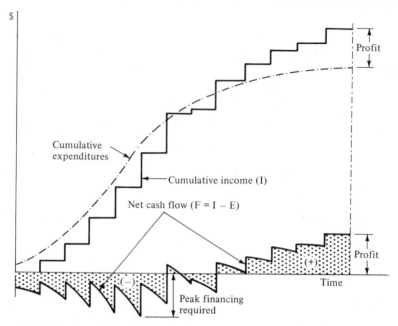

Figure 3-8 Cash flows. From Donald S. Barrie and Boyd C. Paulson, Jr., *Professional Construction Management*, McGraw-Hill, New York, 1978.

level based on the information available. Subsequent design development can supply information to plan to the next level of detail and in this way increase the accuracy of the plan and promote confidence in the estimate and schedule or recognize that more money and time will be required long before construction has proceeded to the point of no return.

Where a fully detailed plan is prepared, a summary reporting system can give the foreman the man-hour cost per square foot of forms compared to the estimate for his area. It can give the superintendent the overall man-hour cost for all types of forms, both by type and area, and it can give the project manager the overall cost of all forms to date compared to the original estimate. Each manager can ignore the operations that are proceeding according to plan and spend his time on the problem areas. See Figure 3-17 for a computerized report developed by an electrical-contractor to monitor weekly and cumulative productivity as well as progress.

PROCEDURES AND RESPONSIBILITIES

Someone has said that for any successful endeavor, the following are musts for the individual or manager:

• Know what to do.

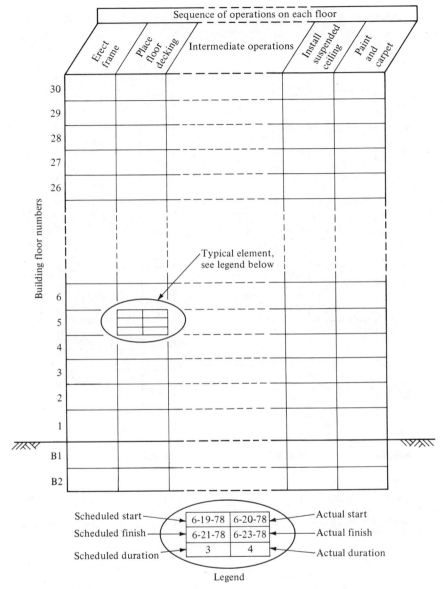

Figure 3-9 Matrix schedule. From Donald S. Barrie and Boyd C. Paulson, Jr., *Professional Construction Management*, McGraw-Hill, New York, 1978.

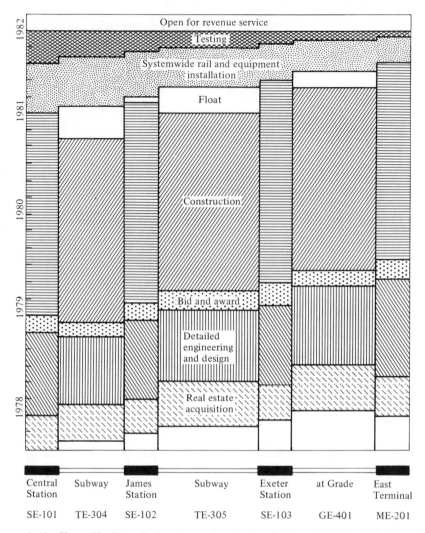

Figure 3-10 Horse blanket schedule. From Donald S. Barrie and Boyd C. Paulson, Jr., *Professional Construction Management*, McGraw-Hill, New York, 1978.

- Know how to do what is required.
- Have the resources to do what is required.
- Have the authority to do what is required.
- Want to do what is required.

Each level of management must know what is expected and must be skilled enough to be able to do it if he or she has the resources and authority to do it. In the construction industry, with few exceptions, the manager

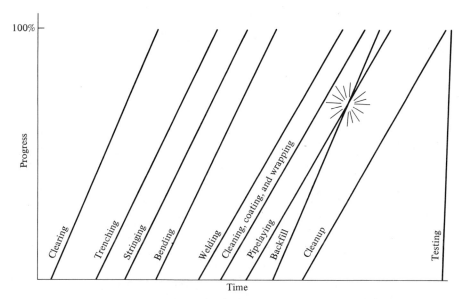

100%

Progress

Clearing

Trenching

Stringing

Bending

Welding

Cleaning, coating, and wrapping

Pipelaying

Backfill

Cleanup

Testing

Time

Figure 3-11 Linear balance chart. From Donald S. Barrie and Boyd C. Paulson, Jr., *Professional Construction Management*, McGraw-Hill, New York, 1978.

and craftsmen will want to do the work required if higher-level managers provide the prerequisites. Here again procedures are effective if they are developed on a level that fits the facts available and are given to knowledgeable managers who have the resources and responsibility to effectively carry them out.

Basically, the prime contract is the highest-level document delineating the responsibilities of the several parties to the contract and to others such as the engineer or material or equipment suppliers. Each participant in the project must organize his own portion in a way in which the individual manager will be assigned tasks that, when taken together, will hopefully result in a successful overall performance in accordance with the contract, schedule, and budget.

Procedures and work plans for a single-family home may consist of giving the foreman a copy of the plans and the building code and telling him how far he can go in his dealings with the subcontractors. On the other hand, for a nuclear power plant nearly every conceivable operation must be planned and determined in advance to comply with the provisions of the quality assurance program as set forth in Federal Regulation 10 CFR 50, Appendix B.

Therefore, an equally important planning tool consists of advising all participants in the program of what is expected of them and showing each party what is expected of others. A simple project procedure outline for a design-construct or construction management (CM) project may consist of the following items:

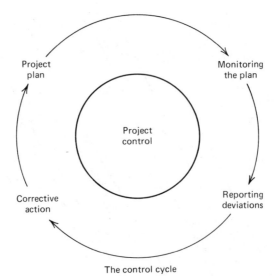

The control cycle

Figure 3-12   Elements of project control.

- General
  - Purpose
  - Key personnel
  - Correspondence requirements
  - Report requirements

- Responsibilities
  - Owner
  - Designer
  - Contractor or construction manager
  - Others

- Home office responsibilities
  - Planning
  - Control and schedules
  - Budget estimate
  - Major procurement
  - Work plan

- Field office responsibilities
  - Detail planning
  - Job schedules
  - Change order estimates
  - Field procurement
  - Safety program
  - Quality control program

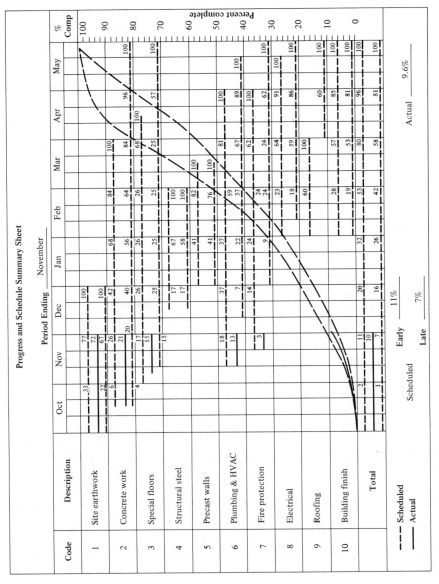

Figure 3-13 Construction schedule summary. From Donald S. Barrie and Boyd C. Paulson, Jr, *Professional Construction Management*, McGraw-Hill, New York, 1978.

Control account number	Description	Recorded costs	
		Current period	Cumulative to date
	Direct cost		
1000.0000	Site development and improvements	$ 32,215	$ 1,279,198
2000.0000	Buildings and structures	602,299	6,275,876
3000.0000	Process equipment and systems	228,836	1,731,133
4000.0000	Utilities distribution	110,560	1,825,050
6000.0000	Distributable directs	41,228	306,689
	Total direct cost	$1,015,138	$11,417,946
	Indirect cost		
7100.0000	Contractors field services	$ 25,789	$ 338,895
7200.0000	Construction plant	11,457	64,273
7300.0000	Construction equipment	9,614	47,749
	Total indirect cost	$ 46,860	$ 450,917
	Total construction cost	$1,061,998	$11,868,863
8100.0000	Engineering, supervision, and procurement	$ 17,337	$ 949,395
8900.0000	Contingency	0	0
9000.0000	Clearings	$ (1,304)	3,571
	Total project	$1,078,031	$12,821,829

Figure 3-14 Summary cost report.

PERIODIC REPORTS

Reporting on a periodic basis in both a qualitative and quantitative manner is an important part of control. Reporting on a single-family home built for an individual may consist of weekly visits to the site to visually monitor contractor quality and progress. On some major nuclear power plants reports literally number in the hundreds, and these include a report to keep track of all reports. Again, the reporting of every conceivable item or items specially selected for each management level can prove counterproductive.

A summary of the principal reports that might be common to commercial, industrial, and heavy construction projects of any size might include a sample monthly report which is intended to brief top contractor and/or owner managers regarding the status of the project compared to the overall objectives developed during the planning stage and modified to suit later experience, increased knowledge, and the effect of external and internal constraints.

Monthly Project Report

1. Summary of overall project status.
   ◦ Design.
   ◦ Procurement.

Open commitments	Cumulative total recorded and committed	Estimated cost		Budget	(Under) or over budget
		To complete	At completion		
$ 132,166	$ 1,411,364	$ 101,497	$ 1,512,861	$ 1,537,800	$(24,939)
247,683	6,523,559	627,477	7,151,036	7,235,000	(83,964)
1,700,729	3,431,862	838,379	4,270,241	4,360,000	(89,759)
1,252,602	3,077,652	753,348	3,831,000	3,815,900	15,100
296,384	603,073	345,122	948,195	1,000,300	(52,105)
$3,629,564	$15,047,510	$2,665,823	$17,713,333	$17,949,000	$(235,667)
$ 10,500	$ 349,395	$ 350,605	$ 700,000	$ 723,000	$(23,000)
3,167	67,440	10,560	78,000	78,000	0
1,251	49,000	0	49,000	50,000	(1,000)
$ 14,918	$ 465,835	$ 361,165	$ 827,000	$ 851,000	$(24,000)
$3,644,482	$15,513,345	$3,026,988	$18,540,333	$18,800,000	$(259,667)
$ 0	$ 949,395	$ 100,605	$ 1,050,000	$ 1,100,000	$(50,000)
0	0	782,000	782,000	1,800,000	$(1,018,000)
2,030	$ 5,601	(5,601)	0	0	0
$3,646,512	$16,468,341	$3,903,992	$20,372,333	$21,700,000	$(1,327,667)

Figure 3-14 (Continued)

- ∘ Construction.
- ∘ Schedule.
- ∘ Cost.
2. Design report.
3. Procurement report.
4. Construction Report.
5. Quality Assurance Report.
6. Schedule Report.
7. Cost Report.

TOOLS AND THE MANAGER

Planning and control tools are merely implements for use by knowledgeable managers much as the skilled craftsman uses his tools of the trade. Tools become dull, need replacement or sharpening, and become obsolete. The knowledgeable manager uses the tool for the job and discards it when it is no longer effective. The manager must control the evolution of the tools and of the technicians who carry out the detailed assignments in both the planning and control functions.

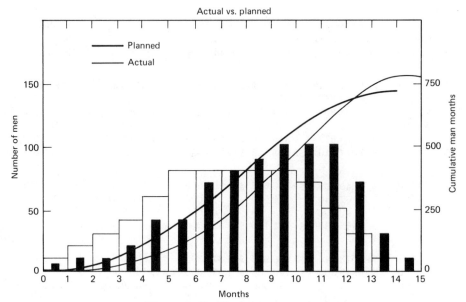

Figure 3-15   Manpower summary.

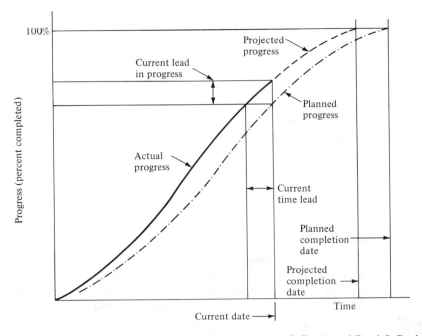

Figure 3-16   Planning and reporting progress. From Donald S. Barrie and Boyd C. Paulson, Jr., *Professional Construction Management*, McGraw-Hill, New York, 1978.

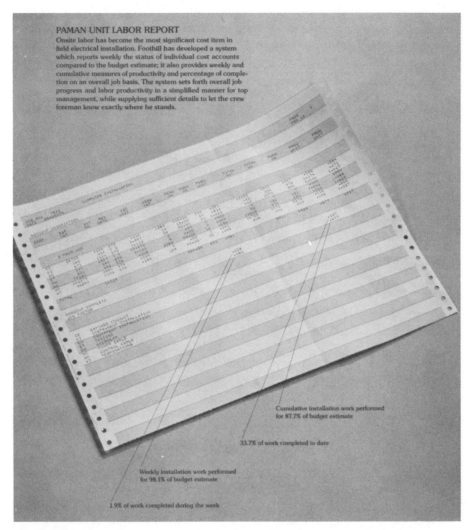

PAMAN UNIT LABOR REPORT

Onsite labor has become the most significant cost item in field electrical installation. Foothill has developed a system which reports weekly the status of individual cost accounts compared to the budget estimate; it also provides weekly and cumulative measures of productivity and percentage of completion on an overall job basis. The system sets forth overall job progress and labor productivity in a simplified manner for top management, while supplying sufficient details to let the crew foreman know exactly where he stands.

Cumulative installation work performed for 87.7% of budget estimate

33.7% of work completed to date

Weekly installation work performed for 98.1% of budget estimate

1.9% of work completed during the week

Figure 3-17 Unit labor report. Courtesy of Foothill Electric Corp. and *The Kaiser Builder*, Summer 1979.

When the computer printout reaches the stage where it is of no value to the manager, the elimination of the program may in itself represent a significant savings in the project. The management boom and the aerospace industry have produced very sophisticated computerized management control systems, all based on fundamental logic but often with questionable reliability for the input data. The industry must begin to evaluate the management tools based on effectiveness rather than theoretical promise, if the promise of the management boom is to be in any way realized.

CHAPTER 4

THE GROWING INDUSTRY MANAGEMENT PROBLEMS

Donald S. Barrie

With the construction revival following World War II, the construction industry began a period of rapid growth with increasing demand in each of the major industry divisions. The rapid economic growth introduced four new conditions that continue to affect the performance levels which can be expected to be encountered on most major and many smaller new projects:

- Project size began to increase substantially in dollar value, peak work force requirements, complexity, and overall duration.
- Design, procurement, and construction increasingly began to overlap as owners endeavored to shorten overall design-construction schedules through phased construction programs.
- Government regulations and the effects of special interest groups began to have an increasingly detremental effect on the cost and scheduled performance as big government and special interest intervenors became increasingly active.
- Owner involvement in the execution phase of many major projects became increasingly important as owner dissatisfaction began to increase.

The number of individual management problems on many major projects may seem to be almost insurmountable. Yet on many smaller or more finite projects, job management has effectively dealt with the same problems in an effective manner. Management problems affecting the construction industry are summarized in the following groups:

- Work force problems.
- Organization problems.

- Contractual problems.
- Regulatory problems.
- Design problems.

To illustrate the potential savings from management action at the super-project level, an analysis of the on-site productivity of craftsmen on a moderately sized project is compared with an average of 15 nuclear power plants. If the United States is to continue in a leadership role in the construction industry, management methods must find a way to improve performance on the very large and complex projects.

CONDITIONS AFFECTING PERFORMANCE

Increasing project size and complexity, increasing use of phased construction programs, increasing effect of government regulations and special interest groups, and the emerging owner involvement in the construction process has given notice that the traditional management methods will not be enough to cope with the interaction of all of the new complexities upon a single major project.

PROJECT SIZE AND COMPLEXITY

Project size and complexity continue to increase in all segments of the industry. In the housing and residential area billion-dollar cities are being developed on new sites in the oil rich middle east. The building industry has produced the Sears tower, the New Orleans superdome, and other previously unprecedented structures with mixed results. Industrial construction has produced billion-dollar steel mills, billion-dollar nuclear power plants, and other projects on an unprecedented scale. The heavy construction industry has the multibillion-dollar Alaskan Pipeline, Mangla Dam in Pakistan, the St. James Bay hydroelectric project in Quebec, and other unprecedented projects. Material and equipment suppliers have fully participated in the program with increasingly larger equipment such as nuclear reactor containment vessels, the production of 150 yd^3 capacity walking draglines, boilers, turbines, and generators of unprecedented size, and similar applications in essentially all industries. Increasing size and complexity present a major challenge to the management team.

PHASED CONSTRUCTION PROGRAMS

The traditional method, still used on many large individual projects, features complete working drawings prepared by an architect, architect/engineer, or engineer. A reasonable bidding period was selected and several contractors prepared proposals and submitted lump sum, unit price, or combination bids. The owner and his designer evaluated the bids and normally awarded the work to the lower bidder. This system has many advantages as set forth in Chapter 2. However, this system's major disadvantage in a period of increasing inflation, high interest rates, and high demand for the finished product is the length of time from start to design to completion of construction. By overlapping the individual phases and the component parts, initial construction can begin after completion of site work drawings. Under such a fast track concept, overall design may not be completed until late in the program. Overall shortening of the total design-construct duration can be sizable on many projects when compared to traditional projects constructed sequentially.

Phase construction programs began to be applied to all sections of the industry on large, medium, and small projects. The added complexities involved in beginning work and completing major components of the work before overall design planning is complete has represented a major challenge to industry management to achieve comparable performance to that demonstrated in the more traditional construction process.

GOVERNMENT REGULATIONS AND SPECIAL INTEREST GROUPS

In the classic traditional construction program, most projects were first fully designed on paper, and, depending on the project location, government regulations and influence of other special interest groups were largely involved in the preconstruction activities such as reviewing or obtaining a building permit, developing building codes, developing or changing zoning regulations and other such activities that were usually fully determined when site construction began. The effect of the regulators on the conduct of the work by the contractor was generally minimal so long as the contractor followed the plans and specifications, adopted good safety practices, and in general conducted a well-managed business.

With the increase in big government every component of the industry is affected by both local and national level government regulations and special interest groups that have grown equally powerful. Not only has the preconstruction period been complicated by the increasing regulatory requirements, the actual construction process is equally affected as the regulator and the intervenor develops on-the-job enforcement and modification programs to insure that regulatory compliance is in fact achieved. Regulatory changes or modifications during the construction phase create a ripple effect that requires management solutions of design, economic, schedule, and responsibility interfaces throughout the life of the project.

OWNER INVOLVEMENT

Under the traditional method owner involvement was generally minimal, with some owners taking a sizable interest in management aspects of the project, while others delegated such responsibilities to the architect, engineer, or other designated party. As the increasing interaction of three of the four emerging conditions resulted in schedule and cost overruns of an heretofore unprecedented magnitude, the owner began to become involved in the management process largely due to the failure of traditional management methods and the new computer-assisted management control systems to achieve performance comparable to planned objectives.

In the utility area many major utilities are developing owner-dominated management teams to lead major projects. The owner took over operational control of construction on the largest project to date, the Alaska Pipeline, prior to completion. The increasing influx of a major task-force-type organization staffed by managers who are many times unfamiliar with the construction industry practices and complications, but are extremely conscious of the overall project costs is presenting additional complications.

The entry of the owner into active management of major construction projects has evolved because of dissatisfaction with industry cost and schedule performance. Whether this new concept will prove effective or counterproductive will await a meaningful performance evaluation over several projects.

PROBLEMS AFFECTING PERFORMANCE

Individual problems have always taxed the ingenuity and skill of construction management and supervision. Such problems are always found on the very smallest to the very largest projects. Individual job and company managers' abilities to solve such problems have traditionally marked the line of demarcation between successful projects and companies and the unsuccessful or marginal performer. The ability of proven supervision using traditional industry management methods to cope with individual problems seems to be far more effective on smaller- to medium-sized projects, on traditional projects, where design and construction do not overlap, where government regulation is not a major factor during the construction phase, and where contractor management is basically responsible for major construction decisions rather than the owner.

WORK FORCE PROBLEMS

Work force problems include those with local labor organizations, those at the national level, and those affecting the individual workmen. It is difficult to generalize regarding individual labor unions. Responsible international officials may be thoroughly frustrated by powerful local leaders. In other cases foresighted local business managers and memberships recognized that employer-union relationships can be mutually helpful rather than destructive. In other areas responsible local officials may be handicapped by less responsible international officers. Some areas of the country are generally known as good places to work. Others have adopted practices that result in an overall climate which discourages productivity to such an extent that many knowledgeable national contractors prefer not to perform work in these sections.

Local Labor Relationship

Historically, local agreements were negotiated by local contractor groups with local unions. Large national contractors coming into the area would accept the wages and working conditions set forth in the local agreement but would not participate in local bargaining and would generally sign interim agreements with the local unions to avoid shutdowns during local wage-bargaining disputes. Since a large industrial project in an area might employ a major fraction of the local labor force, local contractors found it difficult to resist wage demands, since the union could strike local contractors and hold out almost indefinitely a when a large part of the membership would continue to work on the major project that the national contractor was performing under a cost plus a fee contract with the owner.

Local contractors often fought back by negotiating special clauses for travel time, premium wages on large projects, or other working conditions that did not affect most of the local jobs in an effort to hold down the overall settlement as it affected local work.

Local agreements sometimes specify production limitations such as setting maximum production quotas. But more often they introduce organized coffee breaks, excessive tool pick-up time, nonworking stewards, manpower limitations, limitations on operating more than one piece of equipment, and other featherbedding practices.

Equally or more important is the prevailing practice in the area of excessive coffee breaks, early quitting, production limitations, seniority layoffs, local union preference in choosing foremen, and other practices, most of which were covered by the "Ten Commandments" and the formalized "Work Rules Agreements" negotiated by the NCA and the Building Trades during the early 1970s. Of course, in this area individual contractor supervision will often mean the difference between effective control and rampant featherbedding irrespective of other projects in the area.

The local union approach to jurisdictional disputes can have a major effect on work force productivity. Many areas take pride that no union walks off the job because of jurisdictional disputes. Rather such disputes are settled in a well-organized local program with strong union backing. Other areas demand a walk off whenever a dispute is not settled in their favor. As in featherbedding, contractor supervision is often the difference between a minor disruption to the job and a major problem.

The skill of the craftsmen can be influenced by the locals' attitude toward race, color, and sex discrimination as well as by contractor cooperation in apprenticeship programs, training sessions, and other influences.

In many areas there are two sets of rules. One set is for local contractors with an essentially stable work force. Here the union offers minimum or no interference, and local contractor supervision is in full control of the work force. However, on the big project handled by the out-of-town contractor, nonworking stewards may police work rules and jurisdictional refinements with guardhouse lawyer tactics.

Overall, some areas of the country are better than others in achieving a productive climate. Some unions are better or worse than others in assisting to maintain efficiencies, and some contractors show more or less skill than their counterparts in enforcing job discipline, working to achieve a harmonious relationship, and achieving productivity gains. The local contractors who achieve a productive climate generally are far more successful than their less-productive competitors, and in the long run the more inefficient producers will be eliminated from the marketplace.

National Labor Relationships

As industrial construction began to accelerate the NCA became increasingly important in dealings with the labor unions, with other contractor associates, and in endeavoring to influence legislation. However, the major employer organizations, including AGC, NECA, MCA, and NCA, have never been able to subordinate individual objectives to develop a united front in dealing with construction unions or influencing legislation in any way that has been comparable to labor's ability to unite in its lobbying and negotiating efforts.

AGC has historically believed in local bargaining with the building trades, while NCA has increasingly tried to negotiate broad national agreements. Other differences regarding the settlement of jurisdictional disputes have also continued over the years.

At present using Political Action Committees (PAC), the Contractor's Mutual Association, and through a recent attempt to unite in NCEC, the employer groups are again trying to unite at the Washington level. It remains to be seen whether the conflicting individual objectives will prevent a meaningful and beneficial association at the national level as they have in the past.

MAJOR LABOR ORGANIZATIONS. Historically, the large international unions that make up the building trades have held a strong lobbying position in national politics through their activity and location in Washington, D.C. They have also become much more influential locally as the heavy industrial construction sector showed heavy growth.

The Building and Construction Trades Council consists of the following AFL-CIO unions:

- Bricklayers.
- Carpenters.
- Cement finishers.
- Electricians.
- Glaziers.
- Iron workers.
- Laborers.
- Lathers.
- Operating engineers.
- Painters.
- Plasterers.
- Plumbers and steam fitters.
- Roofers.
- Sheet metal workers.
- Other specialty contractors.

The Teamsters are not presently members of the AFL-CIO. However, they normally cooperate with local building trades at the local level.

MAJOR CONTRACTOR AND OWNER ORGANIZATIONS. Dealing with the international unions, attempting to influence local productivity, and also engaging in lobbying activities in the Washington, D.C., area are the following major employer groups:

AGC
NCA
NECA
MCA
Sheet Metal and Air Conditioning Contractors Association.
Numerous specialty associations.

ABC, the sponsor of the Merit Shop, is also active in overall productivity improvement and Washington lobbying in an open shop environment.

Increasingly, joint contractors and owners or owners' associations are becoming more active at the Washington and local levels as well as in endeavoring to increase productivity and to resist excessive wage increases or feather bedding. Major organizations active in Washington, D. C., and nationwide include Business Round Table and Contractor's Mutual Association.

Individual Craftsmen Relationships

Equally important to the improvement of productivity are job relationships between the contractor, the superintendent, the foreman, and the craftsman. Based on a study prepared by Marjatta Strandell of the Pacific Power and Light Company, union workers in power plant construction average only 22 to 34% direct useful work or less than three hours per day. Other studies, generally performed on large power projects have effectively substantiated these findings. See figures 4-1 and 4-2 for results of the Strandell study.

Much of the reason behind declining productivity on major power plant projects as the size of the project increases can be attributed to effects stemming from the nuclear quality assurance program as delineated in Federal Regulation 10 CFR 50. Much of the decline can be attributed to job management problems, use of unskilled workers, or lack of materials or tools. However, much of the decline remains attributable to the individual workman and his attitude toward his craft, his peers, his foremen, and his supervisors.

PRIDE IN CRAFTSMANSHIP. Thirty years ago in construction most craftsmen took a great deal of pride in their work. Most foremen were more knowledgeable mechanics than those they supervised. Most superintendents came up through the crafts and had the respect of the entire crew. The typical craftsman took pride in both the quality and the quantity of

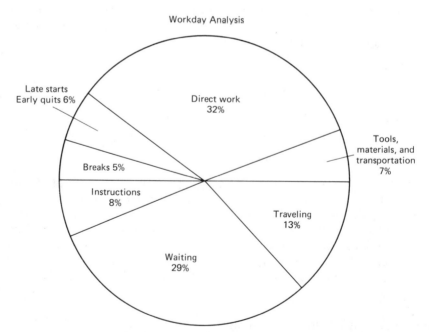

Figure 4-1 Workday analysis. From Peter A. Cockshaw, *Employers Must Regain Their Right to Manage Before Productivity Can Improve,* Plant Facilities, November/December 1977.

Craft	Time in Direct Work (%)
Boilermakers	27
Pipe fitters/welders	28
Electrical workers	28
Laborers	41
Carpenters	42
Insulators	26
Operating engineers	39
Ironworkers	31
Millwrights	32

From Peter A. Cockshaw, *Employers Must Regain Their Right to Manage Before Production Can Improve,* Plant Facilities, November/December 1977.

Figure 4-2   Direct work.

his output. Nonproducers were usually removed from the project by the foreman as a matter of course.

Today, this condition still exists on most reasonably sized projects constructed by local contractors with repetitive work loads. However, this condition does not exist on major power plant projects and appears to be affecting almost every large contractor active in this field.

ORGANIZATIONAL PROBLEMS

Organizational problems exist at all industry levels and are evident on small projects as well as on superprojects. Figure 2-1 showed several alternate organizational approaches for a project. Use of the wrong organizational concept can predetermine a detrimental effect throughout the entire project. Within the framework of an organizational concept, there is the choice of the task force, the functional organization, the line and functional staff, and the new matrix organization. At the job level development of departmental responsibilities, reporting, and accountability relationships can help or hinder overall project control. And finally the selection, training, motivation and promotion of key individuals is becoming increasingly difficult.

Choosing Organizational Options

On a major nuclear power plant jobsite contractor salaried organizations, including nuclear quality assurance, may approach 20% or more of the craft workforce. Add to this the effect of the regulators such as OSHA and the NRC and the on-site forces of the design engineer and the owner. The development of a jobsite organizational to minimize communication difficulties, overlapping responsibilities, and sheer inertia of getting anything done should be approached as a management problem of perhaps greater importance than preparation of detailed procedures. Yet management consideration and theory are seldom directly applied in the development of a major jobsite management organization that in itself will control annual expenditures which are greater than many major corporations.

The interrelationships between the client, the contractor or construction manager, and the designer will depend heavily on the organizational concept chosen and the presence of inherent adversary relationships. These interfaces require knowledgeable top management involvement in order to minimize conflicts, eliminate duplication, and inhibit the formation of other detrimental relationships that may be prevalent on projects of any size level.

The traditional contractors' organization was developed to implement a plan prepared during the bidding phase based on very accurate quantities of work that were "taken off" from fully detailed plans and specifications. On a typical phased construction or fast track program much of the work will begin before overall quantities have been developed. Often the organization is expected to react quickly to major changes and numerous drawing revisions. There is little theoretical understanding of the cumulative effects of superproject size, overlapping design and construction, and outside regulations all impacting on the construction management organization.

CONTRACTUAL PROBLEMS

A nationally known insurance company has stated that one out of four building professionals will either face a lawsuit or arbitration during this year.

Settlements in injury actions are reaching new heights. And it is becoming both difficult and expensive to obtain sufficient liability insurance to insure business continuity in the event of a major problem.

Owners are beginning to expect contractor, design-constructor, and architect-engineer to pay for their errors often including peripheral or consequential damages as well.

Increasingly, contractual decisions are being made by lawyers, and the threat of litigation often dominates many relationships. Yet major lawsuits may take from five to eight years before going to trial. Often legitimate claims would be better forgotten than pursuing them through the unwieldly and expensive judicial establishment. Labor law, discrimination, equal opportunity statutes, safety requirements, and other areas of potential dispute require considerable foresight in order to avoid major problems.

The possibility of double-digit inflation on long-term projects has introduced a large number of devices to attempt to retain the traditional fixed price bid on major projects, while removing some or all of the escalation risk from the bidders. Many times the chosen index introduces additional risks to the bidders and to the owner.

With the rush to overlapping design and construction, drawing revisions have become common on many projects. When fixed price contracts are awarded on one set of plans and drawing revisions make major alterations, claims and conflict are the almost inevitable result.

REGULATORY PROBLEMS

Excessive government regulations were cited as the most significant business problem facing engineers in 1977 according to the American Consulting Engineering Council. The cost of the avalanche of paperwork imposed by the federal government reaches $100 billion per year of which the federal government spends one-third and industry the balance. State, county, and local governments combined may also approach this figure.

Contractors and architects-engineers face almost daily problems in dealing with armies of inspectors who have the authority to fully disrupt any construction project. Relatedly, licensing and permit procedures often inhibit the orderly development of a project and add to the cost to such an extent that many viable projects become uneconomic.

Laws and agency rulings concerning labor relations represent an ever-changing set of separate legal requirements. Policies are set by the National Labor Relations Board, the Federal Trade Commission, DOE, the Environmental Protection Agency, the Nuclear Regulatory Commission, and other agencies as well as laws enacted by the Congress.

Compliance with the tax laws of the federal government, states, counties, and cities is becoming a major undertaking for the construction industry. Additionally, excessive subcontractor listings, minority-contracting programs, ethnic job quotas, and civil rights and other requirements add to the paperwork monster.

DESIGN PROBLEMS

There is little incentive for innovative design solutions when liability considerations favor the use of proven solutions. Yet the United States is losing its technological leadership to countries like Germany and Japan that have found profitable growth through innovation.

Designers have difficulty using lowest-cost materials and methods, since with today's rapid inflation the old rules of thumb in designing for minimum concrete or steel use are no longer cost effective. Also, the overlapping of design with construction has introduced an ever-changing climate, with several projects going through the alphabet in drawing revisions before the job is finished.

The designer, the owner, and the constructor are often in an adversary relationship, with each blaming the other for cost and schedule overruns and quality or utility short-comings. Designers are increasingly being held to be accountable for damages to third parties, and obtaining satisfactory error and omission insurance is becoming increasingly difficult.

SUPERPROJECT PERFORMANCE

While the growing industry management problems are being experienced in all segments of the industry, the most dramatic illustrations of industry-wide management failures can be shown on the very largest projects, often called "superprojects." Perhaps the best illustration of the failure to develop superproject performance comparable to standards achievable on more manageable projects is in the nuclear power plant field where substantial performance data are available. Figure 4-3 shows a tabulation of superproject performance on nuclear power plants comparing mid-1960 performance with 1980 experience.

In the mid-1960s nuclear power plants were being built with a lead time of five years; today, the time has doubled. On-site man-hours have tripled, and design hours have quadrupled. The only consistent fact is that few or no plants have ever been built with the original schedule or within the original budget. Clearly, if current trends continue, the age of nuclear power will require an overall management approach far different from present practice if it is to become a reality.

What does all this mean? A nuclear power plant is made up of concrete, steel, pipe, wire, and equipment much like any other project. Figure 4-4 shows a comparison of the basic hourly units for electrical work on a $35,000,000 experimental Magneto-Hydro-Dynamics (MHD) plant constructed for the Department of Energy in Montana compared to similar units obtained from a 15-nuclear plant average as developed from a study by Dr. John Borcherding, a professor, at the university of Texas at Austin specializing in productivity studies. The MHD plant was chosen because the average conduit and wire (with several exceptions) were quite similar to those found on a typical nuclear plant.

The basic nuclear plant electrical installation of rigid conduit and pulling

	Mid-1960	1980
Lead time (years)	5	10−12
Construction (hours/kw)	3−4	11−12
Design (hours/kw)	0.5	1.4−1.9
Cost ($/kwe)	$120	1100

Figure 4-3 Superproject performance (based on nuclear power plants)

	Project A	15 nuclear* plant average
Project Cost	$35,000,000	$800,000,000
Cable pulling		
Power	0.05	0.17 mh/lf
Control	0.01	0.07 mh/lf
Cable tray	0.52	2.3 mh/lf
Conduit	0.25	1.01 mh/lf
Terminations		
Power	3.40	2.5 mh/ea
Control	0.33	0.7 mh/ea
Weighted average job factor	1.0	3.4
Weighted average productivity	1.0	0.29

Figure 4-4 Productivity comparison. The job factor is man hours per unit compared to 1.0 for a selected $35,000,000 project. Productivity is the reciprocal of job factor.

power and control cable and making the required terminations took 3.4 times as many on-site hours to complete the same amount of work that was completed for 1.0 hours on the MHD plant. Stated another way, productivity on the nuclear plant is only 29% of that on the MHD experimental plant.

POTENTIAL REWARD FOR IMPROVING PRODUCTIVITY

What is the potential reward for achieving substantial productivity improvement on the superproject as exemplified by the nuclear power plant? Figure 4-5 shows a typical billion-dollar project. Assuming that the work of other crafts is affected similarly to that of the electrical work shown in Figure 4-4, 50% improvement in productivity would still result in craft hours being 70% greater than demonstrated performance in our MHD plant. Surely, the nuclear quality assurance programs should be able to be accomplished within a 70% cost increase if more effective management performance can be achieved.

HOPE FOR OUR FUTURE

Many construction professionals have concluded that the computerized management control system has failed at the superproject level. Motivational factors prevalent on smaller projects produce individual and group performance far superior to performance on the larger projects. Yet motivation cannot be restricted to the building trades and the production

*Unit Man Hour Units developed from Improving Productivity in Industrial Construction by John D. Borcherding, Journal of the Construction Division, ASCE, vol 102, no. CO4, Dec. 1976, pg 607

Case I	15 Plant average
Material and equipment	320,000,000
Labor	250,000,000
Indirect cost	130,000,000
Design and financing	300,000,000
Total cost	$1,000,000,000
Duration	8 years
Labor hours	10,000,000
Job factor	3.4
Case II	50% Productivity improvement
Materials and equipment	320,000,000
Labor	125,000,000
Indirect cost	95,000,000
Design and financing	210,000,000
Total cost	$750,000,000
Duration	6 years
Labor hours	5,000,000
Job factor	1.7

Conclusion: Total savings due to productivity increases will be at least double the labor savings.

Figure 4-5   Billion-Dollar Project.

worker. Economy and pride of performance must be found in the contractor's and subcontractor's organization, the designer, the regulatory agencies, and in the owner's organization if the promises of the management boom are to be fulfilled. The following chapters take a more detailed look at the state of the art, the problems, and proposed solutions for future efficiencies. Traditional management methods will not achieve a reversal of current trends. The future is truly in the hands of today's and tomorrow's managers.

PART 2

MANAGEMENT AND ORGANIZATION PRACTICES, PROBLEMS, AND SOLUTIONS

CHAPTER 5

HOUSING AND
RESIDENTIAL CONSTRUCTION*

Donald S. Barrie

By far the largest individual share of the construction market is captured by the housing and residential segment of the industry. During 1979 approximately 1.7 million equivalent homes were constructed with an overall value of almost $100 billion. The industry contractors and subcontractors range from individual entrepreneurs who perform much of the labor themselves to large national builders such as U.S. Home and Kaufman and Broad. New starts are quick to adjust to demand that fluctuates based on interest rates, regional and national demand, inflation rates, mortgage money availability, and all the effects of the business cycle. During boom times almost everyone makes money, and a large number of new firms enter the industry. During recessions demand drops, and a large number of high-cost and marginal contractors are squeezed from the market, and even the industry leaders have difficulty achieving reasonable profits.

EVOLUTION OF HOUSING CONCEPTS

The American dream has been based on a home of your own for every family. In addition, homes continue to become more functional, and new convenience items are introduced yearly. From 1970 to 1977 the median area for new one-family homes went from 1510 to 1720. Homes with two or

*The author is indebted to Don McKechnie, registered plan designer and general contractor, Lafayette, California, for assistance in the preparation of this chapter.

more bathrooms jumped from 48 to 70%; those with dishwashers went from 42 to 82%; homes with fireplaces increased from 35 to 61%; and homes with garages increased from 58 to 68%. Hot tubs, saunas, shampoo bowls, security systems, intercom systems, and even programmable computers are being introduced into the custom market.

As both the size and utility of the median home continues to increase, basic costs for land, financing, and builders' overhead continue to capture a much larger share of the housing dollar. Figure 5-1 summarizes component costs for a typical single-family house for 1949 to 1977.

A new phenomenon in the postwar economy has been the appreciation of the average home at a rate generally in excess of consumer prices and the overall cost of living. For most Americans, the single-family home has proved to be an excellent investment.

Concurrently with the bull market in owner-occupied homes, the apartment and rental property segment of the industry has been more equivocal. Increased taxes, increased government regulations, rent control laws, and other cost factors, coupled with practical rent maximums, have made it difficult to achieve operating profits, with returns being largely achieved through capital gains on the sale of the property. In fact, a thriving current segment of the industry is engaged in the conversion of apartments and other multiple dwelling units to condominiums to eliminate operating losses and achieve higher capital gains through sales to the individual homeowner market than can be justified from sale of a going commercial enterprise. Figure 5-2 provides a comparison of apartment construction costs and rent costs prepared by the Bank of America, San Francisco, California.

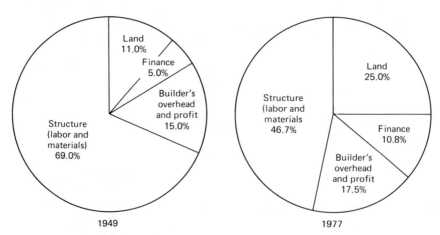

1949   1977

Figure 5-1 Component costs—typical new single-family house, 1949 and 1977. From the National Association of Home Builders.

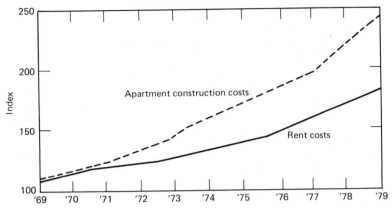

Figure 5-2 Apartment construction costs versus rent costs. From study by the Bank of America, San Francisco.

Clearly, the United States is beginning to rely on multiple dwellings to preserve the American dream in the face of ever-increasing housing and land costs. The promotion of semidetached houses with common walls, town houses, condominiums, and even low-rent subsidized multiple units appear to be America's answer to the problem that fostered the development of multiple housing in Britain and Europe.

TRADE AND CONTRACTOR PRACTICE

The housing industry is unique in that essentially similar products are often produced by the largest builder and the very smallest builder. The techniques used in constructing the house on site are very similar or identical, and the codes, regulations, and local inspection practices apply equally to all firms.

Factory production of individual homes has held great promise ever since the first prefabricated "Great House" was shipped from England in 1624 to Cape Ann, Massachusetts. However, at present, possibly only about 15% of individual homes in the United States are substantially built using assembly line methods in a central factory. In the beginning union pressure undoubtedly handicapped the use of the factory-built home. However, today, much of the home building industry is either nonunion or open shop, and the traditional stick-built house still predominates with prefabrication limited to on-site work and to mechanical and other specialty items prefabricated in the shop or factory, with final assembly at the home site. However, the house trailer industry is growing substantially and is providing an increasing share of functional and affordable housing in well-laid out and maintained mobile home parks. And for the first time, many better mobile homes are beginning to appreciate in value.

All housing contractors rely heavily on subcontractors for specialty items. The typical general contractor may install the concrete foundations, erect the basic frame using prefabricated trusses, and perform the finish carpentry with his own forces while subcontracting everything else. Some very successful developers subcontract all the work and only handle overall planning, land purchases, marketing concepts, and other businesslike duties, leaving the actual construction to others.

Major operational levels in the home building industry include a number of size levels such as the following:

- Individual entrepreneurs build essentially one or two homes at a time on speculation.
- Small businessmen-developers who may perform remodel work on existing homes, construct one or two contract jobs, handle a speculative home or two, and possibly bid on small commercial work in a given geographic location.
- Regional custom or tract home developers who will create new subdivisions or handle groups of homes in existing subdivisions where the basic property development has been by others.
- National tract and custom developers who generally operate nationally through several regional subsidiary companies or divisions who operate much like their regional competitors.

MANAGEMENT TOOLS

Use of management tools in the home building industry varies with the individual firm and with the class of work. As expected the larger the firm the more elaborate the estimating, scheduling, and control systems.

A first-class individual entrepreneur handling one or two houses at a time and subcontracting all the specialty work may handle all the scheduling details in his head yet have the work so well organized that the subcontractors are able to come in on call, do their work without interference or delays, and leave in a very efficient manner. On a large tract housing project a single superintendent may be able to plan the overall approach and direct the individual subcontractors in a similar and equally effective manner. Other builders may use bar charts, CPM diagrams, and other scheduling and progress reporting tools to try to control the construction schedule.

Estimating methods vary equally widely throughout the industry, ranging from the speculative individual entrepreneur in boom times who completes the framing and awards all the subcontracts before he sets his price to elaborate individual estimating systems developed by the regional and national builders. Perhaps the least use of a man-hour base for cost esti-

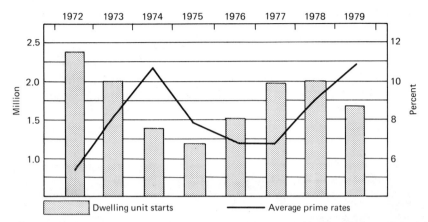

Figure 5-3 Closing the money door for housing. Home buyers are less frightened by high interest rates than in the past, but the harsh fact of economic life remains: a rising prime rate signals less funds ahead for construction loans and mortgage lending. A downturn in housing starts now seems inevitable. Data for 1978 and 1979 are estimated. From *Forbes*, January 8, 1979.

mates and corporate records is found in the home building industry where a repetitive product and a high degree of subcontracting has fostered the use of the unit price or unit cost estimating methods that combine material and labor costs into a single unit which may be as detailed or as broad as the individual builder selects.

The builders who are able to complete their projects within a predictable time frame and who have arranged for sales in advance to avoid today's high interest and other carrying charges will continue to survive and prosper, while their less-foresighted competition will find that long-range survival in the housing market is equally or more difficult than in any other branch of the construction industry. Figure 5-3 compares average prime rates and dwelling unit starts.

Figure 5-4 shows a cost study produced quarterly by the Bank of American covering a standard single-family residence. Figure 5-5 shows a typical construction program listing the inspections required and a typical progress payment program.

Schedules and costs for essentially similar houses may vary substantially, dependent on the skill of the manager or superintendents, the amount of competition, and the ability of the builder to coordinate a large number of subcontractors and to avoid delays and interferences. For example, it may take six months to construct a well-managed custom home of 2500 ft², while a skilled tract builder may turn them out in four months simply by eliminating most of the time spent waiting on subcontractors, along with certain on-site prefabrication advantages due to a large number of essentially identical units.

SPECULATIVE HOME BUILDERS

During good times with a high demand for housing, accompanied by plentiful credit, a large number of individual entrepreneurs enter the home building business. They may arrange to obtain several lots and often are in partnership with others who contribute labor, financing, and/or credit guarantees. These "spec" builders will generally perform much of the basic foundation, framing, and carpentry work themselves and will subcontract

COST STUDY
JULY 1980

STANDARD QUALITY SINGLE FAMILY RESIDENCE SAN FRANCISCO AREA		$ COST AS OF 7/1/80	% CHANGE SINCE		% OF TOTAL DOLLARS	$ COST PER S.F.
			4/1/80	7/1/79		
PRELIMINARY 1.0 AND GENERAL CONDITIONS	.1 Permits, plan checking, temporary power, water, portable toilet, debris box	984	+ 2.2b	+ 4.9	1.6	.63
	.2 Final clean-up (allowance)	325	+ 30.0	+ 51.2	.5	.21
SITE 2.0 WORK	.1 Site preparation and excavation	749	+ 6.8	+ 16.1	1.2	.48
	.2 Flatwork (driveway, patio, walks)	1,509	+ 4.7	+ 14.5	2.4	.96
CONCRETE 3.0	.1 Foundations, slabs, piers	2,388	+ 2.1	+ 11.1	3.7	1.49
MASONRY 4.0	.1 Brick hearth and face veneer at fireplace	429	+ 4.4	+ 12.3	.7	.27
METAL 5.0	.1 Rough hardware	275	0	+ 11.3	.4	.18
	.2 Finish hardware (allowance)	150	+ 20.0	+ 20.0	.2	.10
WOOD 6.0 AND CABINETRY	.1 Rough lumber	5,975	+ 2.4	− 3.7	9.7	3.80
	.2 Finish lumber	295	+ 3.1	− 16.0	.5	.19
	.3 Rough carpenter labor	5,016	+ 9.0	+ 9.0	8.0	3.19
	.4 Finish carpenter labor	1,003	+ 9.0	+ 9.0	1.6	.64
	.5 Countertops (cultured marble and laminated plastic)	888	+ 11.0	+ 19.8	1.4	.57
	.6 Cabinets	2,163	+ 1.5	+ 12.5	3.5	1.38
THERMAL 7.0 AND MOISTURE PROTECTION	.1 Insulation, weather stripping, thresholds	1,364	+ 10.0	+ 13.3	2.2	.87
	.2 Roofing (medium shakes)	3,707	+ 4.6	− 5.1	5.9	2.35
DOORS 8.0 AND WINDOWS	.1 Doors	1,234	+ 6.3	a	2.0	.79
	.2 Garage door	279	0	+ 4.5	.4	.18
	.3 Aluminum windows, glass sliding doors, all with screens	871	+ 3.4	+ 16.3	1.4	.55
FINISHES 9.0	.1 Stucco	3,558	+ 11.3	+ 18.2	5.7	2.27
	.2 Gypsum wallboard, ceiling acoustical spray	2,790	+ 3.0	+ 8.0	4.5	1.78
	.3 Resilient flooring (allowance)	1,300	+ 13.0	+ 18.2	2.1	.83
	.4 Carpeting (allowance)	1,400	0	+ 12.0	2.2	.89
	.5 Painting	2,369	+ 7.3	+ 15.7	3.8	1.51
SPECIALTIES 10.0	.1 Shower and tub enclosures	263	+ 1.9	+ 20.6	.4	.17
	.2 Prefabricated fireplace	580	0	0	.9	.37
	.3 Bath accessories (allowance)	400	+ 14.3	+ 14.3	.6	.25
APPLIANCES 11.0	.1 Built-ins (allowance)	1,000	+ 11.1	+ 17.6	1.6	.64
12.0 13.0 14.0	(No items under these divisions)					
MECHANICAL 15.0	.1 Heating and sheetmetal	2,327	+ 4.4	+ 7.5	3.7	1.48
	.2 Plumbing, including sewer connection	4,912	+ 7.5	+ 11.6	7.9	3.13
ELECTRICAL 16.0	.1 Wiring	1,922	+ 4.0	+ 9.5	3.1	1.22
	.2 Fixtures (allowance)	650	0	+ 13.0	1.0	.41
	SUB-TOTAL	53,025	+ 5.8	+ 8.3	84.8	
A.	Insurance: Workers' Compensation, Social Security, Unemployment	1,264	+ 9.1	+ 9.1	2.0	.81
B.	Overhead and profit 15%	7,954	+ 5.8	+ 8.3	12.7	5.06
C.	Plans and Specifications	301	+ 5.8	+ 9.1	.5	.19
	TOTAL CONSTRUCTION COST	62,544	+ 5.8	+ 8.3	100.0	39.84

SUMMARY		AREA	S.F. COST	TOTAL	NOTES:
	House	1570 S.F.	34.79	$ 54,619	(a) Denotes change of less than 1%.
	Garage	446 S.F.	14.39	6,416	(b) Miscellaneous municipal fees & taxes not included.
	Patios, Driveway, Walks	837 S.F.	1.80	1,509	
	TOTAL CONSTRUCTION COST			$ 62,544	

BANK OF AMERICA

APPRAISAL DEPARTMENT

Figure 5-4 Cost study. Reprinted by permission of the Bank of America, San Francisco.

BUILDING LOAN INSPECTION REPORT

	Payment No.	(This side to be completed by appraiser)	Payment Plan (A)	Payment Plan (B)
Primarily for use in conventional one and two story, single family or small multi-unit residential construction.	1	☐ 1. Foundation complete. ☐ 2. Underground plumbing in and stubbed thru 1st subfloor or slab. ☐ 3. Floor structure and subflooring in including top floor (except 1st floor only if steep hillside). ☐ 4. Framing lumber on site (including siding if applicable). ☐ 5. Garage slab poured.	20%	25%
The appraiser may approve the appropriate payment, recommending a withhold for the following items if not complete: Garage slab, siding on site, furnace installation, appliances and finish flooring. In HUD designated "Special Flood Hazard Areas", an appropriate amount should be withheld for lumber delivered on site but not yet incorporated in the structure.	2	☐ 6. Framing complete. ☐ 7. Roofing complete. ☐ 8. Windows installed. ☐ 9. Siding installed (Lath on if stucco). ☐ 10. Rough plumbing complete. ☐ 11. Ductwork installed. ☐ 12. Rough electrical installed. ☐ 13. Insulation installed except ceiling.	30%	30%
Bldg. Dimensions Agree with Plans Yes ☐ No ☐	3	☐ 14. Ceiling insulation in place. ☐ 15. Gypsum wallboard installed and taped. ☐ 16. Furnace installed. ☐ 17. Stucco brown coat complete, if applicable. ☐ 18. Finish carpentry complete, except for installation of cabinets. ☐ 19. Interior painting substantially complete.	15%	15%
Set-Backs Conform to Plans Yes ☐ No ☐	4	☐ 20. Complete and ready for occupancy (Notice of Completion recorded).	15%	20%
	5	☐ 21. Upon expiration of lien period (SPM 451.7).	20%	10%

Unchecked items indicate reasons for rejection.

Payment No.	Date Inspected	Approved By	Rejected By	Payment No.	Date Inspected	Approved By	Rejected By

REMARKS:

_____
_____
_____
_____
_____
_____
_____
_____
_____
_____
_____
_____
_____
_____
_____
_____

Figure 5-5 Building loan inspection report. Reprinted by permission of the Bank of America, San Francisco.

remaining specialties. They generally obtain plans from a plan designer, plan service, or from adaptation of plans from a previously constructed home.

The selling price for the home may not even be established until most of the entrepreneur's own work is complete and the remaining work is covered by firm price contracts. Many skilled builders-craftsmen prefer to work on speculative houses to avoid the changes and owner interference often found in the custom home market.

In periods of good demand most of the spec homes can be sold prior to or shortly after completion, and the builder may realize an excellent return on his investment and his labor. In periods of increasing financing costs such as the 1978–1980 period where the prime rate went from 8 to 20%, with an increase in the construction loan rate of from 9.5 to 22.0%, many speculative builders find that failure to sell homes promptly resulted in significant carrying costs that often proved fatal to continued existence.

SMALL GENERAL CONTRACTORS OR SUBCONTRACTORS

Many homes are built by small general contractors using similarly situated subcontractors who often act as developers for several speculative homes, may handle a custom home or two, may do major remodeling work, and sometimes submit bids on small commercial work. This type of contractor has often been a skilled carpenter or other craftsman and has progressed from working for others to handling his own business. He usually maintains several full-time employees principally geared to performing the foundation, framing, and finish carpentry work. At one end of the scale the contractor operates from his home, has only one or two people on the payroll, keeps the books himself, and handles all the business aspects of the enterprise, including preparation of bids and proposals. At the other end of the scale the contractor may have a small office, an estimator, office manager, and secretary and maintain a substantial craft payroll.

It represents a sizable jump in dependable volume to justify the expense of going from a one-man business operated from a home with minimal overhead to a business office and staff with fixed overhead costs that will be incurred irrespective of volume. Many growing contracting businesses have failed as the owner shaved his prices to obtain volume to cover his increased fixed overhead costs and found that he was unable to complete the work for the bid price. Small contractors are often subject to an economic squeeze when owners delay payments, and contractors are faced with losing discounts and jeopardizing credit relationships with suppliers through similar postponement or borrowing at substantial interest rates that also affect profitability and the contractors' ability to bond and finance new work.

The small general contractor must become a successful businessman or businesswoman if the enterprise is to prosper in the long term. Government regulation, both at the local and national levels, is also beginning to be a factor in introducing additional record keeping requirements, additional taxes and fees of many natures, and in other regulatory requirements that may differ widely, dependent on the area.

The small subcontractor is in a similar position. Many skilled electricians, plumbers, cement finishers, painters, and other craftsmen have gone into business supplying their specialty services to general contractors. The subcontrator is subject to all the economic uncertainties as is the general contractor and in addition is dependent on receiving prompt payment from the general contractor.

Often during periods of slack demand the owners of smaller firms may perform some of the on-site work themselves, and all owners will generally supervise the work more closely. Individual productivity based on units of output such as square feet of sidewalks, number of concrete blocks, or board feet of lumber per hour are usually very high. Often there is an economic incentive involved to the extent that increased production means increased pay to the individual workman. The successful small contractor has obtained a thorough knowledge of the craft skills but has also learned to be a businessman who can manage his money, his plant and equipment, and his employees and clients in a skillful manner.

Union problems, featherbedding, and counterproductive work practices are minimal except in periods of excessive demand where an insufficient supply of workmen exist. Quality problems will often depend on the care the owner devotes to insisting that plans and specifications be followed without changes unless prior appraval is obtained. The difference in quality of construction between two homes constructed to similar plans can be substantial if one contractor builds to the exact details set forth, while another takes liberties with the quality and dimensional standards not readily noticeable in the formal inspections as required by local law. Failure to delineate overall requirements in the plans and specifications is an open invitation to disagreement and litigation on an individual project.

As the individual custom house continues to escalate in price, most of the young homeowners of the future will probably use some form of multiple housing such as duplex, fourplex, condominium, or town house. As the shift toward multiple residences accelerates, many of the smaller general contractors active in home building may probably change operations successfully to acting as subcontractors for foundations, framing, or finish carpentry for larger multiple residence developments. Others may specialize in remodeling on residential and commercial work where markets may continue to grow as the average building ages and requires substantial periodic remodeling to maintain the overall value.

The smaller general and specialty contractors will continue to survive in the marketplace, since the inefficient operators will be quickly eliminated by more efficient competitors as they have in the past. In many ways the small contractor is far more efficient than his medium-to large-sized competitors, which should enable this class of contractor to continue to perform a substantial share of work in the industry as it traditionally has.

CUSTOM AND TRACT DEVELOPERS

Regional custom and tract developers generally operate quite similarly to the small general contractor in regard to the actual manner of performing the work. Up to a certain volume the developer may subcontract all the work, including framing, foundations, and finish carpentry. After a certain volume some developers may use their own crews for such basic work, while relying on subcontractors for the balance of the specialty work. National developers such as Kaufman and Broad have developed a national organization largely through acquisition of successful regional firms throughout the country.

Custom Developers

A successful custom developer has the foresight to continue to acquire suitable lots so that he may command a premium price for a premium product. Many successful developers make their major profit from profits on developing the property and may allow other builders to participate in constructing individual homes in the completed development. The successful developer of custom homes also requires a certain degree of architectural excellence in his homes and may employ his own designer or have an arrangement with several registered plan designers or architects to produce the finished plans.

The developers of custom homes will usually have several speculative homes under construction that can serve as models for showing quality of workmanship and typical interior designs to prospective customers for custom homes. In view of the substantial costs associated with developing the property, continuing taxes and fees, and the sizeable interest charges, selling the houses prior to completion in the case of the spec home and prior to beginning construction in other cases is important to a profitable operation. This class of builder often employs his own sales force if volume can justify such, or he may enter into a commission arrangement with a local real estate firm at rates considerably less than the standard 6% real estate fees charged for individual homes.

TRACT DEVELOPERS

Tract developers operate much like the custom developers, except that their developments are often considerably larger and most homes are sold through the use of several model homes. For a 300-home tract a builder might have seven basic house types, ranging from 1500 to 2700 ft^2. Each of the homes would have three or four or more different external elevations, and numerous optional items at additional cost would be available. Architectural design is usually very functional and attractive and can be obtained at a surprisingly low individual unit cost in view of the repetitive nature of the designs.

Here the secret is to sell the houses before construction begins. Most of the work is subcontracted, and the builder will publish price lists that are generally not subject to discount for each type of house. The builder has obtained quotations from his subcontractors in a similar manner. Every six months or so, dependent on labor rates and other cost escalation, the builder revises his basic price list accordingly. He probably will set up his own sales force and will handle financing for the customer through previously established channels.

An emerging factor in the tract housing market is the establishment of several different types of dwellings in an overall development often featuring a golf course, swimming pool, tennis courts, or other amenities. The development might have row houses (so-called town houses or condominiums) with common walls in one section. Another section might have duplexes or fourplexes, and several detached or semidetached homes would also be constructed on premium lots. Such an arrangement will allow a much greater density than single-family dwellings and offer considerable opportunity to obtain economies through mass purchasing and prefabrication suited to the repetitive nature of the final product.

COMBINATION TRACT AND CUSTOM FIRMS

Many regional and national firms operate successfully in both tract development and custom development. Combinations of these two have often been successful with condominiums and other multiple housing units using repetitive arrangements, coupled with a smalled number of custom residences, all tastefully arranged around a lake, golf course, park, or other attractive features. Possibly, this type of development offers considerable promise for the future, and both tract and custom developers may find it advantageous to develop their properties using both the repetitive methods of the tract builder, coupled with the individually designed homes in the custom market.

ENERGY-CONSERVING HOMES*

The residential sector of our economy utilizes about 20% of the energy used in the United States. Recent experiments in energy-conserving homes have

*This Section is based upon a paper entitled *Building and Marketing Energy Conserving Homes* Preprint No. 3607 presented by Thomas F. McGoman, Research Engineer, Georgia Institute of Technology at the American Society of Civil Engineers convention and Exposition, Atlanta, Georgia, October 1979.

shown that a 50 to 75% reduction in energy use is achievable at additional costs of about 3% or less of the selling price.

DESIGN AND CONSTRUCTION FOR ENERGY SAVINGS

There are three elements in building an energy-conserving home or in upgrading an existing home:

- Adequate insulation, properly installed.
- Reduced air infiltration and installation.
- Proper sizing and installation of the heating and cooling systems.

One criterion that has been proposed is to adopt a 10-year payback for the addition of energy-saving elements. Such a criterion, of course, will vary dependent on interest rates and initial cost of the facility.

Potential Savings

Present average utility bills represent 16 to 27% of the monthly mortgage payment of new homes built with standard construction and are bound to grow as energy costs continue to increase each year. At only 10% per year fuel and electricity utility cost inflation, it will take from 14 to 19 years for the average utility bill to equal the mortgage payment. An initial investment in energy conservation can cut these bills up to 50% and minimize the cost of future energy inflation.

Builders in Georgia and the Southeast have found a 50% reduction in energy bills is possible through use of energy-conserving construction. One of the most important factors in minimizing energy costs is to avoid an oversized heating or cooling unit that costs more to purchase and more to operate, wastes more energy, and produces less comfort.

SUMMARY

Housing and residential construction capture the largest individual share of the construction industry. Individual entrepreneurs, small business-men–developers, regional developers, and national developers all build essentially similar products using essentially similar methods. Industry prosperity is closely allied to interest rate changes and the state of the economy. In a good economic climate, almost everyone makes money. In periods of low demand and high interest rates, even the most successful firms have difficulty in breaking even.

CHAPTER 6

BUILDING, INSTITUTIONAL, AND COMMERCIAL CONSTRUCTION

Rolland M. Wilkening

The fundamental components of the building process have remained the same for the past several decades. It has been the imposed conditions on the fundamental process that have changed more dramatically in the past several years. The basic components of the construction process are the following:

1. Need.
2. Program.
3. Design.
4. Construction.
5. Use.

Whether we are dealing with institutional or commercial construction, these five components must be addressed. The need for a facility, whether it be a hospital, school, office building, or shopping center, must first be verified. Once the verification of the need has been established, a program must be established that defines the facility, site criteria, and basic use of the facility. With the program verified, the establishment of the design procedure must be carried forward until the execution of final design. On the execution of final design, it is assumed that the decision to construct the facility has been verified. The construction component includes the establishment of costs, developing of procedure, and execution of the construction. On completion of construction, the owner must occupy, furnish and equip the facility, and begin establishing operating and maintenance procedures.

The carrying out of these components, in previous years, was a lock-step procedure—each component following the other in a regimented fashion. In recent years, conditions have been placed on each of the components that have changed the traditional building process. These conditions are as listed here:

1. Control.
2. Natural.
3. Man-made.
4. Demand.
5. Economic.

More stringent zoning and building codes, together with health and safety and social-political controls, have impacted the process. The natural conditions imposed by the environmental impact, environmental analysis, and site analysis have become more prominent in recent years. Man-made conditions relate to architectural and engineering disciplines, building systems, and occupant furnishings and equipment. Demand conditions can be imposed by the user for such needs as function and time of occupancy. The economic conditions all relate to costs, and these could be capital investment, financing, maintenance, operation, and insurance.

THE GENERAL CONTRACTOR

The spiraling inflation of recent years has placed a demand on the entire construction industry for more innovative ideas, together with cost control and expenditure restraints. The general contractor and his subcontractors are becoming more and more aware of more stringent cost control and the attempt to increase productivity. Demands are being placed on architects and engineers to design a facility within a budget that is established by the owner. Owners are restricted in their demands for facilities that are not economically justifiable. No one questions that the building and construction community plays a major role in the U.S. economy. It accounts for over 10% of the gross national product (GNP) and employs over four million workers—making it the nation's largest industry and employer. Added to this are an estimated three million jobs in related construction services that are dependent on the core industry for their livelihood. Construction's rippling effect impacts general purchasing power and the cost of living of every American.

In the traditional construction process, the owner, whether public or private, normally will retain the services of an architect who will work with the owner in determining needs, developing the program and executing the design. Once the design is complete, the entire project, including plans and specifications, is submitted to several general contractors to submit a competitive lump sum bid. Most general contractors perform less than 20% of the project with their own forces. The general contractor relies heavily on specialty contractors or subcontractors for the various components that go into the building other than basic concrete and masonry work. The subcontractors receive their contract from the general contractor and are subject to the conditions of contract. The general contractor has traditionally been the manager of the construction process in whatever form that process has taken. However, the complexities of today's construction techniques and the difficulties in managing the ever-increasing number of highly specialized subcontractors occasionally required new approaches to the methods historically used by the general contractor in his management function.

One such method is the construction management method, and many general contractors are providing that service. This method allows the owner and the architect-engineer to have available to them the services of the general contractor, not only during the conctruction phase, but during the design phase as well.

COST CONTROL

For a general contractor to survive in this highly competitive industry, it is imperative that he operate with an effective cost control system. Many contractors have long recognized the importance of accurate and timely information to effectively manage their construction projects. To provide this information as a management tool, systems have been developed by personnel with professional experience in computer systems and the construction industry. Many contractors use the capabilities of the computer to integrate all functions of the project and to provide management information for controlling project costs. These systems usually provide timely job reporting. The systems monitor project costs and are completely integrated with other related functions of estimating, employee payroll, labor distribution, equipment costs and use, accounts payable, material and subcontract accounts receivable, and general ledger (Figure 6-1). The integration of these related functions provides complete financial reporting of project status. The collection of data for input into the system usually starts at the construction site. The system is designed to use original documents from the field as input data. Once these source documents reach the Data Processing Section, a minimum of clerical effort is required to verify and prepare the documents for input into the computer. This is possible because of well-planned procedures that encourage a high degree of accuracy. The general ledger with a built-in job cost subsidiary is usually the heart of a cost control system. While each of the system modules is designed to operate independently, job-related data generated by other subsystems are integrated into the files of the general ledger and job cost

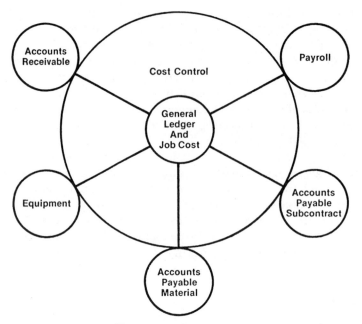

Figure 6-1   Cost control.

module. This integration of data allows all cost information to be recorded in o.1e place and provides a link with all of the system, while maintaining system independence and flexibility.

Profitability of a major project depends on the effective control of labor costs. Controlling such costs begins with the preparation of time sheets used for processing payroll. These sheets are preprinted by computer with the jobsite name, employee name, Social Security number, and general trade classification (carpenter, mason, etc.) to assure that project managers are not burdened with excessive paperwork. Depending on the size of the project, time sheets are filled in daily or weekly by the superintendent who enters a code indicating the type of work performed (such as wall forms, foundations, etc.) and the related hours. The sheets are forwarded to the Data Processing Department to serve as source documents for keypunching. The keypunch cards are then processed by the computer to provide the following payroll records: payroll journal, employee pay statement, and employee check. Other reports are provided (such as labor charge report, labor union reports, and government reports). The payroll data provide information for two important reports: (1) Labor Cost Report (Figure 6-2); (2) Unit and Trade Cost Analysis (Figure 6-3). The Labor Cost Report is a powerful tool that can save vital construction dollars because it is tied directly to the payroll. It provides accurate data that enable management to follow current trends and quickly spot discrepancy between actual and

BARTON-MALOW COMPANY LABOR COST REPORT

		EST.-MGR. B. MAYER	SUPT. A. CARNEY	ADMINISTRATOR J. MILLER

JOB NO 29650 CADILLAC CONSTR WASTE TREATMENT ADDN   W/E 05/29/75

CODE DESCRIPTION	* * LABOR * * ALLOWED	ACTUAL	* * QUAN * * ALLOWED	ACTUAL U	ACTIVITY THIS WEEK LABOR UNITS VAR.	U/COST ALLOW ACTUAL *	UNIT COST ALLOW	ACTUAL	VARIANCE TODATE	COMPLETE
00342 CURBS	792	1,780	480	500 SF *C			1.65	3.56	988	988
00344 PAVING	101b	191	75	175 LF *C			1.35	1.09	90	90
00345 BASES	1,088	2,041	435	460 LF *C			2.50	4.44	953	953
00351 TANK PAD	78	100	60	60 SF *C			1.30	1.67	22	22
00352 PIT/TRENCH BOT	2,314	4,255	1,535	1,610 SF *C			1.51	2.64	1,941	1,941
00354 PIT/TRENCH WALL	22,385	20,995	15,100	15,550 SF *C			1.48	1.35	1,389C	1,389C
00355 RINGWALL	14,630	16,848	14,630	14,260 SF *C			1.00	1.18	2,218	2,218
00356 MAT AT LG TANK	1,620	591	830	830 SF *C			1.95	.71	1,028C	1,028C
00357 INTERIOR PITS	11,281	13,373	6,560	6,406 SF *C			1.72	2.17	2,592	2,592
00358 SUMP IN PITS	180	557	6	6 U *C			30.00	92.93	377	377
	65,937	74,029			*** SUB-TOT.-PREM. COST	672.91			8,092	8,092
00361 REINF STEEL	12,330	15,199	90	95 TON*C		137.00		159.99		2,869	2,869
00362 MESH	225	222	4,500	4,500 SF *C		.05		.05		2C	2C
	12,555	15,421			*** SUB-TOT.-PREM. COST	90.53			2,866	2,866
00371 FLOAT FINISH	4,454	4,089	380	306 HRS*C			11.72	13.36	364C	364C
00376 RUBBED FINISH	1,100	1,079	2,300	2,300 SF *C			.48	.47	20C	20C
00379 FIN TOP OF WALL	930	673	3,100	2,716 LF *C			.30	.25	256C	256C
00380 BONDING AGENT	50	36	5	4 HRS*C			10.00	9.09	13C	13C
	6,534	5,879			*** SUB-TOT.-PREM. COST	274.11			654C	654C
00386 SET LOOSE M.I.	2,155	2,171	220	184 HRS*C			9.80	11.80	16	16
00387 ANCHOR BOLTS	2,073	1,284	161	146 U *C			12.88	8.79	788C	788C
00390 EXPANSION JOINTS	79	131	225	300 LF *C			.35	.44	52	52
00392 UNISTRUT	460	384	230	172 U *C			2.00	2.24	75C	75C
00393 CONTROL WATER	3,000	4,132	315	352 HRS			9.52	11.74	1,132	1,132
00394 R/R GRATING	3,500	3,700	350	304 HRS			10.00	12.17	200	759
	11,267	11,803			*** SUB-TOT.-PREM. COST	186.28			536	1,096
00610 MISC. CARP	1,499	3,245		*C					1,745	1,745
	1,499	3,245			*** SUB-TOT.-PREM. COST				1,745	1,745

	183,394	193,978	61,878	83.81		VARIANCE SUBTOT			12,642	13,202
						.42 P/R TAXES			5,310	5,545
		61,322	83.81			TOTAL			17,952	18,747

Figure 6-2 Labor cost report.

BARTON-MALOW COMPANY

TOTAL UNIT AND TRADE COST ANALYSIS

DATE RUN 03/25/80

TRADE HRS/ PER UNIT	CADILLAC PKK-STRUCT 29992	DET.WATER- PC422 30057	FORD HOSP BID PAK1 30125	PONTIAC CA R PARKING 30274	O.C.C. PAR K STRUCT 30321	DET ARENA BM-CONC 50853	ARENA PRK DECK 50883	BEAUMONT REC. BLDG 51907
CODE 0301 MUD MAT - POUR								
CARPENTERS	CY	CY	.3600 CY	CY	CY	CY	CY	CY
LABORS	CY	CY	1.0500 CY	CY	CY	CY	CY	CY
UNIT ACTUAL			17.31					
UNIT ALLOWABLE			10.00					
CODE 0302 PILE CAP FTGS- POUR								
CARPENTERS	CY	.1168 CY	.0584 CY	CY	CY	.1875 CY	.0516 CY	CY
CEMENT FIN	CY	.5876 CY	.4880 CY	CY	CY	.5000 CY	CY	CY
LABORS	CY	.0182 CY	CY	CY	CY	.6875 CY	.6630 CY	CY
RESTEEL								
UNIT ACTUAL		8.09	6.78			19.20	14.51	
UNIT ALLOWABLE		6.92	8.62			18.14	22.25	
CODE 0303 WALL FTGS- POUR								
CARPENTERS	CY	.0811 CY	CY	CY	CY	CY	CY	CY
CEMENT FIN	CY	.0541 CY	CY	CY	CY	CY	CY	CY
LABORS	CY	.5554 CY	CY	CY	CY	CY	.1481	CY
UNIT ACTUAL		9.33					10.30	
UNIT ALLOWABLE		7.02					8.00	
CODE 0304 GRADE BEAMS - POUR								
CARPENTERS	CY	.0074 CY	CY	CY	CY	CY	CY	CY
CEMENT FIN	CY	.5110 CY	.2438 CY	CY	CY	CY	CY	CY
LABORS	CY	CY	CY	CY	CY	CY	CY	CY
UNIT ACTUAL		6.60	3.09					
UNIT ALLOWABLE		3.60	9.00					
CODE 0305 WALLS-PIERS - POUR								
CARPENTERS	.2206	.0126 CY	.0363 CY	CY	CY	.0357 CY	.0147 CY	CY
CEMENT FIN	CY	.0434 CY	CY	CY	CY	.0217 CY	CY	CY
LABORS	1.0588 CY	.4717 CY	.5237 CY	CY	CY	.6087 CY	1.5828 CY	CY
UNIT ACTUAL	15.31	6.50	6.92			8.34	19.93	
UNIT ALLOWABLE	14.00	6.90	10.58			5.40	14.69	
CODE 0306 COLUMNS - POUR								
CARPENTERS	CY	CY	.1131 CY	CY	CY	CY	CY	CY
LABORS	CY	CY	.9770 CY	CY	CY	CY	CY	CY
UNIT ACTUAL			13.26					

Figure 6-3 Total unit and trade cost analysis.

allowable labor cost. The Unit and Trade Cost Analysis report serves two major purposes. It provides a detailed look at each unit by cost code. The actual labor cost per unit and the allowable cost are compared for each job. The unit cost is the time required of each trade to put one unit in place. This reveals the current trade mix per unit and serves as an indication of production. It is an important historical factor for future estimates.

The material-subcontract accounts payable module processes major subcontracts and material orders that are dispersed in a series of payments with retention part of the agreement. The material-subcontract cost report (Fig. 6-4) is generated from invoices entered into the two accounts payable modules. This report shows allowable and actual costs with resulting variances for materials and subcontracts. Early indication of excess costs provided by this report allows management to make timely adjustments.

Since equipment represents a major asset, it is important that the contractor establish tight control over equipment inventory. Each time equipment is moved from a contractor's yard to a jobsite or from one jobsite to another, a transfer slip is prepared to record the quantity and type of equipment being moved. The transfer data are input to the computer system to generate a detailed equipment location report and rental invoice. Similar records are prepared when equipment is rented to other contractors.

The accounts receivable system is designed to record and maintain sales, cash receipts, and retention. When the data are recorded, management reports can then be produced as an aid to improve collections and increase cash flow.

The cost reporting system is the function of the general ledger and job cost module. However, it is supported by all other subsystems to provide an integration of all accounting data. Timely cost reports are prepared for each project. To attain maximum benefits, these reports are shared with all levels of field management.

GOVERNMENT REGULATIONS

A Commission of Federal Paperwork was established by Congress to do a comprehensive review of federal paperwork processes and to recommed improvements in those processes. The commission had a statutory two-year life that expired late in 1977. During its existence, the commission was instrumental in focusing attention on a great many improvements that could be made in the federal paperwork process and made hundreds of specific recommendations to improve or eliminate individual paperwork requirements. One of the key recommendations was that Congress review its role in spawning unnecessary paperwork and regulations as well as the role of the executive branch; and several bills have been introduced that attempt to do more in this direction. With the adoption of Proposition 13 in California, this sort of legislation has probably now achieved a much

BARTON-MALOW COMPANY   MATERIAL-SUBCONTRACT COST REPORT   ADMINISTRATOR

JOB NO.30000   WASTEWATER TREATMENT PLANT ADDITION-ST JOHNS, MI

FST.-MGR. R. MAYER   SUPT. J. MCLAY   J. STRANG   M-E 03-31-80

OPER	DESCRIPTION	* MATERIAL * ALLOWED	ACTUAL	* QUAN * ALLOW	ACTUAL	U	* UNIT-COST * ALLOW	ACTUAL	* SUBCONTRACTS * ALLOWED	WRITTEN	VARIANCE TO-DATE
00105	ENGINEERING	.00	71.13				.00	.00	.00	.00	71.13
00106	O.S.H.A.	.00	.00				.00	.00	.00	.00	.00
00107	TRAVEL EXPENSE	10,000.00	8,953.67	26	20	MOS	384.62	447.68	.00	.00	1,261.20
00109	TESTING SERVICE	1,141.55	.00				.00	.00	358.45	493.40	134.95
00110	PHOTOGRAPHS	.00	197.67			U	.00	.00	7,000.00	2,707.13 NP	197.67
00111	OFFICE SUPPLIES	500.00	550.96				.00	.00	.00	.00 N-V	50.96
00112	PROJECT SIGN	400.00	208.60	1	1	U	400.00	208.60	.00	.00 *C	191.40CR
00116	ARCH. FIELD OFFICE	4,700.00	3,204.20	26	20	MOS	180.77	160.21	.00	.00	411.20CR
00117	B-M FIELD OFFICE	5,850.00	3,937.20	26	20	MOS	225.00	196.86	.00	.00	562.80CR
00119	TELEPHONE	7,800.00	8,340.39	26	20	MOS	300.00	417.02	.00	.00	540.39
00120	TEMPORARY TOILETS	60.00	.00	26	20	MOS	2.31	.00	.00	.00	.00
00121	WINTER PROTECTION	2,500.00	2,855.24	650	500	HRS	3.85	5.71	2,800.00	2,251.11 NPN-V / 58.50	413.74
00122	POWER	5,000.00	10,888.81	25	20	MOS	200.00	544.44	.00	.00	5,888.81
00123	WATER	500.00	122.94	25	20	MOS	20.00	6.15	.00	.00	277.00CR
00124	TEMP ROADS	.00	349.84				.00	.00	.00	.00	349.84
00126	TEMP. FENCE/PROT.	200.00	.00	157		HRS	1.11	.00	1,000.00	1,065.00 NPN-V	.00
00127	PROGRESS CLEAN-UP	200.00	.00	180		HRS		.00	.00	.00	1,416.25
00129	FINAL CLEAN UP	100.00	.00	360		HRS	.56	.00	1,500.00	2,916.25	.83CR
00130	CLEAN DIGESTER	.00	.00	120	1	HRS	.83	.00	.00	.00	293.00
00134	FIRE INS.	19,500.00	15,293.00	26	20	MOS	750.00	764.65	.00	.00	1,790.00
00135	BOND PREMIUM	46,000.00	47,790.00			LS		.00	.00	.00	2,899.68CR
00136	PAYROLL TAXES	59,867.00	30,625.79	100	56	PCT	598.67	546.89	.00	.00	1,331.00CR
00137	O C P INSURANCE	4,600.00	3,269.00			LS		.00	.00	.00 *C	3,356.00CR
00151	RENTAL	7,000.00	2,243.92	25	20	MOS	280.00	112.20	.00	.00	2,189.20CR
00157	TRUCKING	3,000.00	210.71	25	20	MOS	120.00	10.54	.00	.00	951.84
00162		170.00	.00				.00	.00	500.00	1,451.84	1,898.28
00198	BUSINESS EXPENSE	.00	1,898.28				.00	.00	.00	.00	.00
00200	EXCAVATION	.00	.00				.00	.00	471,659.00	471,659.00	170.22
00214	CONTRACT PROCEED.	.00	170.22				.00	.00	9,000.00	8,417.98 NP	.00
00215	DEMOLITION/ALTER.	180.00	.00	330		HRS	.55	.00	35,410.00	35,410.00	.00
00261	ASPHALT PAVING	.00	.00				.00	.00	8,375.00	8,375.00	.00
00271	FENCE	.00	.00				.00	.00	.00	.00	.00
00289	SEEDING	.00	.00				.00	.00	2,500.00	.00 NP	.00
00320	CONCRETE	.00	.00				.00	.00	1204,171.20	1204,171.20	2,211.08
00361	REINFORCING STEEL	.00	591.08				.00	.00	218,166.00	219,786.00	.00
00380	PRECAST CONCRETE	.00	.00				.00	.00	29,875.00	29,875.00	.00
00400	MASONRY	.00	.00				.00	.00	140,950.00	140,950.00	.00
00550	MISC. IRON	.00	.00				.00	.00	290,000.00	290,000.00	.00
00555	AC. METAL WALLS	.00	.00				.00	.00	.00	.00	.00
00622	MILLWORK	2,000.00	1,425.00				.00	.00	9,900.00	9,900.00	1,425.00
00710	WATERPROOFING	.00	.00				.00	.00	34,740.00	34,740.00	.00

JOB NO.30000   WASTEWATER TREATMENT PLANT ADDITION-ST JOHNS, MI

		FST.-MGR.	SUPT.	ADMINISTRATOR
		R. MAYER	J. MCLAY	J. STRANG M-E 03-31-80

OPER	DESCRIPTION	* MATERIAL * ALLOWED	ACTUAL	* QUAN * ALLOW	ACTUAL	U	* UNIT-COST * ALLOW	ACTUAL	* SUBCONTRACTS * ALLOWED	WRITTEN	VARIANCE TO-DATE
00711	CONCRETE RESTORAT.	.00	.00				.00	.00	5,000.00	.00 NP	.00
00740	ROOFING/SHEET MET	.00	.00				.00	.00	64,682.00	62,960.00	1,722.00CR
00790	CAULKING	.00	.00				.00	.00	3,590.00	3,590.00	.00
00811	HOLLOW METAL	10,088.00	10,088.00				.00	.00	.00	.00 N-V	.00
00845	ROLLING STL DOOR	.00	.00				.00	.00	1,771.00	1,771.00	.00
00852	ALUM. WINDOWS	6,730.00	6,982.00				.00	.00	.00	.00 N-V	252.00
00855	STAINLESS STL DOOR	.00-	.00				.00	.00	6,263.00	6,458.00	195.00
00856	ALUM. DOOR/FRAME	.00-	.00				.00	.00	.00	.00 N-V	.00
00870	FINISH HARDWARE	14,639.40	16,007.00				.00	.00	.00	.00 N-V	1,367.60
00885	GLASS/GLAZING	.00	.00				.00	.00	4,500.00	4,500.00	.00
00916	PLASTER	.00	.00				.00	.00	18,748.00	18,748.00	.00
00940	TILE/TERRAZZO	.00	.00				.00	.00	8,994.00	8,994.00	.00
00990	PAINTING	.00	.00				.00	.00	71,500.00	71,500.00	.00
00999	INSTALLATION ALLOW	.00	.00				.00	.00	14,100.00	1,500.00 NP	.00
01010	CHALKBOARD	.00	152.00				.00	.00	500.00	.00 NP	152.00
01018	TOILET PARTITION	186.00	186.00				.00	.00	.00	.00	.00
01025	FIRE EXTINGUISHER	365.00	.00				.00	.00	.00	.00	.00
01040	ENTR. CANOPY	.00	.00				.00	.00	15,000.00	15,000.00	.00
01042	SIGNS	.00	.00				.00	.00	500.00	.00 NP	.00
01050	LOCKERS	545.00	545.00				.00	.00	.00	.00	.00
01054	REFL SCREEN	.00	.00				.00	.00	17,875.00	17,875.00	.00
01071	SAFETY EQUIP.	3,000.00	765.69				.00	.00	.00	.00 N-V	.00
01080	TOILET RM ACCES.	2,576.00	1,930.00				.00	.00	.00	.00 N-V	.00
01160	LAB. EQUIP.	.00	.00				.00	.00	52,025.52	52,025.52	.00
01198	TOOLS/EQUIP.	13,225.00	7,710.36				.00	.00	.00	.00	.00
01260	FURNITURE	5,024.00	400.40				.00	.00	.00	.00	.00
01430	HOISTS	8,750.00	.00				.00	.00	.00	.00	.00
01500	MECHANICAL	.00	.00				.00	.00	3013,957.82	3013,957.82	.00
01546	FILTER MEDIA	10,865.00	11,200.00				.00	.00	46,125.00	46,125.00 N-V	335.00
01547	FILTER EQUIP.	.00	.00				.00	.00	46,125.00	46,125.00	.00
01548	SLUDGE DRYING	14,738.70	.00				.00	.00	35,661.30	35,661.30	.00
01600	ELECTRICAL	.00	.00				.00	.00	905,276.68	905,276.68	.00
		272,000.65	199,164.10	2,154	758				6,753,973.97	6,730,169.73	

SUB. VAR.   2,654.54
MATERIAL VAR.   5,770.31
TOTAL VAR.   8,424.85

Figure 6-4 Material-subcontract cost report.

greater appeal both to the public and to elected officials at all levels of government. The argument of those favoring passage of such legislation is that the federal paperwork and regulatory burden has escalated beyond reason, that the cost of compliance for individual citizens and businesses exceeds the benefits of compliance, that the bureaucracy has been ineffective in limiting the paperwork and regulation explosion, and that the Congress must bear major responsibility for these problems because the Congress has not provided adequate or effective limitation in the legislative process. Unnecessary government regulations increase the cost of public works, and cooperative effort should be taken to reduce the number of regulations and to simplify, standardize, and make more practical application of requirements.

The Associated General Contractors of America (AGC) has long endorsed better coordination and consolidation of public works programs and has supported the establishment of the Federal Department of Public Works. Such an agency would eliminate duplication, simplify fiscal control, and facilitate planning. Conversely, the establishment of new agencies to handle new public works programs is counterproductive, for newly created agencies are slow in functioning and hence delay program effectiveness.

The construction industry is currently subjected to many layers of federal safety inspection, most of which are within the U.S. Department of Labor. They are the Construction Safety Act, the Occupational Safety and Health Act, the Walsh-Healy Act, the Longshore and Harbor Workers Act, the Jones Act, and now the Federal Mine Safety and Health Act of 1977. Add to this, inspections by the federal awarding agencies, such as the Corps of Engineers, Bureau of Reclamation, Department of Transportation, Naval Facilities Engineering Command, to name a few. Virtually every one of the ten listed here has a training requirement, and the contractors have met the obligation. At this point, the secretary of labor must exercise some authority in providing direction to his forces and those of the awarding agency, less the entire federal safety movement degenerates into a program of ineffective mass confusion.

The new Office of Federal Contract Compliance Programs (OFCCP) concerning women in minority goals and timetables went into effect in March 1978. The new regulations apply to all federal and federally assisted construction contracts and subcontracts in excess of $10,000. The goals are applicable to the contractor's or subcontractor's aggregate on-site construction work force, whether or not part of the work force is performing work on a federal or federally assisted construction contract or subcontract. Representatives of the OFCCP have indicated that ongoing private work started after May 8, 1978, will also be subject to the goals and timetables for women and minorities. However, emphasis will be placed on new hirees on private jobs after May 8 rather than on the total number of employees employed. The goals and timetables for women to participate in the total construction work force are as follows: March 31, 1979—3.1%; March 31, 1980—5%; March 31, 1981—6.9%. The problem of additional increased costs to the contractor in complying with such a requirement has been pointed out to the OFCCP; but no explanation is forthcoming at this time from the Department of Labor about who will be paying for the change orders to meet these requirements on private work. The percentage has remained the same but total work force for females has not kept pace with the percentage requirement.

LABOR RELATIONS

The Associated General Contractors of America (AGC) serves each of its member contractors equally, whether the contractor operates with a collective bargaining agreement or without such an agreement. The collective bargaining agreements are usually negotiated by a chapter or as part of a multiassociation bargaining group. The association promotes multiassociation-coordinated bargaining in appropriate areas, determined locally and encourages participation in a national organization comprised of major national construction associations so as to develop an effective single voice in labor relation matters. The association opposes the inclusion of cost-of-living adjustment provisions in collective bargaining agreements. The association opposes the use by AGC members of interim short-form agreements, other agreements written or oral, and national or project agreements containing provisions that require the contractor to continue production employing workmen represented by a local union on strike against or locked out by the local employer-bargaining group. It is recognized that, in some instances, a separate collective bargaining agreement may be necessary for the economical construction of a project because of its location, size, or special nature of construction. The association opposes the execution of collective bargaining agreements between building trade unions and owners who impose working and economic conditions on construction contractors, since the interpretation of such agreements by management negotiators would be by persons over whom the contractors have no control.

The association recognizes the importance of open shop construction as a stabilizing and constructive force in the industry, ranging from a moderate influence in some areas to a dominant influence in others. The association supports the full legal rights of contractors to operate open shop as well as to operate under labor agreements. It is the policy of the association to provide all needed services to open shop members on the same basis as is provided to those operating under labor agreements.

CONSTRUCTION METHODS AND TECHNIQUES

The construction industry is constantly searching for new ideas and innovations that can reduce the overall costs of construction in-place. Recently, *The Handbook of Construction Techniques*, published by McGraw-Hill, cited approximately 40 actual examples of cost-saving techniques that also resulted in a boost in production. The subjects contained in the handbook provided actual case studies on such items as excavation and earth moving, bridges, dams, tunneling, marine construction, foundations, concreting and asphalt production, and paving. This handbook is an example of what is happening on a daily basis when ingenuity is used for money-making concepts.

EQUIPMENT PURCHASE VERSUS LEASE

The use of equipment is a major factor on large construction projects; and it is important to analyze the type of equipment that must be used and the method of using the equipment in the total time frame with which it would be used. Such an analysis would dictate whether it would be feasible to purchase equipment or if it would be financially better to lease equipment for a short term. Does a contractor purchase or rent? This is a decision that is made repeatedly. Ownership of construction equipment can be more expensive than a contractor realizes. If a contractor is assured of high use of new equipment, purchase is probably the first choice. However, if new equipment is not used frequently enough to match the standard revenue-producing and depreciation expectations, it can be a burden on the contractor's profit. In such a case, rental should be considered. Rentals can help the contractor meet tight scheduling or to do a specialized job without increasing capital expenditures for equipment. There are advantages and disadvantages to either approach. Current interest rates are high, and there is no indication of significant reduction in the foreseeable future. These high interest rates, coupled with idle time between jobs, can make it difficult for new equipment to pay for itself. Down payments on equipment can cause a severe drain on a contractor's available cash supply and can eventually lead to short-term loans to meet unexpected cash needs. Income tax deductions for purchase of equipment are limited to interest expense and depreciation. Depending on the use that the equipment gets, it could take several years for depreciation allowance to catch up with principal payments. On the other hand, idle time is not a consideration with rental equipment. You pay rental charges on equipment only while you are using it. In today's construction market, with widely fluctuating government and private spending, it can make quite a difference in the profitability of a contractor's operation. Since sizable down payments are avoided through equipment rentals, available cash supply remains intact. The contractor can meet demands more easily and avoid the added expense of short-term borrowing. Equipment rental charges are 100% tax deductible as an operating expense, which allows the contractor to fully amortize the equipment cost in the same year the corresponding revenue was produced—resulting in a more stable financial condition. In recent months, there has been a strong trend toward the purchasing of equipment. This was been primarily due to the fact that, with inflation, the equipment is appreciating; and companies are looking to it as an investment. Many contractors are looking in terms of good used reconditioned equipment in lieu of purchase of equipment because of the long lead time in delivery. The inflation factor may have some influence on those contractors who have traditionally been leasing their equipment and, as a result, are now considering purchase of either new or reconditioned used equipment.

PUBLIC VERSUS PRIVATE WORK

Many contractors are interested in private work in lieu of public work, primarily to avoid the government agency regulations, together with all the bureaucratic red tape necessary in the public sector. However, because of the fact that, in some cases, private work is not available, many general contractors have entered the public sector for the first time. For some contractors who have adequate financial strength but have not developed a line of clients, the public sector provides an opportunity for that contractor to begin bidding work. This method is often followed by new contractors who have just been organized. Federally funded public work requires a great deal more reporting and regimentation than a similar project in the private sector. There is less flexibility with work in the public sector. Many contractors feel that there is an increased cost to work in the public sector because of the extent of reports and forms that must be filed with the various awarding agencies. In many cases, there is duplication of forms. The requirement for all the paperwork does not discriminate between the large or the small firm. The larger firm can somehow absorb some of the additional load without a dramatic impact on its operation. For the smaller firm with limited personnel, such an experience in the public sector can be quite traumatic.

A CONSTRUCTION MANAGER

DEVELOPEMENT OF A PROFESSIONAL STAFF

The basic responsibilities of a construction manager to provide input into the design phase of a project requires expertise in the following areas:

Job cost control.
Architectural engineering.
Civil engineering.
Construction supervision.
Contract law.
Electrical engineering.
Estimating (architectural, civil, mechanical, electrical).

Inspection.

Labor relations.

Mechanical engineering.

Safety.

Structural engineering.

Testing facilities.

Value management.

Construction management control system.

Computer technology.

For a firm to be adequately staffed in all the disciplines, it is important that a review of in-house talent be made and there is also the necesity of recruiting qualified personnel to fill the various positions necessary to fully staff an organization.

CONSTRUCTION MANAGEMENT CONTROL SYSTEM

The Construction Management Control system is a valuable tool, and it can either be developed within an organization or use programs that have previously been developed. The prime importance of the use of the control system is that all parties who are part of the system be thoroughly familiar with the importance of proper input and control of the system. The control system primarily includes four major subsystems:

1. Narrative reporting.
2. Schedule control.
3. Cost control.
4. Financial control.

The Narrative Reporting Subsystem consists of a monthly narrative report from the construction executive, chief estimator, construction management control system supervisor, project accountant, daily diary, and schedule analysis report.

The Schedule Control System provides network diagrams, schedule updates, computer-generated schedules, and the time-related cost data necessary to plan and execute the planning, design, construction, occupancy, and construction manager's work within the time specified in the contract. The various schedules as shown in Figure 6-5 are as follows:

1. Master schedule.
2. Construction manager's schedule.
3. Design schedule.
4. Prebid schedules.
5. Construction schedule.

6. Purchase order and shop drawing schedules.

7. Occupancy schedule.

A monthly integrated current schedule should be provided that provides for a schedule for all design, construction, and occupancy activities contained in a single network. Design, preconstruction, and construction occupancy schedules should also be incorporated into the single network.

The Cost Control Subsystem should provide timely data detail to permit the construction manager to control and adjust the project requirements, needs, materials, and equipment so that construction will be completed at a cost that, together with all the project costs, will not exceed the maximum total project cost specified. Requirements for this subsystem include the following submissions at these phases of the project life:

1. *Estimates*   Five forms of estimates are required as follows: concepts, tentatives, 50% bid package estimates, monthly current working estimates contractor bid cost estimates.

2. *Control Reports*   Other reports based on construction cost estimates developed by the construction manager and the architect-engineer will be prepared and updated at intervals to detail, summarize, and update costs—first by building system and second by trades—when required for bid and change order reviews.

The Financial Control Subsystem will enable the contracting officer and the construction manager to plan effectively and to monitor and control the application of funds available for the project—cash flow, costs, change orders, payments, claims, and other major financial factors—principally by

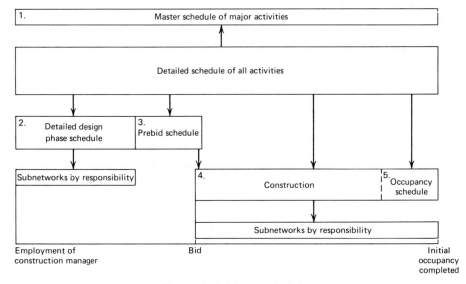

Figure 6-5   Master schedule.

comparison of funds available, funds expended, funds committed but not yet expended, and funds required for commitment in the future. These reports must be such as will serve as a basic accounting tool and an audit trail.

CONCEPTUAL ESTIMATING

The three categories of cost estimates recognized by the American Association of Cost Engineers (AACE) can be roughly correlated with the construction development of a project. Estimates in the first three categories are conceptual (Figure 6-6), since they are prepared prior to the completion of the plans and specifications. The fourth category of estimating is based on completed plans and is comparable to the proposal estimates that are most frequently prepared by a general contractor (Figure 6-7). The four categories are these:

1. *The Order of Magnitude Estimate*   Estimates in this category are intended to have an accuracy of plus or minus 30%. The estimate is prepared at an early stage of the project when the design is limited to schematics and when quantities of work have not been established. It is useful when a rough approximation of the ultimate project cost is sufficient for an owner to determine whether a preliminary study should be abandoned or pursued further. An order of magnitude estimate can be prepared in various ways— the most obvious of which is to make a comparison of historical costs for some repetitive element of the building. For instance, if a school is being considered, the estimator might multiply a specific number of classrooms by historical cost per classroom to arrive at an approximation of the cost. This type of estimate requires very little time to prepare if historical cost data suitably categorized are readily available to the estimator.

2. *Preliminary Estimate*   If the order of magnitude estimate is acceptable to the owner, the project will normally proceed to the stage where a preliminary estimate, sometimes referred to as a "budget" or "feasibility" estimate, can be prepared. Estimates in this category are intended to have an accuracy of plus or minus 20%. A preliminary estimate is often prepared by the parameter method, wherein the estimated total cost of a project is correlated with the estimated costs of its major parameters. As in the order of magnitude estimate, historical cost data from similar projects must be available and appropriately summarized. Analysis of historical cost data will usually establish a definite pattern of cost in relation to building type for each building parameter. The following parameters are typical of those used to accumulate historical costs and to predict future costs:

1. Site work.
2. Foundations.
3. Substructure.
4. Substructure frame.

ALL COSTS ARE IN: U.S.DOLLAR

BARTON-MALOW CO.
DETROIT, MICH.

HISTORICAL PARAMETER ESTIMATE
COST LEVEL 3 (BY CONFIGURATION)
USING MED SPECIFICATION

JOB NO:52600

TYPE PROJECT: 46 HOSPITAL, GEN   FRAME:HEALTH&WELFARE STL HI
LAST HISTORICAL DATE:- 5/76 AVE ESCL/YR   %   REPORT DATE:- 4/25/79

ESCALATION (L- 53.00%),(H- 60.00%) TO 12/1980

FLOOR AREA :   145000 SF   NO.FUNCTIONAL UNITS: 193 BEDS
DETROIT,MICH.1/79   COST/SF:-   99.75, BASE COST/SF:-   45.30

SYSTEM	SYS MEAS	SYS UNIT	FLSF/ SYS U	DIR COST/ SYS U	% LAB COST	% MAT COST	% TOT COST	DIR COST/ BLDSF	TOTAL COST/ BLDSF	LABOR COST	MATERIAL COST	TOTAL COST	M/HRS
01 SITEWRK	127000	SITSF	1.14	2.86	41.57	58.43	2.82	2.50	2.81	150742	211914	362657	6882
02 FOUNDTN	145000	BLDSF	1.00	2.06	42.70	57.30	2.32	2.06	2.32	127714	171376	299091	5812
03 FLOOR	145000	BLDSF	1.00	11.33	40.91	59.09	12.77	11.33	12.74	672166	970847	1643014	29317
04 INT COL	3600	COLLF	40.28	59.51	48.74	51.26	1.66	1.48	1.66	104416	109806	214223	4380
05 ROOF	36000	RFSF	4.03	15.24	39.71	60.29	4.26	3.78	4.25	217856	330709	548566	9295
06 EX WALL	65000	WLSF	2.23	18.83	33.98	66.02	9.51	8.44	9.49	415878	808159	1224038	18853
07 EX GLAZ	68000	PGSF	21.32	20.15	29.64	70.36	1.06	0.95	1.06	40615	96430	137046	1855
08 IN WALL	272000	WLSF	0.53	6.07	49.38	50.62	12.84	11.40	12.81	815936	836444	1652380	38048
09 DOORS	21000	DRSF	6.90	28.90	22.97	77.03	4.72	4.19	4.70	139420	467456	606876	6367
10 SPECLTY	145000	BLDSF	1.00	1.74	22.97	77.03	1.96	1.74	1.95	57819	193945	251764	2581
11 EQUIPMT	145000	BLDSF	1.00	3.99	23.72	76.28	4.50	3.99	4.49	137384	441889	579273	5349
12 CONVEYR	145000	BLDSF	1.00	2.96	35.39	64.61	3.33	2.96	3.32	151778	277042	428821	5910
13 PLUMBNG	682	FIXTR	212.61	1944.33	45.04	54.96	10.30	9.15	10.28	597236	728798	1326034	29892
15 H-V-A/C	580	TON	250.00	3637.89	34.21	65.79	16.40	14.55	16.36	721926	1388051	2109977	36441
17 EL W/AC	145000	BLDSF	1.00	7.63	48.13	51.87	8.60	7.63	8.58	532550	573942	1106492	24740
18 SPC ELC	145000	BLDSF	1.00	2.61	36.76	63.24	2.94	2.61	2.93	139014	239199	378213	6458

TOT DIR COST	12868460.					100.00	88.75			5022452	7846009	12868460	232180
MARK-UP	1595689.					12.40	11.00			622784	972905	1595689	
TOTAL COST	14464150.					112.40		99.75		5645236	8818914	14464150	

TOTAL DURATION(CREW WORK DAYS), ALL TRADES =   4153 CREW/DAYS

Figure 6-6 Historical parameter estimate.

CODE	DESCRIPTION	QUANTITY MEAS	TOT M/H	UNIT L COST	LABOR COST	UNIT M&E COST	MTL&EQP COST	TOTAL COST	PARM
C20.05	STIRRUPS	2463EA	118.94	0.91	2241.	1.02	2519.	4760.	(0.00)
C20.07	#7 RNF BAR	13429LB	66.87	0.09	1261.	0.12	1643.	2904.	(0.00)
C20.08	#8 RNF BAR	35083LB	125.07	0.07	2354.	0.12	4138.	6492.	(0.00)
** MAJOR-COMP. C04.36E	TOTAL	365CY	2161.60	97.01	35409.	95.25	34765.	70174.	(0.00)
	SUB-TOTAL	($ 1.67/BLDSF)	2276.83		37364.		36542.	73906.	
TOTAL . . .		($ 1.67/BLDSF)	2276.83		37364.		36542.	73906.	

RECAPITULATION

DESCRIPTION		TOTAL/SF	TOT M/H	LABOR COST	MTL&EQP COST	TOTAL COST
2-02 FOUNDTN	75.00	($ 1.67/BLDSF)	2276.83	37364.	36542.	73906.
TOTAL . . .		($ 1.67/BLDSF)	2276.83	37364.	36542.	73906.

MARK-UP

	LABOR COST	MTL&EQP COST	TOTAL COST
GENERAL CONDITIONS (5.0%)	1868.	1827.	3695.
SUB-TOTAL	39232.	38369.	77601.
SALES TAX (4.0%)		1535.	1535.
SUB-TOTAL		39904.	79136.
OVERHEAD & PROFIT (4.0%) ($ 79136.)			3165.
SUB-TOTAL			82301.
ESCALATION (2/81) (L 8.0%, M 8.0%)	3264.	3320.	6584.
SUB-TOTAL	44066.	44820.	88885.

TOTAL ESTIMATED COST . . . ($ 2.01/SF) 2276.83 M/H 88885.
(SS & LABOR INS ARE INCLUDED IN DIRECT COST FIGURES.)

Figure 6-7 Construction cost estimate.

5. Exterior cladding and roof.
6. Interior Construction work.
7. Fire protection.
8. Plumbing.
9. Heating, ventilating, and air conditioning.
10. Electrical.
11. Process.
12. Conveyances.
13. General conditions and staff.
14. Fee.

Buildings will differ in their construction, timing, site condition, mechanical and electrical sophistication, etcetra. The parameter method must be used with care, since it does not automatically take these differences into account. Like the order of magnitude estimates, the preliminary estimate requires only a limited amount of effort to prepare. However, it is necessary to do enough preliminary design and engineering to determine the size of the building. Assumptions must also be made about the kinds of subsystems that will be used. In making a presentation of a preliminary estimate to an owner, the preliminary nature of the design information on which the estimate is predicated should be emphasized.

3. *Definitive Estimate*   The next stage is the definitive estimate that frequently is used for the appropriation of funds for the project and sometimes is used to establish a guaranteed maximum price. The owner's representative usually wants a definitive estimate to present to his management in order to obtain authority for expenditures. The desired definitive estimate accuracy is usually in the plus or minus 10% range. This type of estimate can be prepared in a manner similar to the parameter method described previously, except that more detailed studies are required. The major systems and subsystems of the building must be identified, and the purchase cost of major items of equipment should be established. An analysis of the site as well as the building configuration should be made so as to understand the degree of finish and operating complexity required. Sufficient design information to prepare a definitive estimate is usually available when about 50 to 60% of the total design effort has been expended. At that time, the basic engineering design for the framing system is substantially complete, and the mechanical and electrical systems design should be well advanced. Quantity estimates can be made with reasonable confidence at this stage by an experienced conceptual estimator, although he must be prepared to fill in the gaps where design drawings are incomplete. The estimate should include allowances for unresolved items such as building finishes and exterior building treatment. The three stages of conceptual estimates are prepared prior to the completion of working drawings. the conceptual estimate is of critical importance in the construc-

tion management system, since it is the basis on which the financial feasibility of the project is evaluated. If a conceptual estimate indicates that the cost of a project will excel the financial limits the owner has established, a major reevaluation is in order before the subsequent stages of the project development are initiated. A conceptual estimator differs from a bid estimator in that he must be creative. He must search out the things not shown in the documents he studies, continually striving to make the estimate package complete. He must be able to perform conceptual design as an essential adjustment to his conceptual estimating.

VALUE ENGINEERING

Value engineering is a systematic effort directed at analyzing the functional requirements of systems, equipment, facilities, procedures, and supplies for the purpose of achieving the essential functions at the lowest total cost consistent with needed performance, reliability, quality, maintainability, esthetics, safety, and fire protection. In other words, do not build it any better or any worse than it needs to be built. Value engineering should be performed throughout the whole project, and the following questions should be asked, while keeping in mind the principle of "build it no better than it needs to be built": What is the project's function? What does the project do? What will the project cost?

Value engineering combines a deductive program-solving method with creative problem solving in an atmosphere that encourages challenging everything—organization, traditions, procedures, policies, customs, products, and people. The systematic approach of value engineering includes the following:

1. Gathering more than the usual information.

2. Determining the function of each product, component, system, idea, and so on.

3. Placing a dollar value on the function as now performed and comparing it to the dollar value estimate on how it might otherwise be performed.

4. Selecting the largest dollar ratios between the present operational solutions and the possible alternative functional solutions.

5. Determining alternate ways to perform functions through the application of creative problem-solving methods.

6. Investigating the alternative function solutions for their potentials in greater efficiency, higher reliability, reduced weight, better maintainability, and reduced cost.

7. Selecting short-range and long-range possibilities that have reasonably high probability of success if adopted as operational solutions.

8. Developing a value engineering proposal suitable to the decision maker's needs.

The key early steps recycled many times are these:

1. Determine the basic functions of the total subject.

2. Determine if the basic function can be eliminated and hence eliminate the total subject.

3. If the subject is necessary and its function is necessary, then determine alternative ways to perform the basic function.

4. Evaluate the function and select the best alternative.

5. If the basic function is determined to be performed as it is rather than going to some other way to perform the function, then determine the basic function of the individual details of the system or product.

The word *value* has many meanings. There are four kinds of value:

Use value: The properties and qualities that accomplish the function.

Esteem value: The properties, features, and attractiveness that cause us to want it or own it.

Cost value: The amount of dollars or man-hours that must be paid to purchase or produce it.

Exchange value: The properties or qualities that enable us to exchange it for something else we want.

The ultimate benefit of value engineering occurs when the various components of life cycle costing are incorporated into the process. Life cycle costing, in conjunction with value engineering, takes into consideration initial cost impact, collateral costs, replacement costs, and life cycle costs (Figure 6-8).

MARKETING

The marketing of construction management services is not difficult, if the construction management firm meets the major qualifications of an awarding agency. Consideration is usually given to firms or joint ventures meeting the following requirements:

1. Has experience as a construction manager or potential competence to perform construction management services.

2. Has the financial ability to provide the services required by the awarding agency.

3. Is competent in civil, mechanical, electrical, and structural engineering; value management; construction estimating; cost accounting and control; tenant coordination; project management; contract negotiation and administration; construction supervision and inspection; and other related fields.

4. Has experience in constructing buildings in the general geographic area of the particular project in question, or has good recent knowledge of local

Project: Metropolitan Stadium   Date: 9-4-74

System or item: Hydraulic vs. traction elevators   Project No.: 27023

	Original	Alternate
Instant contract		
Initial cost impact	Hydraulic	Traction
1. Base cost	30,000	45,000
2. Interface costs		
(A) Penthouse vs. machine room	1,080	1,900
(B) Electrical power	4,000	2,000
Collateral costs		
Subtotal instant contract	35,080	48,900
1. Other initial costs		
Total initial cost impact	35,080	48,900
Replacement costs		
Life cycle expenditures		
(A) Year 10 at 10%/0.3855	(2,000) 771	(4,000) 1,542
(B) Year 16 at 10%/0.2176	(6,000) 1,306	(12,000) 2,611
Life cycle costs		
Annual owning and operating costs		
1. Initial cost—amortized at 0.1175		
20 Years at 10% interest	4,121	5,746
2. Replacement costs—amortized at		
(A) 10 Years at 10%/0.1175	90	181
(B) 16 Years at 10%/0.1175	153	307
3. Annual costs		
(A) Maintenance	2,400	3,000
(B) Operations	120	240
Total annual owning and operating	8,961	13,627

Figure 6-8 Life Cycle Cost Analysis

conditions in the project area, or has the ability to retain others with such knowledge.

5. Has proven competence in the implementation and maintenance of network-based construction management systems and in the application of systematic cost control throughout the design and construction process.

6. Has a good professional and business reputation and an on-time and within budget preformance record.

7. Has the ability to provide professionally qualified key personnel with a minimum of 12 years' satisfactory experience in the design and construction industries. Satisfactory experience should include the following: (a) Eight years in work related specifically to the duties to be performed in the designated position for the project and (b) four years in positions with the requirements equal to those for the designated position of the project.

AN ARCHITECT-ENGINEER

STAFF

The type of staff organization within an architectural-engineering firm is dependent on the capabilities of the staff. It is to the firm's advantage that its technical staff be organized so that each person is delegated responsibility equal to his or her capacity and potential. In the firm that consists largely of specialists—that is, persons particularly talented in one aspect of production such as design, preparing working drawings, writing specifications, or performing contract administration—a so-called "horizontal staff organization" would be appropriate. In the horizontal organization, each project passes from one department or specialist to another during the phase of basic architectural services that includes the schematic design phase, design development phase, construction document phase, bidding or negotiating phase, and the administration of construction contracts phase. Each specialist, programmer, designer, site planner, delineator, model maker, draftsman, engineer, specification writer, color specialist, construction contract administrator, and project representative contributes his efforts at the proper time and place under the direction of the project architect. Under this arrangement, several projects (each at a different stage of development) may be in process by the firm at any particular time. A specialist or department may be working on two or more projects at any one moment. In the smaller firm, the principal and his most trusted associates or employees will perform most of these functions, giving their attention to each phase of each project as circumstances require. The "vertical staff organization" is implemented if the firm has several generalists—that is, architecturally trained or experienced persons having capabilities in all or several phases of an architect's services. Under this organization, each project is assigned to a project team under a project architect. Programming, design, structure, mechanical systems, working drawings, specifications, and construction contract administration are all tackled cooperatively by the project team. Some members of the team serve during all phases, others during only one or two phases. The organization of many firms may be a combination of horizontal and vertical patterns and may be altered from time to time to adjust to changing conditions and personnel capabilities.

PRODUCTION

The advantages of using the architect's regular office force for a project are obvious. A means of enabling an architectural firm to undertake more or larger projects than would otherwise be possible is to secure the services of other firms as associate architects or as participants in a joint venture. The production staff of an architectural-engineering office is usually controlled by a director of production. In most firms, this is handled by one of the principals of the firm. It is his responsibility to orchestrate all the disciplines necessary to effectively carry out the project from initial inception to final occupancy. The director of production must communicate and maintain constant liaison with each department head as well as the project manager assigned to the project. A typical example of this communication would be weekly meetings with each of the project managers, together with all the parties in the architectural-engineering office involved on a specific project. Such a meeting provides an opportunity for the director of production to receive a firsthand update regarding the status of the project from a representative of each of the departments. Within such a meeting, the monitoring of time expended on the project by each of the engineering disciplines is reviewed and discussed. Also, on a regularly scheduled basis, the director of production meets with each of the department heads to review in depth the overall work-load of the firm. The project manager may or may not be the designer, but he will direct the project from start to finish. The project manager and the principal responsible for the project, if the project manager is not a principal, maintain contact with the owner. He may be assisted in the operation by a job captain. In some circumstances, the project manager and the job captain will be the same person. The project manager assumes major responsibility for the project for the other partners, the owner, and the public. The job captain is directly responsible to the project manager. Generally, all negotiations with the owner are carried on by the project manager, but the job captain attends all meetings and prepares reports of the same for distribution to those concerned. It is the job captain's normal responsibility to see that the project work is done efficiently and in accordance with established standards of the firm. The time the job captain spends managing and overseeing the work of members of his team may be of more value to the firm than

the time devoted to drafting. The job captain sees that engineers, specifications writers, consultants, and so on, are given the proper drawings and all
other information needed. When the working drawing specifications are
complete the job captain sees that they are thoroughly and completely
reviewed prior to the bidding period. He also reviews all correspondence
and meeting notes to determine that all items have been accommodated.

MARKETING

The function of marketing in architectural practice is threefold. Marketing
allows pursuit of the kind of work the architect wants to do; it creates
contacts among the kind of clients the architect wants to serve; and, as a
result, it provides opportunities to execute the kinds of buildings the architect is most qualified to do. The size of the professional firm has nothing to
do with the applicability of the marketing functions. If the firm wishes to
have better control over or improve the type, location, and quality of commissions, it should have a marketing program. It is important to recognize
that architecture is not a market itself, but a service that is performed in
many different markets. The individual architect usually lacks the training
and knowledge to perform services for every market; therefore, the first
step in establishing a successful marketing program is to identify markets
that are most compatible with the capabilities of the firm. Six elements are
required for a marketing program. They are as follows:

1. Identification of local markets.
2. A capability to serve a particular market.
3. A system or process for selling the capability to that market.
4. Public relations to support the effort.
5. A marketing organization and financial capability to carry out that
process.
6. A marketing plan that includes an outline of what the marketing objective is and what results are expected to be achieved.

   The marketing plan will indicate where to place the marketing emphasis,
how much effort should be applied and what results can reasonably be
expected. If the plan is developed and followed as outlined, experience in
many firms indicates that the goals will in due course be achieved. Once the
architect decides to conduct a formal marketing program, being selected for
any one particular job does not greatly matter. Win, lose, or draw, the
committed professional will find more than enough incentive to try again.
The lesson of the marketing process is that architects can and should be
more than merely responsive to potential new business opportunities.
Those who seek out and develop opportunities can do much to influence
the quality, quantity, and interest of the commissions they undertake.

PROJECT SPECIALIZATION

Architects have traditionally been taught in school to believe themselves capable of designing any type of building for any location. Many firms have developed a multidisciplined organization that embraces all architectural and engineering services within a single entity. Such a firm is capable of designing any type of commercial or institutional facility. An architectural firm should realistically assess its capabilities of performing work in a variety of markets. It is important to recognize that architecture is not a market itself, but a service that is performed in many different markets. To locate a potentially fruitful market, it is necessary to determine the factors that will help the architect decide whether the market has potential for the firm. In selecting a potential market, the analysis must be very specific. Education, for example, is not an architectural market of itself. Public schools, private schools, community colleges, vocational-technical schools, and colleges are individual markets with quite different criteria when it comes to professional services. For the architect, some markets are as specific as an individual type, such as libraries, warehouses, or theaters. The health care and medical field is a totally unique market in itself, requiring the architectural firm to maintain multidiscipline personnel capable of serving the entire health care community. A manufacturer approaches a specific market with a product that, as a result of research and acquired knowledge of a client's needs, is tailored to that market. Otherwise, that product will not sell. The architect's product is capability, and it is just as important that his individual capability be matched to the market being sought. Many times an architect is noted for certain types of projects, whether office buildings, hospitals, or educational facilities. Such stereotyping can be both an asset and a liability, depending on the total availability of work in the marketplace. The importance of matching the firm's capability to the market cannot be overemphasized, particularly for the small firm. Given a large enough marketplace, there is a place for every kind of practice, large and small, specialized or generalized. For the majority of firms, the market determines what that place is. The professional who wants to engage in a particular type or size of practice must recognize and act on the obligation to locate the segments of the market where the capability of the firm is accepted and desired. If it is felt that the combined capacities of the firm's personnel are not equal to the marketplace test, three options are available. First, the firm can develop the needed capability, either through hiring qualified staff or associating in a joint venture or otherwise with a firm that already has the needed expertise. Second, the firm members can make a conscious decision to attempt to sell their current capabilities despite the conditions of the market and accept the consequences in terms of the greater difficulty of securing commissions and the lower initial yield on the marketing effort. Third, the firm can stay out of this market and devote its entire efforts to markets more suited to its capabilities.

A TYPICAL OWNER

SELECTION OF THE ARCHITECT-ENGINEER

Normally, a new construction program to be performed for the typical institutional owner is handled through a building committee. As an example, for a hospital, the building committee might be made up of members of the board of directors, members of the medical staff, the hospital administrator, and other appointees from the community. As a rule, most of the members of the building committee have limited knowledge of the construction industry. In recent years, several institutions have retained retirees of the construction industry as advisers to the building committee. Usually, one of the first tasks for the building committee is the selection of the architect. There are three methods most generally followed. The type of project will very often influence the method used. The importance of a careful choice in the selection of an architect for a proposed building project cannot be overstated. For most owners, this is a once or twice in a lifetime endeavor. A building project carried from its earliest concept to the realization of an attractive functional structure should be a rewarding experience for the building committee. The following three general methods are used in selecting an architect for the proposed building:

1. Direct method.
2. Comparative method.
3. Design competition method.

The particular method followed is very often determined by the type of client and the type of project. For example, the direct method is most often used by a group of people or building committee, and the design competition method is most frequently used for large civic and monumental projects. Although all methods are available in the consideration of any project the great majority of architectural commissions are awarded as a result of either direct or comparative selection. Therefore, the description of the selection methods will be limited to the direct and comparative method only. Whether the selection is made by an individual or by a group of people, the procedure follows three basic steps:

1. A review of an architect's qualifications and experience resume, together with photographs of executed work.
2. A personal interview to afford the investigator an opportunity to find out more about the architect's attitudes, philosophy, and personality.

3. An investigation of the architect's former clients and project, preferably through visitation of buildings. This step will give insight into the architect's ability and ingenuity in solving a problem and the degree of satisfaction attained.

DIRECT SELECTION

By this method, an architect can be chosen with relative ease and without additional expense in the process. The selection is made on the basis of the architect's reputation, personal acquaintance, or recommendation by former clients. Frequently, the architect will be appointed as a result of the procedure outlined previously, whereby the three basic steps are followed. An individual often decides in favor of a personal acquaintance or on the recommendation of friends and satisfied clients. In any case, the architect is chosen on the basis of talent, professional experience, and taste as evaluated by the client in terms of his needs and inclinations.

COMPARATIVE SELECTION

This procedure may be pursued in several different ways, but essentially the architect is chosen from among a group who have presented the necessary qualification data in the form of written application and a subsequent interview. The application may be requested in a limited way for a restricted list of architects, or it may be called for by public announcement, which may result in responses from many applicants. The invitation to submit an application should include a description of the project under consideration, giving the approximate budget for the work and the time schedule proposed. All applicants should be asked to submit a complete statement of the training and experience of key personnel, the size and type of organization, and a representative list of projects done by the firm. After the applications have been received, they should be carefully reviewed so that a selected group may be invited for interview. Of the total number of respondents, not more than three or four should be considered further. Through the interview, the potential client will want to know more about the architect's professional standing, his experience and projects, and the conduct of his practice. And he will find out about the architect's attitudes, compatability, and philosophy of design. The client will frequently be concerned about whether the architect under consideration has had experience in work of similar size, type, and complexity. The young architect should not be ruled out because he does not have many buildings to his credit. He may be well qualified in other respects, although he should be able to prove competence in such work as has been entrusted to him. The size of an architect's office is generally less important than the efficiency of his organization. The professional office is usually organized to handle work within established price limits, and the potential client can be guided accordingly by considering representative work done by the firm. The final selection of the architect should be made on the basis of good standing in his profession and in the community on his creative and artistic ability, his technical competence, his business capacity, his integrity, his good judgment, and on his ability to cooperate with all those involved in the project.

Regardless of the method used by the owner in the selection of an architect, he should be chosen as a person with whom there can be a relationship of absolute confidence and trust. He should be given complete information pertaining to the project, and his judgement should be fully respected. When the decision to award the commission has been made, the owner and the architect should conclude their negotiations with a written agreement so that all matters between them are thoroughly understood by both.

TYPE OF CONTRACT

Once the owner has entered into an agreement with the architect, it is necessary to give consideration about the type of construction contract that would be used for this particular project. The procedures for selecting the organization to supervise and perform building construction and the types of contracts available for use have proliferated in recent years because of the increasing complexity of building designs, escalating costs, legal constraints, magnitude of public projects, accelerated social needs, and increasing demands on the owner's staff. The general contractor selected under any of the contracting methods should be selected by the owner on a completely objective basis—taking into account his skill, integrity and responsibility in equal and fair competition with his peers. The four most commonly used types of building contracts are as follows:

I. Lump sum contract
   A. *Definition.* Agreement to perform the work for one fixed price, regardless of cost to the contractor.
   B. *Selection Method.* Competitive bidding among general contractors for construction of the entire project under a single contract is preferred. Bidding may be from a preselected list of bidders or from anyone who wishes to bid. In public work and some private work, the bidders must furnish proof of financial capability such as a bond or certified check. When using a preselected list on private work, the owner and his architect-engineer should carefully and objectively weigh capabilities of the contractors while assembling the list. After the list is determined, when the bids are received the owner should award the job to the lowest bidder. Preselection is not possible on most public work.

C. *Owner's requirements*
1. Completed detailed plans and specifications.
2. Adequate professional inspection and supervisory personnel experienced in construction, either in-house or from architects and engineers.
3. Staff and consultant proficiency in planning, budgeting, construction feasibility, and marketing construction.
4. Marketable job.

D. *Advantages*
1. Economy of contractor effort with his own money at risk.
2. Objectivity of selection on private work.
3. Final price known (assuming no changes in plans and specifications).
4. Less bookkeeping and auditing expense.

E. *Cautions*
1. Owner and contractor may have opposite financial interest.
2. The complicated procedures required to process changes and the resulting cost to both parties.
3. Delay in start of construction until plans are 100% complete and bids taken.
4. Reliance on consultants to provide practical construction advice, budgets, and schedules prior to receipt of bids.

II. Cost plus contract
A. *Definition.* Agreement to perform work and be reimbursed on the basis of actual cost, plus a percentage (or fixed amount) fee for the contractor.
B. *Selection Method.* The owner should make a careful objective review of the qualifications of interested general contractors and make an award to the one best qualified who submits an acceptable fee.
C. *Owner's requirements*
1. Sophistication required to determine the need for this form of contract and the best contractors for the particular project.
2. Staff and consultant ability to make prompt decisions and maintain a completed drawing and specifications flow to keep up with the job.
3. Staff proficiency in monitoring costs and auditing.
D. *Advantages*
1. Start construction before plans are complete or even before all requirements are known. This may be particularly desir-

able where an owner wishes to quickly get into production with a new manufacturing process, for example.

2. Flexibility to make changes at their actual audited cost.

3. Can be used on jobs that are not easily marketable because of size, lack of definition of scope, and so on.

    E. *Cautions*

1. Final cost not guaranteed.

2. More work for the staffs of the owner and architect-engineer in monitoring costs, bookkeeping, and auditing.

3. Burden on owner and architect-engineer in selection of general contractor experienced in this type of contract who is efficient, has management experience to act as a team member, and knows how to keep proper books of account.

4. Early construction start can cause delays or additional expense if design is changed.

III. Guaranteed maximum or upset price contract

    A. *Definition.* Agreement to perform work and be reimbursed on the basis of actual cost plus a percentage or fixed fee, with the contractor guaranteeing that an agreed maximum price will not be exceeded. Costs above this price are borne by the contractor. Savings below the guaranteed price, after the contractor takes his fee, are often shared between the contractor and owner.

    B. *Selection Method.* Basically the same as the cost plus contract. This method often starts as a cost plus contract and is converted to a maximum price contract when plans sufficiently define the scope of the work. Competitive proposals can be taken by the owner or architect-engineer and award made to the lowest bidder, but this is not advisable when the plans and specifications are not complete because of the varying assumptions made by the preselected bidders.

    C. *Owner's Requirements.* Basically the same as on a cost plus contract, except that the owner need have less concern for his cost-monitoring input because of the price guarantee.

    D. *Advantages.* Can combine the advantages of the lump sum contract with price guarantee from a risk-taking general contractor and the flexibility in scheduling and project development implicit in a cost plus contract.

    E. *Caution.* Same as for a cost plus contract, except that there is a price guarantee.

IV. Construction management contract

    A. *Definition.* This is an agreement to perform the services and the work for a percentage or fixed fee, with the qualified general contracting organization serving as the construction professional and expert on the building team with the owner and architect-engineer from the beginning of design throughout the completion of construction. (For a more detailed definition refer to the booklet entitled *Construction Management Guidelines,* published by AGC, as adopted on March 9, 1972.) The contract can be converted to a guaranteed maximum price contract when the plans are sufficiently complete to define the scope of the work.

B.   *Selection Method.*   the owner should make a careful objective review of the qualifications of interested general contractors, giving due consideration to their experience in working with architects and engineers on work of similar character during design development and make an award to the one best qualified with an acceptable fee.

C.   *Owner's requirements*
1.   Staff involvement and ability to make prompt decisions after weighing the building team's recommendations.
2.   Selection of architect-engineer who is willing to operate as a team member and be receptive to the construction manager's recommendations.
3.   A job where flexibility to change is important, whose time allowance precludes waiting for completed bid documents, or that is not easily marketable because of lack of definition of scope or size.

D.   *Advantages*
1.   Creates a "team" with the owner, general contractor-construction manager, and architect-engineer before plans are developed. General contractor-construction manager is available to give his advice on construction feasibility, cost, site selection, and scheduling.
2.   Time and cost saving by starting construction before all plans are complete.
3.   Ability to competitively bid, including public work in a public-letting situation, all the trade contracts on the job, while at the same time having a qualified general contractor on the team from the inception of design through final completion and acceptance of the project.

E.   *Cautions*
1.   Final cost not guaranteed (unless converted when plans are sufficiently completed to a guaranteed maximum price contract).
2.   Burden on owner in selection of a general contractor experi-

enced in scheduling, cost control, plan and specifications review, and so on, and who has management experience to act
as a team member and qualified to direct the work of the
individual trade contractors.

3. Under many public-bidding statutes, a construction manager is precluded from performing work with his own forces.

FINANCIAL AND CONSTRUCTION FEASIBILITY

Feasibility, finances, location, and analysis form part of the foundation of
the design phase of an architect's basic services. In recent years, feasibility
and locational studies have become customary—part of the additional services of many firms. As the techniques of such activities are refined and
detailed, they require the increasing attention of the architect and expand
his responsibilities and costs. Some of these services are more properly of a
business nature rather than of a professional nature. Often, the owner finds
it to his best interest to seek the services of outside firms that are more
readily qualified in providing a broader background in real estate, finance,
and taxation. Some of the items to be considered under a feasibility study
are as follows:

1. Is there a need for a new facility?

2. How can this need be accomplished, and what should be the method of
accomplishment? Is it possible to remodel and renovate part of the existing
facility to meet the needs in lieu of total new construction?

3. To meet the need requirements, what is the total economic
requirement?

4. Should consideration be given to relocation in lieu of constructing adjacent to an existing facility?

5. What personnel requirements should be incorporated?

6. What are the legal considerations?

The financial analysis should include the following:

1. Operational financing.

2. Capitalization of project.

3. Land values and availability.

4. Taxes and insurance rate.

5. Interim financing.

6. Long-range financing.

If positive responses can be generated to each of the foregoing items, those in charge can move the project forward, being confident that all the major economic and legal considerations have been totally addressed.

MAJOR INDUSTRY PROBLEMS

As president of a major general contracting and construction management firm in the building, institutional, and commercial construction industry, I recognize two problems relating to our industry. These two problems are general enough in nature, and all firms are confronted with them. They are manager development and productivity improvement.

In discussing manager development, I would like to look at this subject in the broad sense of developing managers from a superintendent level to the midmanagement level. Strange as it seems, there is a reluctuance for some individuals to want to move into a higher-responsibility position. Many are content to forego a major advancement within a corporation because of the increased responsibility. The general attitude is that increased compensation is not worth all the headaches and pressure. There is a somewhat general feeling that people are just not willing to work as hard as they used to, and the old work ethic has eroded. The attitude of unwillingness to work has led to our attempts at productivity improvement. Since productivity in our industry is so directly related to our costs, it becomes a major concern in our overall operation. The annual lack of productivity improvement has had its impact on inflation, with its continuing increase of construction costs. Productivity has not kept up with the annual wage increase, and, as a result, actual construction costs have accelerated at a greater rate than the annual percentage wage increase.

Management has attempted to introduce techniques and methods that would minimize the human factor in production. The production of a product in a controlled environment other than at the job site has been introduced into the building construction industry. Such components as precast concrete structural systems and concrete reinforced fiberglass wall systems are examples of what can be done in the way of prefabrication off the site. Recently, a totally integrated system consisting of a structural core, finish floor and ceiling, and all mechanical and electrical components was constructed off the site with the intent of merely transporting it to the site and making the necessary and final utility connections. This total system was perhaps one of the most radical departures from conventional construction methods.

In reviewing both the problems of developing managers and productivity improvement, the underlying factor with both of these problems is a lack of motivation. Fear, money, and work organization reliance on the work ethic are losing their effectiveness as motivational tools. Our economy is not the unbeatable, dynamic, ever-growing world force it was in the first-quarter century following World War II. Our productivity is falling for many reasons: the cost of energy, the crippling effects of government regulations, the distortions of inflation, environmental costs, a slackening of investment, a shift to services, and so on. But careful studies show that, collectively, all these factors can account for only a fraction of the present slippage. If you look at changing American attitudes toward work, you can catch a glimpse of what is a major factor contributing to the decline. People who work at all levels of enterprise, particularly younger middle-management people, are no longer motivated to work as hard and as effectively as in the past. Reasons abound for downgrading the centrality of motivation, in enhancing effectiveness, efficiency, and productivity. Many of the people in top management positions are trained in finance, engineering, or production. While they are not comfortable with the intangibles of human behavior, they are comfortable with the more tangible areas of business.

There tends to be a growing mismatch between incentives and motivation. The incentive system does not work as well as it used to. Formerly, management had the tools for motivating people adequately in order to ensure ever-increasing productivity. This is no longer true. People's values and attitudes have changed faster than the incentive system, creating a mismatch. Yankelovich describes a few areas from which the incentives of the future are going to come or be shapped. One of the most important sources of incentive in the future will be derived from innovative and ingenious ways of using time—not just the restructuring of the use of time, but vacations, sabbaticals, informal schedules, in freedom of flexibility. Customized feedback mechanisms on achievement and on keeping the individual's own balance sheet represents another potential area of incentives. Such feedback mechanisms have been incorporated with many companies, with the establishment of an annual personnel evaluation.

Over the years, various solutions have been suggested for improving productivity, and they are as varied as the people making them. Some suggestions include the following: (1)The establishment of a separate set of labor laws for construction that equalizes the bargaining power of contractors and the union and recognizes the uniqueness of construction labor situations. Construction was regarded as different enough to be excluded from the Taft-Hartley Act, so there is no reason why this is not different enough to have its own labor laws; (2) establishment of compensation rates based on skill and productivity, independent of existing rates; (3) establishment of regional bargaining. While a single company and a single union can set a pattern for the entire automotive or steel industries, several hundred contractors in any given area may have to bargain with 100 or more separate local unions, many representing the same trade. This creates an unstable labor market and produces wage spirals as individual unions vie for the best contract terms.

Many of today's contractors believe that, in our free society, it is impossible to legislate productivity or build conscientious workmanship into a contract, unless those being controlled are also concerned. Managers cannot develop unless they are qualified and ready and willing to take on the duties of responsibilities of management. No longer can a job be created for those who have no desire to work for their pay.

SUMMATION

Demands placed on the building construction community have changed dramatically in the last decade. In response to these demands, the industry is reawakening to calls for greater efficiency to meet the needs of society. To meet these needs—despite the changing availability of resources, excessive costs, increasing regulations, and conflicting priorities—there is an unwritten mandate to the building community to improve productivity. Because of this growing awareness and widespread interest, the Building Research Advisory Board (BRAB) has focused full attention on the issue of productivity in the building and construction community. BRAB is a nonprofit organization that is acting as a catalyst to harness the resources of the public and private building and construction sectors to confront the issue. An attempt will be made to bring together all elements involved or impacting on building and construction to delineate the problems of productivity and recommend plans for resolution. BRAB feels that it is impossible for anyone in the industry to be complacent. All segments (residential, commercial, institutional, industrial, or civil works)—whether a firm, corporation, sole proprietorship, governmental agency, financial institution, realtor-investor, craftsman, or professional—have a stake in improving productivity in the building and construction process. The demands for change in operational and management philosophy, research and development, and financial and regulatory burdens are evident. No one can be satisfied with the status quo, because what each individual does today with an idea or technique is part of an additive evolutionary process that in sum affects the whole community. Whether the interest is focused on the private or public sector, the issue of productivity cannot be ignored.

CHAPTER 7

INDUSTRIAL CONSTRUCTION

Donald S. Barrie

Industrial construction is broadly defined as being that class of work involving the construction of manufacturing and process plants designed to produce bulk commodities such as steel, aluminum, and cement; petroleum refineries and petrochemical plants; fossil-fueled and nuclear power plants; heavy manufacturing plants; and facilities designed to supply a wide range of products essential to our utilities and basic industries. In general, the process or manufacturing sequence is highly complex with the machinery, equipment, and service requirements, dictating the shape and nature of the structures as distinct from building construction, where the structure serves as an overall housing for people, materials, or other commodity.

BACKGROUND AND GROWTH

Industrial construction played a major role in the growth of the United States and Canada in the decades following World War II. While this branch of the industry uses all the performance options (traditional single contract, design-construct, and construction management), the early years saw the emergence of the design-constructor as the dominant force. Owners in a rapidly growing economy increasingly began to try to minimize the overall design-construct duration from concept to start-up. Payout times for new facilities were often extremely favorable, and shortening the construction schedule often became a major objective. The invention of PERT and CPM offered an opportunity to manage the project in such a way as to concentrate resources on the critical items in order to minimize the overall construction schedule. Most of the major projects began to be awarded to engineer-contractors who performed both design and construction work usually under some form of a reimbursable cost plus a fixed fee contract.

THE NATIONAL CONSTRUCTORS ASSOCIATION (NCA)

NCA was formed in 1947 and rapidly became the leading industrial relations spokesman for the engineer-contractor operating nationally. It is not surprising that the overall policies of AGC and NCA were very divergent. AGC, while organized nationally, was basically a regional association with almost all the power being vested in the local chapters that historically negotiated wages and work conditions with the basic craft unions. Most agreements had some form of local grievance procedure, and disputes were generally settled locally between the local chapter and the local labor unions. AGC contractors were typically working on lump sum or unit price competitively bid jobs, and most contracts had provision for time extensions in the event of strikes, lockout, or other labor disputes. The contractor's economic survival was in part based on the skills of the negotiators in holding down unreasonable wage increases and possibly was equally important in eliminating make-work items, featherbedding, or restrictions output. Thus AGC contractors as a whole were generally fully prepared to take strikes over economic demands in order to achieve reasonable contracts through the collective bargaining process. In fact, originally, wages in many areas were negotiated as firm for the duration of the job so that the contractor would not have to anticipate wage increases over the life of the contract. Most jurisdiction in building work, light industrial work, and heavy and highway work was fairly well established for the area, and the National Joint Board for the Settlement of Jurisdictional Disputes did not play a major role initially in affecting job performance.

NCA, on the other hand, was made up of leading companies that generally operated under national agreements with the labor unions calling for the adoption of local agreement practices regarding wages and most working conditions. However, two significant departures from local practice are evident. The national agreements negotiated by NCA called for the adoption of a new grievance procedure that completely bypassed the local agreements and provided for the international union representatives to meet with the employer representatives to settle disputes that could not be settled with the local union. The other significant departure was the inclusion of a no-strike-no-lockout article that paved the way for the national contractor to continue working in the event of local bargaining strikes. Since the large national contractor was operating on a cost plus contract with a client who was vitally interested in keeping the job going to minimize overall construction schedules, a retroactive wage adjustment or at least a continuation of work under the old agreement was generally placed in effect. In areas where large numbers of men were working on a major project the unions learned to effectively keep most or all their membership working for the national contractor, and this virtually allowed them to hold out for long periods of time to secure larger wage increase and more restrictive work practices than would have been possible prior to the influence of the national contractor. In many areas the local bargaining group retaliated by negotiating restrictive work practices, higher wages, or excessive travel time applicable only to the national contractor's projects.

Another significant departure from local AGC practice was the large amounts of overtime the national contractors used to attract in qualified journeymen in a labor short area and in an effort to "crash" the work as indicated by the critical path. Often the local employer group was forced to concessions that would never have been made if the normal economic pressure of a strike had been applied equally to both union members and the employer group.

The economic cycle in the United States has included periods of expansion and recession in the postwar economy. During the periods of recession many owners began to realize the many evils that had crept into the construction scene, and they began putting the pressure on the engineer-contractors to do something about low productivity and poor work practices that had become common on many major projects. NCA responded by first negotiating a work rules agreement with the International Building Trades Unions informally called the "Ten Commandments." Most of these agreements were aimed at restoration of employer control over the work force. Contractors and owners joined in denouncing the effects of scheduled overtime; many owners began to instruct national contractors to shut down the work to support local bargaining.

AGC and NCA have made several abortive attempts to unite at the national level in order to present a common front to the ever-growing political power of the international unions that had already effectively reached accord in political matters. At present, another attempt is being made with final results as yet unknown.

The influence of the growing open shop movement is challenging both the traditional AGC union contractor and the engineer-contractor. NCA has tried to meet this challenge by promoting project and national agreements that provide for concessions on the part of the union in working conditions, overtime premiums, or travel allowances negotiated during the go-go years. The National Industrial Construction Agreement between the building trades and NCA calls for several major concessions in southern and border states where open shop work is especially strong. AGC, on the other hand, has begun actively accepting open shop contractors into its membership and is fast assuming a dual role with many organizations going double-breasted with both a union and nonunion company under generally separate management or an open shop company which may sign labor agreements for a particular project. The emerging Merit Shop movement promoted by ABC is developing a substantial number of specialty trade contractors to enable open shop to complete directly with the union contractors on small-to medium-sized projects.

The twin effect of government regulations and the overlapping of design, procurement, and construction has produced a climate of constant change in the heavy industrial and utility construction environment. Traditional management methods have been able to cope with the fast track schedule and the regulator on more finite projects. Yet on the larger projects, a marked deterioration of performance, morale, and professionalism or craftsmanship of all parties involved in the building process has been clearly observed. New concepts and approaches must be pioneered and developed if the industrial construction industry as we know it is to survive in the ever-changing environment of the future.

Perhaps the overall management concepts developed during the management boom can achieve their highest workability in a well-managed, small-to medium-sized design-construct or design-manage project that is based on engineering integrity, sound planning, and historical data supplemented by a thorough understanding of local or other unique conditions that must be accounted for in the work plan. To illustrate the integrated approach to management planning and control, a theoretical example project has been selected. The state of the art is illustrated through the use of several exhibits that will describe the major construction planning and control tools which have been adopted in one form or another by most successful design-construct companies or major construction companies specializing in the heavy industrial area.*

A well-managed project may be divided into a number of management steps that, while often overlapping, develop the management plan for the program. such a program is summarized as follows:

- Fact finding.
- Conceptual planning.
- Detail planning and organizing.
- Operational control.

FACT FINDING

A successful construction program must be developed to fit the individual objectives, requirements, and characteristics of all the numerous entities that make up a complex industrial project. There is the client who may or may not understand or communicate his or her overall objectives or who may know exactly what he wants and how he expects to achieve it. Many times the design-constructor must evaluate and cope with conflicting demands from a client organization. For example, one level of a client organization may desire redundant components to insure operational availability, while another level may not be prepared to pay the cost of achieving the

*Many of the exhibits illustrating the state of the art used in the example project have been derived from material made available by Jim McCloud, President, Kaiser Engineers, Inc.

highest reliability. Client objectives may not always mesh with control requirements as in the desire of the client to keep track of costs for depreciation and tax considerations as opposed to cost accounting to maximize control during construction.

The designer will have objectives and requirements that will impact the construction process. Often individual designer preference may be in conflict with overall cost objectives for the program. Designer manpower availability may impact heavily the optimum design-construct program. Overall quality requirements may have a significant effect on the cost and duration of the construction phase as well as the operational period. A comprehensive site visit is essential if those items peculiar to the work site are to be taken into account in developing the program. On many major industrial projects proposed for remote areas, the location of the construction camp, access and supply routes, and the availability of manpower will have a major effect the cost of the project and the length of the construction program. Expected weather conditions will dictate overall construction methods and costs. Planning and building a project in southern California is vastly different from doing the same for one located in northern Canada or Alaska. Certain areas of the country are known to have militant and difficult labor unions. Other areas may have manpower surpluses and cooperative craft unions. Local contractors and local business agents can often contribute valuable information regarding local conditions if sufficient interest is expressed by the design-constructors during the site investigations. An understanding of area practice and the history of previous or current jobs in the area is very important. Anticipated productivity for use in making the estimate and in determining the overall schedules is at best an educated approximation. However, the more known about the local area including current problems and business practices, the more accurate will be the initial planning that will serve as the baseline for measurement of project performance. Table 7-1 shows a simplified checklist for performing a site and area visit. Finally, the results of the area and site visit must be reduced to certain conclusions and assumptions that can be communicated to the scheduler, estimators, and organizational planner so that an initial program can be developed which has an excellent chance of setting realistic conceptual goals for control of the overall project.

CONCEPTUAL PLANNING

After the facts have been developed, a formal work plan can be prepared for use by all entities in proceeding to execute the project. The initial plan must be prepared on a conceptual basis using broad parameters, including a conceptual estimate, conceptual schedule, project construction concept, organizational requirements, choice of management planning and control tools, project procedures, and delineation of individual responsibilities.

The plan must be both descriptive and quantitative so that overall proj-

TABLE 7-1.   Area Investigation Guidelines

---

1. Site Description
    (Vegetation, trees, terrain, depth of topsoil, drainage, existing structures, existing utilities, access, etc.)
2. Utilities serving site
    (Electricity, gas, water, sanitary sewer, storm sewer, railroad, highway, railroad siding, etc.)
3. Building department
    (Contact, telephone number, building code, plan check time, fees, zoning, licensing, etc.)
4. Labor unions
    (Membership, manpower shortages, manpower surplus, current agreements, wage rates, expiration dates, etc.)
5. Recommended contractors
    (List recommended general and trade contractors for further consideration)
6. Materials and methods
    (List favored local materials and methods, including current quoted price for readi-mix concrete, lumber, imported granular base, plywood, masonry, and other key items)
7. Equipment rental
    (List local prices or key local quotations)
8. Climatological data
    (List average maximum and average minimum temperature, precipitation, and other significant data by months)
9. Other projects
    (Visit other projects noting productivity, favored methods, favored materials, subcontractors, etc.)
10. General appraisal
    (Summarize results of site and area visit and recommend significant conclusions to be taken into account during the planning of the program)

From *Professional Construction Management,* McGraw-Hill, 1978

ect objectives are communicated to all parties early in the program. The plan must be sufficiently specific to set forth cost, schedule, and quality objectives for use as a baseline in monitoring detail planning and detail development throughout the program.

The following selections from a proposed work plan for a 600 MWe power plant were prepared in advance of commencement of detail design or construction:

Work package description.

Equipment list.

Conceptual estimate.

Conceptual schedule.

Alternate construction programs.

TABLE 7-2. Model Power Plant Work Package Description

1. Sitework, phase I
Site grading, roads, railroad, excavation, embankment, culverts, fencing, drainage, parking, etc.
2. Miscellaneous yard buildings
Plant warehouse, construction warehouse, guardhouse, construction offices, miscellaneous structures, construction utility, and service supply
3. Substructures
Including concrete for main power plant, substation and transfer yard substructures, underground electrical and piping support, and miscellaneous foundation concrete
4. Underground electrical
Electrical duct banks, underground electrical, and first-stage electrical work, including construction power supply
5. Underground piping and utilities
Includes water supply, fire water supply, construction utilities, rough-in underground, sanitary, and sewer and water piping
6. Circulating water system
Includes complete installation of circulating water system piping and mechanical work
7. Structural steel
Includes boiler room structural steel, turbine room, office area, coal bunkers, and miscellaneous steel
8. Coal handling structural
Includes all concrete foundations, structures, slabs, buildings, equipment foundations, conveyor supports, and other work, except mechanical, electrical, and equipment installation
9. Equipment erection
Includes erection of heavy and miscellaneous equipment, transformers, bridge cranes, compressors, condensers, and associated miscellaneous piping and vessels
10. Ductwork and fan installation
Includes installation of induced draft and forced draft fans and breeching
11. Power plant superstructure
Includes turbine room, office area, boiler plant, turbine foundation concrete, slabs, equipment foundation and building finish items, including HVAC, plumbing, building electrical, miscellaneous work, and steel
12. Ash handling structural
Includes site development, grading, culverts, roadways, drainage, and miscellaneous concrete
13. Power and process piping
All high-pressure piping, including off-site fabrication and installation of all on-site high-pressure piping, service air, water, condensate, and other services
14. Power wiring
Includes all power wiring for the power plant and associated structures. Will include remaining work on substations and transfer yards if not previously awarded

TABLE 7-2   (continued)

15. Instrumentation
    Includes all pneumatic and electrical instrumentation and installation
16. Painting
    All remaining field painting, including power plant, miscellaneous buildings, substations, tanks and bunkers, and power piping and electrical
17. Sitework, phase II
    Includes remaining grading, paving, curbs, roads, parking lots, etc.

The following equipment is assumed to be obtained on a design and construct basis:

1. Steam generator
2. Turbine generator
3. Electrostatic precipitator and ducts
4. Scrubber
5. Ash handling equipment
6. Coal handling equipment
7. Fire protection
8. Chimney
9. Cooling tower

WORK PACKAGE DESCRIPTION. The following work packages have been developed to facilitate control of design and construction work. Seventeen installation packages have been developed to achieve complete portions of work for a phased (fast track) construction program. Nine design-build packages have been developed for competitive bidding to major equipment suppliers. The 17 installation packages can be handled as a part of a CM program featuring a separate construction manager with competitively bid subpackages or as a part of a design-manage program developed by the design construction. Packages can be further subdivided to suit local conditions as warranted for any of the conceptual construction programs. The installation packages can also be handled by a single general contractor on a negotiated cost plus a fixed fee or guaranteed maximum cost type contract. Alternately, the design-constructor may act as the general contractor subcontracting the specialty portions of the work as deemed appropriate. Table 7-2 shows a simplified work package description for the project.

EQUIPMENT LIST. The single most important item in developing the overall work plan, including the cost estimate and the overall construction schedule, is an equipment list that can be used to obtain vendor price and delivery quotations. The list also serves as the starting point for the structural, service, and support requirements for the plant and serves to outline the scope in sufficient detail to provide a common baseline for all entities engaged in developing the work plan.

Table 7-3 sets forth a simplified equipment list for the 600 MWe plant, including preliminary quantities and sizes for use in developing the overall program.

CONCEPTUAL ESTIMATE. Conceptual estimates can be developed based on different levels of information. See Figure 3-6 for a tabulation of a number of estimate accuracy levels ranging from type 1 to type 6 depen-

TABLE 7-3   Equipment List Model Power Plant

Item	Equipment description	Quantity
I.	Turbine building	
A.	Operating floor	
1.	Turbine generator, tandem-compound, fourflow, single-reheat, condensing steam turbine	1
2.	Feedwater heaters, two closed, two strings (trains)	4
3.	Boiler feedwater pump	1
4.	Booster feedwater pump	1
5.	Turbine drive for boiler and booster feedwater pumps	1
6.	Lube oil tank, pump, and coolers for drive turbine and feedwater pumps	1
B.	Ground floor	
1.	Condenser, two shell	1
2.	Condensate pumps and motor drivers, one standby pump and motor drive	3
3.	Steam packing exhauster	1
4.	Condensate polishing system, one standby filter demineralizer	3
5.	Condenser air removal pumps and motor drives	2
6.	Condenser waterbox/vacuum priming pumps and motor drives	2
7.	Sixth-point heater drain cooler	2
8.	Sixth-point heater drain receiver	2
9.	Stator water cooler	1
10.	Generator carbon dioxide gas purge storage system	—
11.	Service air compressors and drive motor	2
12.	Service air receivers	2
13.	Turbine plant sampling system	—
14.	Generator lead cooler	1
15.	Potential transformer cubicle	1
16.	Neutral ground equipment	1
C.	Mezzanine floor	
1.	Feedwater heaters, sixth and seventh point heaters mounted in condenser neck perpendicular to turbine and condenser centerline	4

TABLE 7-3   (continued)

Item	Equipment description	Quantity
2.	Vacuum priming tank (located directly above vacuum priming pumps at mezzanine level)	1
D.	Above turbine operating floor	
1.	Turbine building overhead crane	1
E.	Auxiliary bay—above turbine operating floor	
1.	Deaerator heater	1
2.	Deaerator storage tank	1
F.	Auxiliary bay—operating floor	
1.	Feedwater heaters, two closed, two strings (trains)	4
G.	Auxiliary bay—ground floor	
1.	Bearing cooling water pumps	2
2.	Bearing cooling water heat exchangers	2
3.	Start-up feedwater pump and motor drivers	1
4.	Instrument air compressors and motor drivers	2
5.	Instrument air receivers	2
6.	Instrument air dryers	2
7.	Chemical feed pumps	5
8.	Chemical feed tanks	4
II.	Lube oil building	
1.	Main turbine lube oil tank	1
2.	Clean lube oil storage tank, pump and motor driver	1
3.	Dirty lube oil storage tank and transfer pump with motor drive	1
4.	Hydrogen seal oil unit	1
5.	Turbine lube oil conditioner with pump and motor driver	1
III.	Water treatment building	
1.	Ferric sulfate mix tank	1
2.	Ferric sulfate feed tank	1
3.	Alkali feed tank	1
4.	Raw water chemical pump	1
5.	Gravity filters	3
6.	Filtered water pumps	3
7.	Clearwell tank	1
8.	Water softeners	3
9.	Softened water pumps	3
10.	Caustic tank	1
11.	Caustic pump	1
12.	Acid tank	1
13.	Acid pump	1
14.	Sump pumps	2

TABLE 7-3 (continued)

Item	Equipment description	Quantity
IV.	Boiler building	
1.	Pulverizers and motor drivers	8
2.	F. D. fans and motor drivers	2
3.	P. A. fans and motor drivers	2
4.	I. D. fans and motor drivers	4
5.	Coal bunkers	8
6.	Air preheaters and motor	2
7.	Circulating water pumps and motors	4
8.	Furnace ash hopper	1
9.	Coal feeders and motors	8
10.	Igniters	56
11.	Soot blowers	168
12.	Economizer	1
13.	Bottom ash sump pumps and motors	2
14.	Bottom ash water pumps and motors	2
15.	Slurry pumps and motors	2
16.	Bottom ash transfer tank	1
17.	Pyrites transfer tank	1
18.	Precipitators	4
V.	Yard area	
1.	Cooling towers	1
2.	Circulating water pumps and drive motors	2
3.	Service water pumps and drive motors	2
4.	Make-up water pumps and motors	—
5.	Condensate storage tank	1
6.	Condensate storage tank transfer pump	1
7.	Nitrogen blanketing gas storage system	—
8.	Generator hydrogen gas cooling storage system	—
9.	Fuel oil tank	—
10.	Fuel oil transfer pump	—
11.	Fly ash silos	1
12.	Dewatering bins	2
13.	Settling tank	1
14.	Recirculating tank	1
15.	Sump pump and motors	2
16.	Sludge return pumps and motors	2
17.	L. P. water pumps and motors	2
18.	Fly ash water pumps and motors	2

TABLE 7-3   (continued)

Item	Equipment description	Quantity
19.	Recirculation pumps and motors	2
20.	Track hoppers	2
21.	Emergency hopper	1
22.	Reclaim hopper	8
23.	Vibrating feeders	11
24.	Coal crushers	3
25.	Coal stacker	1
26.	Bradford breaker/unit	1
27.	Single 60 in. conveyor belt	700 ft
28.	Double 48 in. conveyor belt	1300 ft
29.	Coal samplers	3
30.	Stack	1
31.	Coagulators	2
32.	Brine tank	1
33.	Main transformer	1
34.	Service transformer	1
35.	Auxiliary boiler	2
36.	Hypochlorinator	1
37.	Retention basin pumps	1

dent on different levels of information. Figure 7-1 shows a summary page from the conceptual estimate for the 600 MWe power plant that can be classified as a Type 2 Estimate. For an integrated program it is important to express labor in man-hours as well as in dollars. Using man-hour information, planners and schedulers can apply alternate production factors and time durations to predict alternate manpower requirements throughout the construction period. Table 7-4 shows the man-hours of on-site installation effort from the cost estimate tabulated in accordance with the chosen work packages. These man-hours will be used by the planners and schedulers in evaluating alternate programs and in assessing jobsite productivity under varying conditions.

CONCEPTUAL SCHEDULE. The conceptual schedule is prepared using equipment delivery dates from vendor quotations, preliminary drawings developed during the initial design period, and man-hours developed from the estimate. Figure 7-2 shows a modified arrow diagram on a time scale for the overall program, including design. Figure 7-3 shows a CPM precedence

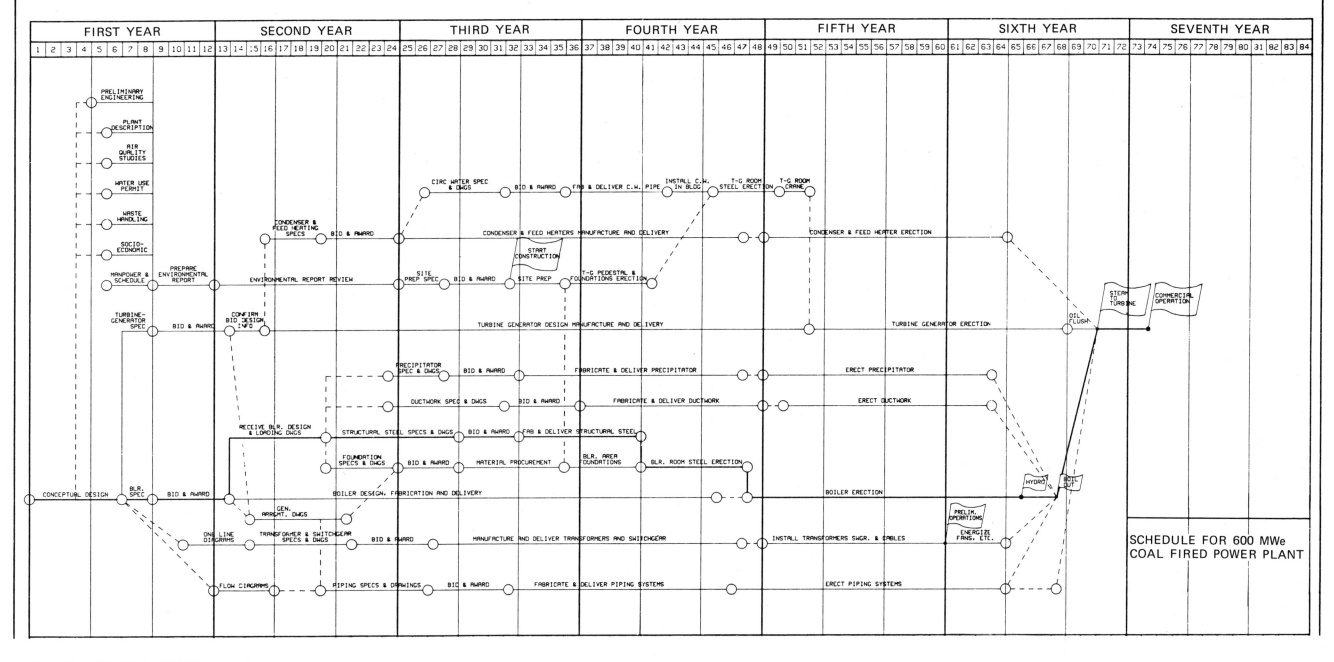

Figure 7-2 Schedule for 600 MWe power plant.

Account	Description	Man-hours	Labor	Material	Subcontracts	Equipment	Total
1000	Structures and improvements	1,460	29,200	40,000	40,000	5,000	114,200
2000	Boiler plant	1,000	2,200	6,000	30,000	60,000	98,200
3000	Turbine plant	915	18,300	4,000	10,000	25,000	57,300
4000	Electric plant	800	1,600	3,600	25,000	5,000	35,200
5000	Miscellaneous plant	105	4,100	4,000	4,000	8,000	20,100
	Subtotal direct cost	4,380	55,400	57,600	109,000	103,000	325,000
	Contractors' cost				30,000		30,000
	Construction plant				5,000		5,000
	Home office and fee				5,000		5,000
	Design engineering				10,000		10,000
	Subtotal indirect cost				50,000		50,000
	Estimated total cost		55,400	57,600	159,000	103,000	375,000
	Escalation						75,000
	Contingency						50,000
	Grand total estimated cost						500,000

Figure 7-1   Conceptual estimate, 600 MWE power plant (all costs in $1,000)

TABLE 7-4   Assumed Work Packages 600 MWe Model Power Plant

Direct effort design packages	On-site man-hours
1. Sitework I	30,000
2. Miscellaneous yard buildings	49,000
3. Substructures	240,000
4. Underground and miscellaneous electrical	75,000
5. Underground piping and utilities	70,000
6. Circulating water system	250,000
7. Structural steel	50,000
8. Coal handling structures	230,000
9. Miscellaneous equipment erection	20,000
10. Ductwork and fan erection	50,000
11. Power plant superstructure	400,000
12. Ash handling structures	70,000
13. Power piping	885,000
14. Power wiring	515,000
15. Instrumentation	50,000
16. Painting	37,000
17. Site work II	39,000
Total direct hours	3,060,000
Man-hours/K We	5.1
Design and Build Packages	
1. Boiler	550,000
2. Turbine generator	80,000
3. Electric precipitator	150,000
4. Scrubber	330,000
5. Ash handling equipment	45,000
6. Coal handling equipment	50,000
7. Fire protection	10,000
8. Chimney	65,000
9. Cooling tower	50,000
Total design and build hours	1,320,000
Man-hours/K We	2.2
Total	4,380,000
Man-hours/K We	7.3

diagram for a portion of the project. Figure 7-4 shows a summary bar chart showing early and late start programs. Figure 7-5 shows manpower scheduled for a 40-month construction period. Figure 7-6 shows manpower scheduled for a 46-month construction period. Manpower peak requiremenst for the 40-month program is shown to be 1650, compared to 1250 for the 46-month program.

Legend of symbols:

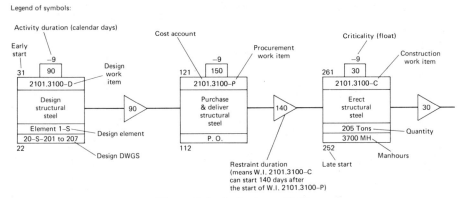

Figure 7-3   Preliminary CPM.

ALTERNATE CONSTRUCTION PROGRAMS. The primary on-site supervisory organization will vary, dependent on the conceptual construction method chosen and the individual requirements of the particular program. Figure 7-7 shows a conceptual organization for construction services for the plant. Figure 7-8 shows a similar organization using the CM approach.

DETAIL PLANNING AND ORGANIZING

Detail planning and organizing may be performed by various organizations and to various detail levels, dependent on the conceptual construction approach chosen for the project and to the degree of detail favored by individual clients and contractors. In a design-build program one organization will perform all the detail planning (except for subcontractor efforts) for the program. For a design-manage program, it is considered good practice for the design-constructor to prepare detailed fair cost estimates and milestone schedules in order to monitor development of the conceptual program and to develop actual quantities and schedule requirements for use in the control phase of the project. The individual bidders will develop bid estimates and their own schedules as a part of their efforts to obtain the contract.

Alternate Program Concepts

Detail planning can be counterproductive on many industrial programs, resulting in excess administrative costs and a lower level of project control. For the 600 MWe plant we explore a design-manage and design-build program, although good practice using either a single negotiated general contractor or a separate construction manager would use an essentially similar approach.

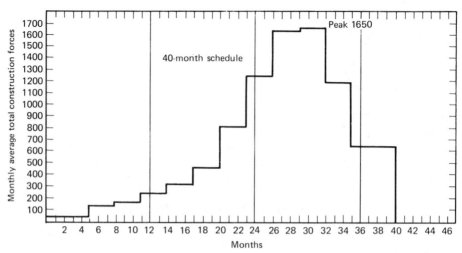

Figure 7-5   Manpower schedule—40-month program.

DETAIL PLANNING FOR DESIGN-CONSTRUCT. On a design-construct project a single management team can fully integrate design and construction plans and operating decisions simply because everyone is working for the same organization. This concept in theory is heavily promoted by the design-construct companies. In practice, this concept as well as all other management concepts has mixed results. Some companies plan to very detailed levels in the home office. Others plan to conceptual or control levels in the home office, with detail planning delegated to the field. Others plan to detailed levels in either the home office or the field but summarize to a level comparable to the conceptual estimate and schedule for overall control purposes.

Figure 7-9 shows an outline on a classification of cost accounts that permits the development of conceptual estimates to compare with more detailed estimates to follow. Figure 7-10 shows the accounts using the work breakdown structure concept. As detailed estimates are prepared, the summation of the fair cost estimates can be compared exactly to the original concept and potential overruns or underruns detected at an early date.

Levels of detail for scheduling listing overall and intermediate milestones can be prepared using the results of each of the estimates to permit comparison with original concept milestones at a summary level (looking backward) and to develop intermediate milestones for use in measuring actual performance (looking forward).

In any well-run program, weekly installation schedules to fit overall summary objectives are best developed at the field level, since adjustments must be made continually to cope with the weather, equipment and material availability, productivity of work force, and all the other variables that

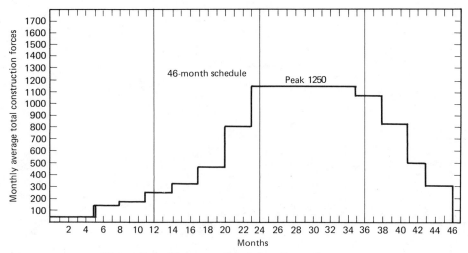

Figure 7-6   Manpower Schedule—46-month program.

make field construction management and supervision such a challenging and ever-changing art.

A similar level of detail for fair cost estimating permitting comparison with later periodic estimates to complete prepared by field forces is also used in a well-run integrated program in which man-hours form the common parameter between estimater and scheduler.

DETAIL PLANNING FOR DESIGN-MANAGE. In design-manage, detail planning subsequent to the fair cost estimate level is often counterproductive when performed by the design-manager either in the home office or at the jobsite, since the individual project contractors must do their own planning for day-to-day operations in order to control their own economic performance. Similarly, estimating to exhaustive levels of detail may be counterproductive when overall cost performance is measured by lump sum bids and the base for progress payments and measurement or progress to a summary level is more fully consistent with owner control objectives.

OPERATIONAL CONTROL

Conceptual and detail planning summarized to levels consistent with the actual ability to measure field performance form the basis for operational control for the project. True control enables the manager to observe actual results and trends compared to planned results at an early enough level to permit replanning and other management action to help achieve desired results.

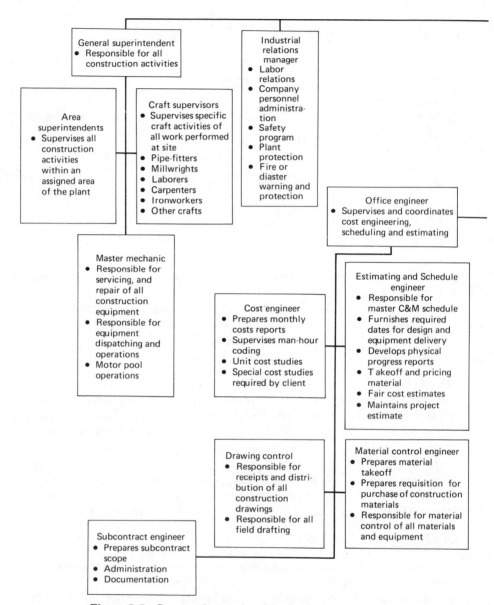

Figure 7-7 Construction services functional organization.

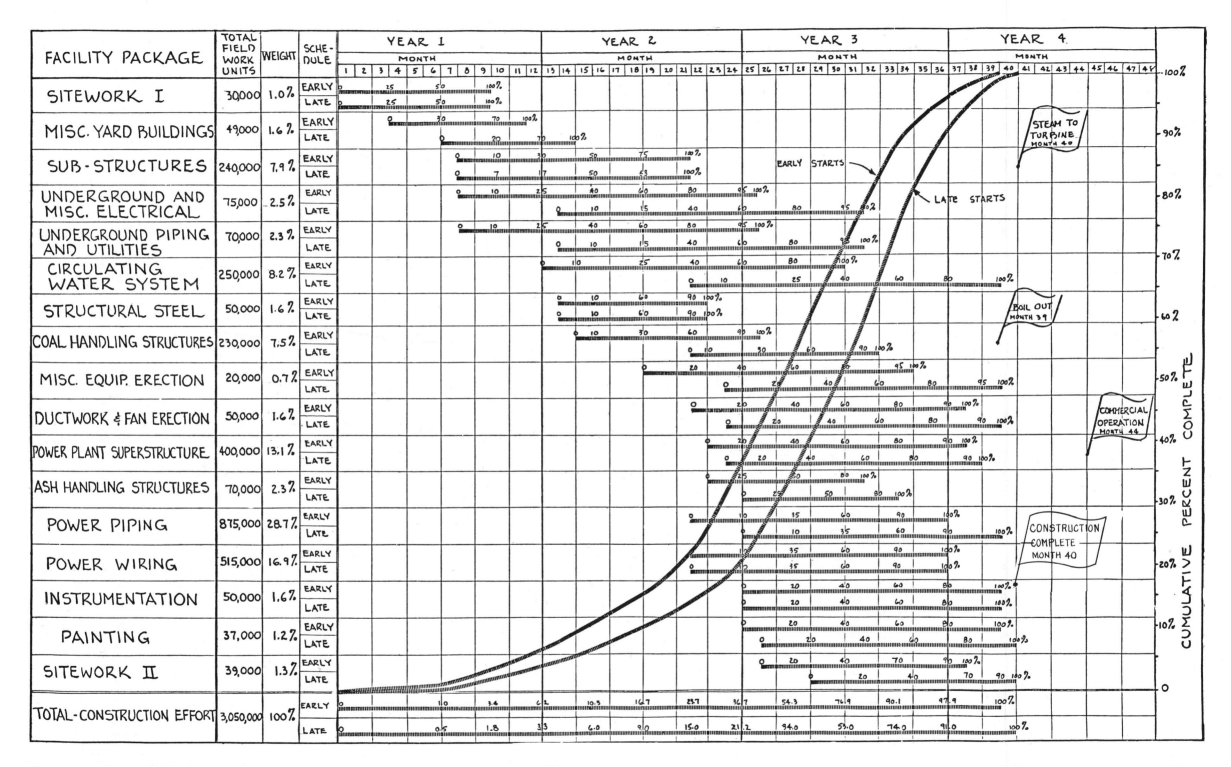

Figure 7-4 CPM physical progress.

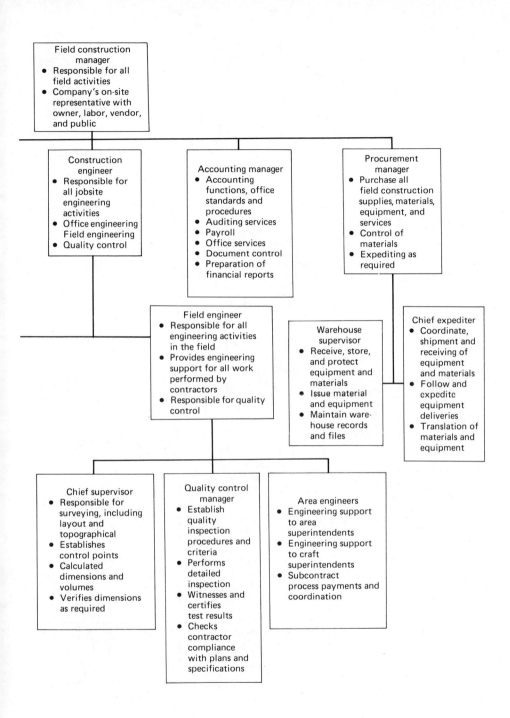

Figure 7-7 (Continued)

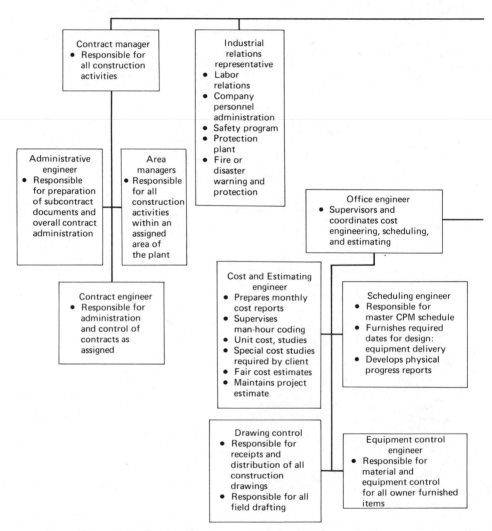

Figure 7-8 Construction management functional organization.

600 MWe power plant
Construction management functional organization

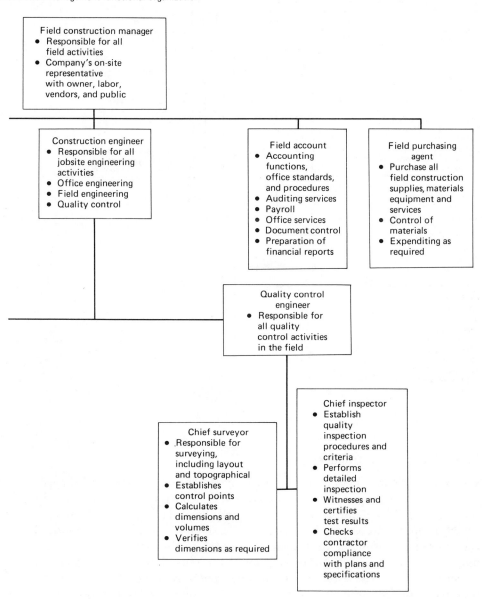

Field construction manager
- Responsible for all field activities
- Company's on-site representative with owner, labor, vendors, and public

Construction engineer
- Responsible for all jobsite engineering activities
- Office engineering
- Field engineering
- Quality control

Field account
- Accounting functions, office standards, and procedures
- Auditing services
- Payroll
- Office services
- Document control
- Preparation of financial reports

Field purchasing agent
- Purchase all field construction supplies, materials equipment and services
- Control of materials
- Expediting as required

Quality control engineer
- Responsible for all quality control activities in the field

Chief surveyor
- Responsible for surveying, including layout and topographical
- Establishes control points
- Calculates dimensions and volumes
- Verifies dimensions as required

Chief inspector
- Establish quality inspection procedures and criteria
- Performs detailed inspection
- Witnesses and certifies test results
- Checks contractor compliance with plans and specifications

Figure 7-8   (Continued)

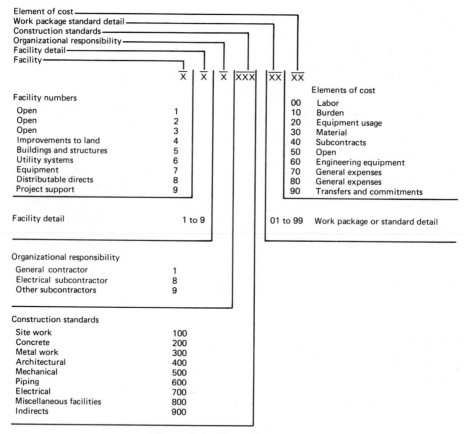

Figure 7-9   Chart of accounts.

Control for Design-Build

Where actual construction is performed by the design-constructor, a negotiated general contractor, or the individual subcontractor, control to both the very detail level and to various summary levels is required. Figure 7-11 shows a summary cost and comparison to estimate report that summarizes the overall performance and anticipated cost of the project itemized by major facility as shown by level 2 on the Figure 7-10 work breakdown structure. An alternate report can also be issued by work package to compare with the estimate shown in Figure 7-1 or by organizational responsibility. In the days before the digital computer, one or the other method was generally chosen (each with its advantages and disadvantages) because of the heavy clerical and accounting requirements. However, with a properly designed cost accounting system, results and anticipated performance for schedules and costs can be reported by work package, area (individual building or component), responsibility, and major discipline (electrical, mechanical, etc.).

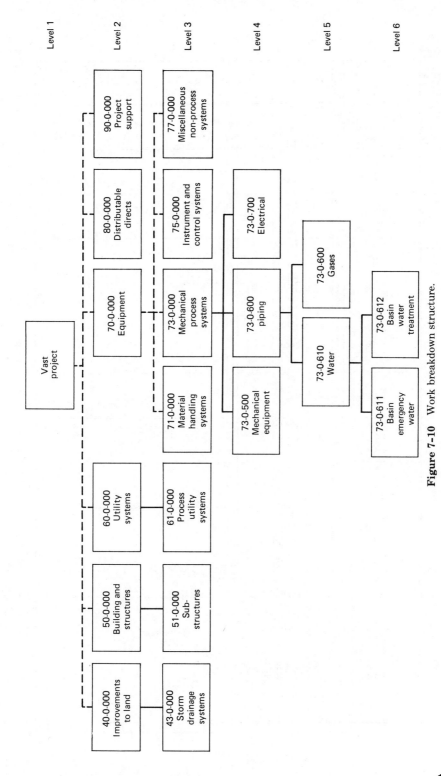

Figure 7-10 Work breakdown structure.

149

Description	Recorded Costs		Open Commitments	Cumulative Total Recorded & Committed	Estimate to Complete	Estimate at Completion			Official Estimates			Variance Over (Under) Title II Official Est.
	Current Period	Cumulative to Date				Current	Previous	Increase (Decrease)	Title I Control Estimate	Change	Title II Official Estimate	
DIRECT COST												
400.00000 Improvements to Land	$ 91,071	$ 91,071	$ 0	$ 91,071	$ 1,608,929	$ 1,700,000	$ 1,700,000	$ 0	$ 1,700,000	$ 0	$ 1,700,000	$ 0
500.00000 Buildings & Structures	436,610	6,527,960	0	6,527,960	11,454,040	17,982,000	16,430,000	1,552,000	16,430,000	0	16,430,000	1,552,000
600.00000 Utility Systems		1,000,000	0	1,000,000	0	1,000,000	1,000,000	0	1,000,000	0	1,000,000	0
700.00000 Equipment	649,170	8,066,150	3,150,000	11,216,150	20,905,850	32,122,000	29,370,000	2,752,000	29,370,000	0	29,370,000	2,752,000
800.00000 Distributable Directs	0	0	0	0	2,000,000	2,000,000	2,000,000	0	2,000,000	0	2,000,000	0
TOTAL DIRECTS	$1,176,851	$15,685,181	$3,150,000	$18,835,181	$35,968,819	$54,804,000	$50,500,000	$4,304,000	$50,500,000	$ 0	$50,500,000	$ 4,304,000
INDIRECT COSTS												
910.00000 Construction Field OH	$ 208,000	$ 2,475,000	$ 0	$ 2,475,000	$ 5,025,000	$ 7,500,000	$ 7,500,000	$ 0	$ 7,500,000	$ 0	$ 7,500,000	0
TOTAL INDIRECTS	$ 208,000	$ 2,475,000	$ 0	$ 2,475,000	$ 5,025,000	$ 7,500,000	$ 7,500,000	$ 0	$ 7,500,000	$ 0	$ 7,500,000	0
TOTAL CONSTRUCTION COST	$1,384,851	$18,160,181	$3,150,000	$21,310,181	$40,993,819	$62,304,000	$58,000,000	$4,304,000	$58,000,000	$ 0	$58,000,000	$ 4,304,000
920.00000 Home Office Services	$ 7,000	$ 200,000	$ 0	$ 200,300	$ 300,000	$ 500,000	$ 500,000	$ 0	$ 500,000	$ 0	$ 500,000	$ 0
930.00000 Escalation	0	0	0	0	5,950,000	5,950,000	5,950,000	0	8,500,000	0	8,500,000	(2,550,000)
940.00000 Contingency	0	0	0	0	3,983,000	3,983,000	4,900,000	(917,000)	7,000,000	0	7,000,000	(3,017,000)
TOTAL PROJECT	$1,391,851	$18,360,181	$3,150,000	$21,510,181	$51,226,819	$72,737,000	$69,350,000	$3,387,000	$74,000,000	$ 0	$74,000,000	$ 1,263,000

Figure 7-11 Cost summary.

150

AREA NO.	AREA DESCRIPTION & RESPONSIBILITY	BUDGET MANHOURS	WEIGHTED VALUE % AREA	WEIGHTED VALUE % PROJECT	SCHEDULE COMPARISON
4000	IMPROVEMENT TO LAND				
	SUBCONTRACTED ITEMS	56,000	100	4	EARLY / ACTUAL / LATE
	SUBTOTAL AREA 4000	56,000	100	4	EARLY / ACTUAL / LATE
5000	BUILDINGS & STRUCTURES				
	GENERAL CONTRACTOR	190,000	27	13	EARLY / ACTUAL / LATE
	SUBSIDIARY ELECTRICAL CONTRACTOR	70,000	10	3	EARLY / ACTUAL / LATE
	SUBCONTRACTED ITEMS	454,000	63	32	EARLY / ACTUAL / LATE
	SUBTOTAL AREA 5000	714,000	100	48	EARLY / ACTUAL / LATE
6000	UTILITY SYSTEMS				
	SUBCONTRACTED ITEMS	50,000	100	3	EARLY / ACTUAL / LATE
	SUBTOTAL AREA 6000	50,000	100	3	EARLY / ACTUAL / LATE
7000	EQUIPMENT				
	GENERAL CONTRACTOR	410,000	60	29	EARLY / ACTUAL / LATE
	SUBSIDIARY ELECTRICAL CONTRACTOR	60,000	9	1	EARLY / ACTUAL / LATE
	SUBCONTRACTED ITEMS	210,000	31	15	EARLY / ACTUAL / LATE
	SUBTOTAL AREA 7000	680,000	100	45	EARLY / ACTUAL / LATE
	TOTAL VAST PROJECT	1,430,000	100	100	EARLY / ACTUAL / LATE

Timeline columns: 1979 (1, 2, 3, 4), 1980 (1, 2, 3, 4), 1981 (1, 2, 3, 4), 1982 (1, 2, 3, 4)

Right axis: CUMULATIVE PERCENT COMPLETE (0 – 100)

Annotations on chart: DATA DATE, EARLY START, LATE START, ACTUAL

Schedule comparison progress bars (cumulative percent complete figures):

4000 SUBCONTRACTED ITEMS
- EARLY: 5 5 5 5 5 23 65 95 95 96 99 100
- ACTUAL: 5 5 5 5 5
- LATE: 2 5 5 5 5 17 35 41 41 41 42 64 100

SUBTOTAL AREA 4000
- EARLY: 5 5 5 5 5 23 65 95 95 96 99 100
- ACTUAL: 5 5 5 5 5
- LATE: 2 5 5 5 5 17 35 41 41 41 42 64 100

5000 GENERAL CONTRACTOR
- EARLY: 6 26 50 70 78 85 93 100
- ACTUAL: 6 26 50 70 78 85 93 100
- LATE: 6 26 50 70 78 85 93 100

SUBSIDIARY ELECTRICAL CONTRACTOR
- EARLY: 3 13 27 44 56 67 78 90 100
- ACTUAL: 3 13 27 44 56 67 78 90 100
- LATE: 3 13 27 44 56 67 78 90 100

SUBCONTRACTED ITEMS
- EARLY: 3 8 14 21 27 42 52 64 73 82 92 100
- ACTUAL: 3 8 14 21 27
- LATE: 3 8 14 18 23 31 45 56 65 74 84 93 100

SUBTOTAL AREA 5000
- EARLY: 4 13 25 37 44 56 66 76 83 89 95 100
- ACTUAL: 4 13 25 36 42
- LATE: 4 13 25 34 49 61 71 78 84 90 96 100

6000 SUBCONTRACTED ITEMS
- EARLY: 18 69 100
- ACTUAL: 17 68 100
- LATE: 15 66 100

SUBTOTAL AREA 6000
- EARLY: 18 69 100
- ACTUAL: 17 68 100
- LATE: 15 66 100

7000 GENERAL CONTRACTOR
- EARLY: 3 7 15 27 40 53 65 78 90 98 100
- ACTUAL: 2 5 13
- LATE: 4 7 11 22 35 47 60 72 85 97 100

SUBSIDIARY ELECTRICAL CONTRACTOR
- EARLY: 8 27 36 49 63 77 91 100
- ACTUAL: 8
- LATE: 8 22 36 49 63 77 91 100

SUBCONTRACTED ITEMS
- EARLY: 3 12 22 31 42 54 68 81 88 92 95 99 100
- ACTUAL: 2 8 17 26 38
- LATE: 0 13 22 38 46 59 72 85 92 95 99 100

SUBTOTAL AREA 7000
- EARLY: 1 5 9 16 24 36 47 60 71 81 91 98 100
- ACTUAL: .5 4 8 13 22
- LATE: 1 6 11 17 28 41 53 66 77 87 96 100

TOTAL VAST PROJECT
- EARLY: 2.5 9 17 27 35 47 59 71 79 86 93 99 100
- ACTUAL: 2 6 15 25 33
- LATE: 1.8 5 14 23 30 41 53 63 72 80 87 94 100

Figure 7-12 Summary construction progress schedule.

Figure 7-12 shows the actual physical percentage complete for the project compared to forecast early start and late start CPM programs developed at the conceptual level.

Figure 7-13 shows actual overall job productivity by major discipline compared to detailed estimates prepared from completed plans and specifications.

Figure 7-14 shows a detailed unit man-hour report showing performance of electrical work compared to the budget estimate for one portion of the project.

Figure 7-15 shows that portion of the physical progress report pertaining to subcontractors used in developing the overall percentage complete shown in Figure 7-12.

Figure 7-16 shows the relative labor schedule and cost variance for those portions of the project performed by the electrical contractor and the final anticipated result as developed from the previous exhibits.

Figure 7-17 shows actual manpower compared to forecast manpower for the overall project.

Figure 7-18 illustrates a detailed CPM bar chart schedule as generated by a computer.

Figure 7-19 shows the network CPM calculation applicable to the bar chart.

Figure 7-20 shows a typical equipment status report as generated by a computer that lists the status of major equipment procurement which is critical to the success of the project.

Figure 7-21 shows a unit cost report that develops individual unit costs compared to the budget estimate.

Figure 7-22 shows a project cost summary organized by major facility as is commonly done for design-construct project.

Many other reports can be generated by the integrated approach using a central file or common data bank, but the workwise manager will recognize the overall capability of the computer and the computer technician to produce just about anything. He will limit the program to those items for which accurate information can be developed and that will actually be helpful to job management in monitoring and improving overall project performance.

Control for Design-Manage

When the design-constructor acts as a construction manager with individual contracts or subcontracts, a somewhat different control requirement is apparent. A similar control requirement is imposed on a separate construction management firm or on the owner if he acts as his own construction manager.

Where individual work packages are based on completed design and bids are obtained on a fixed price basis progressively throughout the program as

Unit cost—summary by standard	Labor hours (man-hours)		Cost trend (man-hours)		
	Period	To Date	Period	To Date	Job Factor
Group No. 1					
Totals of 1000 site work					
• Quantity—man-hours	41	21334	543–	3164–	0.88
Totals of 2000 concrete					
• Quantity—man-hours	104	67844	99	637–	0.99
Totals of 3000 metal work					
• Quantity—man-hours	235	7592	0	3894–	0.72
Totals of 4000 buildings—arch, coatings, etc.					
• Quantity—man-hours	347	6093	350	2951	1.97
Totals of 5000 equipment (engineered)					
• Quantity—man-hours	478	14992	377	11035–	0.58
Totals of 6000 piping and insulation					
• Quantity—man-hours	4538	49985	1491	1937	1.04
Totals of 7000 electrical (quantities and man-hours are zero) (All work subcontracted)					
Totals of 8000 instrumentation					
• Quantity—man-hours	318	3001	276	1401–	0.68
Totals for group No. 1					
• Quantity—man-hours	6061	170841	2050	15243–	0.93
Job totals unit cost—summary by standard					
• Quantity—man-hours	6061	170841	2050	15243–	0.93

Figure 7-13   Job factor/productivity report. Cost trend: actual man-hours over or under budget unit multiplied by actual quantity. Work to date has been completed for 15,243 man-hours less than budgeted. Job factor: cumulative man-hours divided by budget unit multiplied by actual quantity. Performance to date is 93% of amount budgeted or an improvement of 7%.

a part of a fast track of phased construction program, the total project construction cost is committed as soon as the last contract is awarded. Of course, changes, unforeseen conditions, or other unpredictable occurrences may develop claims and change orders that can modify the contract prices and influence the total project cost to the owner.

Cost control in this type of program is limited to items that take place prior to contract award for the basic contract and for appraising changes or changed conditions which develop after the award. Therefore, cost and comparison to estimate reports for this type of program are best organized by construction contract rather than by facility, building, or area, which is often the case for design-construct or negotiated construction contracts. The fair cost estimate can be summarized by area, facility, or some other breakdown, adjusted for actual contract awards and change orders and used for owner depreciation requirements without duplicating accounting requirements to detailed work items throughout the program. Once the price has been determined, accounting and cost forecasts to the detailed accounting and cost forecasts to the detailed account level are not only needlessly expensive, but also are counterproductive, since a simple tabulation of contracts and anticipated changes is considerably more accurate.

Schedule control for construction management is again best restricted to summary levels to determine whether the contractor is meeting predetermined milestones and keeping up with contract schedule requirements. An overall physical progress report can take the form of Figure 7-15. However, the backup calculations and the level of detail have been considerably simplified for purposes of overall job control. Detail schedule control continues to be the responsibility of the individual contractor who may choose methods found most successful by his own experience.

By monotoring actual total manpower expended by the contractor from required force reports and man-hours earned by the contractor from the physical progress report, the construction manager can often identify productivity problems encountered by the contractor. A productivity report prepared by a construction manager would take the form of Figure 3-15, which summarizes the project by contractor rather than Figure 7-13, which summarizes the project by major work discipline. In this method productivity is defined as actual manpower expended by the contractor compared to the estimated manpower from the fair cost estimate adjusted by change orders. This productivity can be quite different from that computed by the contractor, since the base man-hour estimate prepared by the two parties many vary considerably. Such a program has long-range advantages to the construction manager, since unlike a general contractor, labor productivity feedback from CM jobs is not generally available.

The fundamental control concept for CM is that all the tools and concepts of force account construction apply but at a much higher and consequently simpler level without the exhaustive detail required for a force account project. On CM projects the detail control is provided by the con-

Cost account
10000000

Code	Estimated material	Estimated man-hours	Revised date	Estimated unit	Period material	Period man-hours	Period unit	Total material	Total man-hours	Report unit	Progress unit
Consolidated report											
CE	29340	5028	378	0.171	1240	159.00	0.128	12164	1414	0.116	0.678
CP	5870	560	378	0.095	0	0.00	0.000	0	0	0.000	0.000
CR	56190	2342	378	0.041	0	0.00	0.000	29790	674	0.022	0.536
CT	3200	215	378	0.067	280	8.00	0.028	660	32	0.048	0.716
CY	192	105	378	0.546	0	0.00	0.000	0	0	0.000	0.000
EG	7	326	378	46.571	0	0.00	0.000	3	100	33.333	0.715
EQ	89	1108	378	12.449	0	0.00	0.000	2	24	12.000	0.963
ET	400	730	378	1.825	0	0.00	0.000	0	0	0.000	0.000
GR	3449	935	378	0.271	0	2.00	0.000	398	35	0.087	0.321
HC	14900	1185	378	0.079	0	0.00	0.000	0	0	0.000	0.000
HT	114	740	378	6.491	0	0.00	0.000	0	0	0.000	0.000
LD	332	147	378	0.442	9	30.00	3.333	9	128	14.222	7.556
LF	512	964	378	1.882	4	13.00	3.250	4	13	3.250	1.809
LI	64	115	378	2.878	16	14.00	0.875	44	91	2.068	0.718
LM	272	783	378	1.796	0	0.00	0.000	0	191	0.000	0.000
MH	0	0	0	0.000	0	0.00	0.000	0	0	0.000	0.000
OH	0	600	378	0.000	0	0.00	0.000	0	0	0.000	0.000
PP	0	0	0	0.000	0	0.00	0.000	0	0	0.000	0.000
RC	100	200	0	2.000	0	0.00	0.000	0	85	0.000	0.000
TP	0	0	0	0.000	0	12.00	0.000	0	371	0.000	0.000
WC	157750	3343	378	0.021	1500	10.00	0.006	5280	47	0.008	0.380
WT	4700	1355	378	0.288	0	0.00	0.000	0	0	0.000	0.000
XW	0	0	0	0.000	0	0.00	0.000	0	7	0.000	0.000
Total		20781				248.00			3212		

Direct accounts	Period	To date
Man-hours budgeted	333.00	3879.00
Man-hours expended	236.00	2643.00
Job factor	0.71	0.68
Percent complete	1.6	18.7

Figure 7-14 Unit man-hour report. This report shows that the electrical work is 18.7% complete and has been performed for 68% of the direct hours budgeted.

GROUP NO.	ACCOUNT CODE	SUBCONTRACT GROUP DESCRIPTION	BUDGET MANHOURS	WEIGHTED VALUE		SCHEDULE COMPARISON
				SUB	PROJ	
1	44-9-100	FENCING	3,000	.4	.2	EARLY / ACTUAL / LATE
2	51-9-100	BUILDING EXCAVATION & PILING	4,000	.5	.3	EARLY / ACTUAL / LATE
3	51-9-200	REINFORCING STEEL SUBSTRUCTURE	70,000	9	4.8	EARLY / ACTUAL / LATE
4	73-9-600	PROCESS PIPE FABRICATION & OTHER	150,000	19.5	10.5	EARLY / ACTUAL / LATE
5	61-9-600	PIPE UTILITIES	20,000	2.6	1.4	EARLY / ACTUAL / LATE
6	61-9-700	ELECTRICAL UTILITIES	30,000	3.9	2.1	EARLY / ACTUAL / LATE
7	52-9-200	REBAR SUPERSTRUCTURE	75,000	3.9	2.1	EARLY / ACTUAL / LATE
8	52-9-300	STRUCTURAL & MISCELLANEOUS STEEL	50,000	6.5	3.5	EARLY / ACTUAL / LATE
9	73-9-700	PROCESS ELECTRICAL	60,000	7.8	4.2	EARLY / ACTUAL / LATE
10	52-9-400	ARCHITECTURE & BUILDING FINISH	300,000	3.9	2.1	EARLY / ACTUAL / LATE
11	43-9-100	STORM DRAINS	20,000	2.6	1.4	EARLY / ACTUAL / LATE
12	42-9-100	ROADS & PARKING	30,000	3.9	2.1	EARLY / ACTUAL / LATE
13	41-9-100	LANDSCAPING	3,000	.4	.2	EARLY / ACTUAL / LATE
		TOTAL VAST SUBCONTRACTS	770,000	100	53.8	EARLY / ACTUAL / LATE

Figure 7-15 Subcontracted progress schedule.

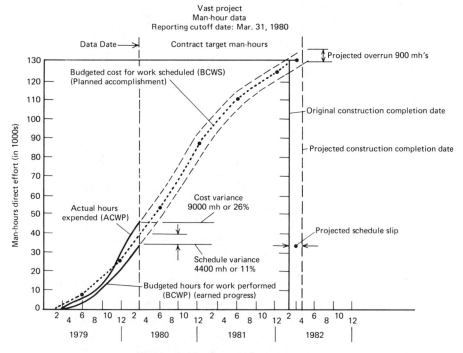

Figure 7-16   Cost performance report.

tractors themselves. The successful contractors prosper and grow; the unsuccessful contractors go out of business.

In the long run, design-constructors, general contractors, and construction managers operating in a cost reimbursable atmosphere are also subject to the laws of the marketplace. Firms that develop successful projects for clients will obtain repeat business with minimum sales costs. Firms that depend on the hard sell and minimum fees at a sacrifice to performance will run out of clients and will eventually also go out of business.

AN APPRAISAL OF INDUSTRIAL CONSTRUCTION

The problems and job conditions affecting the local contractor operating in a known environment competing against known competition are vastly different from the construction problems facing a design-construction operating nationally or internationally in new areas on phased construction programs featuring overlapping design, procurment, and construction phases. Add the special problems associated with coping with nuclear quality assurance and quality control as set forth in Federal Regulation 10 CFR 50 and one begins to realize that the man-hour production data previously cited, while possibly being typical for each class of work, is not directly

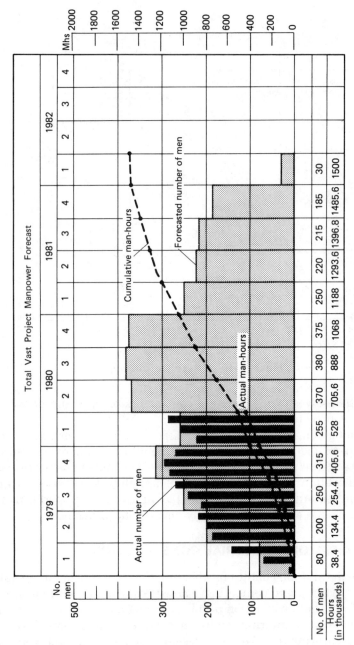

Figure 7-17 Total project manpower forecast.

PROJECT—
LOCATION—

JOB NO.
TIME NOW
RUN DATE
RUN NO.

WORK ITEM	DESCRIPTION		1972										1973			
		MAR	APR	MAY	JUN	JUL	AUG	SEP	OCT	NOV	DEC	JAN	FEB	MAR	APR
2100.000	PLANT BUILDINGS														
2101.000	PRIMARY CRUSHING BUILDING														
2101.1400-C	ENGINEERED BACKFILL 9000 CY					CCCCC*									
2101.2100-C	BUILDING FOUNDATIONS 135 CY				CCCCCCCC*										
2101.2300-C	SLAB ON GRADE 170 CY						CCCCCC*								
2101.3100-C	STRUCTURAL STEEL 205 TONS								CCCC*CC						
2101.3200-C	MISCELLANEOUS STEEL 15 TONS									CCCC*					
2101.4300-C	ROOFING AND SIDING 24500 SF									C*CC					
2101.4400-C	VERTICAL LIFT DOORS 4 EA									*CCCC					
2101.4800-C	GENERAL CONSTRUCTION LOT									CCCCCC*					
2101.8100-C	INTERIOR ROOMS-COMPL 1186 SF										CCCC*CCCC				
2102.000	COARSE ORE STORAGE BUILDING														
2102.1400-C	EARTHWORK 2000 CY			XXX											
2102.2100-C	BLDG FDNS & WALLS 3800 CY					XXXXXXXXXXXXXXXXXX			*						
2102.3100-C	STRUCTURAL STEEL 510 TONS														
2102.3200-C	MISC STEEL 21 TONS														
2102.4300-C	METAL ROOF DECK 22000 SF														
2102.4800-C	GENERAL CONSTRUCTION LOT														
2102.5800-C	EQUIPMENT INSTALLATION LOT														
2102.6100-C	HEATING AND VENTILATION LOT														
2103.000	CONCENTRATOR BUILDING														
2103.1400-C	EARTHWORK 4000 CY			CCCC	*										
2103.2100-C	BLDG FDNS 1600 CY			CCCCCCCCCCCC			*								
2103.2300-C	SLAB ON GRADE 390 CY					CCCCCCCC		*							

C=CRITICAL (30 DAYS OR LESS FLOAT)   X=NON-CRITICAL (MORE THAN 30 DAYS FLOAT)   *=LATEST COMPLETE DATE   PAGE 1

CPM SCHEDULE
Bar Chart

The "Bar Chart" printout reflects the CPM calculations in a graphic format. The activities are printed on a time-scale with a bar representing duration and criticality as follows:

ccccc	Critical	30 days or less total float
xxxxx	More than 30 days total float	
*	Late finish date	

Figure 7-18 Project schedule.

NETWORK CALCULATIONS

WORK ITEM	IDENTIFICATION / DESCRIPTION	STATUS CODE	DURATION	EARLY START	EARLY FINISH	LATE START	LATE FINISH	CRITICALITY
EVENT-01	START PLANT BUILDINGS	4	0	01MAY2	01MAY2	31MAY2	31MAY2	30
EVENT-02	START PRIMARY CRUSHING BLDG.	4	0	01JUN2	01JUN2	06JUN2	06JUN2	5
EVENT-03	COMPL PRIMARY CRUSHING BLDG.	6	0	31DEC2	31DEC2	31DEC2	31DEC2	5
EVENT-04	START COARSE ORE STORAGE		0	01MAY2	01MAY2	27JUL2	27JUL2	87
EVENT-05	COMPL COARSE ORE STORAGE		0	24JAN3	24JAN3	20FEB3	20FEB3	27
EVENT-06	START CONCENTRATOR BLDG		0	01MAY2	01MAY2	31MAY2	31MAY2	30
EVENT-07	COMPL CONCENTRATOR BLDG		0	20FEB3	20FEB3	20FEB3	20FEB3	0
EVENT-08	COMPLETE PLANT BLDGS		0	20FEB3	20FEB3	20FEB3	20FEB3	0
2101.1400-C	ENGINEERED BACKFILL 9000 CY		30	16JUL2	15AUG2	21JUL2	20AUG2	5
2101.2100-C	BUILDING FOUNDATIONS 135 CY		45	01JUN2	16JUL2	06JUN2	21JUL2	5
2101.2100-D	DESIGN BUILDING FOUNDATIONS	1	90	01MAR2	30MAY2	09MAR2	06JUL2	7
2101.2300-C	SLAB ON GRADE 170 CY		30	15AUG2	14SEP2	20AUG2	19SEP2	5
2101.2300-D	DESIGN SLAB ON GRADE		60	01JUN2	31JUL2	21JUN2	20AUG2	20
2101.3100-C	STRUCTURAL STEEL 205 TONS	4	30	28SEP2	28OCT2	19SEP2	19OCT2	-9
2101.3100-D	DESIGN STRUCTURAL STEEL	1	90	01FEB2	01MAY2	22APR2	22APR2	-9
2101.3100-P	PURCHASE & DEL. STRUCT STEEL		150	01MAY2	28SEP2	02NOV2	19SEP2	5
2101.3200-C	MISCELLANEOUS STEEL 15 TONS		14	28OCT2	11NOV2	06MAY2	16NOV2	21
2101.3200-D	DESIGN MISCELLANEOUS STEEL		60	15APR2	14JUN2	05JUL2	05JUL2	21
2101.3200-P	PURCHASE & DEL. MISC STEEL	4	120	14JUN2	12OCT2	19OCT2	02NOV2	-9
2101.4300-C	ROOFING AND SIDING 24500 SF		14	28OCT2	11NOV2	22MAY2	02NOV2	21
2101.4300-D	DESIGN ROOFING AND SIDING		60	01MAY2	30JUN2	21JUL2	21JUL2	21
2101.4300-P	PURCHASE & DEL. ROOF & SIDE	4	90	30JUN2	28SEP2	02NOV2	19OCT2	21
2101.4400-C	VERTICAL LIFT DOORS 4 EA	5	14	25NOV2	09DEC2		16NOV2	-23
2101.4400-D	DESIGN VERTICAL LIFT DOORS	1	60	20JAN2	20MAR2	16NOV2	16NOV2	-23
2101.4400-P	PURCHASE & DEL. LIFT DOORS		250	20MAR2	25NOV2	17SEP2	16NOV2	5
2101.4800-C	GENERAL CONSTRUCTION LOT	4	30	11NOV2	11DEC2	16NOV2	16DEC2	47
2101.4800-D	DESIGN GENERAL CONSTRUCTION		60	01AUG2	30SEP2	16NOV2	31DEC2	-23
2101.8100-C	INTERIOR ROOMS-COMPL 1186 SF		45	09DEC2	23JAN3	27JUL2	10AUG2	87
2102.1400-C	EARTHWORK 2000 CY		14	01MAY2	15MAY2	10AUG2	08NOV2	41
2102.2100-C	BLDG FDNS & WALLS 3800 CY		90	30JUN2	28SEP2	11JUN2	30JUN2	41
2102.2100-D	DESIGN BLDG FDNS & WALLS	4	60	30JUN2	30JUN2	08NOV2	11NOV2	27
2102.3100-C	STRUCTURAL STEEL 510 TONS		30	12OCT2	11NOV2	11JUN2	08DEC2	27
2102.3100-D	DESIGN STRUCTURAL STEEL	1	90	15FEB2	15MAY2	08NOV2	08DEC2	27
2102.3100-P	PURCHASE & DEL. STRUCT STEEL		150	15MAY2	12OCT2	11JUN2	08NOV2	34
2102.3200-C	MISC.STEEL 21 TONS		21	11NOV2	02DEC2	15DEC2	08DEC2	48
2102.3200-D	DESIGN MISC STEEL	4	60	01MAY2	30JUN2	18JUN2	05JAN3	48
2102.3200-P	PURCHASE & DEL. MISC STEEL		120	30JUN2	28OCT2	17AUG2	08NOV2	27
2102.4300-C	METAL ROOF DECK 22000 SF		14	11NOV2	25NOV2	08DEC2	05JAN3	71
2102.4300-D	DESIGN ROOF DECK	4	60	01MAY2	30JUN2	17AUG2	15DEC2	71
2102.4300-P	PURCHASE & DEL. ROOF DECK		120	30JUN2	28OCT2	18JUN2	22DEC2	61
2102.4800-C	GENERAL CONSTRUCTION LOT	4	60	11NOV2	25NOV2	16NOV2	16NOV2	61
2102.4800-D	DESIGN GENERAL CONSTRUCTION		60			17SEP2	31DEC2	27
2102.5800-C	EQUIPMENT INSTALLATION LOT	1				16NOV2		60
2102.5800-P	PURCHASE & DEL. EQUIPMENT					27JUL2	10AUG2	57
2102.6100-C	HEATING AND VENTILATION LOT					10AUG2	08NOV2	68
2102.6100-D	DESIGN HEATING & VENTILATION	4				11JUN2	08DEC2	30
2103.1400-C	EARTHWORK 4000 CY					08NOV2	08NOV2	30
2103.2100-C	BLDG FDNS 1600 CY					11JUN2	05JAN3	40
2103.2100-D	DESIGN BLDG FDNS	1				15DEC2	17AUG2	30
2103.2300-C	SLAB ON GRADE 390 CY					18JUN2	15DEC2	30

CPM SCHEDULE

NETWORK CALCULATIONS

This is the basic output of the CPM program and lists all work items or activities. For each activity the duration, early and late start, early and late finish and the days of "float" are shown.

The Work Item list can be sorted to various levels according to the classification of accounts.

Figure 7-19 Network calculations.

PROCUREMENT SCHEDULING & STATUS REPORT

FAC. CMP. SHP EQ. ITEM	COST-CODE SPEC/REQ NO	P.O. CO AMOUNT	DESCRIPTION & QUANTITY VENDOR & ORIGIN	SCHED CLASS	REQ-DTE BID-REC	KE-RECM CLNT-OK	AWARDED	ENGNRNG RELEASE	SHIP EX PLANT	ARRIVE AT JOB	EARLY START	DIFF CPM
46-0960-00-00-00	1501-5700	46001-00	STEAM METER #2	04	A08FEB2		A30MAR2	02MAY2	31JUL2	15AUG2	01SEP2	17
46-1010-00-00-00	1501-5700		HEATEXC FOR HOT WATER SYSTEM	06	A30MAR2	13MAY2	28MAY2	07JUL2	24NOV2	09DEC2	15SEP2	85-
46-1020-00-00-00	1501-5700		HEATEXC FOR HOT WATER SYSTEM	06	A30MAR2	13MAY2	28MAY2	07JUL2	24NOV2	09DEC2	15SEP2	85-
46-1030-00-00-00	1501-5700		HEATEXC FOR HOT WATER SYSTEM	06	A30MAR2	13MAY2	28MAY2	07JUL2	24NOV2	09DEC2	15SEP2	85-
46-1040-00-00-00	1501-5700		HEATEXC FOR HOT WATER SYSTEM	06	A30MAR2	13MAY2	28MAY2	07JUL2	24NOV2	09DEC2	15SEP2	85-
46-1060-00-00-00	1501-5700		DOMESTIC WATER HEATER	06	F05JUL2	19AUG2	03SEP2	13OCT2	02MAR3	17MAR3	30APR3	44
46-1080-00-00-00	1501-5700		DOMESTIC HOT WATER CIRCULAT-	03								
46-1110-00-00-00	1501-5700		HOT WATER CIRCULATING PUMP	06								
46-1120-00-00-00	1501-5700		HOT WATER CIRCULATING PUMP	06								
46-1130-00-00-00	1501-5700		HOT WATER CIRCULATING PUMP	06								
46-1300-00-00-00	1501-5700		SUMP PUMP FLOOR AREA 100 GPM	05								
46-1310-00-00-00	1501-5700		SUMP PUMP FLOOR AREA 100 GPM	05								
46-1350-00-00-00	1501-5700		BRINE PUMP	03	F21JUN2	26JUL2	10AUG2	09SEP2	08NOV2	23NOV2	30NOV2	7
46-1360-00-00-00	1501-5700		BRINE PUMP	03	F21JUN2	26JUL2	10AUG2	09SEP2	08NOV2	23NOV2	30NOV2	7
20-0001-00-01-00	2101-3100	101-00	PRIMARY CRUSHING PLANT	00	A18JAN2		A01MAR2	F10FEB3	F01APR3	F15APR3	01MAY3	16
20-0001-00-02-00	2101-3200	101-00	PRIMARY CRUSHING PLANT	00	A18JAN2		A01MAR2	F10FEB3	F01APR3	F15APR3	01MAY3	16
20-0001-00-03-00	2101-3200	101-00	PRIMARY CRUSHING PLANT	00	A18JAN2		A01MAR2	F10FEB3	F01APR3	F15APR3	01MAY3	16
20-1100-00-00-00	2101-4400		VERTICAL LIFT DOORS MOTORIZED	06	A 0MAR2	17MAY2	01JUN2	11JUL2	11NOV2	25NOV2	02NOV2	23-
20-1110-00-00-00	2101-4400		VERTICAL LIFT DOORS MOTORIZED	06	A 0MAR2	17MAY2	01JUN2	11JUL2	11NOV2	25NOV2	02NOV2	23-
20-1140-00-00-00	2101-4400		VERTICAL LIFT DOORS MOTORIZED	06	A 0MAR2	17MAY2	01JUN2	11JUL2	11NOV2	25NOV2	02NOV2	23-
20-1150-00-00-00	2101-4400		DUST SEAL SWING DOOR 44" W X	06	F18SEP2	02NOV2	17NOV2	27DEC2	16MAY3	31MAY3	31MAY3	
30-0550-00-00-00	2102-4800		MCC PRESSURIZING UNIT 6000	03	F19MAY2	03JUL2	18JUL2	27AUG2	14JAN2	29JAN3	31MAR3	61
30-0600-00-00-00	2102-4800		VERTICAL LIFT DOORS MOTORIZED	06	A30MAR2	17MAY2	01JUN2	11JUL2	28NOV2	13DEC2	31MAY3	169
30-0360-00-00-00	2102-5800		MONORAIL HOIST 3 T 10L 20'RUN	02	F26MAY2	25JUN2	10JUL2	30JUL2	08SEP2	23SEP2	31JUL3	311

PROCUREMENT SCHEDULE AND STATUS REPORT

The PSSR reflects the status of engineered equipment/material items for a project. The reports show the following:

Facility no., equipment no., component no., item no., shipment no., cost account no., spec./req. no., description, schedule class, requisition date, bid received date, recommendation to award date, award date, engineers release date, date due to ship, arrival date, CPM early start date, difference between arrival date and early start date.

Figure 7-20 Procurement scheduling and status report.

UNIT COST REPORT

** PROJECT NAME ** JOB NO. PERIOD ENDING DATE PAGE 1

ACCOUNT	UNIT	QUANTITY PERIOD	QUANTITY TO DATE	QUANTITY AT COMPL.	QUANTITY BUDGET	% COMPL.	RECORDED COST PERIOD	RECORDED COST TO DATE	UNIT ANALYSIS PERIOD	UNIT ANALYSIS TO DATE	UNIT ANALYSIS EST. AT COMPL.	UNIT ANALYSIS BUDGET	COST TREND PERIOD	COST TREND TO DATE	JOB FACTOR
* DIRECT ACCOUNTS															
:: 2000.0000 BUILDINGS AND STRUCTURES															
.: 2100.0000 CONCENTRATOR PLANT															
: 2101.0000 PRIMARY CRUSHING BUILDING															
. 2101.1400 EARTHWORK															
2101.1401 BACKFILL S/C #0101															
. QTY-MHRS	CY	3550	6375	8500	9000	75	463 MH	827 MH	0.13MH	0.13MH	0.13MH	0.11MH	69-MH	119-MH	1.17
. SUB-CONT							8500	15000 MH	2.39MH	2.35	2.35	2.50	375-	938-	
. FLD.TOTAL							8500	15000	2.39	2.35	2.35	2.50	375-	938-	
. MANHOURS							0 MH	0 MH					0 MH	0 MH	0.0
. 2101.1400 SUBCN							8500	15000					375-	937-	
. 2101.1400 FLD T							8500	15000					375-	937-	
. 2101.2100 BUILDING FOUNDATIONS															
2101.2101 CONCRETE PLACE S/C #0101															
. QTY-MHRS	CY	0	117	130	135	90	0 MH	818 MH	0.0 MH	6.99MH	6.96MH	6.07MH	0 MH	108 MH	1.15
. SUB-CONT							0	8200	0.0	70.09	85.85	88.15	0	2113-	
. FLD.TOTAL							0	8200	0.0	70.09	85.85	88.15	0	2113-	
. MANHOURS							0 MH	0 MH					0 MH	0 MH	0.0
. 2101.2100 SUBCN							0	9900					0	2113-	
. 2101.2100 FLD T							0	9900					0	2113-	
. 2101.3100 STRUCTURAL STEEL															
2101.3109 STRUCTURAL STEEL FURN & ERECT (KE)															
. QTY-MHRS	TN	52	105	200	205	53	933 MH	1867 MH	17.94MH	17.78MH	18.21MH	18.21MH	14-MH	45-MH	0.98
. LABOR							5600	11200	107.69	106.67	109.27	109.27	82-	273-	
. BURDEN							1650	3300	31.73	31.43	32.20	32.20	24-	80-	
. EQUIP.USE							1500	3050	28.85	29.05	29.76	29.76	47-	74-	
. MATERIAL							22900	48090	440.38	458.00	458.05	458.05	919-	5-	
. FLD.TOTAL							31650	65640	608.65	625.14	629.28	629.27	1072-	433-	

Detail Unit Cost Report

Computer print-out of the detail unit cost report showing the following information:

Account	- account number, elements of cost
Unit	- unit of measure
Quantity	- period to-date, at completion and budget
% Complete	- to-date quantity; at completion quantity
Recorded Cost	- period and to-date
Unit Analysis	- (by element) period, to-date

COST TREND = ACTUAL COST − (BUDGET UNIT X ACTUAL QUANTITY) JOB FACTOR = TO DATE MANHOURS ÷ (BUDGET UNIT X ACTUAL QUANTITY)

Figure 7-21 Unit cost report.

comparable with each other because of vastly different job conditions affecting the project management and the individual workman. Few companies, few individual managers and superintendents, and few craftsmen are broad enough to be able to operate successfully in both of these segments of the industry, and, fortunately because of the fundamental differences, very few individuals are asked to operate interchangeably.

LOCAL CONTRACTORS AND MARKETS

Much of the industrial work performed in major metropolitan areas is made up of additions to and renovating major plants and the development of new projects, dependent on the business cycle. The emergence of the construction manager has affected the role of the traditional general contractor but has not greatly affected the traditional subcontractors who have always performed the majority of the work in this class of project. Most of the work is performed under competitive bid fixed price contracts, although a sizable amount of negotiated work is apparent, usually increasing in the expansion portion of the business cycle. In the south, in border states, and increasingly in the North and West, open shop or nonunion

Account Number	Description	Recorded cost			Recorded and committed	Estimated cost		Budget	Over or (under)
		Current	To date	Committed		To complete	At completion		
1000	Structures and improvements	3,000	50,000	10,000	60,000	50,000	110,000	114,200	(4,200)
2000	Boiler plant	3,000	25,000	80,000	105,000	10,000	115,000	98,200	16,800
3000	Turbine plant	2,000	20,000	35,000	55,000	5,000	60,000	57,300	2,700
4000	Electric plant	5,000	15,000	20,000	35,000	10,000	45,000	35,200	9,800
5000	Miscellaneous plant	1,000	5,000	5,000	10,000	13,000	23,000	20,100	2,900
	Total direct cost	14,000	115,000	150,000	265,000	88,000	353,000	325,000	28,000
	Contractors' cost	1,000	10,000	1,000	11,000	19,000	30,000	30,000	—
	Construction plant	100	3,000	1,000	4,000	1,000	5,000	5,000	—
	Home office and fee	200	1,500	3,500	5,000	—	5,000	5,000	—
	Design engineering	300	5,000	5,000	10,000	—	10,000	10,000	—
	Total indirect cost	1,600	19,500	10,500	30,000	20,000	50,000	50,000	—
	Estimated total	15,600	134,500	160,500	295,000	108,000	403,000	375,000	28,000
	Escalation					27,000	27,000	75,000	(48,000)
	Contingency					50,000	50,000	50,000	—
	Grand total cost	15,600	134,500	160,500	295,000	185,000	480,000	500,000	(20,000)

Figure 7-22 Cost and comparison to estimate (All costs in $1000).

161

contractors are obtaining more work at the expense of the traditional union contractors or subcontractors.

This segment of the industrial construction market is closely allied with the building construction market in the area. In fact, a large proportion of the contractors and subcontractors may operate interchangeably within their geographic area.

This segment closely resembles the organizational structure and management methods applicable to the entire industry some 20 years ago prior to the management boom in sophisticated management control systems using the digital computer. Interestingly enough, productivity of the individual craftsman may be very high per unit of work, and management, support, and servicing personnel represent a smaller fraction of the jobsite organization with much more responsibility placed on the superintendent, general foreman, foreman, and craftsman than on major design-construct projects or on nuclear power plants.

This conclusion is not surprising when one reviews the fundamental competitive nature of the work. To survive, a firm must bid low enough to get the work but must be high enough to make a profit. The firms that do not have the management talent and flexibility to make consistent profits over the intermediate term do not survive and go out of business.

The following list sets forth some of the factors that appear to be important for a firm to survive in the competitive local industrial environmental:

1. Management must recognize its strengths and weaknesses and must be flexible enough to shift objectives, personnel and resources, and capital to those areas representing the greatest opportunity, while minimizing economic risk.

2. A solid organization, including effective management control, estimating, job supervision, and administrative personnel who operate as a team with mutual understanding and respect.

3. Close communication with general foreman, foremen, and key craftsmen. In many successful companies foremen consider themselves as part of management, and may times make decisions that are made at far higher levels on major design-construct or negotiated projects.

4. The superintendents have generally come up from a craft, fully understand required production and workmanship objectives and do not tolerate substandard performance at the foreman or craft level.

5. The superintendent or foreman is in full charge of the work at the jobsite responsible to the home office for the production and schedule goals set forth in the bid estimate. So long as their goals are achieved, the personnel responsible for the work have considerable flexibility in choosing methods and personnel to achieve overall objectives.

6. A top management that supplies economic evaluation, flexibility, vision,

and direction to cope with an ever-changing environment, while respecting the human needs and pride of performance of the entire organization.

NATIONAL DESIGN AND CONSTRUCTION PROJECTS

Design-construct projects handled by NCA members and their other union and open shop competitors range in size from perhaps 5 to 10 million upward. In the 1950s and 1060s most of the leading firms performed the preponderance of the construction work with their own forces under the design-build format. In recent years most of the actual construction work has been performed using independent contractors in what we call the design-manage concept.

Design-Build

The design-build concept featured construction starting shortly after design, and field forces would often be working literally one step behind the drawings. The ultimate objective was to complete the plant at the earliest possible date, and generous use of overtime was often utilized in an effort to attract manpower and to try to achieve planned schedules. The work was normally performed on some form of cost reimbursement type contract, and sizable capital cost overruns were often tolerated by owners so long as increasing demand for the product resulted in maximizing overall manufacturing profitability. Major client objectives were excellence of plant process capability, minimum production cost, and speed of construction. See the September 1969 *Fortune* article entiled "The Big Boondoggle at Lordstown" for an excellent description of the effect of General Motors' objectives on a construction project. See Life in Organizations for a description of the same corporate objectives on the production worker. In periods of contraction of the business cycle, owners were unable to achieve overall profitability goals because of lessened demand and the law of survival required paying more attention to capital costs. Overtime was curtailed, schedules were often lengthened, and the cost plus concept of design-construct became increasingly abandoned by many major owners. User groups such as the Business Round Table began to publicize many of the restrictive work practices that had been uniformly tolerated during the go-go years. NCA stopped selling its customers on its ability to bypass local bargaining strikes and to continue working when local AGC groups were trying to hold down wage increases and restrictive work practices and introduced provisions for supporting local bargaining when requested by their clients. NCA also began to try to improve productivity by negotiating agreements such as the Ten Commandments and the work rules agreement which proclaimed that everybody was for a day's work for a day's pay.

Design-Manage

The high-level pronunciations were not successful in convincing owners that the design-constructor could build economical plants with their own forces when crash programs were not required and the engineer-contractor increasingly began to perform the construction work using several independent contractors generally on a fixed price contract that we have called design-manage.

The design-manage concept featured a phased construction program with overlapping design and construction. The overall objective was to minimize the overall design-construct period by the use of overlapping contracts. Overall economies were to be achieved by competitive bidding and the awarding of several fixed price contracts that taken in aggregate would produce a fixed price for the entire work.

The design-manage approach brought many of the larger local specialty contractors back into the design-manage projects as well as an increasing number of specialty contractors who were operating nationally in the electrical, mechanical, steel erection, and other fields.

In practice, design-manage proved to be no more of a panacea than did design-construct. There have been and will be many very successful design-manage projects. There are also several disasters or near disasters. For a truly successful project all parties should receive fair value. The owner should receive a quality plant, for a reasonably predictable cost, on a reasonably predictable time schedule. The design-constructor should receive a reasonable fee, produce a quality product, and strengthen his overall organization through internal growth. The individual contractors should make fair profit and be able to work under conditions reasonably under their control as anticipated during the bid period.

The strength of design-construct was the ability of field forces to work one step ahead of design in order to shorten the construction schedule. When late information, process improvements, or layout errors required drawing revisions and modifications or removal of completed work, the jobsite supervisor modified the program immediately and could go in and correct the situation as quickly as possible and put on more men or work overtime or both in an effort to preserve original schedules. Excess costs and time delays due to these design changes were seldom appreciated by design-constructor management and were often not even known by the owner, and the true effect of the changes on the cost of the project and the productivity of the work force was generally totally misunderstand. Everyone began to blame labor productivity, feather bedding agreements, and construction supervision for the delays and cost overruns that in reality were often directly attributable to the continual drawing changes received throughout the life of the project and the use of an extended workweek.

With the shift to design-manage, those design-manage projects that featured realistic initial schedules and properly designed contract packages tailored to normal business practices of local or national specialty contractors and were able to minimize or eliminate major drawing changes during the construction period proved very successful, and all parties—the owner, the design-construct firm, and the local contractors—benefited.

However, when design-construct management, owners, or project managers did not set realistic schedules or did not prepare complete bid packages conforming to local practice, the same cost overruns and schedule delays that often were responsible for excessive costs in design-construct suddenly became very visible to the owner. Drawing changes always cause additional costs to a contractor far in excess of his cost if he had received the drawings at bid time. Suddenly, many design-manage projects deteriorated to arguments over the payment for changes and delays to one contractor due to work of another. Some owner and design-construct management endeavored to preserve completion dates by directing substantial overtime. Then, when productivity inevitably deteriorated, major claims and lawsuits were filed by the individual contractors in an effort to make a profit or break even in the face of staggering cost increases related to drawing revisions, modifications, or time acceleration not normally experienced on projects when all the design was completed before bids were taken.

Overall Choice

The design-construct concept remains the most promising method for handling major industrial plants where process requirements dictate the nature of the facilities. The future success or failure of major NCA firms and their open shop competition will depend on their ability to diagnose the major objectives of their clients and choose either the design-build or design-manage concept based on conditions prevalent on particular projects.

Design-build will continue to prove an effective choice when absolute minimum design-construct time is required and when schedules are of major economic significance to the client or where geographic location or other local conditions indicate that one overall general contractor should directly control the work force such as in remote areas where camp, housing, and craft recruiting programs are required. Where technology is advancing rapidly or where designers are unable to obtain information in time to prepare completed drawings, this method permits timely direct action to make changes or modifications without the necessity of using business strategy to insure adequate payment for the change.

Design-manage will generally prove to be an effective choice where adequate skill, competition, and manpower are available using local contractors, where realistic schedules are carefully developed and included in the bid packages, are where intelligently designed work packages are substantially completed prior to receiving bids with few or no changes afterward.

NUCLEAR POWER PLANTS AND OTHER SUPERPROJECTS

Nuclear power plants and other superprojects are designated as a separate part of industrial construction. Some might classify them as more closely allied to the heavy construction industry because of the massive nature of the concrete and civil works. However, the civil portions of a nuclear plant are dwarfed by the massive mechanical, piping, and electrical efforts that in most ways are more closely aligned with heavy industrial construction, including steel mills, cement plants, and fossil power plants. The factors that set nuclear power and other superprojects apart from more finite heavy industrial work for private clients include the 8 to 12-year design-construct schedules, the effects of the ever-changing requirements of the Nuclear Reactor Commission (NRC) and/or other regulatory bodies, and the unprecedented financial resources required to complete a project. Also unprecendented is the observation that there has probably never been a nuclear power plant in the United States which has been completed for either the original schedule or the original budget.

Background and Growth

The first nuclear power plants were designed and built under turnkey contracts by General Electric and Westinghouse. These companies designed and supplied the nuclear steam supply system and allied components and subcontracted the detail facility design and construction to others. Many utilities received a windfall bargain as both major manufacturers found it impossible to build the plants for a cost that was in any way comparable to the fixed selling price, a problem which has persisted throughout the life of the industry. After substantial cost write-offs both General Electric and Westinghouse abandoned the turnkey concept and confined their future efforts to reactor design and fabrication and other technical services and component supplies. Babcock & Wilcox joined the manufacturers, and as of early 1980 a total of approximately 70 nuclear power plants have been placed in operation and are currently under construction. Nuclear power represents about 12% of the total electrical supply in the United States. The requirements of the NRC continue to become more stringent with each passing year; productivity and unit cost per kilowatt continues to deteriorate at rates substantially in excess of any other form of construction; and no permanent solution to the spent fuel storage problem has been effectively demonstrated. Yet in the absence of a scientific, technological, and economic breakthrough in some other emerging concept such as solar power, MHD, laser fusion, or some form of direct conversion of matter to electricity, nuclear power remains the only really viable alternative to the diminishing coal and oil reserves, minimum additional hydroelectric potential, environmental challenges to fossil plants, and political risks associated with foreign fossil fuel sources.

Industry Problem

Nuclear construction projects are an on-line-real time demonstration of the new phenomenon of the impossibility of being able to predict the future based on the experience of the past. Figure 7-23 shows a construction cost trend for nuclear plant construction compared to refineries and coal plants. With the sharply increasing costs being experienced, many prophesy that nuclear power is clearly economically unfeasible in the foreseeable regulatory climate. The conclusion is readily apparent. However, if we could find a way to achieve 50% of the productivity that is routinely achieved by the local contractor who survives in a competitive environment, nuclear power would have no viable economic competition. See Figure 4-5 for the potential cost improvements on a typical 1980 plant.

Many articles and technical papers have been written pointing out the difficulties involved in nuclear plant construction. Turnkey, fixed price, CM, design-construct, and single cost plus general contractor concepts used with success by the balance of the industry have all been found to be economically unsound in the ability to predict or control at completion schedules and costs. All forms of contracts, including lump sum, cost plus a fee, fixed unit price, target fee, award fee, and other concepts have failed to solve the economic problems. For each individual project someone must place the blame. Some blame labor for the low productivity, and for a period it became fashionable to show that the average craft employee in a nuclear plant was engaged in productive work only 30% of the time. Figure

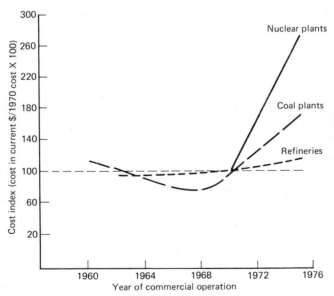

Figure 7-23   Nuclear plant. From Irvin C. Bupp et al., "The Economics of Nuclear Power," *Technology Review*, **77**(4), February 1975, P. 80.

4-1 shows a study prepared by Marjatta Strandell that is typical of the findings. In the real world the owner and job management blamed the project manager. Peter Drucker advises top management that if you have a job on which three managers fail, you should review and change the job, since it is probably not possible to find a mere mortal to fill it. There are few modern nuclear power plants where the originally chosen top on-site construction project manager has survived the project from ground breaking to commercial operation, although it is probable that such individuals may exist.

On the typical nuclear plant the owner blames the contractor or contractors. He also blames the designer. He blames the Quality Assurance/Quality Control (QA/QC) organization, the NRC, the intervenor, and everyone else. The contractor and designer blame everybody in a similar manner.

Using Peter Drucker's analogy on projects as well as project managers, it appears that nobody knows how to manage a project in which the experiences of the past cannot be used to predict future performance.

State of the Art

Any nuclear plant is made up of a finite number of design and construction operations, none of which is in anyway beyond the state of the art. Yet conventional management, supervisory, and engineering methods that prove successful on other projects do not bring together all the parts into a workable whole. In this case the sum of the parts does not equate to the overall whole.

Perhaps the very large industrial or utility project constructed under changing criteria best illustrates the failure of the management boom to achieve performance levels equal to the state of the art as achieved on more finite projects. Figure 7-24 shows the actual cost of nuclear power plants from inception to completion when compared to the original estimate for the plant. The observation that final cost is about three times estimated cost is surprising when one realizes that each successive conceptual estimate was based on the historical cost performance of prior plants. As of 1980 this "rule of three" seems to understate the problem and no new plants are being started for both social and economic reasons.

Figure 4-4 shows actual man-hour units for basic electrical work on an experimental plant constructed for DOE in a western state compared to similar units achieved on an average of 17 nuclear power plants. Possibly productivity can be improved if foremen and craftsmen on major projects are given more responsibility similar to those working for local area contractors on competitively bid work where productivity has been found to be far superior and where craftsman morale is equally improved.

However, the entire regulatory approach as set forth in Federal Regula-

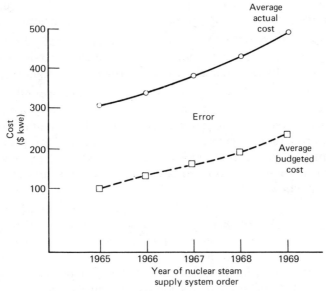

Figure 7-24 Comparison of reactor standard costs and plant actual costs. From Irvin C. Bupp et al., "The Economics of Nuclear Power," *Technology Review*, **77**(4), February 1975, p. 6.

tion 10 CFR 50 Appendix B serves to effectively prevent such responsibility. On one nuclear project an electrical superintendent responsible for 120 men found that 25% of the hours expended during the month produced no measurable quantity of completed work and were clearly attributable to either waiting for inspection, answering questions, or reworking operations to achieve QA/QC documentation approval. Another superintendent on the same project calculated that the cost of periodically cleaning dust from cable trays had easily required more man-hours than was required to pull the cable.

The suggestions presented next are set forth for study by future top managers who must come to grips with the management failure on the superprojects. Since each of the component parts of the most complex project are within the performance ability of almost everyone on the project, it is clearly evident that the resulting failure to integrate the parts into the whole is an overall management failure and cannot be laid at the door of any of the individuals or companies associated with the project. These are the suggestions:

1. Review the relationships that have promoted successful projects in the

nonnuclear area. Isolate the conditions that seem to achieve superior performance and high morale by all members of the construction team.

2. Review QA/QC requirements to tighten up nuclear safety-related items, eliminating meaningless trivia not related to nuclear safety but which is indistinquishable from important items by the on-site organization.

3. Upgrade the pay scale and qualification requirements of all QA/QC personnel so that inspectors are at least as highly paid as the journeymen and so that they bring to their job a skill level at least equal to that of a qualified journeyman. Demand qualifications and require prior performance on construction-related work accordingly. Restrict procedures to essential items necessary for nuclear safety and for the achievement of first-class workmanship.

4. Appoint a top-level review board of recognized industry leaders for each project similar to boards set up for major dam projects throughout the world. Include recognized nuclear safety, design, and construction experts of stature, along with representatives from each of the skills. This board should review criteria for construction installation procedures, inspection programs, and QA/QC documentation for compliance with applicable law and good practice. However, as in the dam consulting board, recognize that economics, craftsman morale, and productivity improvement are vital, provided that required safety standards are achieved. Let the board rule on interpretation from a sound technical knowledge rather than from the level of the para professional inspector who is not allowed to deviate from predetermined criteria

5. Develop an analysis of the state of the art in nuclear design. Adopt the model plant concept on frozen criteria when safety considerations are affected. Adopt the philosophy that improvement of productivity and shortening of design-construct time in more important than increasing technical innovations which result in continual disruption of the project over period of 10 years or more. Consider an experiment to reduce the overall size of the project to more manageable proportions, since there appears to be no economies of scale in the superprojects.

6. Develop a people oriented management plan for both the design and construction programs that recognizes the past failure of traditional methods and which is designed to enable all individuals from laborer to project manager to have some part in carrying out his tasks and in being able to achieve some pride of accomplishment.

7. Recognize that 10 years is too long and too specialized to tie up the best managerial talent without destroying it. Select the very best managers available and put them on a rotational program of from two to three years with planned replacement through promotion and growth. Coping with all the problems of a nuclear plant for two to three years will prove invaluable

to managers of future projects by giving them an opportunity to avoid problems from experience. Above all, select smart, innovative managers who have demonstrated a thorough knowledge of the design and construction business.

8. Continually review the program with the idea of giving more responsibility and recognition to each level in ways that will not prejudice nuclear safety. If the craftsman knows how to do a first-class job, if he has the tools to do it, and if he wants to do it, the final results will be far superior to the present achievement at a fraction of the cost.

SUMMARY

The heavy industrial construction demand of the postwar environment in the United States and elsewhere produced unprecedented growth, with a major objective of shortening the design-construct schedule. Increasingly, design, procurement, and construction were overlapped, and the design-constructor emerged as the leading force. As growth moderated, owners became concerned at the cost overruns, and economy often became more important than crash programs. The design-constructors recognized this trend and developed phased construction programs featuring several individual lump sum bid packages.

Competition for the design-constructors developed in the emerging professional construction management three-party team approach and in the return to more traditional methods, where time permitted completing all design work prior to starting the program.

However, phased construction programs cannot achieve schedule or cost objectives in a climate of change caused by drawing revisions after award or by government regulations. In the intermediate term the lump sum contractor who cannot bid low enough to get the work while remaining efficient enough to make a profit will go out of business. In the long term the design constructor practicing design-build and/or design-manage will also fail to survive through lack of repeat clients unless he can maintain effective management programs and personnel to enable the cost and scheduled deviation of major projects to be reasonably forecast under today's and tomorrow's ever-changing construction environment.

The special problems of the superprojects are evident in productivity, which is perhaps one-third as great as can be achieved in more finite projects. Perhaps no one has developed a cost effective management organization for superprojects, and the challenge of the future will be to develop an on-the-job climate that will allow all industry paticipants to achieve a measure of self-actualization and to regain the pride of performance and accomplishment which was the heritage of the construction industry.

CHAPTER 8

HEAVY ENGINEERING CONSTRUCTION

George T. McCoy

It is no longer possible to treat all forms of engineering construction similarly. The frequency with which very large projects are now required and undertaken, together with the limited time scheduled for their completion, has given impetus to the creation of a vastly more complex system of contracting than that in existence 25 years ago. This chapter deals with the areas of policy and problems that have emerged in this sphere of operations. The accomplishments of the construction industry, including owners, engineers, and contractors, have been remarkable, although sometimes expensive. But more significant, they have forced the development of many new practices on each of the parties concerned. It is hoped that some of the thoughts presented here will help to avoid costly experiences and promote a better understanding of the many policy decisions inherent in the business.

MANAGEMENT AND ORGANIZATIONAL PRACTICES AND PROBLEMS

When considering the management of today's construction activities in the field of heavy construction, it is necessary to understand the nature of the various types of companies engaged in the field as well as the differences that exist between them. Recent years have witnessed many changes in the scope of individual firms and in their organizational structures. Indeed, the greatest problem many of these companies face is the creation of an internal structure that will permit their many talents to be fully used in an ever-changing marketplace. Some firms, successful in this endeavor, have recorded phenomenal growth in relatively short periods of time while others, unsuccessful, have recorded equally phenomenal failures and are no longer active in the construction business.

It is not possible to fully divorce a discussion of a company engaged in construction from the type of owner or owners for whom they perform or from the breadth of work they perform for that owner. The type of contract, together with the financial considerations and risks undertaken by each party, is most relevant to the structuring of both the owner's organization and that of the firm performing the work. The guarantees required to be suplied by each party will also impact the arrangement under which the work is performed.

Modern heavy construction had its inception in the first 40 years of this century and embraced primarily the fields of water storage and conservation; hydroelectric power projects; fossil-fueled power plants; large bridges, tunnels, and underwater tubes; and some of the larger highway projects. Industrial construction was largely a combination of building, mechanical, and electrical work performed by specialized firms, often local and generally small by present standards.

Many, perhaps most, of the companies performing heavy construction today had their origins in that period and in the marketplace of that era. Toward the end of this 40 year period the first joint ventures were formed to undertake work beyond the financial capabilities of any of the individual companies. Governmental agencies in the United States were the principal owners of the projects constructed. Labor contracts were vastly different; the union organizations were structured around powerful leaders with complete control of their memberships. In nonunion areas working conditions and wages were largely governed by supply and demand.

The construction companies starting in this environment were initially one or two-man controlled and undertook only one major job at a time. In the early joint ventures it was not unusual for the principals of the ventures to move to the jobsite to better protect their investment from the financial standpoint and to direct the methods of construction. The tasks of the project manager were arduous indeed under such supervision.

The survivors of this system, those who were able to prosper and grow as well as survive the generation change when the original owners died or retired, now constitute the principal heavy construction firms in the United States. There have been and are other firms entering the field in subsequent years. Some have been able to meet the steady competition of the more experienced companies. The unsuccessful ones either failed financially or have withdrawn from the arena.

A typical successful major firm in heavy construction today will have in excess of 1000 regularly employed staff personnel and financial resources— net assets, plus available credit—of $100 million or more. Obviously, these firms have come a long way from their early origins. And they have acquired a great deal of valuable experience through the years; they are experienced not only about construction work, but also about qualifying for surety bonds and bank loans; knowing how and when to insure against risks they cannot afford to run, the types of contracts and contract clauses to avoid, and about the owner's access to sufficient funds to finance the work; providing for wage and price increases; and being aware of the differences in labor productivity and how to resolve disputes with the owner. Of course, the list is much longer; these are only a few of the more important items aside from the construction work itself. The main point is that there are many pitfalls on the road to success as a heavy contractor. Most, if not all, of the principal companies in the business have had serious involvements with one or more of these problem areas as they have made their way to success through the years. They well know the continuing vigilance necessary to progress in this highly competitive business.

But there has been more than just growth in size and experience that has occurred in the organizational structures of these companies. These changes are related to increased capability to handle a larger volume of more complex work; increased scope of operations, both regarding the nature of the work and the geographical area of operations; and the increase in internal activities required to comply with new governmental regulations. While it is imperative for a contractor to deal with these factors for his operations in the United States, it is even more important that those contractors operating overseas provide adequate organizational support for their foreign operations.

Before getting into the details of organizational structure, we should mention one other trend that has developed in recent years with several of our major companies. This is the inclusion of design abilities within their company framework. The capability of providing complete installations for an owner, the "turnkey" concept, has great appeal particularly where the customer does not maintain an extensive engineering staff. This approach is especially attractive in developing countries where technology is at a premium and in all countries for projects requiring highly specialized skills such as industrial and nuclear power plant construction. Where the potential constructor is prevented from undertaking both design and construction, usually by owners desiring competition for the construction phase, he is frequently able to secure either the role of construction manager or that of the engineer during the actual progress of the work. Such an arrangement will normally yield reasonable profits with minimum risk for the design effort, plus providing a valuable service for the client who is not staffed to properly administer the work with his own forces. But it is not without problems, which we discuss later.

Once a client has reached the decision to proceed with a project, whether a power plant, resource development, or factory, speed of completion becomes an important consideration. The owner has determined his needs, arranged his financing, and received the necessary environmental clearances at this point; now time is even more important in terms of money. Environmental considerations will most likely have delayed the expenditure of substantial sums for site investigations or design if the project is a domestic one; the uncertainties of foreign politics and financing will often delay large expenditures for projects in the less-developed countries. The start of construction before completion of design has become an increasingly common occurrence. A company able to perform both design and construction with a well-coordinated program is well positioned to offer a finished project in a minimum time period. Lacking is the element of competition, but an organization with a reputation for meeting estimates and budgets presents a desirable alternative to an owner when time of completion is a prime consideration. Even inflation works to the benefit of this fast track performer.

With this preface it is possible to look more closely into the organization practices in use by the major heavy construction companies. Surprisingly, there are major differences in these organizations, even though the components are basically the same.

Consider first the companies whose total structure includes a design capability. That is, they are fully qualified to create the total design for a project. In some cases this capability may be broad enough to cover virtually the entire field of construction; in others it may be highly specialized to cover a narrow field, such as the design, manufacture and installation of a large electrical generator.

Many of these design activities are organized as separate companies, physically separated from the parent, but with a degree of liaison capable of exploiting opportunities to sell the services of the construction branches of their total company. Obviously, the design element is normally the first section of such a firm to be aware of new work, and it may find opportunities to provide the total design and construct package that will maximize its combined talents and provide the greatest opportunity for potential profit.

Then there are those companies that perform little or no design work but have the capability of operating very efficiently in one or more of the areas of construction. Some specialize in earthmoving or tunneling, others in large concrete structures, while many provide a variety of other skills, including mechanical and electrical work. The variety is limited only by the number of major contractors, since no two are exactly alike. Some are divisions of still larger organizations in either related or different fields of activity. The diversification of the conglomerates, both large and small, has created many unusual relationships between companies.

And then we have the specialty contractors and the major suppliers of construction equipment and materials. Often they are in the role of subcontractor, frequently for firms much smaller than themselves. It is no longer possible to think of a subcontractor as a less-important company serving the needs of the prime contractor. The subcontractor may well be the most important figure at the construction site, dictating the schedule and activities of the company holding the prime contract with the owner.

Many of the larger heavy construction companies are organized into profit centers on the basis of dividing their operations into geographic areas. Some will have many complete entities serving different locales and with a minimum of main office control. Others will do most of their estimating of large jobs in their headquarters and use the area approach for actual physical construction operations. There are companies, some quite large, that manage virtually all their work from one office.

The other principal approach is to split the organization based on type of work being undertaken. There may be a group dedicated to dams, another to industrial work, and still another to nuclear construction. These activities may be closely coordinated or each relatively autonomous.

The variety of structuring is limited only by the number of companies involved and the abilities of the staff available to them. There is no one type that has proved greatly superior to the others, and the basic functions that must be performed by each are the same. Some obviously result in more duplication of effort than others but seem to compensate by being able to increase the motivation in their individual sectors, whether they are geographic or product oriented.

A few more words about the basic nature of a construction contractor are in order. Perhaps the most important is the fact that the contractor is in business. The company is motivated by profit and by the ethics of its constituents. Just like any other business, it must make a profit and acquire the confidence of its clients to survive. Sharp practices and other unethical behavior soon destroy the reputation of a firm and will ultimately cause its failure.

A contractor, and indeed the whole industry, will exist only as long as he, or it, can perform a service for the client more efficiently than the client can perform this service for himself. Those companies that strive for cost reimbursable contracts solely to eliminate the normal risks of the business are a detriment to the future of the construction contracting industry. To be sure, there are valid reasons for the use of cost reimbursable contracts, but the best interest of the industry in the long term lies in avoiding them where possible rather than encouraging them.

Being a profit-oriented business, the construction company uses many types of people in its operations. Certainly, engineers are used, but only as a part of the operation to deal with the engineering problems. Equally important are the financial and business people. The accountants and the computer, personnel, safety, insurance, and legal professions all play their very essential roles.

It is the skill with which a company can structure, motivate, control, and coordinate its people that will determine its long-range success. The day of the one-man company is past for the large construction organization.

It is readily apparent that what the construction company has to work with are its people and financial resources. The company must use these assets to perform a service that is efficient and to create a quality product.

STRUCTURING THE MANAGEMENT EFFORT

The owner plays a vital role in determining a basic structure under which his project will be constructed. The degree of his participation in the various stages, the selection of the designer, the form of contract and its terms, who will do construction work, who will provide inspection services are but a few of the decisions he must make. He may well perform any or all of the functions with his own people, or he may select others to perform them on his behalf. Projects constructed by governmental agencies of the United States generally have little latitude, since their actions are normally prescribed by federal or state statutes. In foreign countries a greater range of possibilities is usually present, ranging from systems very similar to the United States to ones allowing the widest discretion by the political agencies or persons in the government.

But even in the United States, where competition is the basic requirement of our laws regulating contracts, some discretionary decisions must be made. Shall the design work be performed "in-house" or contracted to private engineering firms? Large governmental agencies doing repetitive projects generally are staffed to perform their own design. On occasion a particular problem will lead these agencies to another designer who specializes in such work. In most cases they are required to let a contract to public bidding for the actual construction. The design and construct contractor is ruled out of this market on a turnkey basis, except for complex manufactured items whose installation is inseparable from design from the standpoint of guarantees required for performance.

But the private company, even though publicly owned, has no such restrictions and is free to select from the myriad of choices what course it will follow. Only a few possess engineering staff adequate to efficiently design their own facilities, so generally the major decision to be made is whether to separate the design effort from the construction effort.

This decision is often a very complex subject. Private companies are normally able to select a small group of well-qualified construction companies to provide competitive bids for construction work. This insures for them the lowest possible construction costs and a specified time of performance for the physical work. These are significant, if not overwhelming, considerations in most cases. There are some prerequisites to maximizing these benefits; the principal ones are that the design must be reasonably complete, environmental clearances must have been obtained, and the site must be available for the contractor to go to work. The owner's time schedule dictated by the uncertainties of environmental problems and financial management may have prevented the necessary expenditures to complete design at the time he must start construction to achieve his desired completion. This is an all-too-frequent occurrence in today's marketplace, and it greatly complicates the objective of obtaining the benefits of competition and timely performance of the work. The coordination of developing or changing design on a project under construction is one of the most vexing administrative problems facing owners, engineers, and contractors alike. Even the design-construct contract cannot avoid these costs, although they may be less visible under a "turnkey" program.

Enlightened owners have come to realize the importance of their participation in the total program. Since the costs ultimately are for their accounts, it is rarely prudent to completely turn all decisions over to others, even if the owner is fully confident of their integrity and ability. There is always the interfacing of cash flow as well as monitoring the operating characteristics of the installation under construction that becomes evident as design or construction proceeds.

To return to the question of the basic philosophy of how to structure the project, many owners tend toward specifying the final results they desire and then obtaining a fixed price commitment for the necessary work to achieve these objectives from a firm financially capable of absorbing the risks involved. There are few firms financially capable of taking such risks, and they did not obtain their stability by undertaking unknown hazards. The lack of control that exists for the owner in such a circumstance would be a sufficient deterrent in most cases to obviate such a method from consideration.

RISK

So we arrive at the problem basic to most disputes in contracting for design and construction services. Who is responsible for what? How is the risk divided? This rather simple point has been the source of the majority of disputes in the construction industry. Any contract by the owner with either a designer or contractor that does not face this question forthrightly is almost certain to result in serious problems.

While we do not wish to dwell on this subject, there are a few basic principles that, if observed, will eliminate most of these problems. Responsible contractors will watch for them in bidding documents, and responsible owners will strive for clarity when they prepare the documents.

Initially there is the engineer: this person is controlled solely by the owner; he is normally either not capable of assuming risk or is unwilling to do so; he is a professional by nature, similar to a lawyer or doctor. The owner should be responsible to the contractor for actions of his engineer. And it is likely that any financial responsibility of the engineer to the owner should be very limited in nature. The role of the engineer as an impartial arbitrator of jobsite disputes is an out-of-date myth, and the owner had best not rely on it is his dealings with the contractor. The place to start is in the contract by avoiding language that contemplates such a position for the engineer.

With regard to risks in general, the risk of a specific factor should be borne by the party who can control it. Labor productivity is an obvious responsibility of the contractor, while providing the site is a responsibility of the owner. Each party must be responsible for the actions of his employees.

This leaves the area of unknowns. Some can be assigned or partially assigned to the contractor; in this category are the weather, strikes, and floods. They are often partially assigned by allowing additional time for performance but not the costs. Unforeseen underground conditions are best borne by the owner, although many attempts, mostly unsuccessful, have been made to assign this risk to the contractor. A good guide about whether a risk should be assigned to a contractor is to determine if he can buy insurance to protect against the cost impact. If he cannot, the owner will usually find it to his advantage to assume the risk himself. Many owners today specify the insurance to be carried to minimize the effect of unexpected costs that will impair the contractor's ability to perform.

CONTRACT FORMS

Let us consider briefly some of the features present in the major alternatives available for the construction of heavy engineering projects:

1. *Cost Reimbursable Contract with a Percentage Fee*   While this has the advantage of automatically adjusting the fee to the amount of work performed, it has the overwhelming disadvantage of creating a negative incentive with regard to construction costs. This contract's other advantage of encouraging quality workmanship can also be obtained under the second alternative presented next. This form of contract is rarely used today because it fails to reward efficiency.

2. *Cost Reimbursable Contract with a Fixed Fee*   This form of contract often seems to require adjustments to the fee to accommodate changes in either scope or magnitude of the work, but it does eliminate the problem of a negative incentive. It can be successfully used where the owner desires to control portions of the work and does not want to create a dispute with the contractor over the methods he directs. In a sense, the owner is renting a construction team from the contractor (or engineer) for an agreed price. This form of contract will not produce the greatest cost effectiveness, since it lacks an incentive feature such as that in the third alternative.

3. *Cost Reimbursable with an Incentive Fee Based on a Target Price or Target Man-hours*   This form of contract is generally regarded as the most desirable of the cost reimbursable types. It permits cost savings incentives for all parties involved. Appropriate sharing of cost savings with

all parties can create a highly motivated project. It can be used in conjunction with the fixed price contract by allowing reimbursement on a cost basis for items subject to uncontrollable variations. Also the fixed fee contract, in the second alternative, can be used to cover preliminary stages of an incentive fee project—for instance, until plans can be completed and a target estimate agreed on. Obtaining competitive proposals on a target-price-incentive-fee basis can yield excellent results, particularly with a selected bidders' list. This latter procedure can be more complex than it looks at first glance; an owner is well advised to secure competent advice if he is to obtain the maximum advantage from such a bidding procedure. The contractor may be required to guarantee a maximum cost under any of the cost reimbursable alternatives, but reasonably complete plans are a requisite for this safeguard to the owner.

4. *Cost Reimbursable with award Fee*   This relatively new form of contract provides for a wide range in scope and magnitude in the work to be performed. It allows a fee varying in amount based on certain agreed criteria on which the contractor is rated during the performance of the work. The frequency of rating can be any stipulated period but is usually about three months. It is normally expressed as a percentage of cost and can be applied to the period being rated or to the next ensuing period. Typical factors considered include adherence to schedule, cost efficiency, labor productivity, quality of supervision provided, cost savings innovations (value engineering), and safety performance. Usually, a relatively small base fee is provided in addition to cover nonreimbursable costs and off-site overhead. The advantage of this form of contract lies in providing a substantial incentive without the necessity of an agreed target. It eliminates the need for complete design and provides the flexibility to accommodate major changes without requiring extensive negotiation. This contract's greatest drawback is the selection of the rating board. The fairness of the board is a requisite to the successful operation of the award fee contract. This form of contract provides the contractor with specific knowledge of his shortcomings, which must be viewed as a favorable factor in achieving better performance.

5. *Fixed Price Contract*   This form is the best-tested system of contracting for construction in use today. It is used with either the lump sum or unit price. It requires a complete set of plans in advance of bidding and a clear set of specifications outlining the requirements for construction, together with the responsibilities of each party. Value engineering provisions are often used to give incentive for cost savings improvements during construction or in the finished product. Where it can be properly used, this contract provides the most satisfactory form of contracting available today.

Aside from these five major types of contracts, there are others involving some of the features from them, combined in a way suited to a particular situation. For instance, most fixed price contracts provide for the performance of "extra work" on a cost reimbursable plus percentage fee basis for small bits of work the owner may ask to have performed outside the scope of the main contract.

Some of the most important provisions of any contract are those that deal with the directing of changes, unforeseen conditions, and the settlement of disputes. If these matters can be dealt with speedily and fairly during the life of the contract, relations between the parties and satisfactory execution of the work will be greatly aided. Long-standing disputes can be most disruptive to the progress of the work and usually involve substantial additional costs to both the owner and the contractor. Owners with a reputation for fairness obtain highly competitive bids, while contractors with a bad reputation do not get on many bid lists.

THE ENGINEER

How the owner structures the role of the engineer into his project can be of great importance. The design can be performed in house by the owner, a consultant, or the contractor in a turnkey situation. The owner will approve the design in virtually all cases, at which point he assumes full or partial responsibility for it.

The next decision will involve the field administration of the contract from an engineering and inspection standpoint. An owner who designs his own work will normally inspect it as well, and there are no illusions about the engineer's role as a representative of the owner in spite of what the contract may say. Settlement of disputes should be provided for by impartial and expeditious means if lengthy litigation and excess costs are to be avoided. Government contracts have long been a prime offender, and the courts have been the scene of many settlements—very fair, perhaps, but so slow and costly.

Where the design is performed by a design-construct contractor, the owner usually performs nominal inspection for himself or hires an outside agency to perform it for him. The general theory is to keep the responsibility for the finished product and its performance on the design-constructor until the project is complete and functioning. While this is not always as simple to do as it is to say, for instance in the case of a new manufacturing process or technique, the basic objective is sound for work constructed under this form of contract.

In the case of an owner who chooses to hire a consultant for design and a contractor for construction, a distinct decision must be made about who will administer the construction contract and perform the inspection. In this case, the designer is not a party to the construction contract. The owner will usually find it to his advantage to administer the work himself or to hire an independent group to do it for him. This will provide a far clearer overview of both the contractor's work and the quality of the design he has purchased. Use of the designer as the supervisor of construction can often mask many problems of which the owner should be well aware. Nonetheless, this procedure is widely followed because it is convenient.

Some mention should be made of the use of the owner's own forces in expanding existing facilities or in the construction of new installations. This is a method widely used in some foreign countries, usually those that are more socialist than the United States—Australia, for example. It has had some application in the United States, where building trades' unions have achieved onerous work rules and high wages in specific areas. Also, many maintenance-type operations, such as highway resurfacing, are performed by forces employed by the government agency involved. Generally, it can be shown that these operations are uneconomical, but they often present desirable political features that are difficult for private business to combat. This is particularly true where the strengths of the unions in collective bargaining have allowed the unions to include costly provisions (to the employer) in their labor agreements. In support of performing construction work by the owner's forces it is apparent that the costs of contract administration are greatly reduced and that engineering costs can be very low, particularly for routine or repetitive operations.

LABOR

This is a good point at which to think about the role of labor in heavy engineering construction. The unionized construction contractors have proved to be a poor match for their well-trained counterparts from the unions in collective bargaining. The rapid rise in construction wages, much in excess of national averages, readily demonstrate the unionized construction contractors' inability to protect their industry from cost increases exceeding average rates of inflation. Laws and governmental agencies dealing with labor matters have made the contractor's labor relations problems arduous indeed. All-too-frequent use of the strike weapon to enforce unreasonable demands by the unions on contractors facing heavy costs of delay and the normal problems of financing, in a business that has become increasingly capital intensive, has worsened the plight of the union contractor in this uneven contest.

It is little wonder that the nonunion organizations have made such rapid inroads into the construction industry in recent years. Recent statistics indicate that over half of all construction work is now being performed on an open shop basis. The results of this change are of some interest. We find an increasing tendency on the part of nonunion contractors to pay the same or higher wages as the union members are receiving and to provide for union-type fringes, such as health and pension programs. The nonunion contractors have resisted any relinquishment of management rights or restrictive work practices. Estimates of the cost advantage they enjoy as a result of retained total freedom of management range as high as 30% of labor costs, although the average advantage is probably much lower. Nonetheless, it is substantial, and it is greatest in the strongest union areas.

The unions, on the other hand, in their attempts to meet this challenge have negotiated new contracts relaxing many of the restrictive work rules previously quite costly to the union contractor. The presence of nonunion competition is obviously the best weapon the union contractor has in his dealings with the crafts he uses. Union contractors have been able to achieve labor agreements that permit them to be competitive in areas formerly in the total domain of the open shop companies.

The bias of present legislation favoring the unions needs to change to further the long-term good of the construction industry. In any event, the natural trend toward uniformity in both factions of the industry can be stimulated if the legal advantages enjoyed by the organized groups are reduced to a point where the struggle is more nearly even. Today, it is very difficult for a union contractor to operate on an open shop basis, whereas the reverse can be much more readily done.

Where do labor considerations impact our thinking in planning for construction work? The answer is primarily in the actions of the owner on very large projects and in the actions of prospective bidders on somewhat smaller ones.

Most owners are primarily interested in getting their projects completed on time and particularly in avoiding work stoppages during construction. To this end it is becoming quite common for them to negotiate project agreements, where unions are involved, containing no-strike provisions. Some owners do this quite skillfully and can establish a favorable situation that permits bidders to prepare proposals free of allowances for the contingency of labor problems. Other owners may not be so successful and accept very expensive conditions as the price for the no-strike clause. If the owner will seek advice from available contractor organizations, he can usually make a fair compromise.

Contractors planning to bid work in open shop territory have likewise been able to achieve agreements with unions that make them quite competitive. It is most important that such an agreement be negotiated before the bid. Such an agreement in open shop areas is also very much to the advantage of the unions concerned, and its terms can eliminate the problems most expensive and troublesome to the contractors.

MANAGING THE HEAVY CONSTRUCTION PROJECT

If we eliminate design from consideration, the typical project consists of four distinct phases:

1. Bid or proposal.
2. Start-up.

3. Production.

4. Completion and demobilization.

Reviewing the elements and functions involved in each of these phases from a management standpoint should enable us to identify the problem areas as well as indicate direction that can provide solutions.

BID OR PROPOSAL

Not too many years ago it was common to hear earthmoving contractors discussing prospective work as "two-bit dirt" or assigning some other valuation to the major items of work on the job they were contemplating. Fringes, payroll taxes and inflation were swept into this rudimentary estimate because they were of such minor importance. These men based their evaluations on their experiences with similar jobs, and the estimates they arrived at were amazingly accurate. But time has ruled out such basic procedures; the complexity of modern construction, new techniques available, schedule requirements, the variability of specification requirements and wage rates have made the job of estimating a far more demanding and detailed procedure.

Fortunately, along with these new developments has come the computer. It has been of great assistance in keeping costs on ongoing projects and, taken together with engineering input on quantities of work performed, has expedited the gathering of data that can be used in the preparation of estimates. Quantities of work can be readily related to man-hours and equipment usage as common denominators. This then permits the application of whatever wage rate or equipment cost is current to obtain an estimated cost for work to be performed. Some contractors use the computer in preparing portions of their bid, but the number of judgment decisions to be made frequently renders such a procedure cumbersome and risky. But payroll and accounting functions are now greatly expedited by the computer, allowing up-to-date cost analyses (or man-hour studies) on a daily basis if required. Considerable care is required in setting up cost accounts that will not only yield the desired data, but also can be accurately recorded in the field.

The complex and detailed schedules frequently required by owners can also be best handled by modern computer techniques. It is still relatively rare to find field superintendents able to cope with the details presented by the computer scheduling, but they can be readily converted to more usable form for production personnel by office technicians. Meanwhile, the advantages in logistical matters can be fully used in purchasing, inventory control, and engineering.

Given a reasonably precise ability to estimate cost, why then is there so much variation in bids on most jobs? The answer must lie in areas of judgment or perhaps the innovative ability of a particular contractor. What are the principal areas of judgment? Labor productivity is most important in the majority of cases. Depreciation of equipment can create considerable differences where one or more of the competitors owns the items necessary for the work. This is closely allied to estimates of salvage value at the conclusion of the work. Then, of course, the amount of margin added for contingencies and profit can be a source of varying opinions. The contractor must evaluate the return he needs on his resources and people. This will be influenced by the amount of each he has available and what he feels other opportunities will be for their use after the bid currently being submitted.

Basically, there are certain steps to be followed in the preparation of any estimate or proposal. First, it is necessary to obtain a thorough understanding of what the owner requires to be built, including any special methods or procedures he has specified to be followed in the construction. The time for completion, together with any intermediate dates he may have specified for completion of specified components, must be reckoned with. These will usually determine the equipment involved as well as the other resources required to be committed to obtain the result desired. The terms of payment under the proposed contract are important to each party as well as how the elements of risk are divided between them. Any restrictions that will affect either the time or cost of performance must be clearly identified.

The bidder then prepares his plan of construction that will include his schedule of operations, equipment to be used, and the personnel (by type at least) that must be assigned to the project. At this point, he is usually able to determine what plant will be required to support the overall operations: repair shop facilities, office requirements, support required by existing commercial facilities in the area, special items of the plant such as concrete aggregate production facilities, and other items of both a general and specialized nature that will be required in the construction of the project. And also the extent of commitment of financial resources begins to take shape during this phase of the estimate.

Then he is ready to price the costs of performing each of the individual units of work that must be performed to complete the contract. Different bidders will break a job into different components, depending on how their cost keeping methods have been developed. They will try to organize their pricing to provide numbers that can be checked against actual records of production, cost, or man-hours on other work. The pricing must include anticipated costs for overhead, plant, fieldwork, and financing. This latter item of financing can now be determinated by scheduling the cash flow into and out of the project, based on the expenditures required to accomplish the work from the schedule, together with anticipated payments to be received from the owner, determined from payment provisions of the contract. This cost of providing finances for a particular project may vary widely between bidders because of such items as equipment required that are already owned (and idle) by the bidder and available plant facilities he may possess. Both the cost of ownership and the cost of money invested must be dealt with.

Then as a final step the bidder must evaluate the contingencies he faces. How confident is he that his estimate is realistic? Has the estimate been prepared from reliable experience records? Is it optimistic or pessimistic? What are the events that could disrupt his program? He must not only evaluate these risks, but he must assign dollar values to them.

The return on investment of the financial and people resources he requires can then be added to arrive at the price. While this is often referred to as profit, it usually includes a component of main office costs, such as interest on general borrowing and other corporate expenses not related specifically to any one project. As a matter of some interest, heavy construction companies have been able to average a return on sales after tax of approximately 4% in recent years. This translates to a return on capital of from 15 to 25% for them. Both are quite nominal from the standpoint of risk involved and reflect the competitiveness of the construction industry. In spite of inflation, construction has been a good buy for the owner and promises to remain so.

Illustrations of the detail typically involved in estimating major work are shown in figures 8-1 to 8-3.

Figure 8-1 illustrates a cost estimate for loading and hauling rock on a large dam in Venezuela.

Figure 8-2 is a summary sheet for a concrete item in an estimate for a large powerhouse.

Figure 8-3 is a sheet from the schedule used in planning for a powerhouse project.

START-UP

Aside from the preparation of a proper bid or proposal, there is nothing as important to the success of a construction project as its start-up. The detailed planning to supplement the general schedules made during the bid, the consideration and selection of the actual methods and equipment to be used from alternatives that existed during bid preparation, and the assignment of supervision to the project are all matters vital to the ultimate success of the project. Assumptions made must be validated, plant and equipment must be ordered, shipped, and either assembled or installed at the site.

These important functions are rarely handled solely by those assigned to be at the site, although they play a most important role. The on-site people must participate, since they must fully understand how everything is intended to function and they must make it all work to accomplish the required objectives. In short, the plan on which the estimate was based must be totally reviewed—not only by the estimators who prepared it, but also by all the talent available in the construction branch of the company. The more critical this analysis the better, for this is the period when necessary or desirable changes in strategy can be most economically achieved. It is too late to change the price, but it is the right time to look for economy.

Project: __Guri Dam & Powerhouse 2__ Cost Estimate—Item: __Tailrace & P.H. No. 2—Exc. Below 125__ Item No.: __1.7__

Bid Quantity: __5,260,000 m³__ Take-Off: __5,171,800 m³__ By: _____ Date: __9/1/76__ Sheet: __11/19__

Subitem: __Tailrace Rock__

Quantity: __3,113,800 m³__

From: __Upper & Lower Tailrace__

To: __Aggr. Plant__

Grades: __+3%__

Ave. Hauls: __2100 M__

Working Schedule: __9__ Hours/Shift

__2__ Shifts/Day __6__ Days/Week

Haul Cycle: Load/Haul Prod: Efficiency: __40__ Min/Hr

Haul Cycle:	Minutes			
Load	1.85	M	__40__ Min/Hr + _____ Min. Load Cycle = _____ Ld/Hr	
Accl. & Decl.	.50	M	X _____ pay CY/Load = __*820__ P.CY/Hr	
Haul Loaded	4.10	M	__50__ Min/Hr + __9.55__ Min. Haul Cycle = __5.24__ Ld/Hr	
Turn & Dump	.80	M	X __15.9__ pay CY/Load = __83.2__ P.CY/Unit Hr	
Return Empty	2.00	M	* Discounted for bottom work	
Spot & Wait	.30	M	USE: __820__ pay CY/Hr = _____ Haul Units	
Total Cycle	9.55	M		

Description	Unit	Quantity	Total cost Unit	Total cost Total	Materials Unit	Materials Total	Labor only Unit	Labor only Total	Equipment cost Unit	Equipment cost Total
Crew:										
1 Exc. Foreman	Hours	4,220	3.80	16,040			3.80	16,040		
1 Gradeset/Spot	Hours	3,800	2.40	9,120			2.40	9,120		
1-2 Spotters	Hours	4,180	1.80	7,520			1.80	7,520		
2-3 D8H Dozers—Rock	Hours	7,980	36.00	287,280			7.40	59,050	28.60	228,230
2 P&H 2100 Shovels	Hours	6,840	125.70	859,790			32.80	224,350	92.90	635,440
1 Lima 2400 Shovel	Hours	1,140	83.80	95,530			22.10	25,190	61.70	70,340
10-11 773 E.D. Trucks	Hours	38,370	48.20	1,849,430			7.60	291,610	40.60	1,557,820
1 No. 16 Blade	Hours	3,800	20.80	79,040			4.70	17,860	16.10	61,180
1 769B 8M H20 Truck	Hours	3,800	21.20	80,560			5.00	19,000	16.20	61,560
1 Pumpmaster	Hours	3,800	7.90	30,020			3.50	13,300	4.40	16,720
(Dump costs in agg. plant)	Hours						—		—	
Standby Operators	Hours	6,320	2.90	18,330			2.90	18,330		
Standby Teamsters	Hours	8,430	2.70	22,760			2.70	22,760		
				3,355,420				724,130		2,631,290
Unit Cost/M³	M³	3,113,800	1.078				0.233		0.845	

Figure 8-1 Guri Dam and Powerhouse 2 cost estimate.

Project: Bonneville 2nd Powerhouse   Bid Item Description: Concrete Powerhouse   Item Number:

Bid Quantity: 510,000 yd³   Takeoff: 487,645 yd³   Addendum: 2   By: Daniels   Date: Sheet:

DWG. REF. Description	Unit	Quantity	Man hours Unit/Man-hour	Extension	Labor Rate/Man-hour	Unit	Extension
Cost Summary							
Concrete Placing	Yard³	487,645		93,719		2.50	1,106,819
Miscellaneous	Yard³	487,645		299,326		6.50	3,171,694
Forms Ratio 6.96/yard³	Foot²	3,003,140		996,814		3.73	11,194,260
Total Direct Field Cost	Yard³	487,645		1,389,859	11.13	31.73	15,472,773
Add #3 changes		83		4,295	576.00		47,808
		487,728		1,394,154	11.13	31.82	15,520,581
Fixed Concrete Cost	Yard³	487,728				7.26	
Add Signal Man to Fixed Cost		487,728				1.00	
Contingency	Yard³	487,728				0.02	
Total Cost	Yard³	487,728		1,757,223	11.13	40.10	19,557,892
Forms S & S		3,003,140	3.43	875,052		3.27	9,826,857
Pre-Fab		753,993	6.19	121,762		1.81	1,367,403

Equipment		Expended Materials		Permanent Materials		Subcontract		Total		Remarks
Unit	Extension	Unit	Extension	Unit	Extension	Unit	Extension	Unit	Extension	
		0.34	20,193					2.84	1,127,012	
		0.53	256,114	0.03	13,722			7.06	3,441,530	
0.002	6,399	1.15	3,461,045			0.004	11,795	4.89	14,673,499	
0.01	6,399	7.66	3,737,352	0.03	13,722	0.02	11,795	39.45	19,242,041	
		130.22	10,790						58,598	
0.01	6,399	7.69	3,478,642	0.02	13,722	0.02	11,795	39.57	19,300,639	
2.77		1.45		9.06				20.54	10,017,933	
								1.00	487,728	
0.02		0.01		0.04				0.09	43,896	
2.80		9.15		9.10				61.30	29,850,196	
0.001	3,639	0.60	1,789,738		0	0.004	11,795	3.87	11,632,029	
0.003	2,760	2.22	1,671,307		0		0	4.03	3,041,470	

Figure 8–2 Bonneville second powerhouse.

191

C Activity	M	Activity Description	Orig	Calc	Rem	Early Start	Early Finish	Late Start	Late Finish	Free	Start	Finish
										FLCAT		
C*M*10	S	Commence cr ramp	0		0	02MAR81 / 270 M	02MAR81 / 270	02MAR81 / 270	02MAR81 / 279	0	0	0
*M*20	F	Contract work complete	0		0	28JUL82 / 628	28JUL82 / 628	02AUG82 / 631	02AUG82 / 631	3	3	3
C AAAAA		Notice to proceed	0		1	07FEB80 / 1 A	07FEB80 / 1 A	07FEB80 / 1 A	07FEB80 / 1	0	0	0
C ASCONA17		Constrct and pour close key 102+58 to 114+93	20		20	19MAR82 / 537	15APR82 / 556	19MAR82 / 537	15APR82 / 556	0	0	0
ASCONA18		Constrct and pour wkwy and bkpt 102+00 to 115+50	35		35	16APR82 / 557	04JUN82 / 591	21APR82 / 560	09JUN82 / 594	3	3	3
ASCONI16		Constrct and pour wkwy and bkpth ID to 115+50	20		20	27NOV81 / 460	24DEC81 / 479	01DEC81 / 462	29DEC81 / 481	2	2	2
ASCONW01		Constrct and pour appr span 117+45 to 116+85	32	36	25	01AUG80 / 124 A	22SEP80 / 159 A	01AUG80 / 124	10OCT80 / 173	0	0	14
ASCONW02		Constrct and pour app span 116+81 to 116+19	30		30	23SEP80 / 160	03NOV80 / 189	13OCT80 / 174	21NOV80 / 203	14	14	14

		Dur.	Dur.	Early/Late Start & Finish Dates				Day Numbers					TF	FF
ASCONW03	Constrct and pour app span 116+15 to 115+55	30	30	04NOV80	16DEC80	24NOV80	07JAN81	190	219	204	233		14	14
ASCONW04	Constrct and pour app span 115+445 to 114+97	25	25	17DEC80	22JAN81	08JAN81	11FEB81	220	244	234	258		14	14
ASCONW05	Constrct and pour close keys 117+47 to 115+50	18	18	23JAN81	18FEB81	12FEB81	10MAR81	245	262	259	276		14	14
ASCONW06	Constrct and pour app span 100+05 to 100+65	30	30	26MAR81	06MAY81	15APR81	27MAY81	288	317	302	331		14	14
ASCONW07	Constrct and pour app span 100+69 to 101+31	30	30	07MAY81	18JUN81	28MAY81	09JUL81	318	347	332	361		14	14
ASCONW08	Constrct and pour app span 101+35 to 101+95	30	30	19JUN81	31JUL81	10JUL81	20AUG81	348	377	362	391	12	14	14
ASCONW09	Constrct and pour app span 102+05 to 102+53	30	30	19AUG81	30SEP81	21AUG81	02OCT81	390	419	392	421		2	2
ASCONW10	Constrct and pour closure key 100+00 to 102+00	20	20	01OCT81	28OCT81	05OCT81	30OCT81	420	439	422	441		2	2
ASCONW11	Constrct and pour retaining wall No. 1	18	18	28MAY81	22JUN81	01JUN81	24JUN81	332	349	334	351		2	2

Figure 8-3 Project schedule report.

193

Starting the initial work at the site will normally require people in addition to those needed during the production phase of the work, such as specialists who can set up the shop and plant facilities, including payroll and accounting equipment, usually highly automated on today's jobs. Contacts must be made with sources of labor if they have not been made before the bid. Definite agreements with major suppliers and subcontractors must be prepared and signed. On remote sites special logistics and camp facilities may require expert guidance.

It is during this start-up period that initial relationships with the representatives of the engineer and owner are made by those who build the job. While it is highly desirable that these contacts be accomplished in a cooperative manner, it is essential that the parties to the contract understand what each expects of the other. Questionable language in the contract documents should be clarified. It is not rare to find the contractor planning to use methods the owner considers undesirable, nor is it rare to find an owner who has failed to recognize his responsibilities under the contract. It is far better to face these problems forthrightly at the beginning than to postpone them to a time when many dollars may be wasted because they have not been resolved. In many cases the owner may be less experienced than the contractor, and he will not welcome last-minute surprises that he feels are to his detriment. Facing the problems early will avoid the disputes and hard feelings later when their cost can be very high indeed.

PRODUCTION

We must recognize that all preliminary work in the field cannot be accomplished during the initial start-up period. Many operations do not start until much later on a major project. To this extent the start-up procedures may repeat during the job as the beginning of a new phase of operations draws near.

But given this exception, the major procedures during each construction phase become very similar to a manufacturing operation. This is not meant to imply that all the problems have been solved and life will now be a bed of roses. It only means that the problems change somewhat.

Especially important during the production phase of a job are the family of things known as "people relations." More than ever it is necessary to maintain good relations with the owner and his representatives, union officials, suppliers of equipment and materials, staff employees including supervisors, and the work force as individuals. The cooperation of all these groups is necessary to properly complete the work; adversary relationships can be very costly for all the parties involved and should not be tolerated where they can be avoided. A vast majority of people respond favorably to fair and friendly treatment, so whatever group you find yourself in will benefit from treating the others properly. Construction work is often difficult, but achieving significant objectives efficiently and on time can be a source of pride in the accomplishment for all concerned. We should see that it is.

In the interest of completeness, the overworked subject of "communication" should be mentioned. There is no substitute for keeping people informed of all the things that will affect them. No one really likes surprises unless they are very happy ones indeed. This is true whether the person being dealt with is the owner, contractor, or union business agent. Discussions in advance will avoid a great many confrontations.

One of the greatest deterrents to good communication is time. The busy project manager can allow himself to become so engrossed in the technical aspects of his work that he leaves no time for one of his most important functions: the management of people. Providing his staff and workmen with motivation and maintaining good relationships with his other business associates can yield great returns for his project as well as enhance his own enjoyment of his job.

Many books have been written on personnel activities, and we do not dwell further on them here, except for one special relationship. It is essential for a well-run job, from the viewpoint of either the owner of the contractor, that the project managers for both have a good working relationship and respect for each other's position. An unsatisfactory situation between them can ruin an otherwise excellent project. The project managers must deal with each other fairly, and the principals of either party should see that an adversary relationship is not allowed to exist which may interfere with completing the work efficiently and on schedule.

It is during the production period that the flaws in planning and design will surface, as well as the actual costs of doing the work. Performance is rarely what was anticipated; it is either better or worse. Deliveries of critical items change and require scheduling or construction program revisions. Unexpected conditions or events occur that could not have been foreseen. All these things must be reconciled as swiftly as possible to minimize their effect on both schedule and cost. Some will be the responsibility of the owner, and some, that of the contractor. The problems of the engineer generally fall on the shoulders of the owner from the standpoint of the contractor. Resolving these often troublesome matters will test the relationships between the managers as well as measure their abilities to react fairly. Prompt and appropriate resolution of such problems can do much to cement a good relationship or cause extensive disruption if the relationship is a poor one.

Good planning during the production period will result in pointing toward the completion phase. The measurement of quantities of work performed will be kept current and agreed to between the parties, and those quantities that have been completed will be resolved to a final number which requires no further analysis at the end of the job. Owners generally like to see completed portions of the work brought into condition for acceptance, although they are often reluctant to assume responsibility for maintaining them. Nonetheless, it is good policy for the contractor to bring these parts of the work he can complete to a condition suitable for final acceptance as quickly as possible. He will save time and costs on completion of the entire project by giving the owner an opportunity to make any changes he may desire in the final product while other work is still in progress. Contractors rarely make any significant profit on "extra work," and this is particularly true if there is no other major activity underway.

The repair and maintenance of equipment ususally assumes a major role during the production phase of a heavy construction project. Many new project managers with civil engineering backgrounds have discovered there is a large part of the industry they are ill prepared to administer. A good equipment superintendent and business manager can greatly facilitate the project manager's job in keeping equipment functioning, but they cannot do it all. Often it is necessary to modify field operations to accommodate inherent weaknesses in even the best of equipment. In spite of the skill and thoroughness of our equipment manufacturers, we frequently expect machines to do things they cannot do or cannot do over a sustained period. New models tend to be particularly vulnerable to fond expectations or may contain design problems not anticipated until submitted to the rigorous work they encounter on a large construction job.

It is only in rare cases that the basic concept on which a project is started can be changed during the production phase. Any such change usually requires such a large increase in capital investment that it is difficult to justify in all but the few cases where serious errors have been made in evaluating the work. Nonetheless, it is during this period that many small changes in procedures can make relatively great differences in productivity, schedule compliance, and cost efficiency. The project manager and his staff must be vigilant in evaluating their program constantly to achieve the maximum in production with a minimum input. It is usually a question of eliminating the limiting factor until it is no longer economical to do so.

COMPLETION AND DEMOBILIZATION

As a project nears completion, both of the parties to the contract assume roles that are slightly different from those that exist during the production phase. The owner, who has been primarily concerned with the quality and soundness of his structure, now becomes interested in the appearance as well. Specifications rarely cover all the things that the owner can now see as the contract nears completion. Most owners today will face this problem realistically and direct the additional work in a manner that provides payment to the contractor for work he could not have anticipated. There are some, however, who will try to read their desires into general provisions of the specifications.

Generally, it is prudent for the contractor who has been fairly treated through the progress of the work to accommodate the owner in every reasonable way. There are few places that he can spend small amounts of money and acquire so much goodwill. If good relations exist on the job, a little "horse trading" will usually occur between the respective managers that adds a spice to the completed program. Even if relations have been poor, and the contractor feels he has been treated badly, most successful builders will see that they leave a good-looking job behind them as well as a structurally sound one. Owners talk to other owners about contractors, and contractors talk to other contractors about owners. Each will gain with a reputation for fairness and carrying out their responsibilities.

The end of the job marks the time when all the disputes must be settled. Ideally, the disputes should be disposed of as they occur during the execution of the work. Usually there are a few unresolved matters, some significant and some minor, that remain to be negotiated at the end of the work. It is the time for the principals of the parties to meet; the jobsite people are too much involved and convinced of their respective positions to have much chance of reaching agreement. The time has arrived for compromise, unless the facts are very unusual. The representatives who meet to arrive at a solution must come prepared to reach a settlement. If both sides are in the mood to retreat a bit from previous "hard" positions, resolution of the problems can be achieved. Generally, lawyers contribute little to such a meeting. The lawyers' will come if one or both of the parties are so stubborn, or self-righteous, or foolish that they block an appropriate settlement. Both sides must realize that lawsuits today are a most time-consuming, expensive, and nonproductive activity; they can and should be avoided.

The contractor must face the problems relative to demobilizing and moving off the site. Equipment must be transferred to other work or disposed of. People must be reassigned. Overall planning in advance will greatly facilitate these operations. Availability dates for personnel and equipment should be established as soon as possible, and these dates should be incorporated in the planning for other projects underway and for jobs being bid. In today's world of expensive equipment and a shortage of experienced management, both must be used to the fullest.

CURRENT PROBLEMS IN CONSTRUCTION MANAGEMENT

There are a host of engineering and technical problems related to performing specific type projects. Each is unique and associated with a special set of circumstances; also, they are in the field in which both the contractor and the owner are most capable. Although these problems are interesting, we do not attempt to deal with them here. Rather, we will attempt to deal with more general problems of an industry-wide nature.

THE CONTRACTOR'S STAFF

Significant changes have occurred in our society during the late 1950s, the 1960, and the 1970s. They have had a marked effect on the heavy construction industry; probably more than on the smaller localized constructors and other business enterprises that tend to be stable regarding location and are not subject to such wide variations in work load. Senior management in most companies have their background in more conservative times when members of management personnel were happy to cast their lot with a company and stay with that organization through good times and bad. It is not easy for this group to think in terms of today's crop of middle managers, brought up in an era of heavy inflation, working wives, oppressive taxation and excessive regulations; and senior managers have had to learn to cope with these new conditions rapidly in recent years.

All the contractor has to offer an owner is the services of his people that combine to give him an ability to perform, on some contractual basis, work for that owner on an economical basis. It is imperative, then, that the contractor maintain a continuing capability to do this. Without a turnover of people, except by retirement, this would not be too great a problem. Unfortunately, that is not the nature of the industry today.

What are the problem areas? Moving is a basic characteristc of our industry: people must go where the work is located; the work cannot all be done at some designated location. This, along with the growing resistance to moving, financial problems that occur with increasing frequency because the wife or husband is also employed, and the further financing considerations of inflated housing costs, makes the questions related to moving people a very significant problem indeed. Intermittent and inconsistent wage policies mandated by the government, plus the economic limitations necessary to remain competitive, provide the constructor with many headaches, and the solutions do not lie in his past experience.

The obvious answer to these problems lies in the area of making continuing employment with your company attractive to the key employee or manager. It is necessary for the individual to have a good line of communication with his supervisors so his problems can be known and dealt with. And it is necessary for the company to have policies that, while having some degree of flexibility, are uniform enough to avoid internal jealousies and friction.

Virtually all major companies now have retirement plans and health plans in addition to the mandatory coverage by workmen's compensation and unemployment insurance. Some have profit sharing, stock plans, and life plus accident insurance coverage. All these are good, basic employee relations, but they do not provide for the real problem of the construction industry, which is moving from site to site.

Increasingly, this is being dealt with by programs tailored to the demands made on the employees; that is, these programs consider these questions: Will the move be permanent or temporary? Will the employee be in a remote location? Must the employee buy or sell a house or both? And what are the relative costs at the locations involved?

In the early phases of this "social revolution," many companies tried to combat the problem by the simple process of paying attrative salaries. This has not proved successful in the long run, because differences have become magnified and there are difficulties inherent in reducing basic salaries in a low-cost area. Presently, pay allowances, clearly identified as related to the specific area concerned, have met with more success. Some companies have gone so far as to provide or locate employment for the wife at the new location, although this problem provides further complexities when both members of the couple have career objectives.

The most successful programs for maintaining a suitable cadre of capable and progressive managers have accented attention to providing challenging and rewarding assignments to the persons contributing most and exhibiting the characteristics leading to further advancement. These are supplemented with periodic discussions with superiors, on a personal basis, in which the managers progress and areas where additional experience may be desirable are frankly dealt with. Development plans are worked out jointly, and the employee rightly feels he is an integral and vital part of the organization. He, in turn, is expected to maintain the same sort of liaison with his subordinates and to insure that discussions concerning their development or performance are provided in a frank and friendly atmosphere. During these discussions an ideal opportunity exists to discuss the objectives and growth of the company and to emphasize the potentials that exist for advancement in this overall program.

One final thought on this problem: you will not be able to retain everyone you want. It is impossible to be everything for everyone, so be sure your training and development programs are sufficient to supply replacements as well as to improve the capabilities of your managers and potential mangers.

Problem areas for the owner, engineer, and contractor are constantly changing; one day the problem areas are financing, bonding, and taxes; a week later they may be industrial relations or environmental problems; constantly present are the technical problems of doing work, estimating, mechanical maintenance, or production techniques. As in other industries, the work of the manager is primarily problem solving and motivating others. Most important, the project manager should realize that the greater the success he can achieve in delegating work which can be done by others, the more time he will have available to attend to the things that only he can do.

LABOR RELATIONS

There are continuing attempts to deal adequately with union labor by organizations of contractors. These activities are discussed elsewhere in the book. Here we just note that none has been totally satisfactory. And while the nonunion or open shop movement has grown in recent years, the success of this movement has been founded on abuses heaped on management by the power of the unions in collective barganing.

Many have predicted the demise of the unions, with the open shop being the funeral director. This is not a realistic expectation in view of union strength in many sections of the country and in many fields of construction, particularly the energy field. Also, it is not to the long-term benefit of the majority of workmen to be unorganized. Business managements are at a distinct disadvantage today in dealing with unions because of the structure of laws that have been created to curb their activities and favor union interests. A more desirable goal than the destruction of the union movement is to work for equality of management rights under the law so that collective bargaining can take place on an unbiased basis. Such equality would further the long-term welfare of both management and workers as well as enhance our society as a whole.

DISPUTES

The resolution of disputes under a contract can be a most frustrating experience for everyone concerned in the construction industry. As has been previously indicated, speedy and fair settlement of differences arising under a construction contract will contribute greatly to the industry. Contracts should contain language to facilitate such solutions. Resolution in a court of law may be eminently fair, but it is so slow and expensive in the world of today that special efforts are well warranted to avoid it.

Many contractors and owners place disputes at the top of their list of problems, but if good communication can be maintained between the parties involved, together with a willingness to understand, the obstacles to settlement can be readily eliminated.

SUMMARY

Most of major heavy contruction companies operating today had their origins in the first 40 years of the century. Joint ventures began to be formed near the end of this period, and they continue to be popular arrangements to share the risks and to undertake projects beyond the financial capabilities of any of the individual companies.

Current trends have indicated that many of the major companies are obtaining design capabilities in order to better approach the changing marketplace and to be able to compete with their foreign competitors outside the United States. Most of the major companies are also diversifying to include heavy industrial construction, nuclear power plants, and increasingly mine stripping and mining operations.

Heavy construction-oriented firms differ from some of their more industrially oriented associates in their efforts to preserve the fixed price philosophy for major portions of their work, with cost-reimbursable contracts generally in the minority. In this way, the efficiency of the industry is preserved, since marginal or inefficient contractors cannot compete with their more progressive and efficient competitors.

Fixed price contracts must face up to the proper allocation of risk between the owner and contractors. Risk is best borne by the party who has control. Unknowns should be shared generally, assigning insurable risks to the contractor with the owner assuming a major share of uninsurable risks.

Nonunion contractors continue to grow, and union contractors in strong open shop areas are beginning to win concessions. Labor unions continue to be protected by government legislation, and many open shop contractors find an advantage in operating union where it is to their advantage and nonunion as a normal pattern.

Heavy construction projects consist of four distinct phases:

- Bidding or proposal.
- Startups.
- Production construction operations.
- Completion and demobilization.

Modern complexities have introduced a number of constraints operating in each phase. The utilization of the computer and numerous new management methods have proved successful for some companies and less successful for others. The elimination of adversary relationships and disputes among contractor, owner, and engineer is becoming increasingly important if the complexities of governmental regulation, union restrictions, and communication difficulties are to be successfully managed for mutual benefit in the heavy construction environment of the future.

CHAPTER 9

MATERIAL AND
EQUIPMENT SUPPLIERS

Donald S. Barrie
B. F. Thompson
. ### Paul P. Burke
R. H. Verdier

Material and equipment suppliers and manufacturers and their distribution outlets may be responsible for 50% or more of the cost of a typical construction project. Many of the products are sold through distributor, jobbers, and retailers, although many major manufacturers also handle direct distribution. Broad classification may be itemized as follows:

Bulk material suppliers.
Building supply companies.
Construction equipment suppliers.
Machinery and process equipment suppliers.

AN OVERVIEW

This chapter sets forth the ideas of industry executives specializing in one of the major classifications. The following overview reviews some of the broad aspects of the relationships of the suppliers to the construction industry.

BULK MATERIAL SUPPLIERS

Bulk materials include cement, concrete, reinforcing steel, structural steel, lumber and plywood, roofing materials, piping materials, electrical materials, aluminum, lead, zinc, and other nonferrous metal products, and other commodities applicable to construction projects.

Bulk material manufacturers have been subject to divergent forces that include the following:

• Plant obsolescence, inflation, and modernization.
• Governmental restrictions and regulations.
• Foreign and domestic competition.

PLANT OBSOLESCENCE, INFLATION, AND MODERNIZATION

Heavy industries such as basic steel and cement have increasinly automated in an effort to achieve competitive advantage and improve productivity. Cement producers have alternated between dry and wet processes, increasingly larger kilns, and conversion to alternate fuels for both economy and process considerations. The steel mills, cement and gypsum producers, aluminum and other nonferrous metal producers, and other basic bulk commodity manufacturers have been one of the major sources of industrial construction in the post-World War II era. Today, we have some of the newest, most modern plants. Yet much of the existing capacity is nearing obsolescence and is used only in periods of peak demand.

Productivity in many plants has deteriorated as increasingly militant unions have received contracts or less formal concessions involving some form of management or output restriction. Increasing the operating and maintenance costs of obsolete plants has also contributed to increasing costs of production. Foreign competition, especially in steel and nonferrous metals, has both curtained domestic output and narrowed profit margins.

Most plants in the bulk material category operate on a continuous rather than a batch production cycle. Demand fluctuates widely with the building cycle, and prices have tended to rise sharply in periods of heavy demand and moderate during periods of oversupply. See Table 9-1 for the material price components of the construction cost index as published by *Engineering News-Record*.

TABLE 9–1. Cost Trend Index [a]

Year	Materials [b] component	Building cost index	Construction cost index
1979	1430	1900	3130
1969	310	710	1130
1959	280	550	810
1949	185	350	480

From *Engineering News-Record Indexes of Cost Trends* 1949–1979.
[a] For 20 cities. 1913 = 100.
[b] Includes steel, lumber, and cement.

Restrictions and Regulations

Restrictions and regulations in many areas of the country make it difficult or impossible to obtain approval for new plants. On the other hand pollution control, safety requirements, health standards, and other stringent measures require a continuous upgrading of old facilities in order to avoid heavy fines and even total shutdown. Plants that were originally located in unpopulous areas have become surrounded by the growing metropolitan areas and face the decision regarding continual upgrading of facilities to comply with increasingly stringent environmental regulations or to suspend operations.

Foreign and Domestic Competition

Foreign competition has been intense in several of the basic industries, especially steel and copper. In the steel industry the Japanese have been able to purchase high-grade metallurgical coal from British Columbia, ship it to Japan, import iron ore, and undersell West Coast producers in both Canada and the United States.

The industrialization in a number of undeveloped countries is producing several basic industrial plants to produce bulk materials. The effect of these plants becoming operative will intensify foreign competition in the basic materials area. Domestically, the large capital requirements are increasinly fostering takeover and merger as the smaller producers are absorbed by the large integrated companies better able to obtain the required financing.

BUILDING SUPPLY COMPANIES

Building supply companies are essentially distributors. They may range from the corner hardware store and the lumberyard that sell at retail but give "contractor discounts" to large lumber mills, plumbing supply houses, electrical supply houses, and other places that sell all types of material to large and small contractors as well as to other distribution and retail establishments.

The major suppliers will furnish quotations to contractors for substantial portions of the project on a lump sum or unit price basis. Like all other industry participants, the volume fluctuates, dependent on the business cycle as applied to the particular class of construction being supplied.

Sales methods, service facilities, credit policies, and collection requirements continue to require modification, dependent on the cost of money, the state of the business cycle in the particular construction branch, and other external factors affecting the independent businessman.

The building supply company is truly a corporate middleman and is often squeezed by the supplier as well as the customer. The collection of invoices and handling of customer complaints remain sensitive parts of the businessman's responsibilities. The customer is extremely upset when a critical shipment does not arrive on time. Yet in reality it was the manufacturer who defaulted, but the middleman must placate the customer or risk losing him.

Service and the ability to deliver emergency requirements are often the difference between success or failure in a business where individual ingenuity and efforts can result in sizable performance differences as well as in internal profitability.

CONSTRUCTION EQUIPMENT MANUFACTURE, SERVICE, AND SUPPLY

Construction and mining machinery advances over the postwar economy have been unprecedented. During many of the years heavy and highway bid price indexes actually decreased in the face of ever-rising marterial and labor costs. Huge draglines can strip overburden at a cost of a few cents per yard with 100-yard buckets. Off-highway equipment is exemplified from the 35-ton rear dumps of 20 years ago to a 250-ton hauler in use today. Tractors have evolved from a maximum of 144 HP in 1950 for a D-8 Caterpillar to 600 HP today for a D-10. Tunneling machines are at home in hard rock as well as in the softest ground. Huge cranes can lift anything anyone can figure out how to transport. Yet in the past decade the larger and theoretically more efficient equipment has not resulted in decreased or even level construction equipment operating costs, and cost escalation now has become a major problem as it has been in the rest of the construction industry.

Fuel shortages, vastly increased prices, and operator and mechanic training requirements are contributing to an unsettled condition that shear size and individual machine efficiency under optimum conditions cannot overcome. Quality control in the factory and preventative maintenance on the job has become a major problem for many manufacturers, with increasing demands being made on the vendor representative, the distributor, and the individuals who assemble, maintain, and operate the complex equipment. Government regulation limits the utility and applicability of the equipment and contributes to increased costs at both the manufacturer and user level. Yet construction equipment applications to the mining industry continue to offer a substantial opportunity for both equipment manufacturer and construction contractor. And mining equipment today is at an all-time high in every aspect of on-the-job safety as well as in production.

Increasingly, the entire construction industry is becoming more impersonal and less individually oriented. In the heavy growth years of the big dams, tunnels, and massive projects there was almost a fraternity of construction men who knew and respected one another and who took pride in developing recognized although unwritten performance standards that were generally enforced irrespective of a particular company or project.

Perhaps the viewpoint of the equipment salesmen and service representatives who travel from job to job dealing with many different managers, superintendents, and engineers creating opportunities, trying to solve problems, or simply promoting their products in an effort to satisfy both

the ultimate user and the home office bottom line will be helpful in reviewing both the construction and mining equipment service and supply industry and the changing personal relationships throughout the construction
industry.

MACHINERY AND PROCESS EQUIPMENT SUPPLIERS

Nothing sets the pace for a large industrial or heavy construction job like
the major operating and production equipment. Much of the project cannot even be designed until major equipment is selected, detail drawings
obtained, and supporting structures and utilities developed. Installation of
the major equipment is almost always on the critical path, whether it is the
turbine-generator for a hydroelectric power plant, the boiler for a fossil
plant, a continuous caster for a steel mill or a kiln for a cement plant.
Delivery and installation of the heating and cooling equipment similarly
often is critical to housing and commercial construction. Finally, the start-
up period and the checkout, testing, and solving of major and minor operational and equipment problems determine the actual commencement of
production.

Much of the equipment is relatively standard such as electric motors,
speed reducers, compressors, package boilers, and so on. Much of the equipment is tailor-made for a specific use such as the basic oxygen furnace or
continous caster in a steel mill or a vessel for a nuclear power plant.

Each major manufacturer is subject to all the productivity, quality control, regulating, warrantee, and marketing and sales problems faced by any
manufacturing business. Yet the cost to the ultimate customer in break-
downs, failures, or other malfunctions could be near catastrophic as evidenced by the Three Mile Island nuclear reactor failure in 1979.

It is difficult to find a single spokeman to survey the internal achievements, problems, and direction, since this segment of the industry is made
up of diverse manufacturers operating in different areas of expertise. However, the manufacturers share a common bond as major suppliers to the
construction industry. Many of the larger industrial equipment manufacturers are also in the construction equipment business and both share
many common problems. Perhaps the viewpoint of a project manager of a
design-constructor responsible for overall design, construction, and operational checkout for heavy industrial plants can best review the overall state
of the art in this key area.

BULK MATERIAL SUPPLIER*

The relationship between a contractor and supplier can be filled with frus-
tations, disagreements, excitement, and lasting friendships. It is rare when

*This section was prepared by B. F. Thompson, Manager, Sales and Marketing Administra-
tion, Kaiser Cement Corporation, Oakland, California.

everything goes right on a job where many different personalities are responsible for so many different phases of the entire construction process. The human factor cannot be forecast when the project is first conveiced, designed, bid, constructed, and, finally, accepted. Therefore, it is extremely important that each individual be familiar with those with whom he will be working during the construction period. Constant and on-time supply must be planned to such an extent that the contractor can rely on his suppliers without fail and turn his attention to the actual process of completing the work. Similarly, the supplier must be assured that his customer will be able to accept delivery at the time specified and to pay for such material according to the agreed terms.

SUPPLIER-CUSTOMER RELATIONSHIPS

How can all this become a reality? The supplier, whether a manufacturer or a middleman, should be able to expect service from those with whom he does business. Raw materials, labor, and trucking deliveries must be as scheduled to obtain the maximum effect from the effort involved. A customer is the most important individual with whom the supplier will deal during his lifetime as a businessman. Mutual respect between supplier and customer is absolutely necessary.

The establishment of bulk terminals on a permanent basis or the setting up of temporary facilities at or near a jobsite has proved successful in many instances. Permanent facilities are costly as in the case of bulk cement. They should be built on or adjacent to rail services or, where possible, located on water. With the proper equipment, water transport is the most economical. However, rail service has many advantages as it is not subject to tides, storms at sea, and all the ailments that have plagued sailors for centuries. Permanent facilities are often already established in or near the project and sometimes only need updating to be adequate to supply large dams, tunnels, or other projects where large quantities of cement are required on a steady basis. Some producing cement plants have been constructed at great expense to supply one large dam. Careful studies have been made to confirm that such outlay of funds can be recovered after job completion and that the region can absorb the added production capacity.

Temporary unloading facilities are usually located on rail spurs where a bazooka can be placed between the rails under a bottom dump hopper and load bulk cement into a bulk tanker. Today, the use of pneumatic rail cars can eliminate the use of such under the track equipment with less loss through spillage of the project.

The supplier or his representative must place the customer's requirements first in his detail of the project. Which method of delivery will insure the most reliable and constant source of supply? Is one less expensive than the other, and, if so, is it as reliable? If not, what is the cost differential? Many years ago we sold the cement on a southern California highway job to a contractor who was, and still is today, a close personal friend. We convinced this contractor to purchase some 60 acres of broccoli adjacent to a rail spur and erect bulk silos and rail unloading facilities. On receiving the first rail carload, he unloaded it into the bulk silos and then into a bulk truck. Each truck was then weighed, and the total weight of the cement trucks was compared to the amount shown on the bill of lading. The contractor was short 19 barrels of cement. The second, third, and fourth cars showed similar shortages. The contractor complained, and we checked the rail car weights, which were off, the cars having been repaired and altered since they were last short weighted. We went to the railroad and asked that each car to be used in this service be reweighted. We were refused. We then informed the railroad that the job would be supplied by trucks whose owners were willing to haul for the rail rate, and the entire job was delivered by truck. The customer got on-time delivery without loss, and the job was completed. We have since made peace with the railroad, and, over the years the railroad has, almost without exception, given us good service on deliveries.

Today, most of the bulk cement haulers are common carriers and will haul for any cement manufacturer who requires their services. Most carriers make every effort not to play favorites among those who request their services. This may apply, not only to jobsite plants and facilities, but also to ready-mix concrete dealers, concrete product manufacturers, and building material suppliers. Many large ready-mix dealers own their own fleet of bulk trucks and will, in addition to keeping up with their own needs, haul for those cement companies with whom they do business. *Backhauling*, the practice of hauling bulk cement from one plant to point A, and picking up another load coming back for point B, has enabled many truckers to earn a better return on their equipment. One such trucker, now out of business because of the death of the owner, was doing so much backhauling that he had difficulty determining which load of cement was to go where. This trucker's saving genius lay in the man who kept track of the loads and who was seldom wrong. Hopefully, the owner paid him what he was worth.

Some cement companies do supply such equipment at a fair cost to the contractor when available. A monthly rented fee, plus move-in and move-out costs, allows the cement supplier a reasonable return on his investment. On a large and fast paving job, our company told the contractor he had insufficient storage for the amount of cement required on an hourly basis. We told the contractor that we had no equipment available and would not be able to supply any. The contractor decided to go with what he had. The bulk pressurized silo into which the pneumatic trucks discharged also supplied the premix plant that fed two eight-yard mixer drums. Hourly cement requirements were heavy. Additionally, two six-inch pipes were hung from the top of the silo, one on each side, with four-inch Y's at the bottom so the bulk trucks could unload both front and rear tanks at the same time.

At 13 to 14 psi for discharge the pressure on the bulk silo was tremendous. As we were watching the operation on the fourth day and the contractor was commenting on how little we knew about equipment, the dust collection system on top of the silo tore loose from its welds. It headed toward the heavens like a rocket launching an astronaut and trailing cement in a cloud. The unloading bulk trucks, freed from the back pressure, really blew cement. Fortunately, the drivers were able to fight their way through the dust and shut off the engines. Next day, an additional storage silo arrived on the jobsite, and the task of cleaning up four acres of cement was started.

CREDIT AND MARKETING RELATIONSHIPS

Credit can be either a very effective tool or a very traumatic nightmare. This function usually reports to the controller or chief financial officer. However, a more innovative approach has been to make the credit manager reportable to the local sales manager. This establishes informational flow between sales and credit, allowing both managers to know the total market better. A customer with temporary problems can be assisted if necessary according to the rules established by both managers. Final decision rests with the sales manger. This friendly, workable solution allows both to spot trouble before it occurs.

To some, the word *marketing* can cover everything from advertising to delivery. We have used marketing as a support function to the sales department handling rates, relations with carriers, and job forecasting analyses. Sales, marketing, and credit are under one person, a senior vice president with knowledge of all three operations. Because of the closeness of control, each department can complement the other in daily and long-term business. The marketing staff also works with the customers and carriers to assist the smooth on-time delivery required. Of course, sales credit and marketing must adjust to varying market conditions from oversupply when price cutting is rampant to allocation when every producer could sell more than he can deliver.

The supplier's function is to assist his customer to the best of his ability. A good product at a fair price is foremost but not the whole story. The supplier should keep the customer appraised of projected work in the customer's marketing area, assist him in finding needed equipment, and advise him of market conditions. The supplier's main thrust is toward seeing that the customer prospers, because as one does, so does the other. In turn, the customer should keep his supplier up to date on his requirements and needs. Suggestions should be exchanged and welcomed. The supplier and customer help one another through fairness and mutual respect that, in turn, builds lifelong friendships. Over the years, we have worked with and known many fine men, watching their companies grow and often their sons grow with them. Today, it is a great pleasure to visit those who are left and talk about former times and the good old friends who are no longer with us. We have achieved mutual respect to the benefit of both parties.

GOVERNMENT REGULATION

Today, the construction industry and its suppliers are devoting a large part of their valuable time to keeping track of conflicting rules and regulations formulated by people who have never built a dam, powerhouse, tunnel, highway, or a skyscraper. Because of the fear of governmental accusation of price fixing, *associations* is a bad word. You cannot join with others in your field to promote your product or service without the risk of violating a rule or regulation or attracting the attention of the lawyers. You may pour many thousands of dollars into an organization that promotes the "widget" method of placing concrete or erecting steel but cannot attend meetings because competitor personnel will be present. America was built on the spirit of competition and enterprise where each person did his best in order to survive in his chosen field. Today, 3 or 10 or 50 men who use the widget method cannot join together and tell the world how good a method it is without being accused or price fixing or collusion. Undoubtedly, a few misguided individuals have and will try to turn such an organization to their advantages, but today's businessman is smart enough to eliminate these types from his organization.

Abondonment of self-regulation and industry improvement with resulting governmental interference, is clearly counter-productive. Construction contractors and their suppliers are in a fascinating business. In my opinion, no other industry in the world today offers the potential satisfaction and rewards inherent in construction. We, the contractors and suppliers, must treat one another with mutual respect, must strive for complete integrity in our dealings with ourselves and our clients, and must find a way to adhere religiously to the letter and spirit of the law.

BUILDING SUPPLY COMPANIES

Building supply companies are middlemen in the true sense of the word. They produce nothing, yet they are a vital link in the overall building process.

Some building supply companies are extremely sales oriented. An example might be an aggressive hardware company specializing in small tools, rubber goods, and consumable supplies applicable to the heavy construction industry. Such a company might have fully equipped vans manned by driver salesmen touring heavy construction jobs throughout their area. Convenience of delivering and personal knowledge and friendship with their customers must be aggressively maintained if they are to prosper.

Other distributors may have both outside salesmen who endeavor to cultivate favored clients and an aggressive bidding department or division that will quote lump sum for all the specified requirements for a particular fixed price bid job.

Multipurpose Firms

Several building supply companies operate as multipurpose firms, handling just about every item necessary for home building and light commercial work. These companies often operate at both the retail and wholesale level, dealing with major requirements for small contractors and emergency requirements from larger contractors who may purchase basic need supplies from the manufacturer or specialty distributor. Such firms often have sizable retail stores as well as a commercial department that will give quotations to contractors on residential and commercial work. Convenience and willingness to handle the details necessary to provide satisfaction often results in substantial amounts of business at premium prices compared to lower prices for mass purchases with little or no service available from other firms. A similar example is the local independent hardware store that handles similar items geared to the homeowner maintenance and addition market.

Major Manufacturers

Major manufacturers such as General Electric, Westinghouse, and other similar major companies maintain building supply divisions that deal directly with individual contractors in a manner similar to the building supply companies. Some major manufacturers are represented by dealers for certain aspects of the business, yet retain the right to handle national customers or foreign sales directly.

Specialty Supply Firms

Most basic electrical and piping materials for all types of construction contractors are obtained through supply firms specializing in electrical and/or piping materials. Such firms must maintain a large stock of items for their wholesale trade to smaller contractors and for emergency requirements for larger firms. Yet the companies, commercial or industrial departments may be the major business undertanding through supplying price quotations for major projects for delivery directly from the manufacturers.

Similarly, firms specializing in standard products such as steel or pipe sections, specialty hardware, or other building components may act as manufacturer representatives on major projects and as wholesalers to hardware stores and regional building supply companies as well.

Equipment Distributors

Very much allied to the building supply companies are the construction equipment dealers and distributors. The Gardner-Denver Company, for example, basically relies on local dealers to sell and distribute its products in a manner similar to Ford, General Motors, and the other automobile companies. The Caterpillar Tractor Company, possibly the largest and certainly one of the most successful equipment manufacturers in the world, relies on a network of dealers to distribute products to the local market. In overseas and worldwide business this company has worked out a program for sharing commissions with local dealers that has produced excellent results.

Other major manufacturers may set up a network of area distributors as a division of the overall company who will be in competition with dealers or distributors associated with major competitors.

Future Consideration

Service continues to be a major factor in the choice of building supply companies. Those companies of any size that can continue to produce premium service, even at a premium price, will probably prove most successful in the future environment of complexity that will continue to depend on the building distributors to handle emergency requirements and to supply reasonable deliveries from stock for sizable quantities of construction materials.

CONSTRUCTION EQUIPMENT MANUFACTURE, SERVICE, AND SUPPLY*

The past 30 years have seen many vast changes in the manufacturing and equipment service supply business. Many of these changes were positive steps that improved efficiency, but there have been many negative aspects as well which will need correction if our industry is to prosper.

CHANGE IN THE CONSTRUCTION INDUSTRY

Initially, the mining and construction industries were run by the powerful personal giants such as Steve Bechtel, Henry Kaiser, Harry Morrison, Peter Kiewit, Lou Perini, Guy F. Atkinson, Sterton Oman, Tom Walsh, Bill Brewster, and many, many others. When these men bid a job and arranged for the equipment and services, it was done with a personal knowledge of the ability of their people. If Tom Walsh and Jack McDonald of the Walsh Construction company bid a tunnel, they would sit with Clyde Turner, or Lester Huntington, evaluate the ground conditions, and ask of these men, "How many feet of progress can you give me in a day?" Before answering they calculated alternate methods very carefully with the engineers working for the company; yet the final answer was also based on personal experience and knowledge, because they knew that if they told Jack McDonald

---

*This section was prepared by Paul Burke, General Manager, National Accounts, Ingersoll Rand Company, San Leandro, California.

and Tom Walsh they could achieve 43 feet a day, they were going to have to do this not only because it was their responsibility, but also because they were actually going to run the job.

The same situation existed if Harry Morrison were to approach Mike Kennedy, Dugan Graham, or Swede Larson about a project, whether the job involved open cut work or tunneling. A like situation would exist with Steve Bechtel, Henry Kaiser, and the other giants who ran their corporations. When these men selected the equipment and the service supplied for their projects, it was often done on the basis of personally knowing the men who headed the dependable service equipment distributor organizations. Such men will include Eddie Mahoney in New York City, Tom Brown on the East Coast, George Philpott on the West Coast, and many, many other great equipment and supply people. Every one of these men who were accepted as being proficient in manufacturing, service, and sales would think nothing of driving 200 to 300 miles in the middle of the night to bring an essential part to a job to keep it going. Men such as Lou Perini kept up with every progressive new idea and innovative design in the broad construction industry and were constantly young in their approach throughout their very successful careers.

Everyone must realize that the construction and mining industries went into a tremendous acceleration in the 1950s. This rapid growth of corporations such as Bechtel, Morrison-Knudsen, Perini Corporation, Atkinson, Peter Kiewit, and others made it impossible for the founder giants to direct many details personally as had been their previous method of operation. Progress required the delegation of these responsibilities that in turn brought about changed methods of purchasing equipment, evaluating suppliers, and managing the project. From the standpoint of the manufacturer of heavy equipment in the 1930s, 1940s and 1950s, almost all the men who were out in the field selling heavy construction and mining equipment knew how to run the rigs they were selling and could take them apart and fix them. But the rapid growth in the manufacturing corporations brought about radical changes in terms of this. Previously, the president of a manufacturing concern knew all his customers on a personal basis as well as every one of the men working for him. If a particular piece of equipment had to be fixed, he personally knew who the best man was to send to that project; but with the rapid growth of the companies, this became an impossible task, and again the responsibilities were required to be delegated.

In the early 1960s the critical path philosophy was brought into the mining and construction field. A group of very, very smart fellows would get together and draw up a CPM schedule utilizing someone elses computer program. Then they would estimate a job on the results they got. If you were pouring concrete, it was possible to do such and such, which results in so much concrete poured. If you were driving tunnel, you could drill so many holes with a given drill, shoot the rock, muck it, and get so much progress per day. In all phases of heavy construction and a great deal of mining, a lot of people jumped on the bandwagon. The one area that was often forgotten was the human element. It always will take tough, dedicated managers to develop major mines, dams, pump storage, nuclear power plants, pipelines, industrial plants, cities, or other new major construction ventures. These individuals must be competent in all fields if only to be able to know when to replace the optimum output of the CPM with personal judgment, but more important they must continue to identify & train dedicated knowledgeable people as did the powerful personal industry giants.

STATE OF THE ART IN CONSTRUCTION AND MINING EQUIPMENT

There have been a great many positive developments made in the manufacturing of mining and construction equipment, and the manufacturing corporations should be complimented on their research and development in this area. Significant safety improvements include whisperized compressors that reduce the decibel factor to a very safe level, the muffling of sinker drills and jack hammers, back-up warning horns on heavy rolling equipment, and the development of the new hydraulic drills which practically eliminate condensation smog in the headings and reduces the noise level. Safety requirements on the part of the government and the unions are a constant challenge to these corporations, and these corporations are to be commended for their outstanding record.

Significant advances in productivity have been achieved by the new tunnel boring machines that are now capable of handling most classifications of uniform rock, the Japanese development of soft ground tunneling techniques using the slurry face technique, and the numerous developments in drill bits, steel, and mining equipment originating in Sweden.

Cranes, draglines, drills, shovels and ancillary tractors, trucks, loaders, and scrapers have achieved and continue to achieve increased capacity and performance in this traditional area of improved productivity through continuing equipment improvement.

Servicing and maintenance advances include sealed bearings, interchangeable component assemblies to permit rapid repair of major problems, and the use of the computer to both schedule preventative maintenance and to fully identify individual piece and total fleet repair and maintenance costs over the service lifetime.

INDUSTRY PROBLEMS AND SOLUTIONS

This section reviews some of the problems that have developed and some of the directions in which major manufacturers of mining and construction equipment seem to be headed. As late as 1960 many of the major manufacturing companies and their executives had a direct relationship with the customers who ultimately used the products they manufactured. In many situations the general superintendent, project manager, or mine manager would call the chairman of the board, president, or executive vice president at their homes when they had a particular problem. There was a personal relationship and the fur would fly if a complaint on product quality or service was forthcoming. The executives of these major manufacturing companies would take immediate action to satisfy the needs of the customer, a major mining company, or a major construction company. All these manufacturers had numerous men in the field who could troubleshoot, recondition, and run the equipment that was being sold.

In the postwar construction expansion there has been a deterioration affecting almost all manufacturers in the mining and construction field. Reasons for this deterioration are as discussed next.

Changes due to Growth

Essentially, all the major manufacturers have grown 4 to 10 times in their gross sales. This brought about the need to go public for additional financing and led to public trading on the major stock exchanges. This tremendous growth rate required a restructuring of these corporations for the most part. The corporations began setting up profit centers called "divisions." These divisions have a tremendous amount of autonomy. In a sense they are self-contained manufacturing companies within an existing structure, reporting to the top executives. The principals in charge of these major mining and construction manufacturing corporations have been put into a position where they are constantly required to show an increase in profit and in growth every year to satisfy prevailing Wall Street investment judgments. This requirement to be heroes every year has resulted in many choices between the current short-term performance demands and the long-term good of the company and the industry. Many corporations have been required to minimize their research and development because funds normally allotted to this are not forthcoming as a result of the pressure for earnings performance.

This pressure for constant growth in both volume and profit is transferred from the principal executives to the profit centers. These profit centers are pressured to do everything prossible to make sure that the projected growth targets are met or surpassed. This approach can result in marginal decisions on manufacturing product consistency and quality control. The manufacturers in the mining and construction industry prior to the postwar construction expansion had a reputation for quality and total product integrity throughout the world. This reputation is deteriorating in a manner similar to our dollar.

Recommendations for the Future

The following recommendations for manufacturers and contractors in the mining and construction field are submitted to help identify some of the individual industry problems and to help in developing possible solutions:

1. Every four to five years the top executives of any given corporation should go before the stockholders at their annual meeting as well as to the Wall Street analysts and have the guts to say to them: "Ladies and gentlemen, we are not projecting any large increase in profits this next fiscal year. We intent to allot a large amount of our profit to research and development and to the modernization of plant machinery that will result in increased growth and profit for the ensuing four to five years. We intended to continue this policy so that your corporation will be one that will be a leader in new design techniques, product integrity, and quality."

2. Major mining and construction equipment manufacturing corporations today are primarily run by people who have backgrounds in business administration, financial management, and marketing and sales. There is a great need to bring into top management people who have the expertise in plant management as well as an understanding of the requirements of the ultimate user.

3. There is a great need to train more young people to represent these manufacturers who actually know how to run the equipment that is being manufactured and who have the ability to fix it, while helping to install personal pride of performance on the part of the user. This is becoming increasingly more important because of our changing labor market, evidenced in a lack of desire; near security from the cradle to the grave given by many operating companies, along with the unions; and the elimination of the personal relationships that fostered individual operator pride in machine production and maintenance. If the manufacturer will lead the way with dedicated, knowledgeable, quality people in the field, the mechanics, equipment operators, and supervisors in the field cannot help but benefit by this example.

4. Pricing and the cost of products produced by the construction and mining companies grow primarily along the lines of the increases granted as a result of labor contract negotiations between construction corporations, mining corporations, and the representative unions. Development of our internal resources and the preservation of the American way of life may well depend on our ability to economically face foreign competition and to develop increasingly marginal energy and metal sources and reserves. The industry negotiators were often in a difficult position when they negotiated contracts with union representatives. The union negotiators are highly skilled full-time professionals, and negotiation is their primary job. However, the industry negotiators constantly change the negotiating groups with the result that there is often no continuity, accompanied by lack of experience and long-range planning. The net result is that the unions have often gained more than expected from healthy collective bargaining. Unions will get everything that the contractors will give them. It would help our industry if these and other industry-bargaining negotiations would go to the same professional procedure that unions use. Of course, open shop and nonunion contractors are increasingly gaining a larger share of major

projects, and this continual growth is moderating union demands and strengthening contractor negotiations in many areas.

5. The equipment profit centers that are in a sense separate factories and separate businesses within an existing structure must be made to realize that if they turn out a product that is substandard because of pressure from headquarters, meeting a delivery date, or for whatever reason they must be accountable for the bottom line results. When this product gets into the field and fails because of the lack of quality control in the profit center, the ensuing costs will be back-charged to the profit center. These costs must not be put aside, hidden, or absorbed by some field sales organization.

6. If all of us—equipment operator, mechanic, superintendent, contractor, and equipment manufacture—will sit down and make up our minds to get back to increasing productivity through operational improvements and pride of performance we could go a long way to helping ourselves and our neighbors. If the various principals in mining and construction corporations will check into it, they will find that their European and Japanese competitors have tremendous research and development programs which are resulting in a widening gap when it comes to increasing productivity through innovative new equipment and method. Perhaps our universities could help if funding can be obtained from industry.

7. At the present time in Washington, D. C., we suffer from a great deal of organized mediocrity and a lack of purpose on the part of our representatives, whether they are Democrat or Republican. Nobody seems to care about the United States as a whole entity. Everybody is in there with pressure groups and lobbyists to get their piece of the pie and do absolutely nothing about dealing with the current problems. Each individual problem begets many additional governmental regulations that prove more burdensome than the problem they were designed to solve. Our trade balance deficit due to deteriorating domestic productivity is becoming outrageous. Our dollar is shrinking in value everyday. Since we all talk a lot about free enterprise and how great it is compared to a totalitarian system, it now becomes mandatory that the manufacturing companies in the construction and mining business must lead the way and show government how to do the job properly. One small gesture would be a start in the right direction. With the exception of get-your-hands-dirty type service personnel who need pickup trucks to do their jobs, all sales representatives and managers should immediately be put into automobiles that average in city and country driving 25 or more miles on a gallon, and we should adopt all other energy-saving methods in our business and personal lives.

8. The various manufacturers through a group organization should go down to Washington D. C., sit down with the congressmen, point out to them in a very positive way the fact that the European governments and Japanese governments subsidize major overseas projects for the development of mines, the building of dams, roads, and powerhouses. Not only does the American government not help in any way, but also the regulators

are putting through taxes that make it economically impossible for an American engineer or construction or mining worker to go overseas. We have to turn this around now. We have to start telling our government how it should be done, and we have to start taking the lead.

OVERALL FUTURE OBJECTIVES AND GOALS

The American manufacturer in the construction and mining business should take a very serious look at his objectives and goals. He has to get back to realizing that the most important person or corporation or company is the user of the product he manufactures. A lack of progressive product planning, research and development, and field service and subquality products will continue to deteriorate the position of the American manufacturer throughout the world. The American manufacturer's highest priority should be to restructure organizational thinking from the chairman of the board down to the man who works a lathe or reconditions a truck, drill, or tractor in the field. This rededication should provide honest quality through service and product integrity. A restoration of the personal relationships so important to the early industry growth could help to restore overall performance through individual pride in the construction industry and the equipment manufacturing industry and could serve as a model for effective productivity gains through individual involvement for other industries as well.

MACHINERY AND PROCESS EQUIPMENT SUPPLIERS*

One of the major reasons for the prosperity of the United States and the industrial nations of the world has been the ability of the machinery and equipment suppliers to improve their products to enable operating cost improvement and more efficient operation at the manufacturing level. The invention and continued improvement of the basic oxygen furnace in the steel industry, the improvements in the operating process in the cement industry, the increasingly efficient electrolytic reduction cells in the aluminum industry, and other major breakthroughs have created a demand for production equipment of a size and sophistication never before encountered.

In general, the equipment suppliers have been very successful and innovative supplying this demand. However, as owners began to overlap the engineering, designing, procurement, construction, and checkout of project components, coordination problems between the manufacturer and the design engineer and the construction contractor and the owner began to adversely affect costs and schedules on many projects.

*This section was prepared by R. H. Verdier, Project Manager, Kaiser Engineers, Oakland, California.

SUPPLIERS' IMPACT ON CONSTRUCTION

A review of the impact of the major equipment suppliers' role throughout a construction project will show the large number of critical interfaces requiring communication and exchange of information between all entities of a project that are necessary if all parties are to work toward the achieverment of the completed plant in an organized and efficient manner.

ENGINEERING. Construction takes place from the ground up, so the contractors first need engineering for all the building and equipment foundations, embedded utilities, and so on. Most of this engineering is predicated on the process equipment design, so the mechanical equipment supplier must very early in the project provide the necessary design criteria to allow others to produce this information.

Soon after, the construction forces need engineering on the utilities such as power, water, compressed air, industrial gases, and so on. The design of the process equipment also dictates these criteria, so again the equipment suppliers are first links in the chain.

Most construction problems in this area center around lateness of information in the field and changes in the same that run up construction costs by causing delays, rework, or efficiency losses. Conventional commercial arrangements often prevent the owner or contractor from recovering fully the costs involved, even though the root cause was untimeliness or errors on the part of the equipment suppliers.

COORDINATION OF DESIGN INFORMATION BETWEEN SUPPLIERS. In many cases equipment for a project is furnished by several different suppliers. All this equipment must fit together from mechanical, electrical, and instrumentation standpoints so that it functions as a system. It is the equipment supplier's responsibility to see that all pertinent interface information is engineered and available to those with whom his equipment interconnects. For example, a supplier of mechanical equipment supplies all information needed to supply the proper drive motors and controls for the machinery. This type of exchange of information is essential if a viable system is to be the result. Failure to carry out this basic responsibility will result in serious construction problems when equipment is mismatched or otherwise incompatible. Inevitably, construction costs go up, the schedule slips, and owners are unhappy when the system they thought they bought does not fit or function properly.

To successfully combat this problem it is common to (1) hire an experienced engineering firm to coordinate suppliers or (2) lump the supply of several types of equipment in a single package furnished by one prime supplier with overall responsibility. Or (3) an owner, if he has sufficient experienced engineering manpower, may perform his own coordination.

How well this design coordination between suppliers is done directly influences construction costs and schedule because it is far cheaper and faster to correct problems on paper in the engineering stage than it is to do the same thing physically in the field. Equipment suppliers, whose natural interest centers around producing and selling their own equipment, must be made aware of, and accountable for, problems of incompatibility of their gear with equipment furnished by others.

INTERNAL COORDINATION. The physical size and organizational complexity of many major equipment suppliers has multiplied over the years. Many of these companies rank among the very largest in this country. Concomitant with this growth these suppliers have had to internally separate various groups to the point where the groups sometimes function as a separate company within the parent organization. This often results in serious internal communication problems and a breakdown in overall responsibility for the supply of properly engineered and manufactured equipment delivered on time to the construction site.

On one recent large project the regional marketing department of a major supplier successfully won an order for the equipment and made promises for price and delivery. Some months later it was discovered that engineering was lagging because the supplier's engineering department was overloaded and had reshuffled design personnel. The equipment designers did not coordinate with the other interfacing equipment suppliers, and the failure to do so resulted in numerous engineering changes and corrections. When engineering was sufficiently complete, internal manufacturing orders were entered, but the manufacturing group had no knowledge of the delivery promises made by their personnel and scheduled the work in the shops to be done to suit the most efficient production schedule. This was discovered when the engineering firm the owner had retained went into the supplier's plant to find out what was holding up deliveries. It was also discovered that no other group in the company had the authority to make delivery promises, including the sales organization. The matter was finally taken by the purchaser's management to the supplier's executive offices in New York before any action was taken. The net result was that the equipment was late, was not engineered to be compatible with other equipment, and required numerous field changes. The owner's construction costs went up, and the job was delayed on account of these problems caused by the supplier. Relatedly, the supplier's independent field service group at the construction site refused to engineer some corrective changes to the equipment without being paid for the work, and the owner was forced to try to recoup these costs later from the supplier under threat of lawsuit. Unfortunately, problems such as these are not unique and occur more frequently in recent years.

QUALITY AND WARRANTIES. Any purchaser of major process equipment has a reasonable expectation that the supplier will furnish equipment that is properly designed and constructed and which will function satisfactorily. Most reputable manufacturers are willing to warrant the quality and function of their equipment and do so.

Equipment suppliers, however, are not immune to the same economic, governmental, and social pressures that bear on all businesses (including construction contractors), and the result sometimes is equipment of poor design or shoddy manufacture. When equipment of poor quality or with defects that affect its function are delivered, the problems start for the constructor. Sometimes the defects are obvious and can be easily remedied. Other times the defects are latent and are not discovered until the equipment is already installed. In almost all cases some degree of unanticipated rework in the field is required that impacts heavily on the job costs and schedule.

These problems can and should be reduced to a minimum by doing as much factory testing and quality inspection at the supplier's plant as possible. Sadly, this is frequently not the case. For example, the furnishing of a great deal of instrumentation for one recent project resulted in a 35% failure rate in the field of what was supposed to be factory-tested equipment supplied by a prominent manufacturer of this type of standard instrumentation equipment. The facility came on line four months late, and both the contractors and owners suffered the consequences.

As a final caveat, most equipment warranties are very limited, since suppliers have lawyers who review them. Many warranties, for example, cover material replacement only. The fact that it took 10 days and $2000 worth of craft construction labor to change out a $10 defective part replaced by the supplier does not change the legal obligation of the supplier to be responsible for material only. The same is also often true of poor engineering: too often the owner and contractors suffer, since it is very difficult to recover costs for consequential damages.

PREASSEMBLY OF EQUIPMENT. Quality in terms of construction impact is the degree to which equipment suppliers preassemble equipment. There is obviously merit from the construction viewpoint in doing as much shop assembly as possible: it reduces the amount of craft labor, problems uncovered and remedied earlier and cheaper, sometimes simplifies handling, and may reduce the possibility of damage to sensitive parts at the construction site. The amount of shop assembly done varies greatly, depending on the type of equipment involved and the practice of the supplier. It costs the supplier time and money to shop assemble equipment, and it is very wise to stipulate at the time of purchase what equipment will arrive at the site in one factory-assembled package so there are no rude surprises in the field.

DELIVERY OF EQUIPMENT. Every project has an optimum construction sequence. The suppliers of equipment should endeavor to ship equipment as close to this sequence as possible, preferably in advance of when it is needed by the contractor in the field.

As experienced construction men will testify, however, it most often happens that the least critical equipment will arrive at the site first and the most critical last.

The solution to this problem is a joint responsibility of the contractor and project engineer. In the very early stages of the program, the contractor or project engineer should identify the major equipment and the best sequence of installation. The tools required for this task include the development of an equipment list and either a CPM schedule or a detailed bar chart schedule. Once this is done it is vital that the information be communicated to the equipment suppliers. The best time to do this is early in the equipment design stages, since often the manufacture and shipment of equipment follows in the order of the engineering. It is also necessary to update and monitor this information, since field conditions sometimes change and the suppliers often have a tendency to engineer and manufacture "easy" parts first. These natural deviations from the ideal are often rooted in internal supplier management edicts to design and manufacture equipment in a way that maximizes early progress payments and allows the manufacturing group to operate in the most cost efficient manner. While these may be worthy goals from the suppliers' vantage point, they can complicate construction and ultimately end up costing the owner and contractors far more in time and dollars than the supplier saved.

The best way to avoid these problems is to set up an understanding of the order of the work at the time the purchase order for the equipment is placed. From there on it becomes a problem of constant communication and coordination until all equipment is at the site.

SHIPPING. The shipment of equipment from the manufacturing plant to the site is one of the most neglected links in the chain of events leading to successful completion of a facility. The responsibility may be handled by the supplier, owner, or a third party, but whoever directs shipping can play a key role. In the case of major capital process equipment most shipment is by rail or truck. Air freight is sometimes used where the added cost can be justified. Rail is generally slow, but relatively cheap, and heavy parts and assemblies can be handled. Trucking is somewhat more expensive and weight limited but often faster, and there is less chance for damage.

While shipping costs are significant, they often are less than the cost of a delay in construction caused by not having parts when needed at the site. Managers of a project should not fear using different means of transportation to even out the flow of equipment to the field.

It is also important to consider shipping problems early in a project. Special loads should be carefully planned in advance to minimize delays later in construction. On a recent large steel mill project it was discovered in the equipment design stage that the supplier did not have the capability of manufacturing or handling some very large machine parts in his shop, nor could the load be transported to the site several thousand miles away without great difficulty, expense, and delay. The problem was solved jointly between the supplier, owner, and managing engineering firm by arranging for the machinery to be fabricated at another supplier's plant much nearer to the construction site. This had the added advantage of permitting the construction contractor to work closely with the manufacturing plant to complement each other's work and schedule. The final shipment of the parts was by truck, rail, and barge, each means of transportation carefully planned and coordinated to suit conditions and handling at the construction site.

SPECIAL INSTALLATION REQUIREMENTS. In many process industries technology is advancing at an unprecedented rate, resulting in new types of equipment being installed. A prime example is the introduction of sophisticated electronic equipment in heavy industrial facilities such as steel, mining, and cement plants that heretofore used mainly hardwired, heavy duty electrical gear for process control and instrumentation. This places new demands on constructors' abilities to handle, install, and check out unfamiliar equipment. It is a rare contractor who has the luxury of being able to train his people to handle technologically new process equipment prior to a job, so most learning is done during actual construction.

When an equipment supplier engineers new types of components into a process system he has a responsibility to make the constructors aware of any new or unusual skills, tools, or procedures required to correctly install the equipment. Failure to do so can, and often does, results in damage to the equipment or adverse effects on its ability to function as the designer intended. It is also important that the supplier somehow makes known to the installer his intent regarding how the equipment should be tested and operated.

Effective communication devices include explanatory notes on drawings, clear and detailed installation manuals, and provision for trained supplier personnel at the site to aid in supervising the installation and testing of equipment. Such measures can be expensive, however, and it is the duty of the job engineers and contractors to be alert to potential problems and insist on help where it is obviously needed.

As an extreme example of the problems that can be encountered in this regard, a new process line was equipped with sophisticated solid-state programmable electrical controls. The factory-assembled panels were designed with several internal voltages, both AC and DC. A construction electrician making terminations accidentaly shorted a 110V AC line to a 28V DC circuit and ruined several tens of thousands of dollars of electronic assemblies in a fraction of a second. The constructor suffered the loss, and the job was significantly delayed while the equipment was repaired and replaced.

Knowledge of the potential problem and careful training could well have avoided the problem.

There is simply no substitute for construction installers knowing all they possibly can about the equipment. The consequences of finding out too late that installation requires special procedures, expensive tools or unique safety precautions can have a mighty impact on the construction costs, schedule, and satisfaction of the owner.

VENDOR ASSISTANCE. Equipment suppliers can provide, usually at some cost, field engineers, service representatives or erectors to help supervise proper installation, testing, and break-in operation of major equipment. The need for this type of assistance during the construction period can vary from none, or a few days, to many months, depending on the amount and type of equipment being installed. In all cases the potential benefit to the construction forces is the availability of the services of a trained man knowledgeable in all aspects of the design, installation techniques and procedures, and testing and operating requirements for the equipment his firm furnished. These people can be of great help in installing equipment properly and also in being a communication link between the field and the supplier's home office when additional information or parts are needed. Generally, these field service representatives share with the construction contractor an interest in making sure the installation job is done properly, since the reputation of both ultimately rests on the owner's satisfaction with the final results. These people can often fill the construction knowledge gap regarding special equipment installation requirements discussed previously. In practice, however, several problems with supplier representatives can occur, and the construction mangers must be alert to these problems in order to control the overall project. Such problems may include the following:

- Some service representatives are very expensive, partly because the suppliers know these people are necessary for conducting the construction work and hope to make a large profit off the service they provide. If a great many service people are needed the costs can escalate quickly.
- In addition to helping a contractor properly install and test the equipment, supplier service representatives are also well aware of their company's liability to provide high-quality, functioning equipment. Because of this they often tend to be very critical of all other construction factors possibly having an effect on their equipment and make a point of exposing real or potential problems and documenting them for use as future evidence should warranty problems with the equipment show up later. To some degree this is healthy in that it encourages care in workmanship and attention to detail, but it can also get out of hand if not controlled so that the focus remains on installing and testing equipment properly and efficiently.

- Unfortunately, some suppliers to send untrained or inexperienced service people into the field. This can be because they have no experienced personnel available or hope to use a sales engineer or designer to do the work. In this case the construction management must immediately contact the supplier and insist on replacement with a competent field man. It should be noted that some supplier firms make a regular practice of using design or sales personnel to provide field assistance and these people often do an exemplary job with the added benefit that there is useful field feedback to the supplier which can be used on subsequent jobs.

- Commonly, a service representative will be the first to discover a defect in his firm's equipment. Shrewd service people sometimes can use the construction personnel to remedy the problem and avoid payment for the labor by obfuscating the facts. This effectively shifts the cost for warranty work for which the supplier would normally be responsible onto the contractor or owner.

- Particularly if the prospect for other assignments is poor or undesirable, an unscrupulous serviceman will drag out the job he is on by continually insisting on additional requirements or rework during the installation or testing of his firm's equipment.

- It is common arrangement for the owner's project managers to separately purchase vendor assistance and provide the same to the constructor contractor installing the equipment. This can create a delicate situation, particularly on lump sum contracts, of who pays for alleged extra work performed at the direction of the service representative. Both service people and contractors can succumb to the temptation to take advantage of these gray areas, especially when a new type of equipment is involved. The only real solution to this problem is to have a technically competent third party acting in control of the supplier-contractor relationship who can adjudicate conflicts and defend the owner from absolving unnecessary or unwarranted extra costs.

- Service representatives coming onto a union construction job should be briefed regarding local work rules to avoid unneccessary labor problems. Some field service people, although technically competent, do not thoroughly understand the far-reaching effects of breaching the construction contract craft union obligations and can cause great problems. This is especially true for service people who are abrasive or otherwise do not work well with the craft labor who perceive them as a threat and will go to great ends to be rid of them. There are numerous cases of construction labor sabotaging equipment to "get even" with a supplier representative they do not like.

- Generally, an equipment manufacturer will warrant only the workmanship and design of materials furnished by his firm. In practice this creates a responsibility on the supplier's part to replace defective parts at no cost and to absorb the labor cost of revisions to the equipment in the field.

Commercially, however, the supplier often cannot be held liable for the labor costs involved to remove a defective part and replace it with a new one. This is very touchy when the option exists to either field repair or change out parts. If a piece of equipment is repairable in place it may be to the benefit of the owner and installer to do so rather than replace it with a new one. However, straight replacement is often the least expensive choice.

- In dealing with vendor service representatives, the constructors should bear in mind that time is often on the side of the equipment supplier; that is, when disagreements occur regarding who will pay for extra work in the field to make the equipment functional, a service representative can refuse to agree to an equitable settlement knowing that the installer must act quickly to prevent delay of the job. Time is especially on the side of the vendor representative on fast track or penalty type contracts, where delay may be more costly to the constructor or owner than doing the work without a prior agreement that the vendor will absorb the costs. Procrastination by the vendor representative thus becomes a means of entrapping the installer into performing costly extra but unauthorized work.

On the other hand many vendor representatives go to unprecedented efforts to correct malfunction, prevent future problems, solve troublesome operational problems, and train operating personnel. Without the skills and dedication of the knowledgeable vendor representatives, installation, check out, and start-up of today's sophisticated machinery installation would often not be possible.

EQUIPMENT TEST AND CHECKOUT. Subsequent to the installation of equipment the construction forces often are responsible for the equipment's test and checkout prior to turning it over to the owner for actual commissioning and operation. In some cases the constructors are also obligated to provide craft labor and supervision during the commissioning period to stand by and make adjustments to the equipment. In many cases this work is performed under the direction of the owner, his engineering representatives, vendor representatives or a combination of these. Depending on the degree of sophistication of the equipment and the overall facility, this can amount to a significant part of the job in terms of schedule and labor cost. Those planning (or bidding) a total job must consider these factors and include them in the overall scope of work.

The testing of individual equipment components is commonly spelled out explicitly by the supplier and sometimes directed by his representatives in the field. Major problems, however, can surface after all the equipment has been individually checked out, and the constructors then attempt to make all the pieces function as a system. It is vital that the construction managers either know how all the equipment is to operate in concert as a system or have engineering help available to them who do. This is an important consideration, since, as a practical matter, the use of expensive construction labor may be under the direction, and hence the mercy, of others who do not necessarily share the concern for efficient use of the craftsmen. Constructors who lack the specific technical knowledge to control their forces in this situation can find their labor costs rising and schedules slipping very quickly.

Two good ways of dealing with this problem are for the construction contractors to use a provisional sum for standly labor to be provided under the construction contract and to have available third-party engineers or technical personnel who are familiar with the types of equipment and systems involved. Project managers in today's world must give careful consideration to the test and checkout effort in order to achieve a fully functional facility while at the same time controlling schedule and costs.

SUPPLIER WARRANTIES. Although the construction forces are usually liable for good workmanship during installation, equipment suppliers are sometimes responsible for guaranteeing the overall design, quality, and performance of their equipment. this occurs as the result of an owner's desire to assure that the large sums of capital money he spends results in a truly functional facility which will perform as anticipated when the project justification was made and as subsequently promised by the equipment suppliers.

In the case of some facilities the equipment does not perform up to the specification. this is cause for alarm on the part of the owner whose first move is to look to the supplier for some sort of relief such as major revisions to the equipment. The suppliers in turn, facing major unanticipated costs to rectify the problem, have been known to deny their responsibility for the problems and instead blame them on improper installation, checkout, or damage to the equipment by the construction installers. This casts the constructors in the role of defendant to prove that they did, in fact, do their jobs properly.

Success in defending the quality of the installation rests with careful documentation and conduct of the work throughout the job and early identification of problem areas that can result in far-reaching future consequences if not resolved during the installation and testing period. Suppliers must be required to approve the installation prior to turning the facility over to the owner in order to protect the constructors. This is often not an easy task, and there is no substitute for good inspection of all work, knowledge of the technical requirements to properly do the job, and proof that the work was done in accordance with proper procedures.

PART 3

SPECIAL INTEREST GROUPS AND OTHER FACTORS

CHAPTER 10

CONSTRUCTION LABOR UNIONS IN THE UNITED STATES

John D. Borcherding

In the United States organized labor has struggled for over 180 years to gain certain rights and benefits for its workers. The American Federation of Labor (AFL) was started in 1886 by Samuel Gompers, stressing an organization of craft unionism and skilled labor. This federation developed from the Knights of Labor. The AFL was the first union to achieve permanence regardless of economic conditions. Earlier, unions had grown during periods of prosperity but had faded as the economy depressed. Gompers had two policies that guaranteed success where others had failed: (1) National unions were guaranteed trade autonomy and (2) each union was guaranteed exclusive jurisdiction. The primary goal of the AFL was collective bargaining with politics in the background. Perennial demands have been higher wages, shorter hours, improved working conditions, job security, and the right to speak for workers.

Most people acknowledge that unions were necessary in past history, but there is a division of opinion about the usefulness and necessity of the unions today. This chapter covers points on both sides of the issue. The focus is on the building trades unions as listed in Table 10-1. A history of the unions is presented by looking at court rulings and federal legislation that has shaped unions development. The present structure and control of organized labor will be covered. The chapter then examines the advantages and disadvantages of union membership, the problems facing and caused by the unions, and, finally, possible solutions that the unions might attempt in order to benefit their members as well as enhance their public image.

TABLE 10-1.   AFL-CIO Construction Unions

---

1. Bricklayers, Masons and Plasterers' International Union
2. Brotherhood of Painters, Decorators, and Paperhangers of America
3. Granite Cutters' International Association of America
4. International Association of Bridge, Structural and Ornamental Iron Workers
5. International Association of Heat and Frost Insulators and Asbestos Workers
6. International Association of Marble, Slate and Stone Polishers, Rubbers and Sawyers, Tile and Marble Setters Helpers and Terrazzo Helpers
7. International Brotherhood of Boiler Makers, Iron Ship Builders and Helpers of America
8. International Brotherhood of Electrical Workers
9. International Union of Elevator Constructors
10. International Union of Operating Engineers
11. Laborers International Union of North America
12. Operative Plasterers and Cement Masons' International Association
13. Sheet Metal Workers' International Association
14. United Association of Journeymen and Apprentices of the Plumbing and Pipe Fitting Industry of the United States and Canada
15. United Brotherhood of Carpenters and Joiners of America
16. United Slate, Tile, and Composition Roofers, Damp and Waterproof Workers' Association
17. Wood, Wire, and Metal Lathers' International Union

HISTORY

The 1930s can be considered a point of separation for labor unions. The pre-1930s involved the establishment of U.S. labor unions and acceptance, while New Deal legislation and changes in union leadership in the early 1930s brought a new period of labor expansion.

PRE-1930 UNION MOVEMENT

U. S. labor organizations started during the Industrial Revolution and the development of national markets. some of the first unions included the shoemakers (1792) in Philadelphia, the carpenters (1793) in Boston, and the printers (1794) in New York. There were many obstacles in the union's struggle for recognition, including the courts.

The case of the Philadelphia Cordwainers (shoemakers) in 1806 was the first case to deal with labor's attempt to organize. The court found that unions were illegal and the workers guilty of conspiracy. The result was a carryover from English common law that treated as illegal all attempts to raise wages by "concerted" (illegal) actions.

Justice Shaw of Massachusetts ended the criminal conspiracy doctrine in

1842 by ruling in *Commonwealth* v. *Hunt* that workers could join a union and there would be no conspiracy as long as the objectives or means to reach the union were not criminal of unlawful acts.

Injunctions became the next significant device that thwarted union development. An *injunction* is a decree issued by an equity court commanding one or more persons to refrain from committing an act or, in the affirmative, requiring them to perform a specific act. It was used against strikes, pickets, and boycotts—the principal economic weapons of the union. This limited the unions' collective bargaining powers and was effective until 1932, when the Norris-LaGuardia Act was passed.

Antitrust legislation was passed in 1890 with the Sherman Anti-Trust Act. The unions contended that the act did not apply to them, but in the *Danbury Hatters Case* in 1908, the Supreme Court ruled that the unions were within the scope of the act and were found guilty of an illegal secondary boycott.

Having trouble with the courts, labor pushed for legislation that would free it from the restraints of the Sherman Act. Labor's "magna carta" was supposedly the Clayton Act of 1914, particularly Section 6, which appeared to remove labor from the restrictions of the Sherman Act, and Section 20, which seemed to limit the use of the injunction. Labor's elation was short-lived as the decision in the *Duplex Printing Case* (1921) stated that the Clayton Act did not change the fundamental fact that it was the *activities* of a union that determined whether it was in violation of the antitrust laws.

1930 UNION EXPANSION

Following these decisions and the start of the Great Depression, the old unionism based on craft unions and limited membership, deemphasizing politics, and restricting labor goals gave way to a new unionism, under new leadership, that stressed industrial unionism, mass memberships, politics, and the expansion of labor goals to include all aspects of American and world life.

Legislation passed in the 1930s also helped the tremendous growth of union membership. In 1932, the Norris-LaGuardia Act was passed that prohibited the use of an injunction involving a labor dispute unless it was nonpeaceful or fradulent. It also made "yellow dog" contracts (a contract signed as a condition of employment in which the employee agreed not to join a union on penalty of discharge) illegal.

This was followed in 1935 by the Wagner Act, often called the "Labor Relations act", that was prolabor. This act supported and encouraged union activities and collective bargaining (Section 7), defined unfair labor practices (Section 8), and created the National Labor Relations Board (NLRB). Unfair labor practices by management in Section 8 stated that employers are forbidden to do the following:

1. Interfere, restrain, or coerce employees in their union activities.

2. Assist or dominate a labor organization.

3. Discriminate in employment for union membership or union activities or the lack of them.

4. Discriminate for participation in NLRB proceedings.

5. Refuse to bargain collectively with a certified union.

Labor's fortune continued as decisions in three cases in 1940 and 1941 (*Apex Case, Milk-Wagon Drivers Case*, and the *Hutcheson Case*) stated that strikes, boycotts, and picketing no longer violated antitrust laws if the restraint of trade was an incidental consequence of union's pursuit of its primary objective of winning a labor dispute. During this period, unions prospered and grew in strength; some felt that they were too powerful. The Taft-Hartley Act of 1947 was passed to equalize the power of labor and management. This act was an amendment to the Wagner Act, not a substitute or replacement for it. It covered unfair union labor practices, such as secondary boycotts; made closed shop, whereby employees are required to be union members before they can be hired, illegal; created the Federal Mediation and Conciliation Service; and added decertification and deauthorization elections to the representative election created by the Wagner Act. Under the Taft-Hartley Act, unions may not do the following:

1. Restrain or coerce employees.

2. Cause discrimination for union activities.

3. Refuse to bargain with an employer.

4. Engage in secondary boycotts.

5. Charge excessive or discriminatory initiation fees.

6. Featherbed.

The final statute that influenced the development of unions is the Landrum-Griffith Act or the Labor-Management Reporting and Disclosure Act of 1959. It consisted of seven sections—the first six dealt with internal union practices, and the seventh section contained amendments to the Taft-Hartley Act. It had a bill of rights for union members, required public disclosure of financial and administrative details of union government, limited trusteeships (national union takeover of a subordinate local union), detailed election procedures, and created fiduciary relationships between officers and union members.

HIERACHY AND CONTROL

Organized labor can basically be divided into three levels: the federation, national union, and local union.

FEDERATION

The federation is the AFL-CIO, which merged in 1955 after a split of 17 years. The organizational chart is shown in Figure 10-1. The AFL-CIO is a coalition of 106 national and international (jurisdiction in the United States and Canada) unions. The organization's primary role can be described as political, since it does not take part in collective bargaining. Goals are accomplished through such efforts as lobbying for certain legislation, political education through the voluntary contributions of members to the Committee on Political Education (COPE), community services, and research. Within the organizational framework, the AFL-CIO's duties include helping to organize the unorganized workers of the United States, minimizing friction between affiliated unions, and settling disputes between the unions.

Control of the AFL-CIO is regulated by the annual convention, which sets policies as well as elects the Executive Council that consists of the president, the secretary-treasurer, and 33 vice presidents. The Executive Council governs the federation between conventions.

There are nine constitutional departments consisting of trade and industrial groupings for unions with strong common interests, such as the Building Trades Council. These departments have their own executive bodies, hold their own conventions, and manage and finance their own affairs within the framework of the AFL-CIO.

The state AFL-CIO is affiliated with the federation. Membership is open to unions within the particular state and is on a voluntary basis. The structure is similar to the national organization, and its functions are basically the same, except they emphasize local and state activities. In Texas, approximately 50% of eligible unions belong to the state AFL-CIO.

NATIONAL UNION

The second level of organized labor is the national union. There are 1973 national unions that provide the basis of American union movement. While the federation performs basically a political function, the national union performs the economic function of collective bargaining. By virtue of this function, the national union has emerged as the dominant force in the labor movement. In the building trades, collective bargaining is performed on a local level, but that power is delegated from the national union. Each national union has its exclusive jurisdiction in which it claims the right to organize workers and control jobs. An example is taken from the Constitution of the United Brotherhood of Carpenters and Joiners of America:

A. *Section 6*:   The jurisdiction of the United Brotherhood of Carpenters and Joiners of america shall include all branches of the Carpenter and Joiner trade. In it shall be vested the power through the International body to

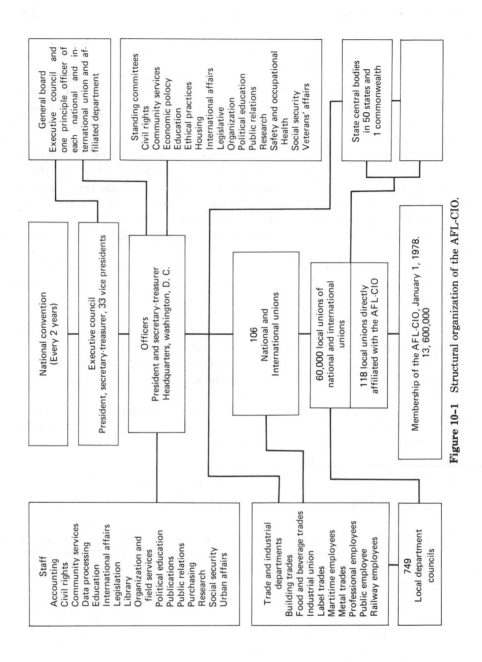

Figure 10-1 Structural organization of the AFL-CIO.

establish and charter subordinate Local and Auxiliary Unions, Districts, State and Provincial Councils in all branches of trade, and its mandates must be observed and obeyed at all times.

There are two categories of national unions: (1) the craft unions whose jurisdiction concerns a particular skilled occupation and (2) the industrial union that defines its jurisdiction in terms of a particular industry and in which membership is a function of employment in that industry regardless of skill or occupation.

Unions have their own officers and manage their own affairs. They are elected by the members. The executive board, which includes the officers, plus one elected member from each district, governs the union between conventions.

Local Union

The third level that is most important for the building trades in the union structure is the local union. Local unions are chartered by the national union and they derive their powers from the constitution of the national union. In the building treades, local unions are fairly autonomous, having collective bargaining rights and jurisdiction for a certain geographic area. The local serves as a headquarters and is responsible for all union activities of that craft within its boundaries.

Local union officials, as with the other levels, are elected by the members. Therefore, the membership is the ultimate authority and has the power to reject or ratify any collective bargaining agreement. Day-to-day affairs are controlled by the business agent, and he is often the contractor's direct contact with the union. Each project has a job steward who represents the union and initially handles any problems.

District councils are two or more local unions located in one city or other designated locality. These districts are empowered to make laws and trade rules for the district.

Building trade councils are local unions of different construction trades that unite on a regional basis. These councils do not engage in collective bargaining for the different locals but act politically and aid in presenting a united front during periods of collective bargaining.

CONSTRUCTION INDUSTRY CHARACTERISTICS INFLUENCING UNIONIZATION

Variables that affect the extent of unionization are the area of the country in which the project is being built and the type of construction. This includes geographic location and the relation to metropolitan areas. Generally, unions are concentrated from southern New England through Pennsylvania over to the Great Lakes and on the West Coast from Canada to Mexico. Nonunion areas include the South, particularly the Carolinas and the Gulf Coast of Texas, excluding the Port Arthur, Orange, and Beaumont areas.

Unionization is inversely proportional to the size of the nearest metropolitan area and the distance from the site. Also, the more centralized the work, then the higher the density of union members. Finally, to a lesser degree, the extent of unionization in other industries nearby affects the construction industry. That is, strong industrial unions encourage equally strong construction unions.

The four major types of construction and the extent of unionization are as presented here:

1. *Residential* Consists of single-family dwellings and low-rise multifamily dwellings. Usually, small firms are involved, and they use subcontractors for the specialized work. It is the least unionized, since it is small, highly decentralized, and away from metropolitan areas. It is estimated that 80% of the work is done open shop.

2. *Commercial* This work consists of stores, offices, warehouses, etcetra. These projects are done by larger, more diversified companies, and these companies are often able to perform some of the specialized work. This type of construction is 55 to 60% unionized, since the projects are often larger and located near metropolitan areas.

3. *Industrial* Work includes large factories, power plants, refineries, etcetra. Usually, the firms are large, have high bid capacities, and are nationwide. It is the most organized type of construction, with 70% union, since there are large work forces in highly industrialized areas.

4. *Heavy* Construction consisting of highways, dams, airports, etcetra. This is more seasonal, using a large percentage of unskilled labor, and involves the least amount of subcontracting. It is the most stable type of construction concerning unionization, with 60% belonging to the union. Work is usually far from metropolitan areas, and is very decentralized. The high union rate is probably due to the fact that the prevailing wage often equals the union wage, so contractors take advantage of the union hiring halls.

UNION MEMBERSHIP

ADVANTAGES

An important factor that leads to understanding the labor organization is the understanding of why workers join a union. Basically, a worker joins if he feels he can get higher wages, better working conditions, and increased job protection. Other factors include status, comradeship, or compulsory membership.

Compulsory membership is often criticized, but it does not seem to affect membership. Proof can be seen in unions existing in the right-to-work states and in the fact that decertification elections held under the Taft-Hartley Act have usually failed.

Unions claim that membership provides security, defense against loss or subversion of hard-won gains, protection of members from unfair or arbitrary treatment by the employer, and insures safe working conditions (5). The contributions of the union to the construction industry from which everyone benefits include the following:

1. Unions have a stabilizing influence on a basically unstable area of business.

2. Through the medium of negotiated labor contracts, fixed wages are established, and much uncertainty of the employment of labor is removed.

3. Unions provide a pool of skilled and experienced labor.

4. Unions help police the industry on both sides by maintaining discipline among their own members and helping to control the entry and actions of irresponsible contractors.

An *advantage* is defined as a benefit resulting from a course of action or a factor or circumstance of benefit to its possessor. Using these definitions, the advantages of joining a union can be viewed by workers as falling into two main categories:

1. Political and social action through COPE; labor presents a united group for prolabor legislation.

2. Collective bargaining.

Since most workers are concerned with economic issues, advantages derived from collective bargaining are listed. Different groups include general advantages, wages, job conditions, and job security.

General advantages include the following:

1. Hiring hall.
2. Apprenticeship.
3. Right to strike.

Wages include the following:

1. Higher pay.
2. Cost-of-living clauses.
3. Deferred pay increases.
4. Overtime benefits.
5. Fringe benefits.
6. Premium differential.

7. Show-up pay.
8. Travel to worksite pay.

Job conditions include the following:

1. Jurisdiction of work.
2. Multishift work regulated.
3. Safety provisions.
4. Tools.
5. Designed working hours.
6. Defined holiday.
7. Time set aside for payday.
8. Foreman requirements.
9. Crew composition.

Job security includes the following:

1. Insurance and retirement benefits.
2. Grievance procedure.
3. Job stewards.
4. Work preservation clause.

DISADVANTAGES

There are disadvantages that must be taken into account. Management cites a loss of productivity and the loss of the right to manage. Management criticizes unions for the following:

1. Loss of control.
2. Crews requiring a foreman.
3. Everyone getting equal pay.
4. Restrictive work rules.
5. Jurisdictional disputes.
6. Less management capability.
7. No loyalty to employer.

There are disadvantages for workers if they join a union including these:

1. Initiation fee.
2. Low or no seniority.
3. Work 1400 hrs/yr versus 1800 hrs/yr (open shop).
4. Must pay dues.
5. No choice of employer.
6. Equal pay.

7. No merit promotions.

8. Lack of profit-sharing program.

9. Cannot work as a team or with friends.

10. Loss of work due to jurisdictional disputes that your union is not involved in.

11. No flexibility in work assignments.

12. Lack of incentive programs.

13. Restricted to certain methods and discouraged from trying innovative techniques.

Before joining a union, each person must weigh all factors and ultimately decide where his best prospects for employment, security, and job satisfaction lie.

PROBLEMS

JOINT PROBLEMS

There are some problems that are common and must be solved by both management and the union. Some of the problems are created by statutes, while others have resulted from court decisions. Most of these deal with equal opportunity, including the following:

1. *Equal Employment Opportunity (1964)*   Title VII prohibits discriminating practices on the part of employers, employment agencies, labor organizations, and apprenticeship or training programs.

2. *Executive Order 11246*   Positive action required to insure minority applicants are employed and that employees are treated during employment without discrimination.

3. *Executive Order 11375*   Added to Executive Order 11246, this order prohibits discrimination because of sex.

4. *Philadelphia Plan*   A sample plan to assure compliance with Executive Oder 11246. The contractor is required to include a statement on affirmative action programs containing the use of minority workers in each trade in his bid. An example would be that by 1973, 20 to 24% of the plumbers in Philadelphia should be minorities. This was accepted as constitutional by the Supreme Court in 1971. Most localities now have a similar mandatory program.

5. *Age Discrimination Act*   Prohibits arbitrary age discrimination in employment and protects individuals 40 to 65 years of age.

6. *Copeland Act*   Prohibits illegal deduction from employees' paychecks and kickbacks. Union dues can only be withheld if the employee consents.

7. *Fair Labor Standards Act*   Contains provisions for minimum wage, maximum hours, overtime pay, equal pay, and child-labor standards.

These laws involve both management and unions, since they are both responsible for their execution. Management is considered by the courts to have the power to hire employees, regardless of provisions of a collective bargaining agreement. Union hiring halls must provide opportunities for nonunion members for employment without discrimination if a union hiring agreement is part of the collective bargaining contract. These laws require proof of action, and employers and unions can no longer just state that they are following them.

The latest case for affirmative action in which the Supreme Court upheld affirmative action was the *Weber case*. This case allows employers to set hiring goals and provide quotas for training programs for minorities.

Another problem that affects the management of open shop as well as union contractors and organized labor is the noncontractual practices that result in decreased productivity. These include the following:

1. Time lost due to late starting, early quitting, or extending lunch hours.

2. Little or trivial problems that are not resolved or explained may cause workmen to reduce their effort.

3. Frequently, foremen are not told what performance the company expects.

4. Spur of the moment emotional decisions may have an adverse psychological effect on the crew.

5. Favoritism and nepotism on the part of the supervisor is common in construction but very detrimental to a project.

COSTS

Union contractors can pass along the increased cost of wages to the owner, so the contractor does not get that concerned with wage increases until he begins competing with open shop contractors whose crews have a lower average pay rate. However, owners are now getting tired of paying these extra costs and more seem to be moving toward open shop construction. In Austin, Texas, approximately 80% of the nonresidential construction is being built under open shop management.

Union contractors increase their percentage of the work when public funds are involved because of the Davis-Bacon Act which requires that the prevailing wage be paid to all workers. The prevailing wage is usually construed to equal the union wage, regardless of whether a high percentage of work was performed open shop at an hourly rate.

Criticisms of union practices that add to cost through lower productivity can be divided into contractual and noncontractual practices (discussed previously). Contractual practices include the following:

1. Restrictive work practices.

2. Preestablished crew sizes and foreman-to-journeymen ratios.

3. Standby labor is sometimes required, even though owner-supplied construction utilities operate unattended.

4. Restrictions on innovative materials or design.

5. More efficient off-site prefabrication and subassembly of components may not be allowed or must be done in union shops.

6. Work times and the length of the workweek may vary for trades, and there may be little opportunity to go to four, 10-hr days to allow make-up days on Friday or Saturday.

7. Jurisdictional disputes may result in slowdowns and work stoppages.

8. Frequently, journeymen must perform unskilled work because of a low apprentice-to-journeymen ratio (1 : 4) and the absence of helpers.

9. Shift work and overtime premiums are too high to be considered as alternatives to adding manpower if the work in accelerated.

10. Foremen, although the first line of supervision, have often displayed more loyalty to the unions than to the contractor.

JURISDICTION*

Of the 10 criticisms of contractual practices previously listed, jurisdictional disputes may be the costliest in terms of lost construction time and dollars. Union craft jurisdiction is best described as the mandate to perform specific work functions and tasks to the complete exclusion of all other trades. As such, it is an integral part of the foundation of organized labor. In effect, it is the adhesive that binds the individual craft union members together. To the craftsman, exclusive jurisdiction means identity, control of work, job furtherance, personal esteem, and employment security. This is particularly true as craft jurisdiction relates to the building trades, where many trades frequently occupy the same workplace. Jurisdiction, therefore, is of great economic and personal importance to the craftsman. It is, of course, a subject of equal importance to the owner or contractor who must economically pursue construction. The construction industry over the years has proved to be the major arena in which jurisdiction is most often spotlighted: therefore, the discussion will be limited to jurisdiction of the building trades unions and industrial construction.

By its very nature, craft jurisdiction has been a continual source of controversy between and among unions. This controversy is best evidenced by the intense personal ferver with which craftsmen proclaim the right to accomplish "their work." Unfortunately, given the right emotional envi-

*The author acknowledges the contribution of D. A. McCormick, Manager, Labor Relations, Kaiser Engineers, Oakland, California, in the preparation of this section.

ronment, there often is no item of disputed work too small or set of ill-conceived or misunderstood field directives too trivial not to warrant a conflict and resultant job disturbance in the form of a slowdown, walk off, or, on occasion, actual physical violence between craft unions that are at odds regarding the "right" to do the work.

Naturally, this penchant for jurisdiction disputes and resultant work stoppages was recognized early in the labor movement, and joint efforts were made by contractors and unions to reach agreements prohibiting work actions in response to jurisdictional disputes. Simply prohibiting such demonstrations would not of itself suffice unless the unions and contractors had some method to resolve the issue and establish, at least for that particular instance, the trade that would carry the work.

Prior to 1919, jurisdictional resolutions were generally reached by the unions themselves. Recognizing the importance of a workable settlement mechanism, and finding none readily available, some unions submitted their disputes to the then-governing body, the AFL. Although many decisions of note were reached by the AFL, most agreements of record during that time resulted from lower-level meetings between the involved unions, and decisions reached were a result of a mutual desire to profitably share the work. Most of those so-called international agreements exist today, and, although dated, they often provide the basis for resolving today's disputes.

In 1919, the Building Trades established the National Board for Jurisdictional Awards. The board served to settle many jurisdictional issues in the rapidly growing construction industry. From this body came the beginnings of the well-known "Green Book" of jurisdictional decisions. In 1927, the Building Trades Department again assumed sole responsibility for such settlements. Unfortuantely, this period is marked by much conflict and confusion, with few meaningful decisions. Around 1937, a so-called National Referee System was established to help the Building Trades Department sort out and arbitrate the issues. Thus the mechanism trudged along until 1948.

Up until 1948, all efforts to determine trade jurisdiction were those of the labor unions. Contractors had no voice in such matters. All that changed, however, as a result of a profusion of job stoppages due to jurisdictional disputes just after World War II. These strikes resulted, in part, in the successful passage of the Taft-Hartley Act. This act, among other things, made contractor involvement in jurisdictional disputes a matter of law. A national contractor organization at that time ratified the Plan for the Settlement of Jurisdictional Disputes in the Construction Industry. The General Presidents of the Building Trades Unions approved the plan, and in May 1948, the National Joint Board for Settlement of Jurisdictional Disputes was created.

Unfortunately, the new plan did not operate as efficiently or fairly as originally anticipated. Unions were unhappy with contractor/employer involvement in the Joint Board. Therefore, in October 1949, a new plan was developed. In essence, the new procedure was identical to the old, except for one major change: the board could no longer issue job decisions universal in scope, that is, covering a specific item of work on all jobs in the industry; the new board would henceforth issue decisions which applied only to the (specific) work item, and the decision could not be used as a precedent for any other dispute anywhere. In effect, it was a one dispute–one resolution system.

The Joint Board continued in that fashion until 1973. Major complaints arose against the board. It was felt that the board was unable to recognize and deal with disputes brought about by new materials and technology. It could not and did not appear to want to adapt to an ever-changing industry. Therefore, in 1973, the Plan for Settlement of Jurisdictional Disputes in the Construction Industry was modified and adopted.

The new plan provides for an eight-man Joint Administrative Committee made up of an equal number of labor and contractor representatives. This committee, in turn, appoints the three-man Impartial Jurisdictional Board (IJDB) matters. The board members, as the name implies, are completely impartial and are not appointed directly from either labor or contractor ranks. Among its many varied responsibilities, the eight-man Joint Administrative Committee appoints special subcommittees—one of which studies changing industry technology as it affects jurisdiction. Another subcommittee is the Appeals Board.

Thus the IJDB exists today. In 1979, dissatisfaction in the labor ranks resulted in a brief interruption of board activity. The unions felt that the Chairman was procontractor in his decisions and asked that he be replaced. The Chairman refused to budge. After about four months, during which no IJDB business took place, he resigned, and a new Chairman was appointed.

Of what is now known as the IJDB, one fact is that actually, only a very small percentage of disputes are presented to it. The majority of disputes are settled at much lower levels. For instance, a typical construction job will often start with a "markup meeting." This is a meeting between the contractor and interested craft unions prior to the start of work, wherein, to the greatest extent possible, all items of work are discussed, plans and drawings are presented (and marked up), and assignments are made.

Keep in mind that the contractor alone has the responsibility to make the assignments. Meetings such as these allow differences of opinion to surface prior to commencement of construction activity and give the contractor the option to delay making an assignment and allow the disputing unions some time to resolve their differences and advise the contractor of their decision at some convenient later date. The contractor usually puts a time limit, say, two or three weeks on such a delay. When he receives the unions' answer, he then proceeds with an assignment he knows will not cause discord later. Of course, if agreement between the unions cannot be reached, the contractor proceeds with what he considers a proper assignment.

The union involved that has "lost" the assignment is then free to seek a decision through the IJDB procedure previously explained. In no instance, however, may the union cause a work stoppage or similar action to reinforce its demands.

Another example of jurisdictional disputes settlement, and one that is by far the most common, starts with an allegation by a craftsman in the field that some other trade craftsman is "doing his work." Here is where the craft steward serves a critical purpose. This craft steward and the one representing the other craft involved meet informally and in most cases either immediately establish proper jurisdiction or, in far fewer cases, do a little horse trading for future work. Sometimes agreement cannot be reached. The stewards then call their respective business managers who seek to resolve the matter in a meeting with the contractor representative. If no agreement is forthcoming, the Union International Representatives are usually called in and in the majority of instances some sort of compromise is reached. While all this is happening, the contractor continues with his work as originally assigned. In fact, the contractor, under the previously discussed Plan for Settlement of Jurisdictional Disputes in the Construction Industry is prohibited from stopping contested work or altering assignments until the unions involved agree to a change or the IJDB dictates some change.

The number and frequency of jurisdictional squables on any given project are often the function of a wide set of variables. Large ongoing projects with seemingly endless work available tend to have fewer disputes proportionally than smaller jobs or jobs that are winding down. As work becomes scarce, the union eye sometimes tends to rove. Indeed, it is considered somewhat a badge of honor for a craftsman to "appropriate" another craft's work and get away with it. In some areas of the country, continual disputes between two trades are commonplace. The chronic battles between such trades are often the result of overeager business agents who may be attempting to establish themselves politically. Fortunately, such empire building is fairly transparent, and sooner or later either the zealot establishes himself and completely overcomes his opposition, or, as is more often the case, this person's contemporaries grow weary of his activities and take internal steps to curtail his drive. This sort of house cleaning goes on frequently in the building trades.

Jurisdictional disputes between unions heavily impact the contractor and client in the form of increased construction costs. Attempts at establishing a universally accepted directory of decisions have been numerous but only partially successful. In large part this has been true because of the profession and a variety of agreements reached around the country. Many agreements are fairly clear-cut, but an unfortunately large number tend to be vague, ambiguous, and contradictory. The problem grows each day as new technological changes are introduced both in material and manner of construction, for example, prefabricated process units and space age electro/mechanical machinery. Since it is clear that protection of jurisdiction is critical to a craft union's future, we must assume that the problem will always be with us, unless strong moves are made by the building trades toward cleaning up their disputes in house, thus making construction with union trades more economically attractive to the construction client and the contractor.

MANAGEMENT

Management's claim that the unions are taking over the right to manage is a serious dispute between the two groups. Unions claim that they do not want to replace management, but it appears that they are usurping authority through collective bargaining.

An unpublished research paper that studied collective bargaining agreements made in Austin, Texas, in 1978 shows this trend. To summarize the paper, a list of 17 management functions that managers considered exempt from collective bargaining was compiled. A review of the collective bargaining agreements showed that management had lost some of its rights. Of the original 17, only 9 management functions remained exempt or in control of management as shown in Table 10-2. Of the 8 functions now subject to collective bargaining, 3 remain the perogative of the general contractor, but some unions have started to gain control of these. The remaining 5 functions show a great deal of union restrictions and influence. These include the following:

1. Determination of job content.
2. Determination of the work force.
3. Determination of policies affecting the selection of employees.
4. Scheduling of operations and the number of shifts.
5. Determination of safety, health, and property protection measures, where legal responsibility of the employer is involved.

The arguments presented in this section, plus those listed as disadvantages in the preceding section, whether justified or not, summarize managers' feelings as well as the perceived outlook by much of the public.

PROBLEMS FACING THE UNIONS

The U. S. labor movement started in the 1700s, and the struggle has continued throughout our history. One of the problems confronting unions is the task of organizing workers who are not presently organized. Today, approximately 20 to 30% of nonagricultural employees belong to a union. Overall union membership increased by only 13% between 1956 and 1976.

TABLE 10-2.   Management Functions (from President's National Labor Management Conference, November 1945)

M	1.	Determination of products to be manufactured or services to be rendered to customers of the enterprise
M	2.	Location of the business, including the establishment of new units and the relocation or closing of old units
M	3.	Determination of the layout and equipment to be used in the business
J	4.	The processes, techniques, methods, and means of manufacture and distribution
M	5.	The materials to be used and the size and character of inventories
M	6.	The determination of financial policies
M	7.	General accounting procedures—particularly the internal accounting necessary to make reports to the owners of the business and to government bodies requiring financial reports
M	8.	Prices of goods sold or services rendered to customers
M	9.	Customer relations
L	10.	Determination of job content
L	11.	Determination of the size of the work force
J/L	12.	Allocation and assignment of work to workers
L/M	13.	Determination of policies affecting the selection of employees
J	14.	Establishment of quality standards and judgment of workmanship required
M	15.	Maintenance of discipline and control and use of the plant property
L	16.	Scheduling of operations and the number of shifts
L	17.	Determination of safety, health, and property protection measures, where legal responsibility of the employer is involved

Key

M = Controlled by management

L = Management control limited by labor contract provisions

J = Jointly determined by collective bargaining between management and union (2)

Evidence suggests that slightly more than 50% of all construction workers are union members, and, proportionately, union memberships in the construction trades has not changed appreciably in more than 30 years (5).

The biggest challenge to the unions is merit or open shop construction. It is estimated that 60% of construction this year will be done by open shop (4). This does not necessarily mean that the unions will lose the total 60%, since many general contractors subout work to union subcontractors. Some arguments for open shop include the following:

1. Absence of restrictive work practices.

2. Absence of jurisdictional disputes.

3. No prefabrication restrictions.

4. Foreman is not part of the union and can aid management as the first line of supervision and can works with tools if necessary.

5. High unskilled to skilled ratios.

Unions face a challenge to the prevailing wage rate and repeal of the Davis-Bacon Act. During the ninety-sixth session of the United States Congress, bills were introduced to repeal or dilute Davis-Bacon. All failed, but the threat still remains. The charge is that Davis-Bacon adds inflationary costs to a project and questions the determination of the prevailling wage rate, based on the 30% rule.

Another problem that the unions face is minority and female hiring goals. According to an Equal Employment Opportunity Commission (EEOC) report of seven major cities, minority hiring increased from 7.2% in 1972 to 8.4% in 1976 for skilled journeymen, which is considered inadequate[*]. The hiring of women is not matching the Federal government goals set. Different reports show that most unions cannot meet their goals despite an intensified effort. There are currently five women in the Carpenters' Union in Austin, a very small minority percentage.[†]

Other problems are falling membership; employment only nine months of the year, even though methods and programs are being studied to smooth out the seasonal peaks and valleys of construction; and strikebreakers hired to overcome the effects of a union strike.

Labor has also decided to fight for common situs picketing—now illegal under the Taft-Hartley Act—and the repeal of Taft-Hartley 14b—the right to work provision. Efforts to pass this legislation has failed.

SOLUTIONS

Solutions to the previous problems are hard to find and harder to put into practice. Cooperation and compromise must exist on both sides. Management should realize that unions and the labor union are here to stay and everyone must work together. This is not advocating a complete turnover of workers to unions. Open shop serves to moderate unions, as unions do to moderate management. Without unions, the exploitation that occurred in the past may not be repeated, but the temptation would always be there.

In a speech to the Bricklayers and Allied Craftsmen Union, John Joyce (then Secretary of the Union) advocated clearly differentiating between open shop and unions by not giving concessions at the bargaining table. This approach, at times effective, would not do much to enhance the unions' image nor add to their membership. Publicity is often the key to a

---

*"GAO Blasts Minority Hiring," *Engineering News-Record*, March 29, 1979, Vol. 202, No. 23, *NY/NY*, 1979, 58.

†"Female Hiring Goals Elusive," *Engr. News-Record*, June 7, 1979 *Vol 202, No. 23, New York, N.Y. 1979, 24.*

successful compaign, and unions are not often shown in a good light; there must be a concerted effort to enhance their image.

Realistic demands should be made during collective bargaining. Demands for higher wages should be met with increased productivity. Management should be given the right to manage, and unions should adopt some flexibility. An adversary relationship with contractors does not help, and both should strive for cooperation.

Frequently, contractors attempt to negotiate project agreements to regain many of their management perogatives. The success of their negotiations is often dependent on an owner's willingness to consider performing the work with open shop labor. The project agreement signed by Union Electric Co., Daniel International Corp., and labor unions in Missouri is an example of a strong project agreement that was brought about by a threat of nonunion construction of Callaway Nuclear Units 1 & 2.

Some efforts have been made, including less featherbedding, arbitration instead of strikes, and an effort to stop the make-work practices. However, unions should not be adverse to changing technology or method improvements. In fact, method improvement studies will often show that it is management's fault for reduced productivity and not the worker, for he often is waiting for materials, tools, and information or another work assignment. Also, study of masonry walls and column costs by C. T. Grimm showed that the productivity of a mason was usually controlled by designers such that many factors over which he had no control adversely affected productivity. Unfortunately, in either case, it is often the workman blamed for lack of productivity and the unions as the ultimate culprit.

It is recommended that both groups undertake productivity improvement programs that identify factors that adversely affect or improve productivity. This can be done through better communication on the site. For example, establishing a owner-management-labor committee to begin to minimize the adverse factors and improve supportive factors previously identified.

Also, using the latest methods improvement techniques such as (1) work sampling (2) time lapse film analysis (3) questionnaire surveys can be beneficial to both groups if techniques are fairly employed on construction sites. Application of behavioral science to construction offers another alternative for both groups to work with one another.

Finally, mangement and the unions must try to minimize the cyclical effects of construction. They must also try to maximize the results of the affirmative action programs or be faced with greater government control.

CONCLUSION

This chapter has reviewed the organized labor movement with emphasis on the building trade unions. The struggle for "more, now" to paraphrase

Samuel Gompers, will continue, but change is inevitable. Open shop contractors recognize training as a major advantage of the unions and have begun to establish training programs to offset the union apprenticeship. This is another signal that unions will face considerable competition in the years ahead. Also, unions must recognize that nonproductive contractual restrictions will lose jobs and money not only for union contractors, but also for their members as well.

The problems and solutions proposed are not new, but the time for resolving the differences is becoming more critical. With shortages in energy and materials, greater productivity is becoming increasingly more important.

To date, unions have had an important influence on general social legislation such as public service programs, minimum wages, occupational safety and health standards, comprehensive national health insurance, and civil rights legislation. Problems still exist, and the solution is increased productivity. Unions can once again take the first step in confronting these problems by promoting methods improvement programs, developing better communication between each group at the construction site, and applying behavioral research to improve job satisfaction as well as productivity.

CHAPTER 11

EMPLOYER AND OWNER ASSOCIATIONS

Raymond E. Levitt
Joel B. Leighton

Most contractors in the United States employing more than one or two workers are affiliated with one or more contractor associations. These associations have developed over the last 100 years either within a single specialty trade (e.g., electrical, plumbing, painting, sheet metal) by a sector of the market (e.g., home building, general building, utilities, heavy engineering, and highway) by contractual position (i.e., general contractor or subcontractor) or by labor relations posture (i.e., union or open shop).

Owner associations can be found in ancient civilizations, and later in the form of medieval guilds. In 1768 in the United States, 20 merchants organized the Chamber of Commerce of the State of New York. In 1792, the New York Stock Exchange was formed. Today, these are the two oldest U.S. business associations in continous existence. However, as far as we know, it was not until 1969 that owners—by which, within the context of this book, we mean the buyers of construction projects—established an association specifically concerned with the management of construction and particularly with the management of construction labor relations.

This chapter presents a brief history of contractor and owner associations in the United States. Tendencies toward fragmentation and other factors that have limited the effectiveness of both types of organizations are discussed. Some recent attempts to achieve unification among associations in construction are reviewed, and the chapter concludes with a look at the future of associations in the industry.

THE DEVELOPMENT OF CONTRACTOR ORGANIZATIONS

Human organizations usually represent a response to evolving economic and social conditions in their environments. Construction contracting organizations have followed this pattern, and we commence with a brief review of their development in the U.S.

EARLY ORGANIZATIONS

The first formal association of contractors in the United States was established in Philadelphia in 1724. Following the tradition of the European guilds, it was an organization of masters within the master-journeyman-apprentice system. Calling itself simply the "Carpenters' Company," it was concerned primarily with prices of work and wages to be paid, and it created a procedure for settling disputes among the members. In the tradition of Ben Franklin's Philadelphia it certainly also provided social activities for its members.

During the rest of the century urban areas grew, the cost of land underwent speculative increases, and financial, and credit arrangements became more formal. The master ceased to be a general contractor—although the term "general contractor" itself was not to come into existence for more than 100 years—and became instead a labor contractor. As time went on, under the pressure of competition, members of the Carpenters' Company cut wages, and thus it was that in 1791 the journeymen responded and formed the first journeymen's trade union in the United States.

NINETEENTH CENTURY

Technology and commerce became the dominant influences on construction during the first seven decades of the nineteenth century. Despite the imposing masonry structures of other civilizations, wood frame construction was almost universal in the United States because of the ready availability of lumber. However, as urbanization progressed, a series of fires devastated large portions of several major cities, two of the most spectacular being the Great Fire of Chicago in 1871 and its successor in 1874. An increased emphasis on masonry contruction was the first result, but with wood framing and wood interiors, the problem of fire remained. Steel frames were introduced in the late 1880s, and the end was in sight for the master carpenter.

Labor provided the impetus for the next stages in the development of contractor organizations. The Federation of Organized Trades and Labor Unions, formed in 1881, became the vehicle around which the fledging building trades unions, notably Carpenters, rallied to push their eight-hour day drive that culminated in a general strike of over 340,000 workers throughout the country in 1886. As a direct response, the first national organization of contractors, the National Builders Association, was formed in 1887.

During this period the one big union—the Knights of Labor—went into decline, and the individual craft unions became dominant, with the power base being that of the local unions in the urban areas. Paralleling this development the National Builders Association also went into a decline and held its last convention in 1899. Local employer associations burgeoned to fill the void, also on a craft basis, primarily to deal with the local craft unions.

Attempts by employer organizations to cope with the problems caused by the fragmented structure of the construction industry provide a recurring theme in the industry. During the period from 1900 to 1905 the local employer craft associations in several of the major urban areas came together and formed building employer associations, although the exact names varied. Many of these organizations have continued in existence right up to the present time.

As technology advanced and as buildings became more complex during the latter part of the nineteenth century, specialty contractors came into existence. Frequently, an owner, working through his architect, would award separate contracts. At other times a builder, frequently one with a background of carpentry or masonry skills, would act to coordinate the construction process. A number of today's general contractors trace their roots in this fashion to the 1870s.

Although national specialty contractor organizations were in existence in the early 1900s, history, in the form of World War I, was responsible for the formation of the first national organization of general contractors. Faced with the absence of any entity through which the federal government could mobilize the construction industry, President Wilson called on the Chamber of Commerce of the United States for assistance.

Accordingly, the Chamber called a meeting in Atlantic City, New Jersey, on July 15, 1918, to set up the National Federation of Building Industries. At that time there were more than 100 national and local contractor organizations in the United States, but none represented general contractors. Observing that their voice was ineffectual among all the other organized contractor groups, 27 of the general contractors present determined to rectify the situation. A meeting was called for November in Chicago. The letter from the chairman of the organizing committee, although somewhat oratorical, probably represents fairly how not only general contractors, but also specialty contractors viewed their condition at that time. It read in part as follows:

> No business is more exacting or requires greater effort and determination than construction. A lifetime may be spent in acquiring experience, judgement and the accumulation of capital, equipment and efficient organizations,

only to have our enterprise meet with disaster of many kinds—commercial or financial discrimination, confiscatory legislation, political extortion, predatory competition, and by the magnitude and concentration of opposing influences—from all of which most of us have suffered.

The contractor is the prime factor in all material progress. Through him all necessary works are built, of public and private interest. He affords a livelihood for millions of men and their families. The contractor is now merely an individual with no influence other than his own personality and his commercial weight. Organized, he can serve his own legitimate interests, open the gates for great prosperity, benefit the country in normal times, and serve it royally in emergencies like the present.

The Chicago meeting launched the Associated General Contractors of America (AGC). The 97 initial members of AGG saw their three main tasks as adjusting relations with organized labor, the adoption of standard construction contracts, and the development of coordination among owners, engineers, and contractors.

There was a substantial expansion of contractor association membership throughout the 1920s, but this trend reversed during the Great Depression. The need for group action was there, but the lack of adequate financing destroyed some organizations, while substantially reducing the activities of most others.

Just as some recovery began to appear, curtailment of most private construction and much public construction during World War II again brought a halt to any expansion of contractor associations. Growth resumed, both in the number of contractor associations and the number of association members, after World War II. In 1972, the U.S. Department of Commerce listed 47 national contractor organizations, including general contractors, general contractors in specialized fields, and subcontractors. Table 11-1 shows a representative list of major construction associations.

CHANGING FUNCTIONS OF CONTRACTOR ASSOCIATIONS

The Philadelphia Carpenters' Company was concerned with self-regulation of business, wage scales, and social activities. These continued to be the main concerns of contractor associations through the nineteenth century.

Then the focus began to broaden. Working agreements with the unions included items other than wages and hours. Actions by state governments required involvement in legislative matters; indeed, several state contractor associations formed at this time for this reason. Lincoln Steffens had written *The Shame of the Cities*. Shakedowns became common on public works.

The reaction by contractors is typified in the first bylaws of AGG, with its concern for public relations; securing just dealings *from* (ital supplied) the public; seeking correction of injurious or discriminatory business methods against general contractors and market protection against governmen-

TABLE 11-1. List of Some Major National Construction Associations, 1979

Associated General Contractors of America 1957 E Street, N.W. Washington D.C. 20006	National Constructors Association 1001 Fifteenth Street, N.W. Suite 1000 Washington, D.C. 20005
The Business Roundtable (owner association) 405 Lexington Avenue New York, New York 10014	National Electrical Contractors Association 7351 Wisconsin Avenue Washington, D.C. 20014
Mason Contractors Association of America 601 Fourteenth Street, #17W Oakbrook Terrace, Illinois 60181	National Insulation Contractors Association 1001 Connecticut Avenue, N.W. Suite 800 Washington, D.C. 20036
Mechanical Contractors Association of America 5530 Wisconsin Avenue, N.W. Washington, D.C. 20015	National Utility Contractors Association 815 Fifteenth Street, N.W. Washington, D.C. 20005
National Association of Plumbing-Heating-Cooling Contractors 1016 Twentieth Street, N.W. Washington, D.C. 20036	Painting and Decorating Contractors of America 7223 Lee Highway Falls Church, Virginia 22046
National Construction Employers Council 2033 K Street, N.W. Suite 200 Washington, D.C. 20006	Sheet Metal and Air Conditioning Contractors National Associations, Inc. 8224 Courthouse Road-Tysons Corner Vienna, Virginia 22180

tal agencies performing construction with their own forces; eliminating waste and lowering construction costs; reducing injury and death to construction workmen; establishing standard contracts to protect the respective interests of owners, general contractors, subcontractors, manufacturers, and dealers; fostering a reasonable credit structure; and securing uniformity of action on principles that are for the good of the industry as a whole. See Table 11-2 for the "purposes" section from the AGC bylaws.

The recovery after World War I saw a development of far-reaching significance. The automobile apparently had come to stay, creating a new segment of the construction industry. The federal Office of Public Roads estimated that all funds available in 1920 for building hard-surface highways would total more than $633 million.

TABLE 11-2. "Purposes" Section of the Bylaws of the Associated General Contractors of America, Adopted November 21, 1918

To make membership in the association a reasonable assurance to the public of the skill, integrity, and responsibility of its members.

To maintain the standards of the contracting business at the level established by its quasi-professional character and to establish members of the association in the public mind as contractors who fulfill their obligations in full faith.

To provide methods and means whereby members may avail themselves of the greater power of combined effort through the association, acting as an authoritative body, in securing just and honorable dealings from the public whom they serve.

To promote cordial and cooperative relations between general contractors and those with whom they deal or have contact in construction.

To seek correction of injurious, discriminatory or unfair business methods practiced by or against general contractors.

To place the business risks assumed by general contractors as nearly as possible on a parity with the risks assumed by other industries of production.

To protect the legitimate market for the services of general contractors against encroachment by governmental or other agencies.

To eliminate waste and reduce construction costs through research and through cooperation with other agencies of construction.

To eliminate as far as possible the occurence of injury and death to construction workmen.

To establish various standard contracts and to coordinate such contracts with each other so that the respective interests of owners, general contractors, subcontractors, manufacturers and dealers may be properly protected.

To foster a reasonable and proper credit structure for the construction industry.

To secure uniformity of action among the individuals forming the association upon such principles as may be decided upon, from time to time, as being for the good of the industry as a whole.

Following the stock market collapse of October 1929, the construction market gradually dried up until the pump priming of the New Deal's $3.2 billion Public Works Program in June 1933. One notable exception was the $49 million contract for the largest single construction contract in history up to that time, awarded in 1931 to a joint venture called "Six Companies"—the Hoover Dam. These projects foreshadowed governmental assumption of increasingly large public works activities.

World War II brought the imposition of governmental controls on the industry—edicts of the War Production Board for contractors and of the Wage Adjustment Board for employees. The Korean conflict saw the reimposition of many of these measures. In 1971 the Nixon Administration imposed wage and price controls on the entire U.S. industry during peacetime, largely because of the inflationary wage increases that were occurring in construction. Of particular interest was the effort made by the Construction Industry Stabilization Commission (CISC)* to rationalize the complex wage and indirect labor cost relationships among more than 30 trade classifications in thousands of localities, frequently differing as well among building, highway, and utilities construction. The commission went out of existence before the results of this effort could become established. In 1979, the Carter Administration once again revived the notion of tripartitie wage control boards, although at the time of this writing, they have power only to advise rather than to regulate.

Particularly since the Great Depression of the 1930s, the government has exerted increasing influence on the construction industry. At first it was the use of construction projects to prime the pump of the economy. Labor legislation then assumed a prominent position, starting with the Davis-Bacon Act in 1931 establishing minimum wages on federal construction projects based on rates determined to be "prevailing" in the area, trade by trade. Earlier in the year the AGC had adopted a resolution at its convention attacking the practice of "many irresponsible contractors" in taking advantage of the unemployment situation to pay extremely low wages. Today, ABC, AGC, and other associations favor repeal of the act, arguing that it was a depression measure, is no longer necessary, and is inflationary.

Contractors as well as industry in general were affected by labor legislation that followed Davis-Bacon—the Norris-LaGuardia and Wagner acts—and finally in 1947 by the Taft-Hartley Act, with its provision outlawing secondary boycotts. But it was the decade of the 1970s in which governmental regulation really took off. New legislation not only affected labor relations—Equal Employment Opportunity (EEO), Occupational Safety and Health Act (OSHA), Employee Retirement Income Security Act (ERISA)—but also business relationships—Minority Business Enterprise (MBE)—and markets—Environmental Protection Agency (EPA).

Today, associations in the construction industry provide a wide range of services for their members. Since, as has been noted, most contractors are small businessmen, they do not have the staffs of specialists to be found in many other industries. To varying degrees, based on their finances and staff, construction associations assume some of these functions, in addition to providing a vehicle to use the strength of numbers in attacking common problems.

In addition to labor relations, legislation, and dealing with regulatory agencies already mentioned, typical activities and programs that may be undertaken by construction contractor associations include the following:

• Publication of newsletters, magazines, special subject bulletins, bidders' unit prices.

*The CISC was the arm of Nixon's Cost of Living Council that regulated construction wage increases. It was chaired by D. Quinn Mills.

- Labor agreements, wage rate data, contract documents, standard forms, and specifications.
- Sponsorship of management seminars.
- Foremen and apprentice training.
- Safety promotion.
- Market promotion (e.g., advocating the contract method as against owners and public agencies performing construction with their own forces; supporting bond issues or appropriations for public works).
- Public relations.
- Crime prevention.
- Promoting equal employment opportunities and use of minority business enterprises.
- Changing building codes.
- Liaison with other segments of the industry.
- Development of recommended industry practices.
- Liaison with government agencies regarding their contracting procedures.
- Disaster assistance programs.
- Operation of group health, pension, and other insurance plans.
- Assistance to members with metric conversion.
- Advice on taxation.
- Operation of plan rooms.
- Providing trustees for welfare, pension, and other funds that are jointly administered with unions or other groups.
- Sponsoring meetings, conventions, and social affairs.

RISE OF OPEN SHOP ASSOCIATIONS

Although many of the national associations referred to previously, as well as their local chapters, are composed of both union and nonunion employers, in the late 1950s an organization was formed with its main purpose being to foster open shop construction and to promote the concept that union and nonunion contractors should be protected in their right to do business with one another. That organization, Associated Builders and Contractors (ABC), claims to have doubled its membership of 7000 in 1974 to 14,000 in 1979 and claims that about 45% are general contractors, with the balance subcontractors, suppliers, and others. Ironically, although ABC's Merit Shop philosophy is deliberately neutral toward union or open shop firms, ABC has emerged—in response, perhaps, to a perceived vacuum of leadership—as the principal political advocate for open shop firms in the industry. The organization has been active in lobbying against common situs picketing legislation* and labor law reform (both supported by the building trades unions) and in favor of the repeal of federal and state prevailing wage laws.

In addition to its national political activities (that have sometimes been supported by AGC and others), ABC has given a heavy emphasis to the problems of its members in manpower recruitment, referral, and training. It also operates a computerized capability profile of its contractor members to answer owner inquiries. ABC performs many functions for its open shop members that unions or union-employer committees perform for union contractors.

ASSOCIATION OF INDUSTRIAL CONSTRUCTORS

In 1947, an organization was formed to represent large national contractors (many of whom are engineer-contractors) engaged primarily in industrial work. This organization, the National Constructors Association (NCA) today comprises some 50 members; however, it accounts for a disproportionately large fraction of the industry's output, because of the large size of its member firms—virtually all are counted among the largest 200 U.S. firms.

As a result of the financial strength of its member firms, NCA is able to offer a broad range of services through its Washington office and packs considerable legislative clout on issues affecting its membership. A recent example was NCA's ability to block changes in U.S. forcing income tax benefits that would have adversely affected construction labor costs for U.S. firms working abroad. As will be seen later, however, the interests of its members have at times conflicted with those of local general or specialty contrators; this has pitted the NCA against the AGC and the NECA in costly economic and legal battles.

OWNER ASSOCIATIONS

Purchasers of construction have had associations for many years—among them, such organizations as the American Public Works Association, American Association of State Highway Officials, American Water Works Association, Buildings Owners and Managers Association International, and International Council of Shopping Centers. However, associations of owners formed for the specific purpose of affecting the management of construction is a recent manifestation.

Although it is difficult to get precise measures of the relative dollar vol-

---

*Common situs picketing would permit employees of one subcontractor to picket all employers on a jobsite. Under current law employees may picket only their own employer and his suppliers at a separate gate.

umes or employment levels of union and open shop construction, the open shop sector has clearly expanded significantly over the last 10 years. In response to—or in some cases contributing to—this recent growth in open shop construction, changes have taken place in the structure and activities not only of contractor associations, firms, and building trades unions, but also of construction users.

TRENDS AMONG CONSTRUCTION USERS

Some of the recent growth in open shop construction has been actively supported—even promoted—by both industrial and commercial users of construction. In contrast, the U.S. government, also a major user of construction, has attempted to find ways to keep unions competitive on government work. This section explores recent trends among all these users and the development of an owner association—the Business Roundtable.

INDUSTRIAL USERS. The construction cost of new plants is a major capital cost item for industrial users of construction. As a result they have presented the most organized efforts of any user group to promote cost-efficient construction. Historically, most major industrial construction projects have been carried out by union contractors. There are two reasons for this: first, until very recently, virtually all the firms with the capability to design and construct major plants were union; thus owners had very little choice; second, if an owner's work force were organized, there was the risk of embroiling this work force in a dispute by engaging open shop construction firms for the construction of new plants and especially for modifications or extensions to existing plants.

During the late 1960s and early 1970s, several changes began to occur that made union construction less attractive to some of these users. First, union construction wages leapfrogged upward at unprecedented rates, fueled by the strong demand for construction. Second, a series of contract and other strikes paralyzed several major projects and created confusion and uncertainly for others. This uncertainty in schedule is intolerable to industrial clients building revenue-producing facilities in competitive markets. Third—and perhaps most significant—the continuing shift of economic activity to the southern part of the United States following World War II has meant that much of the new industrial construction was being carried out in traditionally open shop environments and often for users desiring to have nonunion plant labor forces.

As a result several major industrial owners began considering the unthinkable—building their facilities with open shop labor. After some tentative initial moves in this direction, several major users, notably DuPont, Dow Chemical, and several oil and utility companies, began contracting with open shop firms for a considerable proportion of their new construc-

tion work. At the same time, representatives of the engineering departments of these large user firms began preaching the claimed virtues of open
shop construction at industry conventions and seminars.

Many other industrial users have elected to continue building their
plants with union labor. Recognizing the shortcomings of local collective
bargaining in construction, they have been able to "end run" the problem
by having their contractors negotiate special "project labor agreements"
containing terms that are much more favorable than those in the existing
local agreements. These project agreements are negotiated with all the
local unions that will be involved on the project, sometimes with the assistance of representatives from the international unions, and are binding only
for the duration of the project. Typically, these will tie wages to local union
wages but will have dramatically different provisions regarding such things
as travel pay, shift work, overtime, and use of helpers. In addition, project
labor agreements have often had no-strike, no-lockout provisions. These
are particularly irksome to local union contractors who may find those
involved in a major project continuing to work through a local strike and,
as a result, totally undermining their own bargaining position.

Industrial users have also promoted project labor agreements with non
union construction firms, thereby keeping their construction "union." Nonunion firms—Daniel International is a prime example—have been able to
negotiate project agreements with terms that are more favorable than
those in the local labor agreements and often with terms even more favorable than those in project agreements negotiated by union construction
firms. The motive for the international unions to grant such concessions to
open shop firms is to capture work for their union members that would
otherwise go open shop. From the open shop contractor's point of view, the
project labor agreement does not tie him into any permanent union relationship and at the same time provides him access to the union's labor
pool.

Industrial users have, therefore, found project labor agreements helpful
in the short term to construct their plants union at a lower cost than could
be obtained under the existing local labor agreements and usually without
the risk of strikes. And the unions have been willing to make whatever
concessions seem necessary to the competitive.

In spite of the obvious short-term benefits of project labor agreements to
both industrial owners and their contractors, the long-term effect of these
project labor agreements, especially those containing a no-strike, no-lockout provision, has been to undermine dramatically the position of the local
contractors in their bargaining. The resulting increases in wages and benefits are ultimatrly borne by these users through retroactive wage adjustments on their existing projects, but, more importantly, these increases
help to push up the general levels of union construction wages and benefits
across the country.

PRIVATE REAL ESTATE DEVELOPERS. Private real estate developers are users of construction for whom the price is an important part of their cost of doing business. Whereas they have not organized along the lines of industrial users, they have taken actions as individuals that have in some cases promoted the growth of open shop construction.

Several large developers of commercial property have wholly owned construction subsidiaries. In the past these firms have often been union firms because most of their activity was in downtown areas, where union construction was dominant. Along with the trend in all building construction toward more subcontracting, these in-house firms have generally become essentially construction management firms, subcontracting all their labor. This has provided flexibility to use open shop subcontractors in some cases. A good example of this is the tenant improvement work. This can be performed after the structure is completed and all the basic and mechanical trades are off the jobsite. As a result pickets against open shop firms doing the tenant improvement work are relatively ineffective.

At the same time, some of these developers have extended their operations to shopping centers and suburban office parks outside unionized cities. As a result they are more easily able to use open shop firms on all or the majority of the on-site work.

UNITED STATES GOVERNMENT. The federal government is the largest single buyer of construction services in the United States. Aside from its actions as a regulator of the industry through labor law, agencies of the federal government have exerted some of the same kinds of pressures as private users on construction labor relations. Specifically, the U.S. Department of Transporation, under secretary Coleman, actively promoted the use of project labor agreements, including no-strike, no-lockout provisions (applying also to strikes or lockouts following unsuccessful negotiations to replace an expired contract) for mass transit construction. In fact, in approving the application of Buffalo, New York, for federal financing of its new mass transit system, Coleman implied that a no-strike, project labor agreement between the local authority and local building trades was almost a "sine qua non" for federal funding of mass transit.

This policy was in the interest both of the local transit authorities who benefited from the reduced risks of strikes and of large union contractors who would be working on the project. However, the measure was vigorously opposed by smaller, local contractors in Buffalo, as well as in Baltimore, Maryland, where an even stronger no-strike, no-lockout project agreement was negotiated. The opposition by local contractors, both union and open shop, to these provisions was predictable. Local union contractors feared the weakening of their bargaining position as a result of the large project that would operate through a local contract termination strike. Local nonunion contractors, on the other hand, had conditions imposed on them by these agreements that reduced their competitive advantage over union firms. the Baltimore agreement, in addition to a no-strike clause, had a "no-bumping" clause that prevented nonunion contractors from moving their workers around between different jurisdictions.

These local contractors expressed their opposition through their national associations so vigorously that Secretary Coleman backed off considerably from his initial strong endorsement of project agreements. In June 1977, the new Secretary, Brock Adams, stated that the appropriateness of no-strike agreements would be assessed on a case-by-case basis.

A subsequent project agreement that was used for the construction of bus facilitiies in Denver, Colorado, modified the no-strike, no-lock-out provision to permit strikes in connection with the negotiations of local collective bargaining agreements. This removed the primary objection of local contractors to these project agreements. Thus local contractors who had been unable to stem the tide of project labor agreements on private projects found some success in persuading the U.S. government to stop promoting their use.

DEVELOPMENT OF THE BUSINESS ROUNDTABLE. In addition to their actions as individuals, industrial owners have attempted to influence the structure and outcome of construction labor relations through an association, the Business Roundtable. The Roundtable grew from the "National Conference on Construction Problems" sponsored by the U.S. Chamber of Commerce in the fall of 1968 to discuss the rapidly escalating cost of industrial construction, particularly the rise in labor costs. The Chamber president at that time was Winton Blount, a large Alabama contractor who had become convinced that contractors had serious labor relations problems and that users were exacerbating contractors' problems by their own uninformed and self-serving actions. The conference appointed a task force of user, contractor, and contractor association members to draft proposals for action. The proposals called for the formation of the following:

> . . . an organization of major purchasers of construction. . .to establish a responsible and informed cooperation between purchasers of construction and contractors on the construction industry's labor relations.

Shortly after the issuance of this report, the Construction Users' Anti-Inflation Roundtable was established, with Roger Blough, Chief, Executive Officer of U.S. Steel, as its first Chairman. This group included the Chief Executive Officers of about 60 of the nation's largest companies. A working committee of 15 to 20 members met fortnightly in New York as the executive arm of the group.

The main thrust of "Roger's Roundtable" was to educate users about the impact their decisions could have on construction labor relations. Specifically, the Roundtable tried to dissuade its members (and other industrial users) from having their contractors work through local strikes. The

Roundtable stimulated the formation of independent, local user groups in serveral cities to help "educate" local divisions of member companies as well as nonmember local businesses.

The Construction Users' Anti-Inflation Roundtable has since merged with the Labor Law Study Group (in late 1972) and other business research and lobby groups to become the Business Roundtable. In the process the organization's scope of activities has broadened far beyond construction labor concerns to include environmental, taxation, welfare, and pension issues. However, the working committee of the old Roundtable lives on as the Construction Committee of the Business Roundtable and continues to be the dominant organization of construction users in the United States.

PROBLEMS OF CONTRACTOR ASSOCIATIONS IN BEING EFFECTIVE

FRAGMENTATION

Most of the problems of U.S. contractor associations derive from what has often been referred to as forces for fragmentation that are inherent—one might almost say endemic—in the industry. Looking only at the twentieth century, this fragmentation has been manifested in many ways.

FUNCTIONAL TYPES OF MARKETS. Clearly identifiable and discrete markets exist in home building, general building (commercial, industrial, institutional and public building, and multiunit housing), highways, heavy utilities (sewers ad water mains), tunnels, oil pipelines, power transmission lines, and marine construction.

Generally, a contractor will concentrate on one functional type, rarely on more than two. Different equipment is required as are different worker crafts and different engineering and management skills. Some work with architects exclusively; others, with engineers. Highway contractors deal largely with one state agency: a department of public works. Building contractors deal with many owners—some public, some private.

SIZE OF FIRMS. San Francisco-based Bechtel and Houston-based Brown & Root in 1978 were each awarded over $4 billion in construction contracts (according to *Engineering News-Record*)*. U. S. census data show that over half of all persons calling themselves contractors had no employees, and another 25% had less than four employees in 1972† (data for 1977 were not available at the time of writing but are unlikely to differ significantly).

Based on size alone, the interests of firms are diverse. The large construction firms have their in-house specialists in marketing, estimating, purchasing, operations, labor relations, accident prevention, training, equal em-

---

*Engineering News-Record, Top 400 Construction Firms Issue, April 1979.
†U.S. Dept. of Commerce, Bureau of the Census. *Census of the Construction Industry,* 1972.

ployment opportunity, and in monitoring government regulations. The small firms, without such specialists, look to their associations for assistance in many of these areas, particularly those relating to government regulations and labor relations and to a lesser extent accident prevention and training.

It is certainly to their credit that most of the larger firms are generous in making their personnel available to the associations for the development and execution of much specialized committee activity.

DEGREE OF MOBILITY. Correlated with size, to some extent, is the matter of mobility. Smaller contractors tend to stay in the geographical market area with which they are familiar and in which they have acquired expertise. Larger contractors undertake construction in varying numbers of states, regions, and countries. Often to obtain manpower the larger projects will offer premiums to workers, either in wages or in overtime, pirating them from local contractors. Many of these "visiting" contractors have national agreements. During labor contract negotiations they may decline to invoke the five-day notification clause—if one exists—and keep the project going, while the local contractors attempt to negotiate a favorable agreement. The local union, which has a large body of its members who are at work with the national contractor, will be inclined to keep the the strike going, since often it will ultimately result in a larger wage & benefit increase for them. On the other side of the coin are the instances where local contractors have little work going and decide that this is the year to be tough with the union—at the expense of a visiting contractor who has agreed to support the local association.

GENERAL CONTRACTOR OR SUBCONTRACTOR. As construction projects became larger and more complex, specialists came into being to perform particular work. The master builder became obsolete, and his organizational, coordination, and managerial functions were assumed by a general contractor. Although both general contractors and subcontractors are part of the construction team—the other parts being the architect or engineer and the owner—they frequently are in an adversary role. Disagreements arise over who is to do what work. Progress may be delayed by a general contractor or by a subcontractor, causing the other unanticipated overhead expenses. Disputes arise over the amount of money due on progress payments for work performed to date or on the amount due because of changes in the work made by the owner.

Although it is a generalization subject to many exceptions, particularly among sucontractors in classifications in which technology has become highly sophisticated, historically many subcontractors were former craftsmen who went into business for themselves. Many still hold union memberships. They are closely allied with a single union craft. During the past 20 years, on the other hand, the principals of general contracting firms usually sought engineering degrees that have increasingly included management subjects or, more recently, construction management or pure business degrees. And if such firms perform the basic elements of construction with their own forces, they deal with not one but three to six (or more) crafts.

SINGLE CONTRACT OR SEPARATE CONTRACTS. In October 1923 the Joint Committee of the Mechanical trades requested the Interdepartmental Board of the federal Government to require separate prime contracts on construction projects. Although the board rejected the proposal as uneconomical, several state legislatures, notably New York, have mandated separate contracts on public building construction. The push for separate contracts has died out in recent years, but the bitter feelings engendered by these earlier fights have continued to exacerbate relations between general contractors and subcontractors in many areas.

UNION AND OPEN SHOP. Certain tensions are built into the relationship between union and open shop firms that are reflected in their respective associations' attitudes and priorities.

Open shop firms can sometimes obtain lower bid prices by a combination of lower average wages, freedom from restrictions in the assignment of labor, reduced risk of work stoppages, and other factors. In periods of low employment they will often employ union journeymen with "their card in their shoe" who were trained in apprentice programs financed by union firms. In tight labor markets, on the other hand, open shop firms have problems recruiting skilled labor at any wage less than the union wage. Prevailing wage laws that narrow the wage gap are often a further source of bitter friction and animosity between union and open shop firms (although some union contractor associations have opposed them anyway).

The situation becomes particularly aggravated when there exists, for example, both a union and nonunion plumbing contractors' association in a single state or region.

A new element was introduced into the union versus nonunion conflict in 1971 when the NLRB decided two cases in which it upheld the legality of double-breasted operations—that is, a union firm and a nonunion firm with substantially common ownership. Although the decisions make clear that total separation of the labor forces and day-to-day management staffs must be maintained, particularly those responsible for labor relations, many other factors are looked into on a case-by-case basis, including the interrelationship of operations, the markets, and whether there is an antiunion animus or intent. After an initial burst of interest following these cases, it would appear that the establishment of double-breasted operations has leveled off.

Finally, there has been a recent increase in the acquisition of wholly owned nonunion subsidiaries by many major union firms. For example,

Fluor Corp., a Los Angeles-based heavy industrial constructor, purchased Daniel International, a large nonunion firm based in Greenville, South Carolina, to enable it to build large industrial projects on an open shop basis. A quick analysis of the *Engineering News-Record's* top 400 firms for 1979 identified some 25 double-breasted union firms with open shop components.* Moreover, the top 400 firms included 50 open shop firms, up from 35 in 1978.

To a greater or lesser degree, all the foregoing forces for fragmentation continue today, reinforced by the multiplicity of associations that have lives of their own but which have overlapping as well as competing memberships, interests, and functions.

OTHER LIMITATIONS ON EFFECTIVENESS

Items other than fragmentation influence an association's effectiveness. Closely related are budget and staff.

Association Financing

Traditionally, most trade associations, including those in construction, have derived the bulk of their income from dues or membership fees. Typically, these dues or fees have been based on a sliding scale relative to the dollar volume of work performed by the contracting firm. A few have, in addition, derived income from the operation of plan rooms, and from publications, trade shows, conventions, social events, insurance programs, government grants, and contracts. However, a 1976 survey of 118 construction trade associations carried out by the American Society of Association Executives (ASAE) showed that in the majority of cases none of these other categories accounted for more than 2% of total income.

A December 1977 ASAE survey of 234 construction trade associations showed that 52% had expense budgets of under $200,000 and 21% had expense budgets of under $100,000.

Industry Funds

A long-standing irritation for association members is that a substantial part of the association activities that their membership fees make possible benefits nonmembers who pay nothing. Beginning in the late 1950s industry promotion funds were established by various specialty trades. Financed by employer contributions required as a part of the locally negotiated collective bargaining agreements, they were jointly administered by union and management trustees.

The Chicago lathing and plastering industry was the first group to develop such a fund in an effort to gain back some of the market for its

*Engineering News-Record, Top 400 Construction Firms Issue, April 1979.

products, which had been dwindling for several years. Later the bricklayers' unions and mason contractors' association established funds to promote the advantages of masonry construction among architects and owners.

In May 1960 the Philadelphia Builders Chapter of AGC expanded on this concept to establish an industry advancement program (IAP) to finance a wide range of activities that were listed in the collective bargaining agreement—public relations, education, market development, industry relations, accident prevention, apprenticeship training, and labor relations. By the late 1960s the IAP concept had begun to spread. Today, a high percentage of general contractor and building industry employers' types of associations derive some of their income from IAP funds. Typically, the contributions are 3 to 5¢ for each employee hour worked. Unlike the early industry promotion funds of the specialty trades, the IAP's are administered solely by employer trustees.

The industry-wide fund negotiated by the NECA with the International Brotherhood of Electrical Workers in 1976 was the first nationwide fund. This particular industry advancement fund has been a source of considerable friction between the NECA (which is composed primarily of local firms) and the NCA; in fact, it has led to a lawsuit by NCA challenging the legality of this fund. The basic difference of opinion is whether the activities of the local NECA chapters should be financed from regular dues of their contractor members or whether they should be financed 100% by the industry advancement funds. This issue is presently sub judice.

The Business Roundtable has questioned the propriety of IAPs. The main objections are that some associations may become dependent on such funds for their continued existence and that since the funds are collected as a result of provisions included in collective bargaining agreements the bargaining position of the employers in such cases may be compromised. On the other hand, where the funds supplement and do not replace membership fees, some local user groups have endorsed specific IAPs, recognizing that many of the activities (supporting the construction of a particualar power plant as an example) are of direct benefit to members of the users' groups.

AGC, recognizing that care should be exercised in the establishment and conduct of IAPs, has developed a set of suggested guidelines for its chapters. These are included as Table 11-3.

Association Staffing

The typical state or local association has three or fewer full-time employees. The December 1977 ASAE survey of national, regional, state, and local construction trade associations showed 30% with one or two employees, 18% with three, and 14% with four.

It is difficult for one or two persons, acting as the full executive staff of a small association, to be expert in all the many subjects with which the members are concerned. Such persons frequently end up putting out fires or doing housekeeping chores. By the very nature of such operations, the association becomes dependent on the contributions of time given by the voluntary leadership and the association members themselves.

But here the dog begins to chase its tail, because most contracting firms are small businesses, with one principal, one office executive to assist in estimating and purchasing, one secretary-bookkeeper, and a couple of outside superintendents. Time given to the association by these persons often means they are not producing direct dollars for their firms.

To attempt to solve these problems some associations have engaged attorneys or consultants to perform such varied functions as legislative lobbying, labor negotiations, and public relations. While there are many expert practitioners in these fields, these practitioners have the disadvantage that comes from the lack of day-to-day immersion in the full range of association activities and regular contract with the personalities which comprise the association voluntary leadership. In the field of labor relations, particularly, the day-to-day administration of the contract has a profound effect on the outcome of negotiations occurring every one to three years.

OVERCOMING THE PROBLEMS OF FRAGMENTATION

Since the 1950s various efforts have been made to reduce the problems arising from the fragmented nature of the industry. these have usually taken the form of bringing together existing organizations to attack a specific problem or related problems rather than mergers. The following, while not all, represent what are probably the most significant.

Construction Industry Joint Conference (CIJC)

In 1959 there was established the Construction Industry Joint Conference (CIJC), comprised of the general presidents of international building trades unions and representatives of participating national contractors, associations. CIJC's stated purposes were to preserve and promote the contract system of construction, to seek improved performance and productivity by contractors and by workers, and to provide a continuing forum in which labor-management and industry problems could be regularly discussed, with efforts made to reach constructive and equitable solutions.

In its first year of operation CIJC published a brochure designed to promote among industrial plant owners the contract method for their construction maintenance work. A second brochure in 1961 was designed to promote the contract method generally.

Following the resignation of Professor John T. Dunlop as Impartial Chairman in 1967, the parties failed to agree on its future objectives and the council dissolved. However, partly as the result of early encouragement by CIJC, local labor management groups provide a forum for discussion

TABLE 11-3. Associated General Contractors of America, Industry Advancement Program, Suggested Guidelines

1. The need for the programs should be realized and the programs should be planned *before* the industry program is negotiated or funds are collected. An industry program should not be established merely for the purpose of accumulating large sums of money for which there is no real need. The needs of the industry in the geographical area affected should be closely examined, and programs for fulfilling such needs should be worked out prior to reaching a decision to establish the industry program. The needs of one geographical area may differ from another. However, examples of needed programs may include, but not be limited to, accident prevention; apprenticeship training; education; research into new methods and materials; public relations; relations with architects, awarding authorities, subcontractors and material and equipment suppliers; labor relations; market development and disaster relief.

2. Extreme care should be used in determining the cents per hour contribution to be established in the collective bargaining agreement. Determining factors should include the cost of the programs contemplated, the average number of manhours worked by the trades involved, and the establishment and maintenance of a reasonable reserve.

3. The question of when to negotiate for an industry program frequently arises. It is strongly recommended that such negotiations take place during the regular process of collective bargaining, immediately preceding the termination of an existing agreement. Existing agreements should not be disturbed for the purpose of establishing industry programs prior to their expiration dates.

4. Expenditures from industry programs must be made for programs for the benefit of all contributors rather than for programs for the benefit of Chapter members only.

5. Chapters having industry programs should continue to collect dues from their members and dues payments should not be allowed as credit toward contributions owed to the industry program.

6. When deciding whether an activity or program should be paid for by the industry program or by the Chapter's dues account, the intended beneficiary should be the determining factor. As an example, if a bulletin is mailed to Chapter members only, the cost of preparing and mailing such bulletin should be paid for by the Chapter. However, if such a bulletin were distributed to all employer contributors to the industry program, then the cost of such bulletin should be borne by the industry program. If a management seminar is conducted and only Chapter members are invited, the cost of such a program should be borne by the Chapter and its members. If all industry program contributors are invited, then the cost of the program should be borne by the industry program.

and communication and take action on matters only where there is clear consensus.

Council of Construction Employers (CCE)

In November 1968 eight of the national associations that had been members of CIJC organized a Council of Construction Employers (CCE). It

TABLE 11-3. (continued)

7. The permissive uses for an industry program should most certainly be spelled out in writing and strictly adhered to. Whether this should be in the form of a formal trust agreement or merely in the collective bargaining agreement is the subject of considerable differences of opinion among attorneys, which sometimes varies according to state laws. It is recommended that any Chapter contemplating the establishment of an industry program ask its attorney to give special consideration to this point. Also, it is pointed out that if a trust is created, the industry program becomes a separate entity from the Chapter and could at some future time overshadow the Chapter in prominence and importance. In any event, it is worth repeating that the uses for such funds be spelled out in some form in a written document, and could include such items as those listed in paragraph 1 above.

8. Also it is desirable that prohibitions against the uses of the industry program should be spelled out in writing. Because of the very nature of the program, it should not be used to harm the union which is a party to the collective bargaining agreement. For example, the program should not be used for lobbying or publicizing the promotion of legislation harmful to the union, for subsidizing contractors during a strike, or to the union, for subsidizing contractors during a strike, or for litigation against the union. This is not to say that a Chapter under certain conditions should not engage in such activities, but when doing so, should not use the industry program for those purposes.

9. There shall be no labor representation on the Board of Administration. Whether non-member contributors should be represented on the Board of Administration is a matter for local decision.

10. It is recommended that approximately one year's operating expense be accumulated as a reserve. Many of the programs will be long-range in nature, and collections may be disrupted because of strikes or lack of work. Therefore, a reasonable reserve is both necessary and desirable. Conversely, a large reserve should be discouraged because of Bureau of Internal Revenue limits placed on reserves of tax exempt organizations. In addition, the purpose of an industry program is to meet the needs of the industry and not to accumulate large and unnecessary reserves. Because of the size and nature of industry programs, it is strongly recommended that regular and independent audits be conducted by a CPA and that the results of such audits be made available to all contributors upon request.

11. In establishing an industry program for the first time, many problems will occur which could not be foreseen in the preparation of guidelines. Therefore, it is strongly recommended that Chapters contemplating such programs should confer with the National AGC and with Chapters already managing an industry program.

12. The recommendations and suggestions in these guidelines should not be substituted for competent legal advice. It is recommended that Chapters consult with their attorney or an attorney experienced in setting up Industry Advancement Programs before such programs are undertaken.

employed a full-time staff executive in 1972. At its high point it had 15 members. CCE's major activities included the study and discussion of federal legislation, the exchange of information on collective bargaining and other labor relations matters, and the development of action programs to monitor and promote or oppose government programs affecting the industry.

Under its rules CCE could only take action in its own name if there were unanimity. Each association was represented by its chief elected officer and its chief staff executive.

Contractors Mutual Association (CMA)

During this period yet another national organization was formed to deal with labor relations concerns. The Contractors Mutual Association (CMA) membership was composed of individual construction firms rather than of associations. It was founded in May 1971 by some 40, mostly union, general contractors. Starting out with broad goals of improving labor relations in the industry, CMA very quickly focused its efforts in two principal areas—to continue the operation of the labor agreement data bank initially developed by CISC and to improve the structure of collective bargaining, particularly through the promotion of so-called wide-area bargaining.

During the 1960s partly as a result of the consolidation of local unions by the internationals and partly as a result of efforts by employers to eliminate the effects of leapfrogging of wages and conditions, agreements with individual trades tended to cover wider areas. However, the instances of coordinated bargaining among employers and unions covering more than one trade or craft were rare.

In May 1973 CMA distributed a position paper on coordinated wide-area bargaining to some 2000 contractors in the industry. This was followed up with several attempts to establish wider bargaining units than the traditional local unions in several parts of the United States. CMA also encouraged contractor associations to negotiate with several trades simultaneously in these wide areas. During its existence CISC also attempted to define rational wide areas that would correspond to economic regions with something like a common labor pool.

As a result of all these initiatives, approximately 30 of these wide-area efforts could be identified in 1979. However, given the present structure and positions of construction unions and employer associations, the prospect is that the concept will grow slowly, if at all.

In 1979 the operation of CMA's data bank was assumed by a new Construction Labor Research Council, comprised of CMA, NCA, AGC, and MCA.

National Construction Employers Council (NCEC)

Another step to seek to establish a single management voice on labor relations matters in the unionized construction industry was taken in January

1978 with the formal organization of the National Construction Employers Council (NCEC). It was put together after months of effort by H. Edgar Lore, a past president of the NCA and chairman of CMA. When AGC and other associations comprising CCE voted to cast their lot with the new organization, NCEC was on its way and CCE dissolved. Within months of its formation NCEC had employed as its chief executive officer a man with no previous construction experience but with a background of management administration in several national companies who had been a former assistant secretary of labor, Richard J. Grunewald. By 1979 NCEC's membership numbered 17 national contractor associations.

The main objective of NCEC is to improve the collective bargaining process in the industry, including efforts to reduce fragmentation and to overcome the conflicts between local and national bargaining. One of the organization's early actions was to hold a national seminar in October 1979, "Negotiations Planning for 1980." Topics included the effect of federal pay standards on construction industry bargaining, national construction industry data and trends, elements of sound negotiations planning, local considerations of an economic nature, management bargaining data and tools, and goal setting.

An interesting feature of NCEC is its structure. Policy making and control rest with a board of directors composed of two voluntary elected officers of each of the constituent associations. NCEC also provides for non-policy-making participation by members of national staffs of the member associations through an operating committee that is task oriented. The organization's modest first-year budget of $225,000 provided for a full-time staff consisting of Grunewald, a president, a vice president–labor relations, and support personnel.

National Construction Industry Council (NCIC)

A national organization with even broader participation is the National Construction Industry Council (NCIC). At the invitation of AGC's president, the late Saul Horowitz Jr., representatives of about 20 industry associations met in Reston, Virginia, in August 1974 to explore the possibility of establishing a federation of associations "to speak to other industries and to our nation with a single voice" A study committee was appointed and developed guidelines for the organization. These guidelines were adopted in January 1975.

With more than a sidelong glance at the Canadian Construction Association, NCIC opened its membership to national associations of design and other professionals, suppliers, educators, and managers as well as to contractors and subcontractors. Over 30 national organizations held membership in 1979.

NCIC's broadly stated purposes are as follows:

1. To provide effective liaison between the member associations in order to achieve greater overall efficiency in the construction industry.

2. To provide the means for consultation in matters of mutual interest between the member associations and with the U.S. government on issues affecting the construction industry and the best interest of the public.

3. To provide the means for issuing joint policy statements to the public on issues affecting the construction industry.

Each association has three representatives, one of whom may be a principal staff member, but only one vote. A quorum consists of two-thirds of the members, and a 75% majority is required to initiate action on any matter, except that a 90% majority is required on labor-related items. Meetings of NCIC have been held about four times a year.

NCIC has supported the creation of an office of construction in the federal government, taken positions to alleviate problems of individual employer liability in multiemployer bargaining pension plans under ERISA, and supported President Carter's energy program.

Factors limiting the effectiveness of NCIC are finances and staffing arrangements. NCIC's total 1979 budget was approximately $45,000. The organization employed no staff but rather relied on a prominent Washington multiple-association management firm to handle its administration. On occasion, when a constituent association is particularly interested in a subject, the association will contribute the time of its staff to assist the project.

Before it becomes a significant force in the industry, NCIC will probably have to establish a track record of victories in order to overcome the tendency of most associations to jealously guard their own turf and to reluctantly give credit to any organization but their own. In the meantime it at least provides an established structure for government and others to call on to find out if the various segments of the industry can speak with one voice on a particular matter.

CONCLUSIONS

It was stated at the outset of this chapter that organizations evolve in response to societal and economic needs. Contractor and owner associations in the U.S. construction industry accordingly represent the fragmentation and polarization exhibited by firms in the industry, in an atmosphere of rigorous competition for survival.

Union contractor associations thus far have been unable to completely surmount the centrifugal forces that have been discussed in this chapter. Associations modify and adapt, but even as they are doing so new economic and social forces are evolving in a never-ending helix.

For the near future at least, conflicts between local and national union firms abetting other structural defects in the construction bargaining process in an inflationary environment will foster wage increases above those of other segments of the economy. Coupled with the construction industry's declining productivity during the 1970s, this factor may force the union segment of the industry to be amenable to government-sponsored efforts to restructure the bargaining process to prevent itself from self-destructing.

These, along with other factors we have discussed, will result in open shop firms assuming larger projects. Subcontractor associations that have heretofore been largely union will structure an accommodation to include open shop firms among their memberships, as AGC seems to have been able to do by emphasizing broad membership services outside labor relations. At the same time ABC will continue its membership expansion as an organization dedicated to the active promotion of the open shop.

One development that might radically alter the structure of the industry's associations would be the emergence of a new kind of union firm. Large existing, open shop firms, in the opinion of some industry experts, will be organized on a multicraft basis, by a single union—like an industrial plant. However, the current antilabor mood of the United States Congress makes reform of the nation's labor law—a prerequisite for this type of bottom-up organization of open shop firms—unlikely in the next few years.

CHAPTER 12

OPEN SHOP MOVEMENT

Raymond E. Levitt
Donald S. Barrie

Managers of construction firms have the rights, under U.S. labor law, to unilaterally decide whether they will operate a union or open shop. In contrast to their peers in large manufacturing industries, U.S. construction managers may sign prehire agreements with building trades unions to represent their workers; or, alternatively, they may hire workers directly and negotiate wages and working conditions individually. The short duration of most projects and the rapid turnover of workers make bottom-up organization of a construction firm's labor force almost impossible.

This creates a unique opportunity—or dilemma—for construction company managers. This chapter compares worker wages and benefits and labor management practices between union and nonunion construction. It endeavors to identify some of the advantages and disadvantages of each organization form and to identify to characteristics of projects and locations for which each of the two approaches is most efficient. In the changing climate envisioned for the 1980s, company managers and buyers of construction must evaluate the two options for their types and scales of projects; unions must become aware of changes that they must make to compete in those markets in which open shop firms are now more efficient, and open shop firms (and associations) must continually strive to overcome the limitations of their present structure.

*Some of the material in this chapter was first published in a paper entitled "Union vs. Nonunion Construction in the U.S." by Raymond E. Levitt, *ASCE Journal of the Construction Division*, December 1979, Proceedings paper 15020 and is reprinted with the permission of ASCE.

UNION VERSUS NONUNION CONSTRUCTION

Previous comparisons between union and nonunion construction have been largely polemical in nature. The reasons for this are obvious: (1) The issue is an emotional one for many people; and (2) while labor management practices in the unionized sector of the industry have been well documented, there has been no such source of objective data on wages and labor management practices in nonunion construction. Consequently, in 1976 the Department of Housing and Urban Development (HUD) sponsored a major survey of the construction industry in order to compare and contrast on the basis of recent, unbiased data, the wages and work practices in all types (residential, commercial, and industrial and heavy and highway) of union and nonunion construction.*

The study described in this chapter was carried out by the Department of Civil Engineering at the Massachusetts Institute of Technology (MIT) Cambridge, Massachusetts, in collaboration with the Economics Department of the National Association of Home Builders (NAHB).* The study's primary sources of data were two types of surveys. The first was a wage questionnaire mailed to a large, random sample of all contractors in eight different metropolitan areas—Boston, Massachusetts; Baltimore, Maryland; Atlanta, Georgia; New Orleans, Louisiana; Grand rapids, Michigan; Kansas; Denver, Colorado; and Portland, Oregon. The universe of firms in a Standard Metropolitan Survey Area (SMSA) was compiled by combining a Dun and Bradstreet listing of all firms in construction with membership lists of contractor associations such as NAHB, AGC, and ABC. The response rate to the questionnaires averaged 19%. For cities with a very low response rate a follow-up survey of nonrespondents was used to verify the results of the initial survey (Table 12-1 for a description of the sample and response.). The second source of data was a series of personal interviews on labor management issues conducted with a smaller sample of firms drawn from the union and nonunion sectors of the industry in each of the eight areas. These interviews covered the firms' practices with regard to job descriptions, skill levels, and wage structure; technology and work rules; hiring methods; and training and apprenticeship programs. In addition, the interviews sought to determine the impact of prevailing wage laws on wages and labor management practices, especially for nonunion contractors.

The line between union and nonunion firms is not an absolutely clear one. First, nonunion firms may sign formal project agreements or informal "one-line" agreements that effectively make them union firms on particu-

*Bourdon, C.C., and Levitt, R.E., *Union and Open-Shop Construction: Compensation, Work practies, and Labor Markets*; Lexington Books, D. C. Heath & Co., Lexington, Mass., 1980.

*The study was entitled *A comparison of Wages and Labor Management Practices in Union and Non Union Construction*. M.I.T. Dept. of Civil Engineering Research Report R78-10, Cambridge, Mass; 1978.

TABLE 12-1.   MIT/NAHB Wage Survey Sample, 1976

SMSA (1)	Total number of firms (2)	Total number mailed (3)	Number responded (4)
Atlanta, Georgia	7,023	2,284	298
Baltimore, Maryland	4,056	1,980	386
Boston, Massachusetts	6,058	2,413	481
Denver, Colorado	4,338	1,680	418
Grand Rapids, Michigan	1,809	830	205
Kansas City, Kansas	3,821	1,117	220
New Orleans, Louisiana	3,538	1,450	177
Portland, Oregon	3,815	1,602	375
Total	34,458	13,700	2,560

lar projects. Second, nonunion firms often hire unemployed union members. For the purposes of this study a firm was considered to be nonunion if it indicated that it was "not signatory to a collective bargaining agreement."

The eight large metropolitan areas chosen for the survey were picked to represent both a geographic dispersion across the country and areas that had a substantial mix of union and nonunion construction activity. Both the wage questionnaire and the contractor interviews were designed to permit the comparison and cross tabulation of data by firm type (either general or subcontractor), size (defined either by annual dollar volume or present employment), product market (residential, commercial and industrial and heavy and highway), and union or nonunion status. The purpose of this approach was to permit the comparison of union and nonunion differences in wages and labor management practices, while controlling for firm size and type of construction. The remainder of the chapter presents the findings of this study in the areas of firm size and product markets, wages, occupational structure, work rules and technology, hiring and referral systems, apprenticeship and training, impact of prevailing wage laws, and trends in the construction industry.

PRODUCT MARKETS, FIRM SIZE, AND SIZE OF OPEN SHOP SECTOR

In all eight areas, most of the union firms that responded to the wage survey identified themselves as doing a majority of their work in either commercial/industrial or heavy and highway construction. In contrast, the open shop firms were primarily engaged in residential or commercial/industrial work or both. (Table 12-2 presents a breakdown of union and open shop employment by product market.)

In all the areas surveyed, open shop firms were found to be considerably smaller than union firms doing similar types of construction, for example,

TABLE 12-2. Percentage of Union and Open Shop Employment by Product Market for Study Sample

SMSA (1)	Union, as a percentage			Open shop, as a percentage		
	Residen-tial (2)	Com-mercial/ industrial (3)	Heavy and highway (4)	Residen-tial (5)	Com-mercial/ industrial (6)	Heavy and highway (7)
Boston	11	72	17	55	41	4
Baltimore	2	63	35	49	46	5
Atlanta	0.6	91	8.4	26	65	9
New Orleans	0.5	92	7.5	16	82	2
Grand Rapids	1	48	51	48	49	3
Kansas City	7	61	32	68	32	0
Denver	6	73	21	68	29	3
Portland	11	72	17	67	24	9

in Grand Rapids the median size of open shop firms doing predominantly commercial and industrial work was 18 employees, with a median dollar volume of activity (in 1975) of $1,000,000. Union firms in similar types of construction in Grand Rapids have a median of 37 employees and a 1975 volume of $4,300,000. Despite these general trends, it was evident that there are now a few very large open shop firms, both general and subcontractors, in most of the areas surveyed (see Table 12-3).

The sample was selected to provide unbiased wage data rather than employment data; however, the sample employment figures are suggestive of relative industry levels in each SMSA. The proportion of construction employment in each metropolitan area that was identified as nonunion varied considerably—from a low of 1% in Kansas City to a high of 46% in Baltimore. For other areas the percentages were as follows: Boston—12%, Atlanta—26%, New Orleans—36%, Grand Rapids—20%, Denver—30%, and Portland—10%.

Occupational and Wage Structure

Comparing union with open shop wages to determine how unions affect wages is not any easy task in construction. Even for individual workers classified similarly—say, journeyman carpenter—skills, occupational tasks, and productivity may vary widely both within and between the union and nonunion sectors. These variations, in addition to union bargaining power, may account for a substantial part of a union/nonunion wage differential.

The survey found that, in the union sector, there was a considerable variation in skills and productivity of individual journeymen, even though employers were required to pay all the same minimum hourly rate. Contractors responded to this by keeping the most productive journeymen and firing the least productive; despite the myths of the "restrictive hiring

TABLE 12-3.   Median Size of Respondent Firms

SMSA (1)	Median number of employees		Median dollar volume of construction activities, in thousands of dollars	
	Nonunion (2)	Union (3)	Nonunion (4)	Union (5)
Atlanta				
Residential	6	—	389	500
Heavy and highway	18	—	875	5,000
Commercial/industrial/other	11	24	560	2,042
Baltimore				
Residential	6	5	296	500
Heavy and highway	18	75	1,000	5,000
Commercial/industrial/other	15	25	464	1,750
Boston				
Residential	4	9	169	750
Heavy and highway	30	25	633	2,077
Commercial/industrial/other	8	19	364	971
Denver/Boulder				
Residential	9	7	405	875
Heavy and highway	13	75	450	5,000
Commercial/industrial/other	9	19	453	1,370
Grand Rapids				
Residential	6	7	277	400
Heavy and highway	18	37	1,000	4,333
Commercial/industrial/other	10	20	464	854
Kansas City				
Residential	4	7	189	389
Heavy and highway	—	21	—	1,667
Commercial/industrial/other	9	17	300	857
New Orleans				
Residential	5	30	376	100
Heavy and highway	44	50	3,666	5,000
Commercial/industrial/other	19	25	731	2,500
Portland				
Residential	4	7	311	396
Heavy and highway	14	24	2,000	2,857
Commercial/industrial/other	8	19	460	905

hall," union hiring and referral practices were generally described as being flexible enough to permit this. In contrast, open shop contractors varied wage (and benefit) levels on the basis of individual differences in worker characteristics. They felt this provided a better incentive for individual productivity. In fact, these two approaches may result in equivalent incentives for workers to become and remain productive; that is, union firms adjust the worker to the wage, whereas nonunion firms adjust the wage to the worker.

The wage data, tabulated for each area by trade and skill level (foreman, journeyman, helper, and apprentice), showed considerable variation within and among firms in the open shop sector. Table 12-4 shows the distributions of wages for nonunion bricklayers, carpenters, and electricians in the Denver-Boulder SMSA. These are typical of similar tables developed for all trades in each of the eight cities surveyed. Even though the average open shop wage was substantially lower than the union rate in all cases, the distribution of open shop wages was large enough so that it overlapped the union wage level at the top end. Approximately 10% of the open shop workers in the sample received wages above the union journeyman rate for that trade. This represents wages paid to nonunion lead men or foreman. The substantial differences between union and average nonunion rates may be partially explained by the different types of work done by union and open shop firms—the former concentrating for the most part on larger commercial/industrial and heavy and highway projects and the latter on residential and smaller commercial work—as well as by union bargaining power.

OCCUPATIONAL STRUCTURE

Open shop firms were found to be developing and using important innovations in both occupational and skill structure. Many firms, because of their freedom from union jurisdictional rules, have created new occupations combining different construction tasks most suited to the firm's particular work. Examples of these were "general building mechanics" for general contractors and myriad combinations of electrical, plumbing, insulating, carpentry, and laborers' work among subcontractors (see Table 12-5 for examples). Open shop firms also found it economical to use "helpers" for routine or unskilled work in many trades—particularly in electrical and plumbing subcontracting. To some extent, however, the efficiencies gained by this substitution of less skilled, lower paid labor for craftsmen was offset by the need to provide more foremen as supervisors. The study found that nonunion firms had a foreman: journeymen: helper ratio of 0.5::1.0::0.9, whereas the union firms had a ratio of 01::1.0::0.2 (see Figure 12-1).

On most medium-to-large industrial and public works projects, essentially all union firms are signatory to labor contracts, providing for foreman journeyman ratios not to exceed about 1 : 10 but, more importantly, that after more than five or six men are on the job, the foreman does not work with his tools. On most medium-to-large jobs the foreman is prevented from performing craftsmen's work by the labor agreement, while job management is reluctant to allow him to perform management work routinely performed by the foreman on smaller jobs when the foreman is often a permanent or semipermanent employee of the contractor. Thus union contractors on medium-to-large jobs all start out with a 10% or more produc-

TABLE 12-4. Dispersion of Nonunion Wages (Denver-Boulder, Colorado)

Job data (1)	Number of firms (2)	Number of workers (3)	Hourly wage distribution, in dollars												
			2.50– 2.99 (4)	3.00– 3.99 (5)	4.00– 4.99 (6)	5.00– 5.99 (7)	6.00– 6.99 (8)	7.00– 7.99 (9)	8.00– 8.99 (10)	9.00– 9.99 (11)	10.00– 10.99 (12)	11.00– 11.99 (13)	12.00– 12.99 (14)	13.00– 13.99 (15)	14.00– 20.00 (16)
Bricklayer															
Foreman	16	29				5	5	2	5	—ᵃ					
Journeyman	20	84			1	11	20	19	21	12					
Apprentice	14	47		15	3	21	7		1	5					
Helper	10	44		6	21	12	5								
Carpenter															
Foreman	77	209		1	1	13	57	58	47	15	12	1	4		
Journeyman	82	703		13	128	161	192	133	71	3	2				
Apprentice	47	285		56	134	78	14	3							
Helper	38	154	9	71	65	4	5								
Electrician															
Foreman	21	35		1		2	3	13	8	4	2	1			
Journeyman	17	47			2	4	9	19	7	6	—ᵃ				
Apprentice	15	33		4	16	10	3								
Helper	9	24	3	6	9	6									
Plumber															
Foreman	22	57		6	1	9	13	8	11	2	3	4			
Journeyman	26	99		6	15	17	28	14	14	5	—ᵃ				
Apprentice	15	54		9	20	23	2								
Helper	14	83	1	75	7	3	—ᵃ								
Laborer															
Foreman	37	126	1	11	26	23	25	4	6	1	3	14		5	2
Journeyman	33	211	2	82	50	41	27	7		2					
Apprentice	16	57		11	25	18	3								
Helper	17	132	13	92	13	1	13								

ᵃ Union journeyman's wage rate.

TABLE 12-5.   Union and Open Shop Occupational Titles: Examples

Union (1)	Open shop (2)
	Carpenter
Carpenter	Rough carpenter
Floorlayer	Formsetter
Drywall Hanger	Sheetrock finisher
	Drywall nailer
	Drywall taper
	Framer
	Finish carpenter
	Carpet layer carpenter
	Sheetmetal
Sheetmetal worker	Sheetmetal
	Heating and air conditioning worker
	Refrigeration mechanic
	Aluminum siding mechanic
	Furnace installer
	Welder
	Duct installer

tivity penalty over smaller crews, where the foreman can both supervise and work.

In a very successful union electrical contracting operation operating in a single geographic area with relatively permanent union personnel, it has been shown that crews consisting of one working foreman, two or three journeymen, and an apprentice can consistently achieve high productivity. The same contractor working on out-of-town jobs has found that it requires 15 to 30% more hours to perform the same work when several 10-man crews, each headed by a nonworking foreman and supervised by a nonworking general foreman, are involved. In the local area it has been found that two four- or five-man crews using a working foreman, headed by a nonworking general foreman, can consistently outproduce a single 10-man crew with one nonworking foreman, provided that the foremen and general foremen have sufficient incentive to handle the management duties usually assigned to salaried supervisors and engineers on the larger projects.

While on the surface the nonunion foreman ratios of 1 : 4 or so may appear to be counterproductive, the authors suggest that, as long as the foreman can both work with his tools when required and also perform management work, the optimum-sized crew for maximum productivity is achieved. The small premium paid to the additional foremen is clearly highly beneficial if it helps to achieve increased productivity for the contractor and increased job satisfaction and incentive for the entire crew.

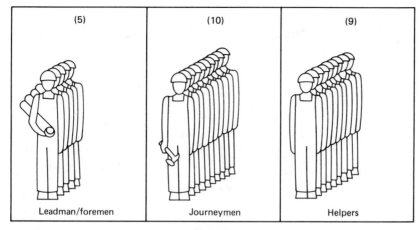

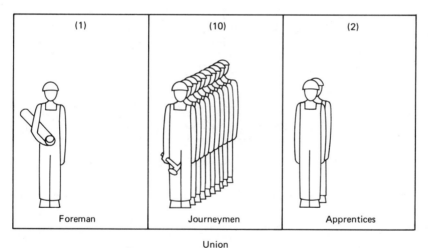

Figure 12-1 Comparison of crew structure in union and nonunion construction (per 10 journeymen in commercial construction, average for all trades, Boston and Denver). From 1976 HUD/MIT study.

The MIT-NAHB survey concluded that the relative efficiency of union versus nonunion labor may be primarily related to the appropriateness of the unions' occupational breadth to a given type of construction. The best indicator of this was the size of the on-site labor force on a typical project for any type of construction. Figure 12-2 shows a map of the industry in which union, nonunion, or mixed work forces are associated with types and sizes of construction projects. Note that the unions tend to dominate the

Sector	Size	Small $2 m	Medium $2–$10 m	Large + $10 m
Residential	Single family	◇	○	⬡
Residential	Garden apartment	◇	○	☐
Residential	High rise	○	○	☐
Commercial//Industrial	Stores and shopping center	◇	○	☐
Commercial//Industrial	Offices	◇	○	☐
Commercial//Industrial	Manufacturing	○	☐	○
Commercial//Industrial	Educational	○	☐	☐
Commercial//Industrial	Medical	☐	☐	☐
Heavy	Utilities	○	☐	☐
Heavy	Transportation	○	☐	☐
Heavy	Water and sewage	○	○	☐

☐ Union   ◇ Nonunion   ○ Mixed

Figure 12-2 "Map" of the industry with a rough assessment of open shop activity.

medium-sized projects, whereas nonunion firms are strong in very small- and very large-scale construction.

The rationale for this is that the small-scale projects are most efficiently performed by broadly trained and used workers. The union occupational structure, which breaks all construction tasks down into approximately 30 discrete trades (within the 15 international unions) is too narrowly specialized for small-scale projects. The union jurisdictional boundaries, if enforced on small projects, result in standby labor or constant turnover of workers within each craft as their work is completed. Blaney[*] found that these jurisdictional rules are not always rigidly enforced by the unions on

*Blaney, James *A Comparison of Occupational structures in Union and Open Shop Construction*, SM Dissertation, Dept of Civil Engineering, MIT; 1979.

small-scale residential projects. Nonetheless, nonunion firms certainly enjoy more flexibility to use and train journeymen on small-scale construction projects—especially on multicraft tasks such as pouring foundations—with attendant increases in efficiency.

At the other end of the size spectrum, multibillion-dollar industrial projects employing thousands of on-site workers permit the economical use of highly specialized workers without standby inefficiencies. For example, workers on these projects may perform repetitive tasks, such as cutting and threading pipe, for weeks or months on end. The union jurisdictional boundaries do not preclude such specialization within their trade's jurisdictions; however, union journeymen are clearly overtrained—and overpaid—for this repetitive, low-skilled work. Nonunion contractors have moved aggressively into this area with advanced, modular-training techniques that are used to teach task modules, each containing a few specific task skills, to previously untrained workers. These workers then perform their specialized tasks at lower wages than their union counterparts, although with somewhat more supervision.

Definite limits to this trend toward increasing specialization arise in two areas. The first is motivational. Studies by Borcherding have indicated that specialized workers on these superprojects tend to become bored and alienated from their work, unlike workers on smaller projects who find construction work to be very diverse, challenging, and satisfying. This boredom and frustration result in lower productivity, quality-control problems, and increased turnover and absenteeism. The second limit to specialization is the increased coordination needs arising from it. Each time one activity is broken into two activities one more interface is created that must be managed. Recent advances in computerized cost, schedule, and technical-coordination techniques have enabled large nonunion firms to extend the number of discrete tasks—and thus the level of specialization—that can be economically coordinated. The motivational problem, on the other hand, remains a serious and potentially limiting constraint to further specialization by nonunion firms.

In the intermediate-sized project range—large buildings and heavy construction projects—the union jurisdictions define an occupational breadth that is very appropriate to the scale and technological complexity of projects. Union fims are, therefore, able to use their journeymen efficiently. In addition, hiring halls permit union contractors to quickly assemble work crews for individual projects. The combination of these two factors results in a domination of this sector of the industry by union construction firms, even in parts of the country that have relatively low levels of unionization.

WORK RULES AND TECHNOLOGY

Rigid and inefficient work rules and resistance to technological change are often thought to be characteristic of the building trades unions. The survey found that union contractors differed considerably in their reactions to these problems. Small firms, particularly general contractors, found various contract or informal provisions relating to manning and crew size to be very costly. However, most larger firms, either because of their scale of activity or influence with union business agents, did not find these restrictions either widespread or onerous. In addition, very few firms reported any serious, consistent efforts by the unions to restrict the use of new materials or techniques.

In contrast to the relative lack of concern about work rules and technology by some union contractors in particular types of work, most union contractors were agitated by extreme variations in journeymen's efforts and productivity. The informal impact of the union, a function of both individual attitudes toward efficiency and political competition among journeymen, stewards, and business agents, was seen to be the most important uncertainty in determining on-site productivity.

HIRING AND REFERRAL SYSTEMS

Few significant differences in hiring practices were observed between union and open shop firms that could not be accounted for by differences in firm size and project duration. In many cases, both types of firms hire key craft personnel through a network of informal contacts maintained by their foremen and key journeymen. Open shop firms supplement this by use of various other sources such as newspaper advertisements or local public employment services; union firms rely on the hiring hall, especially for assembling large crews quickly. As open shop firms have grown in size and activity in various areas, they have come to see the need for a central referral system, both as a means of hiring new workers and in placing those laid off; and local associations of ABC and AGC are creating and operating some referral centers for nonunion workers and member firms. Of course, in relatively slack labor markets it is easy to find workers to recruit. Whether these nonunion referral programs will be able to function adequately in very tight labor markets remains to be seen.

APPRENTICESHIP AND TRAINING

Since 1937 construction labor unions, in collaboration with associations of union employers, have been jointly conducting apprenticeship training. Guidelines for these programs were established by the Bureau of Apprenticeship and Training (BAT) in the Department of Labor and are administered by BAT or by State Apprenticeship Councils where they exist. These guidelines require 144 hr/yr of formal education and varying amounts of informal on-the-job training covering specified work processes. The application of these guidelines, especially at the state level, has tended to require that nonunion apprentice programs conform fairly closely to union programs in order to be certified. Certification conveys two kinds of bene-

fits—federal training subsidies and certification of lower-skilled journeymen as bona fide "apprentices."

Nonunion contractors tend to use significant numbers of semiskilled
workers. In the absence of certified apprentice programs, these workers
must all be paid the full journeyman's rate on publicly funded projects
under the Davis-Bacon Act. However, once nonunion contractors have had
training programs certified, they may pay trainees in these programs an
apprentice's wage that starts at about 50% of the journeyman's wage. This
has been the major incentive for many nonunion firms to join contractor
associations such as ABC. ABC and various associations of nonunion specialty contractors have successfully certified training programs in most
states; however, they enroll sizable numbers in only a few trades—carpenters, electricians, and plumbers—primarily in North Carolina, Maryland,
and Florida. It is now relatively easy for a nonunion contractor or association to certify an apprenticeship program that is set up along union craft
lines. However, nonunion firms have achieved relatively little success in
obtaining certification for multicraft programs, such as "general building
mechanic," or task-based "incentive" programs in which workers can progress at different rates, according to their abilities.

Apprenticeship represents only one particular mix of classroom and on-
the-job training. Whereas nonunion firms have participated relatively little
in certified apprentice programs, they do have considerable needs for training programs, since they do not have access to pools of skilled labor (hiring
halls) like their union counterparts. Thus large nonunion firms (e.g., Brown
& Root or Daniel) have developed very sophisticated training techniques
that are more appropriate to the size and technology of their projects.
They have pioneered "task" or "modular"-training programs that train
previously unskilled workers within very narrow task boundaries. These
workers may later be retrained or upgraded through additional training
modules to perform other specialized tasks. This technique permits nonunion firms to recruit and train large labor forces in remote job situations
or tight labor markets. As a result, nonunion firms are rapidly making
inroads into the market of large petrochemical and power projects, once a
stronghold of union firms.

IMPACT OF PREVAILING WAGE LAWS

A considerable controversy exists about whether the Davis-Bacon act and
other prevailing wage laws significantly raise construction wages or the
costs of construction. The first issue was directly addressed by this study,
the second only indirectly. This is a complicated issue that is usually over-
simplified in the ongoing debate, so the survey results will be summarized
here.

First, the study shows that there is no "prevailing wage" in nonunion
labor markets. The dispersion of nonunion wages for any trade in a given
area means that any attempt to determine a prevailing wage will automati-

cally favor the union rate. As we have shown, this is typically 30% to 50% higher than the average nonunion wage for each trade. Prevailing wages based on surveys and averages of all wages—union and nonunion—for each trade in a given area may be a reasonable compromise; however, this is very costly to administer.

In addition to raising wages above true area average rates, prevailing wage laws impose a considerable burden of record keeping and reporting on contractors engaged in public construction, thereby increasing their indirect labor cost.

The assumption usually made by critics of prevailing wage laws is that labor productivity will be unchanged by higher wages; thus total labor costs will increase proportionally with wages. Economic theory and common sense suggest—and the interviews in this study confirm—that this assumption is naive and incorrect. When required to pay higher wages nonunion contractors select workers more carefully (like their union counterparts); they use public work at higher pay to reward their most productive journeymen, and they devote more attention to managing their labor. All these responses to higher wages result in increased labor productivity. The key question in assessing the impact of the Davis-Bacon Act on construction costs is the extent to which these compensating productivity increases offset the higher wages mandated by the act. The MIT-NAHB study did not measure relative productivity levels; this should be the result of future research. However, we can conclude that prevailing wage laws do not raise costs as much as their most outspoken critics claim they do. However, they do raise wages above average wage levels in many areas with significant nonunion activity, and they impose administrative burdens on all contractors engaged in public construction.

MERIT SHOP LEADERSHIP

While open shop firms have always enjoyed substantial business in certain geographical areas and nationally in the private residential market, the emergence of the Merit Shop concept as promoted by ABC is beginning to eliminate much of the fragmentation inhibiting the growth of the nonunion contractor in the United States. In the Merit Shop concept both union and nonunion firms can coexist. Both types of contractors and subcontractors can compete for jobs in the marketplace. The final choice will be to let the best firm win as determined by their relative efficiency.

BACKGROUND AND EVOLUTION

ABC is a national organization dedicated to the growth of Merit Shop and open shop construction. However, the open shop is certainly not new. The largest open shop contractor, Brown & Root of Houston, Texas, dates back to 1914. Many other nonunion contractors such as the H. B. Zachery Co.,

Daniel International, and others, particularly in the South and Southwest have also achieved considerable longevity, profitability, and substantial continued growth.

In 1950 a group of Baltimore contractors became disillusioned with accepting union control of the industry and established ABC whose members operated on a Merit Shop basis, open shop but not necessarily antiunion. Baltimore was undergoing a construction boom. Unionized firms were having difficulty keeping up with the downtown work let alone tackling the booming business in the suburbs. A similar movement was to take place in other cities in the Southwest and elsewhere such as Houston, Dallas, El Paso, and San Antonio in Texas, and Denver. By concentrating in the suburbs and in the outlying areas, ABC members began building up their strength until today they are beginning to emerge as the majority in their stronghold areas and are making solid gains in almost all the 50 states.

A tribute to the success of ABC is the emergence of the dual role of AGC. Currently, AGC is made up of both union and nonunion contractors. The organization is continuing to negotiate local wage rates and working conditions with local AFL-CIO building trades to establish local agreements for unionized construction in the area. The substantial pressure from the open-shop membership of AGC has helped more than any other single factor to mitigate construction wage increases in the unionized sector during the past few years compared to the unionized manufacturing industries. See Figure 12-3 for membership growth in ABC.

ASSOCIATED BUILDERS AND CONTRACTORS (ABC)

In mid-1979 there were approximately 80 active ABC chapters in 42 states. There are seven chapters in Texas, six in Pennsylvania and Maryland, five in California, and four in Florida. The association has a national office in Washington, D. C., and publishes a monthly magazine entitled *Merit Shop Contractor*, generally similar in content to AGC's magazine, *Constructor*. The magazine is informative on national issues such as labor news, OSHA, the prevailing wage laws, affirmative action, right-to-work laws, and other matters. It also contains educational and instructive information aimed at helping smaller contractors to become more businesslike.

The 1979 ABC publication list offers several manuals, publications, and craft training programs that are available to members at a discount and to nonmembers. A membership directory is available listing all members of the association. The association maintains an active Washington lobbying program promoting right-to-work laws, repeal of Davis-Bacon prevailing wage laws, and other legislation favorable for an open shop climate. The association has also been strong in helping to protect the members from illegal actions by unions.

Other advantages in ABC membership for open shop contractors include the availability of insurance, employee benefit plans, and other programs that can be more economically obtained as a part of a group of employers.

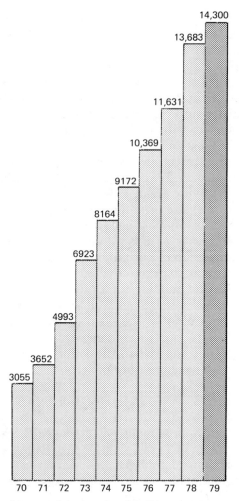

Figure 12-3 Membership growth in Associated Builders and Contractors, Inc. From Associated Builders and Contractors, Inc.

Some local associations are opening referral agencies and are taking the lead in organizing craft training programs.

Perhaps one of the major advantages of ABC association is that open shop general contractors now have a listing of available specialty contractors so that they are able to subcontract substantial portions of the work in a competitive manner. The availability of qualified nonunion trade contractors has influenced several union contractors to establish double-breasted operations and has been a major factor in the rapid growth of open shop construction in commercial, industrial, and heavy areas.

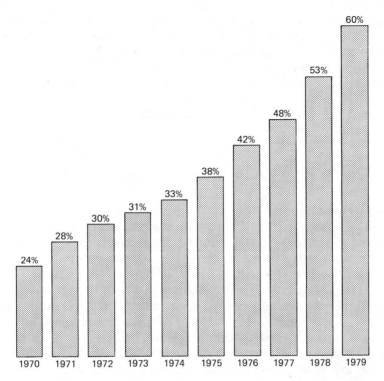

Figure 12-4   Open shop market share. From Associated Builders and Contractors, Inc.

OPEN SHOP GROWTH

The open shop share of the construction industry has grown from about 20% in 1969 to about 60% in 1979 as shown in Figure 12-4. An even more dramatic growth in nonhousing construction is apparent. *Fortune* estimated that open shop construction other than houses has risen from about 5 billion in 1968 to 71 billion in 1979.

Open shop claims 85% of new work in Baltimore, 75% in Washington, D. C., and 83% in Houston, which is up sharply from only about 30% in 1970. In the highly industrialized ship channel, open shop has increased from about 10% to an overall average of 83% for the Houston area.

Political leaders in the Houston area have been extremely supportive of the open shop in a successful effort to minimize the cost of office and industrial space. Houston's spectacular growth continues, illustrating the possibility of achieving both economic prosperity and competitive construction costs. Even the unionized sector has benefited as both union and nonunion firms are in competition for the same project. It is not unusual in Houston to see an open shop general contractor subcontract a substantial portion of the work to union subcontractors through competitive bidding. On one construction management project about half of the contractors were union and half were nonunion. Individual contractors cooperated fully with one another and construction proceeded with no adverse effects. In fact, several union specialty contractors stated that they prefer an open shop general contractor, since they never had any jurisdictional problems on an open shop job. Clearly, in the case of Houston, nonunion competition has resulted in a healthy climate for the area and union and nonunion firms both compete effectively in the marketplace.

TRENDS IN THE CONSTRUCTION INDUSTRY

The apparent substantial increase in the amount of open shop construction can best be understood by focusing on various short-term and long-term conditions and changes in the industry. First, during the last 10 years, the construction industry has been through a cycle of expansion and depression unparalleled in the post-World War II period. The upswing of this cycle created enough dollar volume of activity both to engender the entry of new firms into the industry and to sustain a rapid rise in union wages and power. Open shop firms, which had been small but were growing slowly in residential and suburban construction in the 1950s and early 1960s, expanded rapidly to meet the demand for small-scale commercial/ industrial and institutional building in markets left by the unions. Then the abrupt depression in nonresidential building in the mid-1970s left the unions without markets to support their previous wage and employment levels while providing an amply skilled labor supply for those open shop contractors who specialized in the residential and commercial building that did continue through the recession. Thus the cyclical context of the present period does much to explain the rise and competitive nature of the open shop. Whether this sector is robust enough to continue to expand in a tighter labor market remains to be seen; although initial experience in Houston appears favorable.

Second, over the last 30 years or more, building technology and the scale of projects have continued to evolve in ways that permit the substitution of materials and semiskilled labor for the skills of a craft journeyman. In many important ways, the building trades always have been able to adapt to new technology. Yet technological change has affected various trades in different ways: requiring higher-skill levels in the mechanical trades, for example, while reducing the demand for skilled journeymen in the basic trades. This technological evolution has permitted open shop contractors to compete not simply by their paying lower wages to an equivalently skilled labor force but by their adopting a different skill and occupational structure. This structure substitutes lower-paid, narrowly trained mechanics and more prefabricated materials for the higher-paid journeyman. This technological evolution, with its substantial implications for changes in firm and occupational definitions and in the demand for skills, may provide a continuing source of competitive advantage for many open shop contractors.

By 1980 the open shop sector has grown to the point where it is facing major new problems in organizing and managing larger projects that require access to substantial pools of semiskilled and skilled labor. Thus the open shop is having to develop many labor market institutions such as formal apprentice training programs and referral systems similar to those used by union firms. At the same time the union sector is being forced, by the recession and by competition, to formally differentiate its wages and work rules to fit the competitive climate of particular projects and even entire sectors of construction activity. The union goal of "uniform conditions," even though informally compromised in the past to fit particular market conditions, is now facing a major challenge of formal redefinition if the building trades unions are to compete across all sectors of the construction industry.

INDUSTRY MAKEUP

Based on the results obtained from the HUD study, supplemented by information obtained from the rapid growth of open shop construction in the sun belt areas, union and nonunion firms tend to predominate in different subsectors of the industry, although head-to-head competition in the South and Southwest indicates that substantial change is still underway.

Nonunion firms were found to dominate home building and light construction and are increasingly moving into very large-scale industrial and heavy construction, particularly in the states with right-to-work laws and in the south and southwest. Open shop firms are expanding in the suburbs and in outlying areas throughout the country, even in strongly union areas of the North, Northeast, and Far West.

Union firms tend to dominate in strongly metropolitan areas outside the sun belt in states without right-to-work laws and in medium-to-large projects such as high-rise buildings, large commercial facilities, major industrial plants, and major heavy construction projects.

The Merit Shop program, where both union and nonunion firms coexist on the same project, has shown a remarkable growth in the sun belt and right-to-work states. In these areas both union and nonunion firms compete with one another, and the overall cost of construction work has continued to be competitive, even under extreme growth conditions.

Dr. Herbert R. Northrup, one of the nations's leading experts on open shop construction looks at the future in an interview with *Merit Shop Construction* magazine: "As a result of the economic advantages that it has, the open shop is continuing to increase its share of the construction market. This trend is expected to continue in the future unless we have legislation which inhibits the open shop substantially. If that occurs, it would be a serious blow to the American consumer."

"Open -shop contractors should focus more of their attention on developing better management capability. They have to learn how to hire good people and to delegate authority to them as the firm grows. They have to institute better financial controls and marketing systems like firms in other industries."

"Second, they must do more training. They do a great job in on the job training, but they will need more craftsmen in higher skill areas like the electrical, mechanical, and plumbing trades. More money has to be invested in training to insure an adequate supply of manpower."

"Third, there is a great need to develop better benefit plans for workers that could possibly be transferable. This would give them a countervailing weight against the unions because a union employee knows that he has a benefit plan that he can keep no matter where he goes."

"And finally, wage rates will have to be watched closely to see if they are competitive. If they need raising, they must be raised. I do know that open-shop contractors have been improving in all of these areas. They have been increasing their experience, know-how, and managerial ability. If they keep this up, they will become even more formidable in the marketplace."

SUMMARY

The findings from the HUD-sponsored study permitted an opportunity to make comparisons between union and nonunion construction wages and labor relations practices in eight selected areas of the United States.

Additional information has been developed regarding practices of both union and nonunion firms in the South and Southwest, where because of a favorable political climate, substantial growth, and right-to-work laws, union and nonunion contractors have learned to work together as exemplified by the principles of the Merit Shop.

The major determinant of relative efficiency for a given type and scale of construction project was found to be the occupational breadth (degree of specialization) that was appropriate to the project. Very large industrial projects permit a high degree of specialization to be efficiently achieved. Union journeymen are overqualified—and overpaid—for such repetitive, low-skilled work. On the other hand, very small-scale projects can be most efficiently constructed by broadly trained and used journeymen. Union jurisdictional boundaries create standby problems on these small projects because they are too narrow. In the medium-sized range, especially in building and heavy construction projects, union jurisdiction define very efficient levels of specialization. In addition, hiring halls provide pools of skilled labor so that union firms can man projects quickly, and union-operated benefit plans support the transfer of workers between contractors. Consequently, union firms are likely to continue to dominate this sector of the industry in many sections of the country. However, the sharp growth of the Merit Shop will force many unions to redefine their wage and occupational structures if they wish to compete on very large-scale projects in the future particularly in the sun belt and right-to-work states.

The growth of open shop firms has clearly had a beneficial effect on overall construction costs, including restraint of unionized wages in many areas of the United States. As the open shop firms continue to expand they are encountering problems that could foster a reversal of their sharp growth at the expense of the unionized sector. Unions will undoubtedly come to recognize that the changing nature of the marketplace will require increased productivity and substantial internal reform if craft unions are to survive in the absence of government and customer mandates. To the extent that they are able to adapt to the changing climate of the 1980's, unions may revover considerable lost ground as the economy begins to rebound from its "stagflation" of the late 1970's.

CHAPTER 13

LEGAL AND CONTRACTUAL CONSIDERATIONS

S. R. McDonald
D. M. Bridges

In the last 50 years, the construction industry has been dramatically influenced by the convulsions that have affected our society: World War II, and the industrial boom that followed and the recent economic upheaval wrought by the Organization of Petroleum Exporting Countries. These forces have brought change and limitations to time-honored contracting methods, introduced new contracting concepts and applications, and created some new variations on old themes, all in an attempt to adapt to today's changing society and technology.

This chapter explores a variety of the old and the new in construction contract application and examines each in light of present practices and possible trends in the future. While the fundamentals of construction contracting and contract law have not changed dramatically, as has construction technology, the application of these fundamentals has changed and is still changing. It is the changing application that is reviewed in this chapter.

CONSTRUCTION CONTRACT ALTERNATIVES

Two fundamental methods of construction contracting have been available and widely used for sometime; the single fixed price contract and the design-construct (turnkey) contract. More recently a third method has come into common use—the construction management option that seeks to combine the best of the other two. Actually, each method has its strengths and weaknesses, and the final choice of a contracting method for any project depends on a careful evaluation of many factors.

SINGLE FIXED PRICE CONTRACTS

Fixed price contracts are a very logical and sound way to construct a new facility; completing the design, obtaining firm fixed price bids from several contractors, and choosing the lowest responsive bid. On the face of it, this would appear to be the most economical route to follow. This method was the generally preferred one until the urgency of World War II spurred the use of cost plus fixed fee (CPFF) and percentage fee contracts. Since then, perhaps more than at any time in history, owners have come to know what contractors have known for a long time—time is money. Time is money when financing costs are as high as they are today, when the cost of a facility is escalating at more than 10% per year, and when a later completion can mean losses of substantial profit to others in a rapidly expanding market. Completing design before starting construction (a traditional practice followed for years by the U.S. Bureau of Reclamation and Corps of Engineers, for example) normally requires a significantly longer time from start to completion than a project carried out with design and construction proceeding concurrently, with design leading by a few months. The price advantage of obtaining fixed price bids on a fully defined project is, today, often more than offset by the cost of escalation for the additional time it takes. Yet this method of construction contracting is still highly regarded and used because of the following:

- It provides an owner with a firm price for the cost of the project.
- The firm price offered the owner is the "best price," since it is based on full information and virtually no contingency should be required.

Some of the disadvantages beyond the cost of additional time are as follows:

- Inability to accommodate changes easily or quickly.
- Little or no control by the owner over how the work is performed.

The fixed price or lump sum concept continues to be well used for projects that are of modest scope and are not technically complex and where the design period is relatively short. Thus it is the method for most home building, commercial projects, and some industrial projects that fit this criteria. It is, for the same reasons, generally not the method for large nuclear or fossil-fueled power plants, for research and development projects, and for most large industrial projects where design periods are necessarily long and subject to frequent change. A variation of fixed price contracting, the fixed unit price contract, remains the choice for large heavy construction projects such as dams, tunnels, and highway work where quantities cannot be precisely determined but unit prices can.

In some cases owners have tried to get the best of both worlds by compressing the design period or requesting bids based on incomplete design.

In either case the result is the same—the price really is not fixed because the scope is not. Changes pour in, and the cost soars upward from the original bid. In a few instances owners have knowingly pursued this course of action but have attempted to avoid the problem by including contract language which, in effect, tells the contractor that, even though all the design details are not included, his price should make some allowance for them because there will be no increase in contract for any reason. As a practical matter this approach does not work very well, and the courts have not fully enforced this harsh provision. It is basically not equitable and, fortunately, not widely attempted. The basic theory of successful contracting contemplates the execution of a project that is well defined at the lowest price that still enables the contractor to make a reasonable profit. If the contractor makes an inordinately high profit, then the owner has paid too much; if the contractor loses money, the owner will also suffer, because very likely the job will drag, quality will suffer, and the contractor will claim extras at every opportunity. So the answer is not restrictive contract language but rather a well-defined scope that can be bid competitively and fairly—and that takes time.

In summary, time and technology have challenged the universal application of the fixed price contract and have promoted the search for suitable alternates in those areas where the fixed price concept is most vulnerable. Escalating costs for materials and wages have become a major factor in determining how long a design-construct period can be tolerated. The fixed price method works for well-defined projects of medium complexity and scope, and fixed unit price contracts are still the standard for many heavy construction projects. However, for other projects many owners are turning more and more to a time-phased or fast track method that substitutes a series of fixed price bid packages tied to design progress for the single fixed price package, in an attempt to reduce overall project time requirements yet retain most of the advantages of fixed price contracting.

DESIGN-CONSTRUCT OR TURNKEY CONTRACTS

At some point owners decided that the execution of projects could be greatly accelerated if design and construction were carried on concurrently. Because of its rather indefinite nature this type of contract is most often perfomed on a cost plus fixed fee (CPFF) basis, and, for the same reason, both design and construction are usually carried out by the same firm—thus maximizing coordination and centralizing responsibility. The drastic urgency of wartime caused many, many projects to be performed this way in the 1940s and in the heavy postwar industrial expansion. Today as well many large, complex industrial projects are performed in the same manner. Yet there is now a noticeable trend away from the turnkey project—largely because owners have suffered cost and time overruns resulting from abuse of the method. The most celebrated abuse is the inability to control or predict eventual costs because of the R & D nature of many of the assignments and the results of having design performed only marginally ahead of construction. Some major oil companies and large utility groups have had poor results in the past performing large projects on a turnkey basis, and some have disavowed the turnkey approach, preferring instead the construction management (CM) multicontract method. Yet, properly controlled, the turnkey concept probably results in the shortest design–construct duration, and since time is very much money today the turnkey method continues. It has other advantages too; an owner presumably pays only for what he gets, the responsibility for both design and construction can be centered in one place so that the usual disruptive adversary relationship between architect and builder does not exist; the builder (and the owner) has maximum flexibility in carrying out the work to accommondate changes, late deliveries of equipment, and priority or sequence adjustments—all to achieve the earliest completion date.

Large projects require relatively long durations, and the longer the design-construction period the more vulnerable the project is to cost escalation and delays from weather, strikes, and other causes. So there is more interest today in reducing overall project time for the large complex projects, and the use of cost plus fixed fee turnkey contracts can accomplish that objective.

From a contractual standpoint the cost plus fixed fee turnkey project has in its compensation provisions both its strengths and weaknesses. Typically, the owner pays for all design and construction costs, including overhead and, in addition, a fixed fee (sometimes separately for design and construction). The fee normally does not vary with cost unless the scope of the project is changed. Thus there are virtually no claims or argumentative extras; the owner pays for changes in the normal course of the project as a part of the whole activity. Cost accounting can be structured so that the cost of individual changes or other cost events can be readily identified. If the scope changes the engineer-contractor will request an increase in fee in accordance with a predetermined formula. There can be disputes over extra fee claims, but when they occur they usually are far less intense than those connected with fixed price contracts, if for no other reason than they involve only the "tip of the iceberg"—the fee—and not the basic project costs.

But this relatively easy and dispute-free method of payment is precisely what has alienated many owners. It is in the need for accurate estimating and control of final costs where the method often seems to come apart. The quest for earliest completion means that the design is far from complete when construction begins. In fact, only the earliest few drawings may be available. Most industrial design projects, even if they deal with similar projects most of the time, are subject to the results of design development and refinement as the project unfolds. The development can stem from owners' choices, equipment selections, looking for and finding a better way to do something, and, finally, just plain mistakes or oversights. If a careful and tight scope and cost control system is established at the outset and rigorously pursued final costs are usually predictable at an early date, if not always controlled, for normal industrial projects. However, the problem is accented when the project is of a research and development nature. Where, for example, a new process is involved or sufficient test or pilot runs have not been performed it will be difficult to predict the eventual cost of the project because of the major amount of design development and changes that can be expected. The more control that is exercised by the owner (and it often is necessary as well as desirable) the more time the project will take. So it appears to be a trade-off of time (money) for control (of money)—a decision that will be unique for each project of this type.

There are variations of the basic turnkey approach that can be and are used at times when the circumstances permit. For example, some projects are performed as a turnkey but with separate designers and contractors. Both may have cost plus fixed fee contracts, or, in rare instances, the design work may be performed for a fixed amount. The construction work remains on a cost plus fixed fee basis however, because of the additional time required if it were to be done fixed price. By separating responsibilities a new need is created—a party to manage the construction, which is often the owner. In a real sense this variation is more a construction management approach (with only one rather than several contractors) than turnkey.

Another variation is the lump sum turnkey project—not often used because of some obvious drawbacks. Since a contractor's contingency provision will increase in direct proportion to the lack of information for bidding purposes, this method has application only to relatively standardized types of projects. Cement and coal preparation plants are two current examples where the methods and equipment are fairly well established, and both engineers and contractors who have performed this work before have a good idea of what is required. Nevertheless, to be able to obtain lump sum bids, the owner has to have more engineering and design performed than for cost plus fixed fee, which takes time. Often the bidders will need to do some added design work to be able to bid, which takes even more time. For the trade-off of added time the owner is gaining a "fix" on his expenditure and still can centralize design and construction responsibilities. The disadvantages are found in the additional time required and the real possibility of a higher price due to increased profit and contingency allowances by the contractor to cover the risks and the fact that much information is still unknown. Obviously, this method is best suited to a buyer's market when competition is competent, plentiful, and keen.

Again, as in the case of fixed price contracting, owners have sought alternates to enhance the benefits and remedy the ills of the turnkey approach, and, again, it appears that the time-phased or fast track method is a satisfactory alternate. Not as fast as the turnkey can be, the fast track construction management method is still faster than fixed price contracting and, as an added benefit, brings with it some of the benefits of the fixed price approach.

THE CONSTRUCTION MANAGEMENT OPTION (FAST TRACK)

The preceding sections have made reference to the construction management (fast track) contracting method as a way to perhaps circumvent some of the ills and yet retain the benefits of fixed price and turnkey contracting. Presumably, any method of contracting where design and construction are proceeding concurrently to some degree may be termed fast track; however, in most present usage the term refers to the application for construction management projects under which a construction manager who does no direct work himself directs and coordinates a series of usually fixed price contracts to construct the project.

The fast track method differs from staged construction in the status of design and its relation to construction. For example, a large dam may be built by staged construction with separate contracts being let for (a) the river diversion works and foundation preparation, followed by (b) the superstructure of the dam itself. In this case the design will be completed for a before it is bid and the construction of a will be completed before the construction of b is started. A standard approach to construction of, say, a large modern cement plant might employ the construction management fast track option. Under this method the work will probably be organized more along separate discipline lines rather than separate structures, and the design of one discipline will not necessarily be complete before the first construction contract is awarded within that discipline. For example, when a substantial portion of the foundation design for several structures has been completed a bid package will be prepared and a fixed price contract awarded for that portion. Meanwhile, the design will continue for the balance of the foundation work. When another substantial portion (perhaps all of the balance) of design has been completed another contract will be bid and awarded. It is then quite probable that both contracts will be active at the same time during some period, but one contract will lead the other by several months.

The advantages of this system have already been indirectly stated, but, basically, it offers the opportunity to fix the price of all or most of the work through competitive bidding while performing the work faster than if the entire job were designed then awarded in one fixed price contract. The fast track method is not without some shortcomings of its own, however. The multiple contract approach dictates the need for a separate construction management organization to direct and coordinate the contracts, and, while the construction management group may not be large, it is nevertheless an added cost item. In addition, when more than one contract is awarded within the same discipline (concrete work or steel erection, for example), there is the probability that some economy will be lost through the duplication of contractors' overhead, equipment, and facilities. Finally, the increased number of contracts and contractors means increased exposure to lost efficiency, interference, and claims. A successful construction management organization will minimize this exposure by careful bid package preparation, timely scheduling, and detailed knowledge of the manner in which all the work must be performed. Compared to the turnkey method the construction management approach can often take longer; however, many owners believe that the added time is well worth the much greater ability to fix and/or control construction cost through the use of competitive fixed price bidding. A relatively new method, the construction management (fast track) option has gained many followers and has, today, firmly established itself as a viable alternative within the industry.

THE OWNER AS ADMINISTRATOR, ENGINEER, OR CONSTRUCTION MANAGER

Many owners today feel the need, for a variety of reasons, to take a very active and participatory role in the design/construction phase of projects. Some owners began performing their own design years ago, still carrying on this activity today. Many owners will perform all or a substantial portion of the process design but will have the detail design executed by a separate architect-engineer.

With respect to construction, owners today appear to be adopting a more "hands-on" approach, so we find them acting as their own construction managers of single or multicontract projects and a few even performing their construction. In addition, a relatively new offshoot is being used— that of the integrated organization. It is also quite common on projects of all sizes for the owner to have his own separate construction management group. This group acts to guide, assist, and control the constructor's separate organization, whether carrying out the work itself or managing several separate contracts. This practice could be referred to as the "parallel" approach to construction management. Usually, the owner's group is not nearly as large as the contractors' and acts more in an advisory capacity than in a direct one.

INCREASING OWNER INVOLVEMENT

If there is a trend toward more owner involvement, what has brought this about? In nearly every instance it has to be an unfortunate experience in dealing with the more traditional and separate architect-engineer approach to project execution. The trend is recognizable when dealing with the large complex industrial projects of today. Some owners of large petrochemical and power projects have experienced late completion and substantial overruns on projects where they employed a separate constructor or construction manager. These projects never were completely controlled for reasons that are not necessarily the sole responsibility of the constructor. Whatever the case, the results were unsatisfactory, and the owner's corporate managements were firm that something had to change for future projects—they had to have more control. Then too it may be difficult for owners to believe (perhaps with some basis in fact) that engineers and constructors have the owner's best interest at heart. But the feeling of the need for control of the project is probably the most important factor that drives owners to participate more and more in the belief that if they are in complete control then the substantial overruns of time and money will not occur. Also, owners can argue that if they do the process engineering, why not also the detail engineering and the construction? This reasoning or desire, however runs smack into economics, both regarding the actual cost of the services and the time (hence, money again) it takes to execute a project when one is not in the business on a continuous basis. The very size of some projects such as large refineries or nuclear or fossil-fueled power plants has increased the stakes to an extraordinary level. It is not uncommon for a nuclear power plant today to cost well in excess of $1 billion—a sum unimagined not long ago. The cost of the entire Manhattan Project, which brought forth the atomic bomb was only $2 billion—an extraordinary amount in the 1940s—but perhaps equaled today by such giants as the NASA program to put a man on the moon or the Alaska Pipeline. The significance of the amount is that it attracts a significant amount of the owner's corporate attention for good reason. An owner will be much more interested in actively participating in a $1 billion project than a $1 million one.

Finally, some owners with developed engineering-construction staffs need to keep them occupied, or else such staffs are difficult to justify economically. Since most industrial expansion is cyclical within industry groups, most companies cannot afford the luxury of maintaining the kind of engineering-construction organization it takes to execute major projects.

As with most things the success of owner participation depends on several factors but basically how well the owner can truly recognize and use the real abilities of his own staff and those of the architect-engineer and constructor. The owners' hands-on approach does certainly not only increase the opportunity for control, but also exposes the owner to the results of direct responsibility (for decisions that sometimes others are better equipped to make) and exposure to claims for extras that, in some areas at least, might be avoided. The owner is no longer insulated from direct labor negotiations; and this can have repercussions in the operating labor force. The owner is also subject to significantly greater exposure to liability claims in personal injury and accident cases.

Paralleling this exposure is the increased vulnerability to fines and/or government agency action for safety infractions (although under current legislation the owner of mining projects is the recipient of fines, etcetra., whether he has direct control or not).

On the engineering side the owner, of course, has the full responsibility for all his actions and may bear extra costs for redesign that may have been avoided or not incurred had the design work been contracted. Additionally, an owner may be required to be licensed to practice engineering in the state where the project is located. This is not always feasible or even desirable to an owner and some states have rigorous qualifying requirements that could be difficult to meet.

Finally, it must always be remembered that this added control can be costly. If the owner desires the project (design and/or construction) to be executed along fixed price contract lines, the owner will be effectively barred from actively participating. It is for this reason that most active owner participation is relegated to large, lengthy projects performed on a cost plus fixed fee basis or through the emerging construction management approach.

It is probable that there will be a continued increase in owner involvement in the large, complex, or R&D projects performed on a cost plus fixed fee basis. Such projects are simply too costly and lengthy. The owner wants closer control over how his money is spent. For small-or moderate-sized projects the situation should remain status quo, with some owners trying a bit more actively and some backing off. The tendency to try to actively involve an owner's staff will likely be offset by the desire to fix costs through the use of lump sum contracts. There may well be an increased use of a small owner's construction group acting in an advisory capacity on multicontract construction management projects.

It is difficult to recognize any trend with respect to engineering. The degree of involvement varies with the individual owner and the extent and capability of his engineering staff. If the economy quickens in the owner's particular industry the owner's staff will likely be too busy planning to execute also. When the economy is slack or if the owner has a large in-house engineering force there will be a natural tendency to perform much of the engineering wherever possible.

THE MEGA-PROJECT

Mega, according to Webster, is "a combining form meaning great, mighty . . .," and that perhaps is the best, if broadest, definition to apply to the type of project under discussion. It would be easier, although not necessarily more accurate, to specify such a project in terms of cost and time. But in reality because of changing values and technology it is difficult to do so. For example, a not-unreasonable criterion today would be a project that cost in excess of $1 billion and took six or more years to complete. In terms of pure cost this would eliminate the Panama Canal project from consideration, surely a mega-project by anyone's standards. We need other measurement criteria to acknowledge that such projects are great and not just because of their complexity—both technical and organizational. The Alaska Pipeline comes immediately to mind as a recent example of a mega–project. That project was "mighty" and qualified on all counts: cost, time, and technical and organizational complexity. While these huge projects have all the usual elements of more modest design and construction projects they introduce a new element of their own—the difficulty of management of all the individual pieces.

The modern heritage of the mega-project can perhaps be traced to the Manhattan Project that successfully developed the atomic bomb in the early 1940s. This was an undertaking of extraordinary technical complexity, carried out in unparalleled secrecy at several different geographic locations in the country. Today, in more conventional terms we can consider some of the larger nuclear power plants, large coal gasification plants, petroleum refineries, steel complexes, another Alaska pipeline, several metropolitan rapid transit projects, and some overseas projects such as the construction of an entire city of 70,000 from scratch (Saudi Arabia). These projects have in common the challenge of managing a huge task being performed by a large number of diverse specialty groups to (hopefully) meet a schedule and budget. That these goals were not met in the case of the Alaska Pipeline was widely publicized, but the problems the Alaska Pipeline suffered are found in other mega-projects as well. It seems that, just as sometimes happens when taking an industrial process from the pilot stage to production, escalating established management methods used on smaller projects to these giants gives inconsistent results.

LEGAL AND CONTRACTUAL ASPECTS

So much for the organizational challenge inherent in mega-projects. What about the legal and contractual aspects? Are they the same as those for any engineering-construction project, or is there something unique not found in smaller projects? As with organization, all the legal and contractual elements of any design-construct project are present, but it is the scope and complexity of the effort that sets it apart.

For comparison purposes let us examine the contractual effort in a straight-forward $50 million industrial project involving a standard process and then compare the like effort in a $1 billion-plus megan-project. Interest in such a project in the geographical area of its siting will be vastly greater for a mega-project than for its $50 million distant cousin because of the impact on the community, the state, and possibly the federal government as well. At the outset, this means that all today's time-consuming and complex requirements of permitting will be far greater and probably will require a team of several legal and public relations specialists, together with the engineering and management personnel needed, to generate the basic data for permitting. The legal activity will involve the owner's in-house counsel, of course, but in addition will require one and probably more outside legal firms because of the various special areas affected. In these early stages the legal managers will likely control the project's destiny, working with the project's management teams until permits have been obtained. Contractually, at this stage the normal project might be able to handle these requirements with the use of the in-house legal and management staff with engineering and environmental assistance from only one architect-engineer. Most probably, the mega-project will involve the effort of several architects-engineers in specific areas of expertise. So the very size of the mega–project has a direct effect on the legal aspects and requirements of design-construct activities. This effect is measured not only in time, but also, in significantly increased cost. Oil was discovered in Prudhoe Bay Alaska, in March 1968, but it was not until November 1973 that construction was finally authorized after a long legal fight by various environmental groups. This five-and one-half-year period probably added close to 50% to the project cost through escalation and the cost of the legal effort itself. By way of contrast, environmental and other agency approvals for a $95 million cement plant took only slightly more than a year.

On the practical contractual side it seems clear that as these projects enter the "mega" category (perhaps "super-mega-" in the case of the Alaska Pipeline) their design and construction organizational structure begins to closely resemble that of a giant corporation or even the government. And because most of this structure is comprised of other than the owner's staff there is a profusion of contract agreements with consultants, advisers, architects-engineers, project managers, construction managers, contractors, suppliers, subcontractors, and subsuppliers—tier on tier on tier. The contracts and their terms and conditions may not be especially unusual, but the contractual effort to try to tie them all together and to provide continuity and consistency in carrying out the details of the task is immense. In fact, the contractual process or, more particularly, the execution of it in a real sense will likely prove disappointing and frustrating to the managers at the highest level because of their remoteness from the source of activity. If a dog had a tail a mile long and its tip were stepped on it would be a long time before the dog yipped. So it is with the mega-project's high-level managers.

Contractual language designed to be all-encompassing will not help much, because, again, the problems are the direct result of sheer size and one other factor—the attempt to regulate and control from the very top the things that happen and need to happen at the very bottom. The design and construction work is the same in its basic nature for any project, but in the mega-project this work is heavily insulated from control at the top by size alone. How can one individual, the manager, possibly control $7 billion of work or even $1 billion and do it effectively? The answer is, of course, not very well or not at all. Management theories would say to delegate authority and responsibility and mange by exception, and this is the standard approach, either within the owner's organization or contractually through others. But size interferes. Is too much being attempted at one time?

ORGANIZATION AND CONTRACTUAL VARIATIONS

Some of the largest design-builders in the United States who are tackling the challenge of the mega-project use a divide-and-conquer approach to organization. Instead of trying to manage each and all of the elements of one of these monsters with a large centralized staff who perform the same specialized function for each the entire project is divided into manageable smaller individual projects (subprojects). Each subproject is assigned a complete integrated task force who will do everything for it. This certainly makes sense, but now the trick is to be able to coordinate all these now-(relatively) independent subprojects into the mega-project to meet common schedule and cost goals with management uniformity. From an organizational standpoint this arrangement pushes management control one level closer to the work itself, and that should result in more effective execution of each project. It is also evident that there is a good deal of duplication of effort among the various subprojects, each of which is trying to do the same kind of thing, with some variation, as are the others.

Obviously, control from the top can only be exercised in terms of the broadest of goals, particularly since each subproject may be a very large design construction job itself. Interestingly, this same method—the task force—was the organizational foundation of the Manhattan Project. So far, no one apperars to have devised any better way of organizing these super jobs—although the Corps of Engineers recently is trying a variation that sounds promising for the construction of a $5 billion military city in Saudi Arabia. For this colossal project the Corps is attempting to use fixed price contracting where it has real application and cost plus contracting where the extent of unknowns or risks make fixed prices unattainable.

SAUDI MILITARY CITY PROJECT

The project, which is to support an eventual population of 70,000, includes military organization and support facilities, mosques, schools, a community center, industrial facilities, utilities, a sports complex, a hospital, and ultimately, the Saudi Air Academy. The Corps is responsible to the Saudi government for execution of the project. To accomplish the task the contractual effort is divided into three parts as presented next.

Government-Furnished Property (GFP)

Certain of the material and equipment will be GFP in order to minimize risks for fixed price work, control the quality of materials, provide maximum standardization, reduce the mobilization period, shorten performance periods, and reduce overall cost.

Cost Plus Award Fee

This covers construction of site development and establishing the construction work force community and facilities; construction support such as handling of GFP, aggregate production, vehicle and utility service, and transportation and materials plant operations; life support in the form of camp and work force community management, personnel transportation and communication services and management assistance to coordinate support services, interface construction contractors, allocate resources, review design, perform contract administration, and control reporting.

With the two major elements just cited—GFP and cost plus award fee—completed or known quantities, it is then possible to add the third and final contractual element: the firm fixed price work.

Firm Fixed Price

This covers over 30 separate contacts averaging $100 million each for the permanent project construction.

This overall organizational and contractual approach is interesting on at least two counts. First is the use of a cost plus award fee for diverse and relatively unspecific activities in an attempt to introduce some positive self-motivating performance control into what obviously must be a very diffi-cuualt task from a schedule and cost standpoint. Second is the conscious effort to separate out the high-risk elements of the project and to provide them (the basic construction criteria and environment) to following contractors who will do their work on a fixed price basis. The Corps is trying one additional new twist—the application to construction of the Cost/Schedule Control Systems Criteria (or PMS) used in the weapons manufacturing industry. This is a very detailed and sophisticated system for measuring and monitoring cost and schedule performance from the inception of design and is already finding some use with large domestic governmental design and construction projects.

What does the future hold for the contractual and executional organization of such huge projects? It certainly seems that there will be a continuing demand for supersized projects, since, in general terms, our technology finds economy in size and since the prospect of omnipresent inflation means that economy will be the prime goal. When measured against the kind of performance that can be expected and attained with more modest-sized projects the mega–project comes off as a relatively inefficient way of reaching the goal. Yet to break up, say, the Alaska Pipeline into a large number of truly independent and uncoordinated parts executed over a long period of time would at least lose the benefit of urgency—for that seems to be a prime motivation behind the majority of these projects. For that reason, most resort to design as you go, and construction is carried out on a cost plus fixed fee basis with its attendant risk of lack of cost control. The example discussed previously—the Corps of Engineer's project in Saudi Arabia—seems to point the way to solving part of the mega-project's problems. We probably will see more of this kind of thoughtful dissection of huge projects and the use in the typical project of several kinds of similar contractual approaches tailored to the particular demands of each special portion. Whatever direction is taken, the challenge is there, and all the solutions remain to be discovered.

ACCELERATION—IMPACT AND EFFECT—RIPPLE EFFECT

The concept of acceleration of performance as a recognized basis for additional compensation was a natural outgrowth of the factors discussed in the preceding sections. Extremely complex interrelated tasks were required to be planned on a critical path schedule prior to completion of design. An early example was the missile base program of the Air Force in the early 1960s. Contractors, plagued by a combination of delays, scope changes, and government indecision, found that the costs of their work under such conditions bore little relationship to what was originally contemplated.

As a result, the government was ultimately required to pay not only the cost of additional work ordered during the performance period, but also for the additional cost of performing the original scope of work. This additional cost resulted from the "impact and effect" of the changes on each other and the original work. This, in turn, had a "ripple" effect, resulting in further increased costs. Productivity declined with fatigue, and equipment utilization became less efficient. Additional supervision, recruitment, and other overhead costs were incurred.

THE ACCELERATION CONCEPT—PUBLIC AND PRIVATE

The litigation which stemmed from this controversy settled the point that the foregoing types of costs were compensable consequences of the ordered changes. Since compliance with the change orders required additional manhours within the same time frame, a "constructive acceleration" had been ordered, and the contractors were compensated for the cost thereof and the cost of the "ripple" effect of the changes on the other work. Acceleration has since become a standard compensable item in the construction industry.

Federal Procurement Regulation 1-7.602-3, which is the changes clause required in fixed price government construction contracts, was changed to expressly recognize this new principle. It now provides, in pertinent part the following:

(a) The Contracting Officer may, at any time . . . by written order . . . make any change in the work within the general scope of the contract, including but not limited to, changes:

. . .

(4) Directing acceleration in the performance of the work.

. . .

. . .(d) If any change under this clause causes an increase or decrease in the Contractor's cost of, or the time required for, the performance of any part of the work under this contract, whether or not changed by any order, an equitable adjustment shall be made and the contract modified in writing accordingly. . ..

As private projects such as nuclear power plants, developmental energy pilot plants and advanced technology complexes in the extractive industries have approached and passed the level of complexity and magnitude of the missile base construction, the acceleration concept has found acceptance in the private sector.

In many instances, owners adopted the approach of the FPR; acceleration was treated as an unquantified contingency to be dealt with in the future through negotiations. Unfortunately, the results have been less than satisfactory in many cases. The incidence of staggering cost overruns in both private and public projects is clearly too high. Many in the industry believe that the advent of ultrasophisticated technology has rendered current estimating practices obsolete. Pertinent to this discussion is the fact that the acceleration and "ripple" effect theory is sufficiently flexible to allow the formulation of a colorable claim on almost any large project. Any delay by the owner, any change or refusal to change a completion date, and any adjustment to scope of work can be alleged to be a change requiring acceleration of some (or all) of the work and impacting the cost and time of all other work. Moreover, when a change order has not been issued, claims can be founded on an asserted "constructive change," for example, a specification regarding concrete viscosity could be said to be overly stringent, causing delay in the work and thus requiring acceleration. In the extreme case, the acceleration theory becomes similar to the "cardinal change" theory where the contract is voided by the magnitude and/or nature of the changes and the owner is saddled with all costs incurred by the contractor. This tendency is a factor in some owners' disenchantment with turnkey contracting, as discussed in an earlier section.

OWNER RESPONSE AND RISK AVOIDANCE

Owners have responded with varying techniques to avoid massive acceleration adjustments. One approach is to abolish the constraint of a completion date and require the contractor to use only its "best efforts" to complete on schedule. This cannot be done when the on-stream or startup date of the project is crucial to the owner and certainly does not guarantee that the project will not encounter either claims or overruns.

Another response has been the development of exculpatory clauses, whereby the contractor is required to waive any claim for acceleration and its consequences. This too is an imperfect solution. Prudent contractors will increase bid prices in the face of such stipulations, resulting in an unnecessary increase in project costs. In most jurisdictions, a contractor seriously damaged by the operation of such a clause can get to court by using a legal theory that avoids operation of the exculpatory clause, such as fraud in the inducement of the contract.

Staged construction of major projects tends to avoid acceleration problems. The project is divided into several relatively small, manageable packages of contracts that are awarded and performed sequentially. Each assignment is of relatively short duration, and the owner is not committed to the next stage—in theory—until the completion of the current work is assured. Therefore, neither the owner nor any contractor runs the risk of acceleration of the project as a whole or of the attendant pyramiding of impact and effect costs. As a practical matter, staged contruction carries a built-in premium in time and money. The theoretical advantage of not committing stage 2 until stage 1 is virtually complete is not always attainable or compatible with the need to complete the project. It could be questioned whether the diffusion of responsibility inherent in staged construction is good for the construction industry.

The relative of sequential staged construction, fast track construction management of multiple packages, runs more risk of acceleration and impact claims but does offer opportunities for schedule adjustment as each contract is awarded that the single fixed priced contract does not. It is also possible to accelerate only one portion of the work (package) without, theoretically at least, affecting the other parts.

The costs of acceleration and of its impact and effect on other work are genuine costs of the large complex project. Methods of avoiding acceleration situations and claims on such projects have costs of their own that are incurred whenever these methods are used. In the absence of other constraints, such as the availability of project financing, it may in the long run be the least expensive solution to recognize the acceleration possibility and provide for its occurrence. If there is no acceleration of the project, the built-in costs of other solutions will have been avoided.

The Federal Procurement Regulations treat acceleration in a very general way. This may be appropriate in the private sector, depending on the relationship between owner and contractor and on the nature of the project, but it can result in unforeseen cost overruns. In many contracts, it is possible to quantify the extent of exposure through use of schedules for compensation of premium time, standby time, equipment use, overhead, and other items of cost.

Such schedules are not completely comprehensive, but they can obviate the need of much cost reconstruction by the parties. This type of compensation arrangement reduces the contractor's risk of loss and hence reduces the need, and incentive, for disputes and claims.

ARBITRATION

Agreements by contracting parties to submit disputes to neutral third parties for binding resolution were originally unenforceable in court. The concept of settlement of controversies by the arbitrary decision of a private person rather than in accordance with the law's allocation of rights and duties was regarded as contrary to public policy.

The Industrial Age resulted in a great increase in technical disputes and other controversies that clogged the dockets of the courts. Pressure to legitimize the arbitration process led to legislation that sanctioned the concept in the 1920s and 1930s. In 1955, a Uniform Arbitration Act was proposed and has now been adopted by 37 states. All states but Oklabhoma and Vermont have some form of arbitration act. The Federal Arbitration Act, 9 U.S.C. §§ 1-14, provides for arbitration of disputes arising in interstate commerce or maritime transactions. All these statutes make agreements to arbitrate valid and binding.

The desire for arbitration has promoted the existence of associations that administer arbitration proceedings. The American Arbitration Association has promulgated the Construction Industry Arbitration Rules, which are widely adopted in construction contracts. In the field of international contracting the International Chamber of Commerce (ICC) offers its ICC Rules of Arbitration for adoption in contracts and provides a Court of Arbitration to administer proceedings. The rules provide that the arbitration will take place in a neutral country and the arbitrators will not be nationals of the country of any party. American contractors must bear in mind that many overseas entitities, particularly those of a governmental nature, are precluded by constitutions or other organic laws from submitting to the jurisdiction of any tribunal, except the courts of their country. Absent this problem, ICC awards are enforceable in any country that is a party to the United Nations Convention on the Recognition of Foreign Arbitral Awards. The United States became a party to the convention in 1970; see 9 U.S.C. §§ 201-208.

CURRENT CONCEPTS IN ARBITRATION

The judicial attitude toward arbitration has completely changed. In the major commercial centers, many state court systems are requiring that all matters before the court when the amount in controversy is less than a stipulated sum be submitted to arbitration. The amount is sometimes as high as $50,000, and this trend is likely to continue. Unlike arbitration pursuant to agreement, this court-required arbitration is subject to judicial review in the same manner as the decision of a trial judge.

The premise underlying contracts that submit disputes to arbitration is that the parties prefer such dispute be resolved quickly, economically and finally, by an expert in the field involved. Modern arbitration is structured to perform this function.

The American Arbitration Association can provide a panel of arbitrators from its list of over 5000 experienced construction arbitrators. These arbitrators come from a variety of construction-related backgrounds, including architects, engineers, constructors, and attorneys. Many combine two or more of these disciplines. While the availability of qualified arbitrators is a potential difficulty in some fields, there is no such problem in construction.

Modern-day arbitration statutes are designed to produce a quick and economical result. The arbitrator must render an award within the time period specified in the arbitration agreement. If no time is specified, the courts will fix a time on petition of any interested party. While the need to present voluminuous evidence will extend the time required for arbitration and increase the expense (arbitrators' fees and expenses may be split by the parties or borne by the losing party or allocated in the discretion of the arbitrators) it can be said that most relatively simple construction cases can be resolved in less time and at lower costs by arbitration than by litigation in the courts.

Arbitration proceedings are less formal than courtroom litigation. Rules of evidence are treated with liberality, and traditional limits on the questioning of witnesses do not apply. Many statutes provide that the parties may agree to waive the right to be represented by attorneys, although this waiver is almost universally made revocable.

Under most statutes, depositions may be taken from witnesses unable to appear at the arbitration proceedings for use as evidence. Discovery depositions and other discovery procedures used in the courts to require the production of documents and things are prohibited or curtailed in arbitration. Some statutes make an exception to this rule for disputes involving personal injury or death.

In construction cases, the arbitrator's expertise often enables him to adjudge the amount of costs and damages involved. This may reduce the quantum of proof of damages required (although few attorneys would accept the risk of submitting less than all probative evidence).

The arbitrators' award need not contain an explanation of the reasons behind the decision. Once rendered, the award is subject to only limited judicial review. Generally, it can be vacated by a court only if the court finds that (*a*) the award was procured by fraud or corruption, (*b*) corruption existed among the arbitrators, (*c*) a party was prejudiced by misconduct of an arbitrator, or (*d*) the award exceeds the powers of the arbitrators under the arbitration agreement. Errors of fact or law are not grounds for the vacation of an arbitration award. Many statutes require the court to correct rather than vacate the award whenever possible or to order a rehearing by the arbitrators in the event an award is vacated. A valid award or a corrected award must be confirmed by the court on request. A confirmed award may be enforced like a judgment.

All these features tend to expedite the resolution of the dispute in question. This is not to say that all disputes under all construction contracts should be subjected to arbitration.

On the contrary, great care should be exercised in drawing the scope of an arbitration clause. Problems on construction projects are generally recurring ones, for example, the existence of and responsibility for overruns or delays. Whether this means such problems are simple or not will depend on the magnitude and nature of the project and the contractual format. While practically all questions can be made subject to arbitration, it must be remembered that the arbitrators' decision is virtually always final and binding, despite errors of fact or errors of law. On high-risk projects where the possibility of serious losses exists, agreement to arbitration will act as a waiver of the right to correction of such errors through the appellate process if the clause is overly broad.

It is usually preferable to limit arbitration clauses in this type of contract to resolution of specific factual questions such as the quantities of work (earthwork, concrete, etc.) performed during specified periods. Another approach could be to reserve from arbitration all legal questions and have the facts resolved by the arbitrators.

The contractor must also recognize that the common practice of each side nominating an arbitrator, who then chooses a third arbitrator, will result in one of the arbitrators tending to be partial to each party. The usual result is that the award is a compromise, meaning that the claimant can generally expect to receive less than his full claim even when he prevails.

The advantages of arbitration tend to become dissipated in complex multiparty disputes. Time and money increase with the volume of the record, and, in some cases, the advantage of arbitration will disappear. This possibility must be considered when drafting the contract.

Liberalized rules of procedure and evidence and circumscribed discovery are not always advantageous. The rules of evidence are designed to select the best proof and to exclude dubious material. Discovery is essential to the prosecution or defense of a claim when one is not in possession of the facts. From this standpoint, valuable protections and rights may be forfeited by an overly broad arbitration clause.

Finally, arbitration is not always feasible in projects with complex contractual relationships. An engineer who is bound to the owner by an arbitration clause may be exposed to multiple claims by the prime contractor, other contractors, or subcontractors, if they are not all similarly bound to the owner and also to the contractor and to each other. This is because these other parties may pursue the engineer in court, while the engineer may be precluded by an arbitration clause from joining the owner as a party to the litigation. In the courts, rules for asserting jurisdiction over all parties who must be bound in order to resolve the dispute are well developed. This is not true under the arbitration statutes. Legislation in the major commercial states may in time solve this problem, but many commentators urge that the introduction of developed rules regarding joinder and consolidation would be contrary to the purpose of arbitration: the quick and economical resolution of disputes. Moreover, arbitration is based on contract, and there is no provision allowing the arbitrators to bring in another party who may be necessary to the resolution of the dispute but who has not agreed to arbitration.

Arbitration in its present form is a quick and economical way to resolve disputes between two parties in relatively simple cases. This remains true even if the necessary evidence is voluminous. In complex projects and multiple contract situations, the rights foregone by arbitration agreements can be more valuable than the benefits of the arbitration process. Care should be exercised in drafting the scope of the arbitration clause in such cases.

LIABILITY

This section briefly summarizes the apparent trends in the law's allocation of the risks inherent in construction projects as such allocation affects the engineers, architects, and contractors who make up the construction industry. No attempt is made here to present a comprehensive study of judicial decisions, statutes, or regulations. For such a study, see Acret, *Architects and Engineers, Their Professional Responsibilities* (McGraw-Hill, 1977).

INCREASING EXPOSURE TO RISK

Risk allocation as a matter of social policy is tending to place the burdens of modern life on those best able to bear them and to distribute them evenly to the general populace. This is the theory underlying modern product liability law that places the monetary loss resulting from defective automobile design, for example, on the manufacturer, and hence the purchasers of all cars, rather than on the unfortunates involved in a particular accident. Whether this principle should be applied to those who provide construction services rather than manufactured products is certainly debatable, but the present trend is in that direction.

One precursor of this trend was the abolition of the doctrine of privity of contract. It is now generally accepted that the engineer, architect, or contractor may be held responsible for damages caused by him to those with whom he has no contractual relationship. The courts have concluded that the professionalism of the engineer does not allow him to ignore the interests of all except his client.

Moreover, the standard of conduct required of the professional engineer and contractor is higher than that required of the average man in the street. The professional is required to exercise that degree of skill and care practiced by similar experts; conduct that does not meet this standard is negligent and exposes the engineer to liability for reasonably foreseeable harm caused thereby.

Nor is it always sufficient defense to establish the absence of careless or negligent conduct. Some courts have applied the product liability standards just discussed to the designers and constructors of mass-produced homes. The only questions to be resolved are the existence of a defect and resulting damage. The often-applied rule that violation of a statute or regulation intended to provide for safety is negligence per se produces the same result. The plethora of safety rules promulgated by divisions of industrial safety at all levels, and under the Occupational Health and Safety Act, create an ever-increasing area of strict liability.

In addition, the law is recognizing new types of injury or damage as compensable. In some states, mental anguish or economic dagage are actionable torts without any physical injury having occurred. The tendency appears to be relaxation of the law's former distaste for claims that can be established only by the testimony of the claimant.

The increase in potential claims resulting from the foregoing trends is compounded by the increasing complexity of construction projects, discussed earlier in this chapter. With complexity has come a great increase in reliance by general contractors on specialized subcontractors. More and more often, subcontractors cover not only the entire construction portion of a certain specialty, but also specialized aspects of the design and, therefore, the supervision of the work (construction management).

This huge increase in the number of contractors involved in a single project has resulted in many problems related to cost and time that are discussed elsewhere. Several effects are pertinent to this discussion. First, the increase in subcontracting brings with it an increase in the likelihood of multiparty claims simply because of the complexity of the relationships. The risk of being held to answer for the acts of another under agency principles is naturally increased.

Second, this aspect of modern construction has contributed to the acceptance of the comparative negligence doctrine, adopted from admiralty law. Under the common law, tradition had it that a claimant who was himself at fault to the slightest degree (contributorily negligent) could recover nothing. Comparative negligence posits that the damage should be allocated in proportion to the fault of the various parties involved. This is arguably a principle more properly applicable to construction services than the concept of strict liability discussed previously, because it tends to reward competency and to discourage incompetency.

Third, the increasing complexity of the large construction project has created a particular problem for the architect-engineer in his role as the arbiter of disputes. The courts are finding that such an arbiter has a quasi-fiduciary responsibility to the parties to the dispute to be fair and impartial in determining the resolution of the question. Such a duty often may conflict with the architect's contractual duty to protect the interests of his client. The architect as a professional enjoys a relationship of trust and confidence with the client, and such a relationship has distinct overtones of fiduciary responsibility. The potential for conflict of interest creates an exposure to responsibility for constructive fraud arising from violation of the fiduciary responsibility.

CONTRACTUAL RESPONSES TO LIMIT LIABILITY

There are several developing responses to these problems. Perhaps the most promising is in the insurance field, discussed in the following section.

A reaction to be questioned is the refusal of some designers to accept complete supervision responsibility, thrusting that burden back on the owner. This contributes to increasing involvement of the owner as manager. Correspondingly, there is an associated decline in professional responsibility and in the availability of professional services.

Another response has been the widespread use of indemnity clauses that seek to absolve the party with sufficient bargaining power from all responsibility for anything, specifically including his own conduct. Several states, including California, Delaware, and Illinois, have declared such an agreement void as a matter of public policy regarding damages resulting from nonprofessional conduct or design defects. Many owners, contractors, and designers now use standard contractual language that accepts responsibility for damages caused by their sole negligence.

Those who provide construction services argue with some justification for reasonable limitations on such responsibility vis-á-vis the owner. The rationale is that limits allow insurance at reasonable prices, which reduces the cost of construction, and that the occasional catastrophic loss should properly be borne by the owner, who can better pass the cost on to society.

Current trends do not indicate any lessening of the exposure of the construction fraternity to liabilities of ever-broader scope. Whether the construction industry or society in general can bear such a cost indefinitely is one of the legitimate questions of the day.

INSURANCE

The increased risk of liability faced by the construction industry has resulted in a steadily growing demand for insurance coverage for all aspects of construction operations. In addition to workmen's compensation insurance, which is required by statute, other forms of coverage are becoming commonplace on large projects.

Builder's risk insurance to protect the physical project may be carried by the contractor or the owner. Contractors are forced by the enormous value of today's projects to limit their responsibility for damage to the project to the proceeds of builder's risk insurance. Owners find with increasing frequency that they can achieve economies by carrying the builder's risk policy themselves and naming their contractors as coinsureds.

General liability insurance is also imperative. The contractor on any large project must be protected against claims for personal injuries and property damage arising from the performance of the work. Owners are, therefore, forced to bear the cost of this insurance in the prices quoted by their contractors. The owner of a large project can realize considerable savings by using a project "wrap up," all-risk insurance package. Under this concept, the owner places all required workmen's compensation and builder's risk and liability insurance, covering itself and all the contractors and subcontractors. The contractors then carry no insurance and include no insurance costs in their prices.

Engineers and architects face a problem in securing adequate professional liability or errors and omissions insurance. Coverage is scarce, and rates are extremely high. Claims under such policies are to be avoided because of the cancellation risk. As a result, such policies are often reserved for catastrophic losses, and minor claims are absorbed by the engineer without recourse to the insurance policy. The problem is further compounded by the unwillingness of insurers to write a policy that will cover claims arising from work done prior to the commencement of the policy period.

As the permitting process becomes ever more tedious, and government intervention more pervasive, more support is being sought from the insurance industry.

Business interruption insurance has been sought to protect against delays in project completion as well as interruption of operations.Generally, delay in completion cannot be insured on a true transfer of risk basis. Insurers have been willing to provide a loss stabilization fund against which the insured can draw to meet costs during the delay period. This is actually a form of secondary financing rather than insurance.

Private insurance coverage of political risk is in its infancy. It is interesting that the United States is the area of major concern, and the reason is regulatory lag. The Alaska Gas Pipeline Project is a good current example of a project that may not be privately financeable because of interminable preconstruction regulatory proceedings. The world market capacity for insurance of this type is quite limited, but Lloyds of London reportedly has put some such coverage together, and it may be expected that others will follow.

COST-INFLATION INDEXING

Tying costs or prices to some kind of reference point or index is not a particularly new or novel idea; it has been used since the final decades of the nineteenth century in the form of consumer price indexes called then and in the early 1900s "cost-of-living" indexes. While the government prefers today to refer to such a standard as a consumer price index the earlier term is still probably more familiar to most people. Today, this is a very newsworthy and notorious index that affects everyone. Originally published as a statistic to reflect price movement, the indexes and their numerous variations have been more recently commonly used by labor and management in wage negotiations and are built into many industry agreements. Under such agreements index changes result in automatic wage adjustments for millions of employees. The construction industry relies heavily on the *Engineering News-Record* (ENR) Building Cost and Construction Cost indexes to provide a reasonable guide to forecasting future cost based on historical data. This industry index does what other similar indexes do by measuring the average country-wide increases in the cost of selected kinds of construction labor and materials. Obviously, there can be and are different variations regionally in these same categories, so the U.S. average may not reflect the cost trend accurately in selected areas or cities. ENR also provides similar indexes or the raw data for them for such areas. The ENR index deals with the cost of construction—not of manufacture, so for an owner to judge what may happen to the cost of a project planned today but to be built three or four or more years from now he must also consider the cost trend of manufactured equipment. The U.S. Bureau of Labor Statistics provides a wealth of statistical price and cost data, including prices and wages in numerous manufacturing industries.

In earlier sections it was emphasized that the degree of cost/price inflation we have been and are experiencing in recent years is a significant factor in determining the type of construction contracting arrangement that may be chosen for a project where a free choice exists. For short-range projects in a relatively steady cost trend period (whether rising or falling at a relatively fixed rate) lump sum or fixed price contracts are certainly viable. A contractor can fix his costs using his knowledge of present wage structures and what existing agreements provide in the short term and by using fixed price material bids for delivery in the short term. Any variations from these factors probably will not be great and will fall within the reasonableness of risk evaluation for such work. However, if it is necessary for the contractor to predict the cost of construction labor or material and permanent equipment several years in the future or if he finds himself in a rapidly changing cost/price period for certain commodities, he will be understandably reluctant to place a fixed price on the work. Should he be forced to do so in order to compete he will attempt to add a considerable contingency to protect himself from these unknown conditions. The owner may ultimately suffer either by paying too much or by finding himself with a near broke and defaulting contractor. One way to handle this kind of situation on a more equitable basis is through the use of cost indexing. The contractor by tying certain portions of his bid to readily identifiable items such as the cost of specific kinds of labor or materials at the time of bid provides a means for adjusting the bid to the actual cost of those same items at some date in the future. In this way the owner receives the benefit of a fixed bid to the extent that the contractor can fairly control it and then pays only the increment that varies. The contractor still accepts the burden for establishing the quantity and the unit cost base from which cost increases will be measured.

The use of formal cost indexing is not widespread at present in construction contracting but was quite common in the purchase of major long lead equipment (one year or more) in the changing economy of 1972-1975. At that time manufacturers could not or would not fix prices for equipment other than to say "price in effect at time of shipment." To cope with this blank-check approach many purchasers resorted to negotiating orders with established prices that were subject to variation as measured by agreed on indexes. Copper recently has been a very volatile commodity, with the result that electrical contractors and other purchasers of wire and cable are unable to fix prices, except for a very short term. So bids are tied to the price of wire and cable that the contractor used and "indexed" for the copper price adjustment. It is obvious that the entire selling price or manufacturing cost of an item is not directly proportional to the cost of material, so a formula must be agreed on to reflect the proportion of the product that is affected by material price changes. Labor varies too, and sometimes prices or contract bids are tied to the cost of labor at the time of bid—but more commonly restricted to performance within a period when the labor costs are known. Usually, a supplier or contractor has a better handle on labor cost, because he employs labor and is closer to its fluctuations. But materials are different and largely seen as outside the contractor's control.

There are numerous U.S. government industry, and private indexes—all of which may have application to a specific case. The main difficulty in using indexing is in the initial agreement—or lack of it. It is vitally important to be sure both contracting parties are in *specific* agreement on the index to be used, the commodity or portion of the order/contract affected, the period covered, and the limit, if any, to be placed on total escalation. Most difficulty with escalation clauses arises from a lack of specificity in the initial agreement. If the original agreement is well drawn there usually is no difficulty with the use of indexing other than somewhat more involved administration.

No one possesses a clear vision of the future, but it seems safe to say that significant inflation and commodity price variations will be with us for a long time, if not forever. The recent dramatic rise in worldwide oil prices has had a tremendous effect on the economy of the entire global market.

Rising energy costs have impacted almost everything traded and are indirectly resulting in uneven price changes in many markets. If we accept the premise that this situation is likely to persist for some time then we can expect not only continued but increased interest in the use of escalation clauses. As their use becomes more widespread there may be a trend toward the use of fewer accepted indexing standards and a standardized method of calculating the escalation costs. Because of the great variety and types of items affected, including labor, the list of standard accepted indexes can never be very short, but at least there would be the expectation of some convergence on the major and most representative ones.

Is all this complexity necessary? Of course, it is not, but under the changing cost/price conditions being experienced the alternate is to let the contractor guess at future costs. In these circumstances the prudent contractor adds more than enough to his bid to try to cover himself, and the owner pays the bill.

Guessing has no place in serious construction contracting. Equity produces a better result for all parties. So escalation clauses will stay and probably proliferate.

ALLOCATING CONTRACTUAL RISK

As the stakes involved in large construction projects have increased, increasing efforts have been made to shift the risks of the project from the owner to the contractor. The superior bargaining power of owners has resulted in contracts written in accordance with their desires. Whether the sought-after results have been attained is a different question. This section attempts to review the more common forms of contractual risk allocation and the practical problems with their use.

GUARANTEES

The simplest way to shift risk from the owner to the contractor is to require the contractor to guarantee the results of the project. Various forms of guarantees are in current use.

Workmanship

The most common is undoubtedly the guarantee or warranty of the contractor's workmanship and materials. Many standard forms now require the contractor to correct defects that appear after completion of the project. To keep inordinate insurance costs out of bids, owners usually acquiesce in the contractor's desire to limit the duration of this liability. The most common term is one year from final acceptance of the work. A variation imposes an additional year from the completion of any corrective work required during the initial period. There have been and are attempts by owners to require the contractor to guarantee different parts of industrial projects for different periods, all exceeding one year (buildings, for example, for five years). The contractor will seek a dollar limitation as well, perhaps offering to perform remedial work beyond the limit at cost. The result depends on the owner's policy and the contractor's bargaining strength. The same is true of the contractor's responsibility for vendor-furnished items that are warranted by the vendor. Some owner's will agree to look only to the vendor with respect to defects covered by the warranty, while others may attempt to obtain through a contractor an extension of the usual one-year warranty. Contractors will try to limit the extent of their guarantee to the owner to that they receive from the vendor. Contractors accept some form of workmanship and materials guarantee as a fact of life.

Guaranteed Maximum Price

Much less clear is the desirability of forcing the contractor to guarantee the cost of the work to the owner. The lump sum price does provide cost stability on projects of defined scope and design, with few or no unknowns, subject to such things as subsurface conditions, weather, or others beyond the contractor's reasonable control. It will also allow an opportunity for increased profit to the contractor on such projects. However, lump sum pricing is not desirable on complex or undefined projects or those that carry the risk of adverse foundation conditions or the like. In these situations, it is virtually impossible for the bid to be accurate, and either inordinate contractor profit, or more likely, losses, claims, and litigation will result. The problem can be exacerbated by use of the guaranteed maximum price contract, combined with a provision allowing changes at no increase in price. Typically, a guaranteed maximum price contract requires the owner to pay the actual cost of the work, plus an agreed fee, but only up to the stated maximum price. Any cost beyond that are borne by the contractor. Adding to this the requirement that the contractor make necessary changes at no cost to the owner results in a very high-risk venture. Such documents are more productive of litigation than of satisfactory projects. Most owners are now using unit prices or some other form of cost contract on projects that are not suited for maximum price guarantees.

Time of Completion

While the time of completion can also be made the subject of a contractor guarantee it is patently true that it is beyond the power of any contractor to guarantee that a project will be completed on a specific date, similar to the guaranteed maximum in the case of price. As a result, the guarantee generally takes the form of an imposed penalty for late completion and is discussed subsequently in connection with penalties.

Performance

The satisfactory operation of the project itself on completion can often be guaranteed by the contractor. Performance guaranty tests for pipeline throughput, process plant capacity, and similar attributes are common in the industry. Failure to meet the tests will delay acceptance, require additional work, and may call for the forfeiture of a penal sum. In some cases, should the plant or a critical part never reach the guaranteed production rate, the contractor is required to pay a stipulated sum based on the lost production for a prescribed number of years. Often these guarantees involve vendor-furnished equipment of a special nature, and the guarantee provisions will involve the vendor either wholly or in part. The benefit of the performance guarantee test is not available on projects using proprietary technology that is the property of the owner under its own patents or by license from a third party. In such cases the owner must rely on its own experience with the technology or that of the licensor.

In summary, the owner can benefit substantially from contractor guarantees of aspects of the project that are reasonably within the contractor's control.

PENALTIES

The most common form of penalty is the provision for liquidated damages in the event of late completion. There was a need for such a clause to cover those situations where actual damages were extremely difficult or impossible to determine; hence the parties agreed on an amount per period of time to represent the damages for late completion. Such clauses have never been popular with the courts, and the legal constraints on enforcing such provisions vary from jurisdiction to jurisdiction. Even where enforceable, there are disadvantages to the owner in using a liquidated damage clause. Generally, its use will result in higher bids as contractors include a contingency amount. The contractors may insist on a corresponding bonus provision. Both can lead to cutting corners and a lower standard of performance because of pressure to meet the schedule. Finally, use of the liquidated damage clause is not indicated on projects where there is substantial likelihood of owner-caused delay, for example, in furnishing materials. The contractor will attribute any delay to the owner, and the resulting litigation can cancel any benefit hoped for from the penalty clause.

INCENTIVES

The most common forms of incentive clauses are related to the cost and/or completion date of the project and most often, but not always, are found in connection with cost plus a fee contracts.

Contractor sharing in cost underruns has been used by the federal government as a means of cost control for many years. The standard cost plus incentive fee contract establishes a target cost and a target fee. The target fee will diminish to a specified minimum if the target cost is exceeded and will increase up to the stated maximum if the actual costs are less than the target cost. The same approach is found in private practice, although the incentive fee contract as such is rare. More commonly the contractor may share in the underrun or overrun of the target up to the amount of his fee. In some cases a neutral zone is established just above and below the target cost in which the contractor does not share either overrun or underrun.

The bonus for early completion is generally used in conjuction with a penalty for delayed completion. This can often be a dubious bargain from the owner's point of view, because the penalty provision is difficult to enforce and usually will not be operative if the contractor can establish that delays were beyond his control. The bonus, on the other hand, gives the contractor the benefit of any fortuitous circumstances that make possible the early completion of the work. Still, early completion is obviously very important to the owner, or he would not have provided a bonus in the first place. If the contractor is lucky and earns the bonus the owner is also rewarded by attaining his goal of timely completion.

Bonus-penalty clauses can be an effective tool for use by concerned owners to attempt to have the contractor share some of the risk in cost plus contracts and thus to provide some added measure of cost and schedule control. Critics of these incentive provisions have pointed out that their use tends to produce inflated cost estimates, unrealistically long schedules, and lower-quality work. These disadvantages may be avoidable if the use of incentive clauses is restricted to projects where the owner is in a position to accurately assess the cost and time actually required.

RESTRICTIVE PROCEDURAL CLAUSES

In an effort to limit contractors' claims based on changes and extra work, many owners in the public sector and in private business insert onerous procedural requirements as a prerequisite to the assertion of any claim. Such clauses generally require written notice within a brief period after the event giving rise to the claim, sometimes as short as 24 hours; often detailed calculations of the cost involved will also be required. While some procedure is desirable for orderly contract administration, little purpose is served by making the procedure overly stringent. A well-organized contractor will tend to generate more claims in such a situation rather than less. The owner's interest would be better served by a reasonable procedure designed to identify, quantify, and resolve genuine disputes at the earliest possible moment.

PRICING OF RISKS

On projects where delays and suspensions of the work are foreseeable or likely, much effort and controversy can be avoided by agreeing to price provisions that quantify the risk. By agreeing upon rates for standby time and equipment rental, the owner may avoid a later claim for acceleration of the work carrying a much higher value. The same approach can be applied to extra work when the parties cannot readily agree on a price. The owner would have the right to direct that the work proceed on a time and materials basis, at rates previously agreed on. In some cases, this method can be applied to units of work that are difficult to estimate, such as foundation excavation or dewatering. A given number of units are compensable at an agreed rate. Such price schedules do add to the owner's cost but usually in a lesser amount than would otherwise be spent on claims and litigation.

REGULATORY RISK

In these days of increasing governmental involvement in all aspects of the economy, any major construction project faces a creditable risk of suspension, temporary or permanent, by government order. Since acts of the government are generally events of force majeure, neither the owner nor the contractor is to be regarded as in default under the contract. However, this does not resolve the question of how to deal with a prolonged suspension. The interminable payment of standby costs is not satisfactory to either the owner or the contractor. Many contracts for large projects provide that either party may terminate the contract in the event of suspension exceeding a specified period. The contractor is then paid for the work done and receives a reasonable allowance for profit, together with his termination costs.

MINIMIZING DISPUTES

As construction costs soar, the burdensome expense of claims and litigation becomes less and less affordable for owners and contractors as well. Consideration of practices that may help to reduce the incidence of disputes is worthwhile for all connected with the construction industry.

BASIC CAUSES OF DISPUTES

One basic cause of disputes is the underfunded project. Special purpose government agencies and even private owners sometimes make the mistake of putting a project to bid without adequate capital available. As construction costs begin to exceed the funds on hand, claims and litigation inevitably follow. At the same time, contractors may submit losing bids in the effort to gain business. This practice can seldom be made profitable by resort to claims.

A second fundamental cause of disputes is the unreasonable construction schedule. The owner takes some risk in imposing a tight schedule, particularly when his own acts can influence the time of performance. To avoid this problem, many owners have been requiring the contractor to calculate his schedule and include it in his bid. The owner then reviews the feasibility and desirability of the schedule.

Another recurring problem is the difficulty faced by the contractor in estimating the cost of a project that is not completely designed. Optimism in estimating work to be shown on drawings to be issued after the contract is awarded is often penalized by disputes and claims.

AVOIDING DISPUTES

Many problems can be avoided by a thorough prebid review of the legal and administrative provisions of the contract documents. The areas where problems are likely to arise generally include the clauses dealing with changes and extra work, delays and suspensions of the work, and subsurface or latent conditions. If the contractor insures that his field supervision is familiar with these aspects of the contract before the job starts, many difficulties can be avoided or minimized.

Accurate record keeping is essential on any construction project. There is no substitute for daily records of work accomplished, labor force, problems encountered, and contacts with the owner. Of particular importance are records of material received and of construction drawings issued or revised. Written records of orders and other communications are essential. Dated progress photographs reflecting the status of the work should also be maintained. Failure to keep adequate and comprehensive records has caused the abandonment of many valid contractor claims for additional compensation. It is virtually impossible to substantiate a claim of any complexity without adequate project records.

Similarly, the contractor must be diligent in notifying the owner or engineer of any circumstances that will or might give rise to a claim for additional compensation. The idea that such notices serve only to annoy the owner overlooks the fact that most owners would prefer to receive prompt advice of developing problems rather than stale claims raised at the end of the job.

Finally, both owners and contractors can benefit from a willingness to compromise and settle claims. Relationships between joint venturers and co-owners can sometimes result in arbitrary refusals to entertain compromises. A prompt but partial payment of disputed amounts in lieu of costly and protracted litigation is more often than not in the interest of all concerned.

CONSTRUCTION CLAIMS

Claims filed in connection with construction contracts are a part of everyday life in the industry today. "Claims," in this sense of the word, does not refer to a request for payment for work done on a regular basis, such as sometimes is the case under government contracts, but rather refers to those items of work that are disputed between the contractor and the owner. Typically, the owner orders the contractor to perform certain work that the owner believes is a part of the contract. To the contrary, the contractor believes it is extra work and that he is entitled to additional payment but is bound by the provisions of the contract to carry out the work. Obviously, the contractor needs some method through which to recover costs, and this is through the route commonly referred to as claims.

Claims almost always arise because the contract provisions are not clear. It is the owner's opinion that certain work is a part of the contractor's obligation under the contract, and the contractor thinks otherwise. In this situation the burden of proof is on the contractor, for he usually is required by the provisions of the contract document to do the work first and attempt to recover his cost later. A contractor who attempts to coerce the owner into making a settlement before the work is done on the threat of not carrying out the work runs the risk of a serious default under his contract that can easily have much greater repercussions than an attempt to recover for the disputed work.

In the usual situation where the contractor performs the work and seeks recovery later the process puts an additional financial strain on the contractor. Not uncommonly, this financial strain can cause definite and sometimes major problems. In recent years a number of large joint-venture projects, worldwide, have run into this situation, and, in some of those cases, some of the contractors in the ventures have been bankrupt as a result of being unable to contribute their share of carrying the financial burden of claimed work until a final settlement was reached.

Often the owner will want to delay the settlement of claims and use the economic strength of retention and final payment at the end of the contract to achieve a minimum settlement of the cost of disputed work. The contractor, on the other hand, is usually anxious to settle disputed claims as they arise and as soon as possible after costs can be determined in order to ease his financial burden and reduce the ultimate negotiating strength of the owner.

The federal government has several administrative levels through which a contractor moves in an attempt to try fairly to settle a dispute and obtain an agreement on the claims before the dispute reaches the courts. The private sector operates somewhat differently and does not provide the latitude in administrative remedies that the government does. Usually, attempts are made to settle contract disputes at the job level and then at the level of the owner's home office. Failing either of these two, the dispute will probably move to either arbitration or litigation.

Claims are rarely completely avoided in most large construction contracts, but a clearly drawn contract fairly interpreted, will usually avoid any serious problems.

CONCLUSION

This chapter has attempted an overview of the more notable changes and trends in construction contract application today. Some progress appears to have been made in solving old and new problems—such as how to handle constructive acceleration or how to maximize the benefits and minimize the drawbacks of fixed price/turnkey contracting; other problems remain to be solved. How can we best handle the mega-project and the trend to transferring more and more risk and liability to the engineer-contractor? New methods and applications are needed. The evidence today suggests that solutions are being sought and will continue to be sought in the future as change follows change. The rise in usage and increased attention to the development of the CM fast track approach to contracting demonstrated again that the search for a better way will produce a responsible and viable result. The demand for flexibility and innovation in the construction industry will continue unabated.

CHAPTER 14

EDUCATION AND TRAINING

Keith Crandall

The complexity of many current construction projects is requiring a redirection and focusing of attention of various aspects of performance. Herein lies the need for a careful evaluation of the entire education and training process. There are many individual perspectives on the concept of the "proper training" for each position within the construction process, but most will agree on the requirement to develop and encourage the development of certain abilities so that each individual can perform at the peak of his own capability. This assumed attitude toward training does not ignore the fact that some individuals are jealous of their knowledge, considering it as job security, and are reluctant to share it with others. Instead, the attitude is based on the realization by most managers of the necessity to have qualified individuals available to handle the increasing complexity of modern projects. Without attempting to endorse one method or another, various training and educational programs will be described in this chapter so that those interested in extending current programs may draw their own conclusions and tailor a program based on their unique needs.

BASIC PERSPECTIVES

There exists in the construction industry many successful mangers, field superintendents, foremen, and skilled craft laborers, each with completely different backgrounds in formal and informal training and education. One cannot classify success on actual work classification or on an arbitrary scale such as degree or certificate received from a formal educaion process but if the skills that one has acquired are fully used, it is then possible to correlate such things as success with skill level. How does one go about acquiring the necessary skills? Is there a single best procedure or sequence of training to follow? Does everyone require the development of the same skills? These are typical questions that result from the diverse attitudes which exist in the construction industry.

There are many successful individuals in every work category who have had little or no formal training, as there are others who have completed advanced college programs. Each views the training question from his own perspective, with a strong bias toward his own training. The fact is that each individual responds to different stimuli and that there is no single correct educational or training process. The only official requirement appears in the administration of the various states' license requirements and the federal apprenticeship programs.

To more closely focus on the training options open to the industry, the remainder of this chapter is divided into the broad classification of craft labor training and supervision and management personnel training. Although the author realizes that such a distinction is arbitrary, since many skills are the same for each category, it is easier to view the existing processes if this distinction is made.

CRAFT LABOR TRAINING

Ultimately, the success of any project depends on the availability of a well-trained work force who comprehends what is to be done and how to accomplish the completion of each task. Many contractors rely on the individual crew foreman to complete these daily tasks without due consideration for any additional skill requirements. Since much of the work is repetitive and most foremen have worked for an extended period with their employers, this is not entirely an absurd position but it is worthwhile to view the general training received by various components of the craft labor force in view of this assumption.

APPRENTICESHIP PROGRAMS

Apprenticeship programs are formalized training, administered by governmental agencies. In addition to the requirements of Title 29 CFR (Code of Federal Regulations), Part 30 of the Department of Labor, many states have their own requirements relating to the selection of applicants, record keeping, and reporting procedures. These governmental agencies establish criteria relating to age, prior training requirements, a schedule of skills to be learned, formal training sessions, and training facilities.

The administration of these programs are, in part, controlled by law and also by the local apprentice councils. The councils have labor and management representatives and perform essential functions of establishing standards and often are involved in the overseeing of individual programs.

The apprenticeship programs are funded by industrial funds that represent a token amount for each hour of labor used and by federal support for federally approved programs. Many local unions and contractors have established training facilities such as welding work stations in their own or community institutions. These facilities constitute a capital investment in training and are often part of a larger community effort at the high school or community college level.

The apprentice is paid a percentage of the journeyman's scale while in training, The actual education process combines classroom theory, skill development, and on-the-job training. To be certified, the individual must complete the program, which often takes several years, and show a proficiency in the designated skills.

Although the apprenticeship programs provide a well-defined procedure for the training and testing of skill development, there are several critical assessments of individual programs. These include achievement skill levels well below those anticipated, inequities in the candidate selection process, the inadequate number of trainees processed, and the extensive time required for training. In most of these cases, the criticism is the manifestation of other local problems such as a lack of qualified journeyman over a period of peak construction. In those instances where the criticism is based on valid problems, the local construction industry must work through the apprenticeship councils to correct the situation. See Figure 14-1 for a tabulation showing typical apprentice pay rates.

Article XXI, wage rates
The following wage rates shall become effective the first full payroll period after April 1, 1977:

Classification	Base wage
April 1, 1977	
Carpenter journeyman	$ 9.86
Carpenter foreman (2 or more men)	10.36
Carpenter foreman (12 or more men)	10.86
Millwright journeyman	10.11
Millwright foreman (2 or more men)	10.61
Millwright foreman (12 or more men)	11.11

Apprentice wage rates (percentage of journeyman's base wage)
    First 6 months—60%
    Second 6 months—65%
    Third 6 months—70%
    Fourth 6 months—75%
    Fifth 6 months—80%
    Sixth 6 months—85%
    Seventh 6 months—90%
    Eighth 6 months—95%

Figure 14–1   Typical apprenticeship pay rates.

NONAPPRENTICESHIP PROGRAMS

There exist several formal and informal programs for the training of skilled and semiskilled craftsman. One of the most common is the designation of a "helper" category, where an individual works with and receives training from a journeyman. This informal program provides excellent on-the-job training. The deficiency in this program rests mainly in the lack of a well-balanced preparation for a trade and is heavily dependent on the skill of the journeyman and his ability to train. Finally, there is no certification for the newly trained individual that readily identifies his ability. Since any-one can claim having received such training, contractors are often reluctant to hire such an individual even when they become somewhat desperate for skilled craftsman.

Federal equal employment opportunity requirements have created a de-mand for programs involving the training of minorities. Governmental pro-grams have assisted many individuals in receiving training with minority firms while working on federal projects. Many of these individuals are find-ing their may into organized craft labor pools but in insufficient numbers to meet existing and proposed regulations. Often, as with the helper trainee, the skill level of these individuals is questioned and further on-the-job training is warranted or required. The deficiency in qualified personnel has created a great demand for such training programs, including those not well defined in terms of goals and objectives.

The recent decision to include a fixed percentage of minority contractors on all major federal projects will increase the numbers of minority crafts-men but not necessarily the quality of training received. The industry must support those programs that provide viable training if qualified craftsmen are to be available in reasonable numbers.

There is a recent move by those involved in the Merit Shop concept to provide intensive specialized training to create a craftsman skilled only in those areas required by a particular project. Referred to as "Task Train-ing," contractors have often carried the training right to the job site itself. This effort represents formal training programs in that the trainee receives both classroom and skill training, with a certification of the obtained skill level. These programs not only provide a reasonably flexible method of creating trained personnel in an area where skilled craftsman are not oth-erwise available, but also create an opportunity for continued on-the-job training and ultimate classification as a journeyman. This program also allows an individual to receive training in more than one of the traditional craft skills, which may provide for longer tenure with a contractor and a particular project.

CURRENT ISSUES

There is no question that the industry has a significant stake in the im-proved training of skilled craftsman. Contractors rely on these skills and many, including those in the Merit Shop movement, are taking an active role in this training. It is more difficult for contractors involved on a national level to justify training of union and nonunion personnel who may not stay with the company, since the benefit of such training will likely be realized by competitors. The real benefit accrues to the individual receiving the training, and, if it is administered properly, the individual is grateful to those making it possible. The improvement in overall productivity resulting from knowledgeable craftsman and the improvement in the image by which the public views the construction industry are two positive incentives for creating more training opportunities.

The issue of skill level designation, currently limited to helper, apprentice, and journeyman, is one of the issues to be resolved in the forthcoming years. There are many work assignments that require a "paraprofessional" rather than a skilled journeyman. The skills required are not met by the helper or apprentice designation and often represent the capabilities of some individuals who show specialized talents but never reach the skill status of a journeyman. The current practice of designating such individuals as journeyman after a period of years is a disservice to the qualified journeyman and to the contractors. The paraprofessional designation would identify the skills the individual actually possesses and assures him of satisfactory and productive work assignments and, at the same time reserves those assignments requiring complete knowledge of the trade for journeyman. The benefit of such a designation is that it would recognize the actual skill level and provide recognition to those at the journeyman level, while providing employment opportunities to those who have no desire to reach that level of qualification.

A similar problem relates to the mobility of skilled craftsmen. There is significant unemployment in many areas where others are in desperate need of these excess skills. The question of relocation is, in part, a problem of personal choice, where it is difficult to uproot a family and move at the completion of a project. There is no easy answer to this dilemma. There are many barriers that are created however that can be addressed, and answers to exist. Primary to this category are those barriers that restrict benefits to a local area and the lack of a recognized system of universal classification of obtained skill levels. There is a necessity to remove any possible stigma from those who are skilled and yet join an itinerant work force moving as necessary to follow the varying demand for construction; in fact, these individuals must be recognized as an elite group who will attract the younger generation into promising careers. There is no question that there is a bias against careers as skilled craftsmen compared to the learned professions, yet these individuals are as an important a segment of society as the professions and more important than most others and must be made more attractive in relation to their importance.

Finally, there is a question of the international craft labor market and the role our labor force can anticipate in the future years. The current policy of many developing countries to train and export construction labor has had a significant impact on the use of U. S. labor forces on overseas construction projects. The productivity ratio that in the past indicated the advantage of production in favor of the U. S. laborer is dropping to equality—and in special instances to a point where the foreign labor is superior. The use of craft labor overseas is being restricted to that of an instructor or an operator of very specialized equipment. There is a need to develop and enhance the future role of our skilled craft labor. This may require additional training and the assumption of a supervisory role, since there is a lack of qualified and experienced supervisors.

MANAGEMENT TRAINING

In order to clarify the definition of the term "manager," it is used to designate anyone functioning in a supervisory, planning, design, or control function in addition to those involved in the management of the business part of an enterprise. It is obvious that such a definition implies a diversified training requirement, and current response to this need has created many excellent programs. Several of the more successful programs will be described under the separate headings of nonacademic and academic programs. This distinction represents the two major sources of construction managers namely, those who advance from the ranks of craft labor and those who attend professional programs in engineering and business.

Regardless of the initial background, those who enter the ranks of management require continued opportunity for training and a motivation for learning. Much of this training, by necessity, takes place in the form of on-the-job training, but it must be recognized that at various times in their professional development, managers require specific specialized training to prepare them for new responsibilities.

Since time is a constraint, specialized training is usually obtained through participation in professional societies, short intensive seminars, in-house specialty conferences, and, occasionally, by taking sponsored extension courses. Each manager must continue to appraise his own strengths and weaknesses as he selects the various opportunities to delete the areas of weakness.

During the early stages of development, potential managers often require the support and encouragement from superiors in order to develop proper initial motivation. Outstanding craftsman need encouragement to enter supervisory programs, and young engineers may need encouragement to learn business skills and so forth. Qualifications necessary for senior management assignments include leadership and incentive. With these qualities a potential manager will eventually seek his own formal and informal training opportunities.

NONACADEMIC PROGRAMS

The nonacademic programs ultimately become the most significant as a manager continues his development and therefore require attention and support from the industry. Without question, the most meaningful of these programs are those developed in house, based on adopted company policy. In this regard trainees not only learn the various issues at stake, but also solutions in terms of approved company policy. It is therefore the responsibility of every manager to view training needs of subordinates and provide opportunities, guidance, and the evaluation necessary for this type of training.

Industry-Supported Programs

There are programs directed at the advancement of skilled and qualified craftsmen that use their abilities and enhance their leadership characteristics. Two of these programs are sponsored by contracting organizations. The first is AGC's Construction Supervisor Training Program, which is an outgrowth of work done by AGC of Colorado and its Construction Advancement Program. This program provides formal training for potential superintendents and foremen. The individual sessions are designed to encourage active participation of trainees in a case environment where various roles can be examined and perspective gained in attitudes of various groups. The foreman training program covers the following topics:

Supervisor's role.

Leadership.

Motivation.

Problem solving.

Communication.

Training and learning.

Planning and organization.

Safety.

Material handling.

Evaluation

The superintendent program is still undergoing development, with the following topics to be included:

Construction supervision: leadership and motivation.

Oral and written communications.

Construction problem solving and decision making.

Interpretation of drawings and documentation.

Construction planning and scheduling.

Cost awareness and production control.

Construction safety.

Construction employee and labor relations.

Construction productivity improvement.

Construction project organization and control.

The second program is sponsored by ABC and is called "Profits and Advancement through Construction Education." This program also provides formalized training based on the use of an audiovisual system that synchronizes an audiotape with a continuous loop film strip. The training program is subdivided into several large categories such as "Construction Management," "General Safety," "Free Enterprise," and "Warehousing." Each category has many separate sessions aimed at a specific topic such as "How to Read and Analyze Your Financial Statement." These packages can be used by individuals or large groups, and, if coordinated with in-house programs, could provide for an interaction between participants that is currently lacking.

Company-Sponsored Programs

Many of the large construction or design-construct companies have developed in-house training programs designed to qualify promising managers for overall top job responsibility or for upgrading managerial skills. These programs may take the form of a formal program developed by a training supervisor and administered through the personnel department. Other less structured programs may be developed by individual executives, division or department managers, or others designed to develop overall managers through carefully selected on-the-job assignments.

Formal Training Programs

Typical formal training programs may involve individual courses in specific skills such as CPM, formal management theory, negotiating theory, estimating theory and practice, and many other functional and general skills and knowledge required by managers in today's complex environment.

Other companies designate selected college graduates to participate in a formal program intended to last several years in which the selected potential manager is given three-to-six-month assignments in various functional departments in order to teach the basic managerial and technical skills in a work environment. After conclusion of the formal program the trainee is evaluated and assigned to a division or department by mutual agreement.

Problems associated with formal training programs have been substantial. Nonselected or functional personnel may resent the interest and status shown to the trainee, and the actual responsibilities, encouragement, and training may be wholly dependent on functional supervisors who may differ widely in their approach to management. The lack of significant actual responsibility on completion of the program has led to a high turnover rate among young managers who are eager to assume greater responsibilities than are available to the program graduate.

Informal Mentor Programs

Many effective top managers owe much of their success to selection by a senior manager or mentor who has aided the development of the manager through the selection of responsibilities designed to equip the budding young manager for higher responsibilities as well as through offering sound career and individual task advice and training in a relaxed informal manner. One of the major contributions of a mentor can be to publicize the skills and potential of the young manager among the persons in the company who will be responsible for the selection of general management or functional openings and a willingness to transfer the manager to other divisions or departments when solid career growth is apparent.

Of course, the mentor program can also become nonproductive when the senior executive's concept of career growth is different from that of the manager or when the mentor fails to recognize that all successful managers outgrow their mentors at some point in their careers.

Other Programs

There are programs available through most colleges and junior colleges that allow individuals to gain expertise, during evening extension courses, in a variety of topics, including the aspects of organization, business and accounting, estimating, and specific techniques such as scheduling. These programs require that an individual be in the same area during the academic session, which extends from 10 to 15 weeks.

Many professional societies offer intensive short courses of from one to five days, in conjunction with their annual meetings or on an ad hoc basis in specific cities during the year. The fees for these sessions are nominal, and the instructors are normally recognized leaders from industry. Programs of this nature are offered by groups like the American Society of Civil Engineers, the American Association of Cost Engineers, the Project Management Institute, and many specialty organizations. Figure 14-2 shows a typical program.

Some organizations, for example the American Management Association, specialize in seminar presentations that relate to a broad spectrum of topics important to the construction industry, including supervisor training, scheduling, productivity, and construction management. These seminars normally last from to three days and are offered in large population centers. The fees are significantly higher than those charged by professional societies, but the preparation of supporting course material is more professional.

Many of these organizations offer prerecorded audio or audiovisual presentations that can be used as part of a well-rounded in-house training program. These require a minimum investment in support equipment and normally a fee for materials for each individual participant.

ACADEMIC PROGRAMS

The increasing complexity of major projects manifested by the scope of work, government regulations and other external constraints, technological problems, monetary considerations, and time pressures has, over time, cre-

ASCE CONTINUING EDUCATION

COURSE OFFERINGS in conjunction with the ASCE Annual Convention and Exposition
ATLANTA, GEORGIA,—October 19-27, 1979

October 19-20
CONSTRUCTION CLAIMS: ANALYSIS, PRESENTATION / DEFENSE • CONSTRUCTION COST ESTIMATING & BIDDING • ECONOMIC EVALUATION OF ENGINEERING PROJECTS • ROCK SLOPE ENGINEERING • MODERN DEVELOPMENTS IN WIND ENGINEERING: WIND EFFECTS ON BUILDINGS & STRUCTURES

October 22
CABLE-STAYED BRIDGES • THE ENGINEER AS AN EXPERT WITNESS • FIELD INSTRUMENTATION FOR SOIL & ROCK MECHANICS • MANAGEMENT OF PROJECT PAPERWORK

October 22-23
EVALUATION OF FIRE SAFETY DESIGN FOR BUILDINGS • URBAN STORM & FLOOD WATER MANAGEMENT

October 23
EFFECTIVE MARKETING OF PROFESSIONAL SERVICES • A NEW DIMENSION IN COMMUNICATIONS—PART I & PART II

October 25-26
CONSTRUCTION PROJECT ADMINISTRATION & FIELD MANAGEMENT • THE DESIGN & CONSTRUCTION OF REINFORCED MASONRY STRUCTURES • AN INTRODUCTION TO SITE PLANNING

October 25-26-27
OPERATING A CONSULTING FIRM

October 26
FIELD CONTROL OF PILE INSTALLATION & CONCRETING OPERATIONS

COMPLIMENTARY CONVENTION REGISTRATION

Each course participant will automatically receive a complimentary registration to the ASCE Annual Convention and Exposition.

REGISTRATION DISCOUNT

10% discount given on total registration fee when a person registers for more than one course or a firm sends more than one person to any of the courses.

GENERAL INFORMATION

Certificates: Each course participant will be awarded a certificate of completion indicating the number of CEUs (Continuing Education Units).

Time Schedule: All courses will run from 9:00 a.m. to 5:00 p.m. with a break for lunch.

Course Location: Atlanta Hilton Hotel.

For complete details and registration information. Write or phone—Patricia Irmen, Manager, Continuing Education Services, ASCE, 345 East 47th Street, New York, N.Y. 10017 (212) 644-7668.

ASCE

Please send me information on the course offerings to be held in Atlanta, Georgia October 19-27, 1979.

NAME _____ TITLE _____

FIRM _____ STREET _____

CITY _____ STATE _____ ZIP _____

Figure 14-2 Typical continuing education program.

344

ated an environment in which more and more potential managers are entering the industry from an academic instead of the traditional craft background. Academic training creates individuals capable of solving technical problems generated in modern projects but at the same time produces individuals whose experience and knowledge of traditional construction practice is well below the level of their technical ability. It is, therefore, imperative that these individuals obtain field experience as part of their early professional development. The difference between these individuals' technical and practical knowledge depends, in part, on the type of academic training they receive, since programs vary in length from two to five years with a few taking even longer.

Before describing typical types of programs that are available, it is worthwhile to define the differences in philosophy that are readily apparent in the academic community regarding such programs. These differences are a result of the same reasoning that lead to the separation of engineering from the "pure sciences," and that is the question of the practical versus theoretical treatment of problem solving. Some educators feel that the practical aspects should be obtained solely from later industrial experience, with academic emphasis on theoretical concepts. Others argue that an academic program based solely on theory creates a distortion of reality and that a realistic program must be a blend of the theoretical and practical. With the exception of technological programs, each type of program described has institutions that support each of these philosophies. Although there are firms that support the idea that one or the other of these philosophies is superior, the facts tend to indicate that the probability for success in the construction industry is excellent regardless of the emphasis. There is nevertheless merit in the development of the technical capability that either emphasis provides.

The methods of instruction vary from institution to institution as do the basic qualifications for admission. Some programs are designed to augment the skills of those actively involved in construction. Late afternoon or night classes are also offered. Even with these differences the typical program available for those interested in construction can be classified as follows: technology programs, engineering and other undergraduate programs, engineering and other graduate programs, and graduate business administration programs. Each of these is described subsequently in terms of their general characteristics. With the exception of the Master in Business Administration (MBA) programs, many programs of each type, offered all over the county, are listed in AGC's *Construction Education Directory*, published by the AGC's Education and Research Foundation. This directory is the single best reference of institutions offering construction programs.

Technology Programs

These programs normally require two to four years of training and accept applicants directly from high school, with a minimum academic requirement. The courses in these programs emphasize practical aspects of a given topic and minimize the theory required. Graduates are not prepared for professional registration, since the goal of these programs is to train office personnel in the skills of estimating, cost control, reading of blue prints, and so forth. These individuals are prepared to perform in an active role immediately on graduation or certification.

The two-year programs have been highly successful and are often supported by local employer groups who have a need for office personnel in such areas as estimating and for timekeepers, quantity surveyors, and cost clerks. Courses typical of those offered in the two-year program include the following:

- Construction mathematics—algebra, trigonometry, plane geometry.
- Construction drafting—frame design, sketching, codes, and specs.
- Construction industry—role of industry in contemporary society.
- Construction surveying—layout, leveling, vertical and horizontal controls.
- Construction materials—concrete, wood, soils and interface with specs.
- Construction detailing—shop drawing, mechanical and electrical interface.
- Construction management practices—bidding, field office administration.
- Construction estimating—material, labor, overhead costs.
- Inspection practices—includes those tests common to construction work.
- Quantity estimating—based on practices for unit price contracts.
- Construction scheduling and cost control—interface with estimating.
- Construction law—legal aspects of codes, licenses, workmen's compensation.

The four-year programs are more rigorous and require a minimum amount of science in addition to the construction technology courses from the two-year programs. Graduates from these programs have been quite successful in industry, especially with smaller firms. their background is adequate for many to achieve a position in the top management of these small firms. One word of caution for those who may desire professional registration or graduate level studies at a later date is that these educational programs are not recognized by the Engineer's Council for Professional Development (ECPD), state professional licensing boards, and many colleges and universities. It is therefore more difficult for graduates from these programs to fulfill professionally oriented goals. Figure 14-3 shows the course content for one typical program.

Engineering and other Baccalaureate Programs

Baccalaureate programs are of two major categories. First, there are programs with a major such as civil engineering or architecture and a minor emphasis in construction. Second, those with a major emphasis in Construction and a minor such as civil engineering or architecture. These programs have grown from the two philosophies mentioned earlier and, in part, reflect the attitudes imposed by the physical departments in which they are housed and the accreditation group monitoring their programs.

The programs in engineering or architecture departments with a national reputation offer primarily a professional course of study, with the opportunity to take a minor in several areas, including construction. These programs normally specialize at the graduacte level with high-quality programs. These programs provide an "emphasis" in construction by offering courses as electives within the normal program and amount to less than 10% of the entire program of study. Graduates of these programs are technically qualified in their profession and are prepared for the construction specialty in that they have an overall knowledge of the industry. They require additional training for an in-depth knowledge that is often provided during the indoctrination phase of employment. Graduates of these programs have been very successful in the construction industry in both field and office activities. See Figure 14-4 for typical construction-oriented courses available in such a program.

Four-year baccalaureate programs that stress construction aspects require a less rigorous academic program in the areas of basic science and mathematics but include a significant number of construction courses throughout the four-year period. Some require or encourage an intern program during the last two summers. There has been a problem of accreditation, since these programs do not comply with the traditional requirements for engineering (ECPD) or architectural accreditation. Many institutions offering these academic coourses are members of the Associated Schools of Construction and within this association are trying to resolve the accreditation question. Graduates from programs are well qualified for careers in the industry and lack knowledge only in the areas that require strong technical backgrounds. This training is not generally recognized as fulfillment of a requirement for professional registration.

Graduate Programs

Graduate programs are available to develop the technical and business specialization required by the increasing complexity found in the industry. The demand for graduates from such programs has mushroomed in recent years, and many institutions have initiated programs in response to this demand. As in the baccalaureate programs, the graduate program can emphasize either the theoretical or practical aspects of the industry. Some of the successful institutions such as the University of California at Berkeley or Stanford University, California, have a well-balanced mix of these subject areas.

A graduate program cannot replace experience gained from field involvement and should not attempt to replace this essential training. Rather,

Freshman and Sophomore Curriculum

Freshman year	Credits
SSC 211 American institutions	3
EH 111 Comprehensive English	3
MS 102 Algebra and trigonometry	5
BCN 101 Construction materials	4
PL 101 Physical education	1
	16
SSC 221 American institutions	3
EH 121 Comprehensive English	3
MS 201 Analytic Geometry and calculus	5
GY 220 Engineering geology	4
PL — Physical education	1
	16
SSC 222 American institutions	3
EH 122 Comprehensive English	3
HUM 211 Humanities	4
PS 201 Applied physics	5
PL — Physical education	1
	16

Sophomore year	Credits
HUM 221 Humanities	4
CBS 211 Biological sciences	3
PS 202 Applied physics	5
AE 113 Architectural drawing	4
	16
HUM 231 Humanities	4
ATG 201 Accounting	5
BES 259 Cybernetics and society	5
	14
CBS 221 Biological sciences	3
EH 303 Business communications	4
BCN 201 Construction mechanics 1	5
Elective	4
	16

Upper Division Curriculum

Prerequisites are mandatory, including satisfactory completion of freshman and sophomore courses.

Junior year

First quarter	Credits
BCN 301 Construction surveying and drawing	5
BCN 311 Construction mechanics 2	5
BCN 321 Construction techniques 1	5
	15

Second quarter	
BCN 312 Structures 1	4
BCN 322 Construction techniques 2	5
BA 402 Business law	5
	14

Third quarter	
CIS 302 Introduction to computer programming	2
BCN 313 Structures 2	4
BCN 323 Construction techniques 3	5
BCN 331 Quantity surveying	4
	15

Senior year

First quarter	Credits
BCN 414 Structures 3	4
BCN 432 Construction estimating	4
BCN 441 Environmental technology 1	4
BCN 451 Construction management 1	4
	16

Second quarter	
BCN 402 History of construction	4
BCN 443 Environmental technology 2	4
BCN 452 Construction management 2	4
BCN 454 Construction planning and construction	4
	16

Third quarter	
BCN 403 Site development	4
BCN 445 Environmental technology 3	4
BCN 453 Construction management 3	4
Professional-technical elective	4
	16

Figure 14.3 Typical four-year construction program without a strong engineering emphasis. *From the Requirements of the University of Florida Construction Program.*

Program in Civil Engineering 180 units

	Fall	Units Winter	Spring
Freshman year			
Mathematics 1A-1B-1C, Calculus	4	4	4
Chemistry 1A-1B, General Chemistry	4	4	—
Physics 5A-5B, Physics for Scientists and Engineers	—	3	4
Computer science 1, Introduction to Programming	—	—	4
Engineering 25, Descriptive Geometry	2	—	—
Engineering 26, Engineering Graphics	—	—	2
Humanities and Social Studies Electives	5	5	—
	15	16	14
Sophomore year			
Mathematics 51C-51A-51B, Differential Equations and Related Topics	4	4	4
Physics 5C-5D, Physics for Scientists and Engineers	4	4	—
Statistics 25, Probability and Statistics for Engineers	—	4	—
Engineering 36, Engineering Mechanics I	—	—	3
Engineering 45, Properties of Materials	—	—	4
CE 10, Engineering Survey Measurements	4	—	—
Humanities and Social Studies electives	4	—	4
Free Elective Units	—	2	—
	16	14	15
Junior year			
ME 104A, Engineering Mechanics II	4	—	—
CE 118, Engineering Geology	3	—	—
CE 130A, Mechanics of Materials	4	—	—
CE 165A, Elementary Fluid Mechanics	3	—	—
CE 110, Properties of Structural Materials	—	3	—
CE 121, Soil and Foundation Engineering	—	4	—
CE 131, Introduction to Structural Analysis	—	4	—
CE 165B, Elementary Fluid Mechanics for Civil Engineers	—	3	—
CE 133, Theory of Reinforced Concrete Design, or 134, Elements of Metal Structures	—	—	4
CE 140, Water Resources Engineering	—	—	4
CE 170, Introduction to Transportation Engineering	—	—	4
Humanities and Social Studies Electives	—	—	4
	14	14	16

Figure 14-4 Typical program with a civil engineering emphasis. From the Catalogue. University of California, Berkeley.

Senior year

CE 141, Water Quality Management	—	3	—
CE 192, The Art and Science of Civil Engineering Practice	—	1	—
CE 194, Economics and Management of Engineering Systems	5	—	—
CE Upper Division Electives (15 units)	6	6	3
Humanities and Social Studies Electives	5	—	—
Free Electives	—	5	12
	16	15	15

Elective Courses

100, Control Surveys	4
102, Route Surveying	4
112, Aggregates for Civil Engineering Construction	3
113, Concrete and Concrete Materials	3
114, Soil Properties and their Engineering Application	2
115, Asphalt and Asphalt Mixtures	2
119, Introduction to Geological Engineering	3
122, Soil Mechanics and Foundation Design	3
129, Introduction to Industrialized Building Systems	4
173, Highway Design and Construction	4
180, Concrete Construction	3
181, Engineering Construction	4
182, Polymers in Construction	3
190, Engineering Reports	3

Figure 14-4 (Continued)

graduate programs can provide in-depth knowledge regarding engineering methodology, business requirements, tools necessary to manage human and material resources, and involvement in the decision-making process. The graduate is then prepared for a role as manager once he gains the required field experience. Many of the more successful graduates are those who enter these programs after gaining their field experience. They have by then an understanding of their strengths and weaknesses and are thus able to take full advantage of this educational opportunity. (Although this background is desirable it is often difficult to accept the economic consequences of returning to college for a year or more).

There are two types of graduate programs that attract future construction managers: first, those in construction management and engineering and, second, those in the MBA type of programs. The latter tends to focus on business aspects and industrialized corporations. With an engineering baccalaureate the MBA program adds business breadth, while not providing additional development of technical aspects. Each of these training approaches has its proponents, depending on the role envisioned for the future manager. See figures 14-5 and 14-6 for typical programs.

EXISTING PROBLEMS IMPACTING EFFECTIVE TRAINING

The construction industry has characteristically resisted any major changes, claiming that it is significantly different from the other principle industries that make a significant contribution to the GNP. There is no doubt that these claims are based on a recognitition that actual practices are less repetitive than other industries, because of the one-of-a-kind nature of many construction projects. There have been significant advances in the construction planning function which focuses attention on the potential gains in the productivity possible on large projects that characterize the recent market. One would conclude that these large projects represent an opportunity for the industry to make significant improvements in productivity and the basic technological base from which the rest of the industry could benefit. This has not been the case; in fact, the impersonal nature of these projects, coupled with the difficulty in design and management, has lead to many new problems that will require special considerations in regard to the training of the craft and supervisory work forces. Several issues that have surfaced in the past few years are described in some detail in the following discussion, since it is felt that these issues are representative of those that can be resolved by proper training, better communications, or a reevaluation or current practices.

IMPACT OF THE CRAFT WORK FORCE

The craft labor force for large projects is subjected to many negative stimuli not found in the smaller projects. These can be lumped under the umbrella of impersonal relations but include such items as repetitive work, a large percentage of rework, little personal satisfaction, in part, the result of slow progress, delays caused by changing regulations or supplies, and no close tie with members of supervision. It is difficult to establish a team spirit and a sense that each individual is important to the successful completion of these large projects. The following are specific problems and suggested remedies that might be applied.

A journeyman is not able to use his diverse skills on a large project, since the magnitude of the work effort and attempts at efficient scheduling create an environment of specialization. An electrician may only have to pull

CE 129 (4) Introduction to Industrialized Building Systems

Selection, design, production, and construction of industrialized building systems. Construction aspects of precast concrete systems are emphasized. Homework assignments are based on case studies of actual buildings.

CE 180 (4) Concrete Construction

Consideration of the broad aspects of use of concrete in construction; technical requirements; selection of materials; control of quality; types of concretes used for construction of buildings, highways, airfields, canals, bridges, dams, and hydraulic structures.

CE 181 (4) Engineering Construction

The construction industry: its development, components, organization and importance, construction methods and practices, applications and limitations; factors involved in selection of plant equipment and material, principles of planning, organization and operating construction forces, and estimating costs.

CE 182 (3) Polymers in Construction

Consideration of broad aspects of polymers in construction, particularly urban housing structures; technical requirements and performance specifications; selection of materials; relationship of mechanical properties to microstructure; fire safety; weatherability; manufacturing techniques, use of sealants and coatings on structures.

CE 194 (5) Economics and Management of Engineering Systems

Principles of economic and management techniques applied to the planning, design, construction, and operation of civil engineering systems; professional relations; contracts and specifications.

CE 266A (3) Construction Scheduling and Resource Allocation

Planning, scheduling, and allocation of resources for construction projects. Material will include critical path methods of network diagraming and calculation; consideration for allocating constrained resources; and variation of schedules to optimize costs. Computer and non-computer solutions will be presented.

CE 266B (3) Construction Organization and Management

An introduction into the business aspects of construction management, including organization and financial concerns during entry into business and for continued operations. Topics include legal, financial, labor relations, and accounting practices as they affect decision making in the construction industry.

CE 266C (3) Marketing of Construction and Engineering Services

Business development for contractors, engineers, and the engineer-constructor-manager. Selection and analysis of markets, prequalification, proposals, bidding strategy, brochures, change orders, contractural terms, and negotiations. Presentation of engineering, architectural, and construction ideas in letters, conferences, and personal calls.

Figure 14-5 Typical graduate program with a civil engineering emphasis. From the Graduate Program Department of Civil Engineering, University of California, Berkeley.

CE 266D (3)   Management of International Construction and Engineering
Organization and management of projects in international and multinational construction and engineering. Planning, investigation, procurement, logistics, construction geography, personnel, relations with host area, environmental considerations, communications, financing, special engineering, and management controls. Construction under adverse climatic conditions, including desert, tropical, mountain, and arctic regions.

CE 266E (2)   Applications of Operations Research to Construction Management
Analysis of risk relating to bid strategy, optimization of scheduling costs, aggregate and borrow optimization, and decision theory. Relevant problems from the construction industry will be reviewed.

CE 266G (3)   Construction Quality Assurance
Methods and considerations associated with construction quality-assurance programs. Types of existing programs, identification and role of participating organizations, development of standards and specifications, and initiation of programs.

CE 267A (3)   Advanced Foundation Construction
Evaluation of soil and structural problems connected with the construction of deep foundations for major high-rise buildings and subways. Integration of engineering, cost, scheduling, political, environmental, and management factors. Application to current major projects in urban environment.

CE 267B (3)   Advanced Concrete Construction
Selection and evaluation of construction methods and planning for pre- and posttensioned concrete; lightweight, high-strength, and architectural concrete; precasting and segmental construction. Application to buildings, bridges, pressure vessels, pollution control structures, ocean structures, and cryogenic containment.

CE 267C (4)   Construction of Harbor, Coastal, and Ocean Structures
Construction methods and equipment for construction of cofferdams, caissons, wharves, marine terminals, outfall sewers, power plant intakes and discharges, submarine oil and gas pipelines, dredging, offshore platforms, Arctic Ocean structures, subsea and deep ocean facilities.

CE 267D (3)   Advanced Construction Estimating
Estimates used by heavy, engineering, building, and specialty contractors. Preparation of cost estimates, including planning of methods and program evaluation of labor, material equipment, subcontract, and indirect costs. Rational assessment of risk and profit margins. Value engineering.

CE 298 (3-6)   Group design projects in a multidisciplinary environment
These stress the feasibility, design, and construction of potential projects in the Bay Area. Communication among a multidisciplinary team is also stressed.
Additional courses on construction management techniques and quality assurance are offered as CE 298 seminars.

Figure 14-5 (Continued)

CE 299 (1-12)   Individual Research or Investigation in Selected Advanced Construction Topics

EDA 224 (3) Sp   Advanced Building Methods and Processes
Implications of industrialized building components and systems; design, fabrication, and erection.

EDA 269A (3)   Construction Law

NA 290E (3) W   Vehicles for Ocean Engineering
The construction and design of vehicles for performing engineering functions in the ocean. Topics include environment, deep ocean tasks, vehicle types, design requirements, motion stabilization, structural problems.

Figure 14-5 (Continued)

wire, a carpenter build forms, and a laborer move the same type of material day after day. This creates the feeling that one is on an assembly line, and once the task reaches the state of boredom something is required to motivate the individual. The industry needs to review the work done in the manufacturing industries to improve motivation. Solutions include the rotation of journeymen so that they can maintain proficiency in several of their skills. (This may be difficult on a project that is at a stage where the majority of the work effort requires only one or a limited skill). Use of the journeymen in a training capacity is another method of recognition and motivation. It is extremely important that communication be established between management and the work force; this should include official recognition of work progress, opportunity for suggestions by craft labor regarding solutions to production problems, and an involvement by management to reduce the frustrations created by the work environment.

This specialization creates an attitude among the newer members of the craft labor force that there is little need to increase their skill levels. Given the current system of union wage scales, there is no incentive to improve once the journeymen scale is achieved. There appears to be advantages to the Merit Shop approach that rewards an individual for increasing skill levels. Even so if a proper training program in instituted in a union environment, it should include a survey of job opportunities as a function of individual skills so that members could realize that transfer after the completion of the current project will likely require a new discipline of skill levels.

There is little opportunity to recognize superior performance, since the factory atmosphere does not lend itself to an effective evaluation process. There have been situations where individuals have been selected as the "outstanding employee" of the week or month and other attempts made to compare relative performance by crews so that the outstanding crew can be recognized. There must be a recognized method to honor these individuals, and the selection process must be completely fair and free of bias. (The worst possible situation would be to recognize other than the best, since the workers themselves know who are the top performers.)

The following eight courses are required for this program:

Bus e300

Construction Contracting: the construction process and the operating environment; company management and organization; program formulation and marketing of construction services; business methods; relations with public officials, professional groups, subcontractors, suppliers, sureties, financial institutions

Engr e380

Construction Materials and Processes: introduction to construction materials, including terminology, specifying, ordering and identifying; materials handling methods; quality-control procedures for testing, inspecting, and evaluating government and private construction work; economical uses of materials; emphasis on the relationship of materials to the Uniform Building Code; fabrication and processing technology for conventional materials of construction

Engr e390

Construction Methods and Equipment Utilization: identification of the construction process in terms of a functional breakdown for equipment application in project planning; field operating conditions and working environment; equipment economics; cost, time, and production records; equipment financing; maintenance and operation policy; operational safety and code requirements; equipment characteristics and their selection for optimal utilization

Bus e310

Construction Accounting: an examination of the functions of construction accounting, including corporate accounting and its financial aspects, job or project cost accounting and records, payroll management, allocation of overhead, forecasting profits, depreciation, taxes, insurance, cash flow requirements, the need for the application of management information systems, relevant accounting opinions

Bus e320

Legal Aspects of Construction: overview of the legal system; contractor's license law; contracts and specifications; specific contract clauses; arbitration; contractor's liability in tort-negligence; mechanic's liens; labor contracts; subcontractor claims, land development and real estate law; home improvement contracts; public contracts; contractor responsibility in proposal and bid submission; owner, contractor, design professional relationships

Bus e330

Estimating and Bidding: conceptual estimating; quantity surveys; pricing labor and materials; functional perspective of cost estimator's role in project development/planning and proposal formulation; parameter estimating methods; bidding strategies and markup; computer-based estimates and statistical methods; workshop project

Figure 14-6 Typical program in Construction Management. From the Program in Continuing Education offered by San Francisco State University, in cooperation with the Business School.

Bus e340
Construction Project Management: analysis of construction operations using
critical path methods; project planning, budgeting, and scheduling; resource
allocation and leveling; time-cost optimization of project plan; project control;
review of available network models for construction manager; reporting and
administrative interfaces

Bus e350
Industrial Relations and Construction Supervision: overview of labor management relations on national, state, and local levels, including structure of labor
management system; labor law; methods of settling disputes; management
personnel policies; project supervision and hiring practices; productivity on the
job; occupational welfare for workers; employee relations

Figure 14-6 (Continued)

IMPACT ON SUPERVISION

These large projects have had a marked impact on management, since it
had little precedence regarding the increase complexity required by such
undertakings. Specializations have developed in functional areas, such as
estimating, scheduling, cost control, quality assurance, and organizational
structure. The sheer magnitude of these projects have created an environment for management quite similar to that faced by the work force. In
many cases additional research and innovation will be required before
some of the typical problems described subsequently can be resolved.

Communications is one of the key issues involved with the control function of these jobs. It is difficult to establish and maintain communication
channels especially when there are many pending revisions in various
stages of approval. This, coupled with the difficulty in establishing an overall picture of the status of construction, design, regulations, and all other
activities that directly impinge on the completion of the project, requires
an unusually flexible yet complete communication network. There is a
need to review possible processes that will enhance this communication
requirement. Computers are playing an important role in this area, but
they cannot solve the problem of interpersonal and work force communication. This problem requires a definition of responsibility to be borne by
each segment of the project manpower and a recognition of the team aspects right down to the last laborer on the site. Many of the current roadblocks are due to the attitudes of various individuals toward other groups
participating on the project. There is a necessity to train all involved personnel in the importance of their effort and the importance of teamwork.

These projects have created a significant demand for qualified managers.
The required talents are diverse, but the magnitude of activity has created
an unusual amount of specialization. Compared to more traditional projects the young manager may obtain a much greater depth of knowledge in
a specialized area that can lead to a dead end as far as career development

is concerned. The manager of the smaller projects is truly a decision maker. He must weigh less-than-perfect knowledge against the absolute need to make a decision and thereby keep production moving. Those who spend extensive time in a specialized area eventually feel that with a little more effort that speciality will eventually create the needed perfect information. This in turn tends to create an individual who in a manager's role waits for the picture to be clarified with improved information. This process accounts for many lost opportunities, and when decisions are made the alternatives are ususally narrowed to the point where the remaining decision is obvious. The young manager must take every opportunity to learn as much about the work around him as possible and to exercise judgment in addition to analysis.

Not only is it difficult for young managers to obtain the necessary breath, but also it is extremely difficult for senior managers to evaluate the performance and potential of younger personnel. Performance on small projects is easier to evaluate for two reasons, both related to more direct contact with the younger employee. First, judgment is viewed firsthand as suggestions made by the younger manager directed to his senior. Second, the variety of assignments and requirements for individual attention provide a much sharper image of the young manager's abilities. Seniors must recognize this difference in performance, and younger individuals must keep in mind that their performance will eventually require evaluation on an individual basis.

As a major consequence of the changing role of management resulting from the number of these large projects, new methods of management must be implemented that blend theoretical and practical training to achieve effective results. New controls must be developed to obtain a perspective of the total project progress, new organizational and management theories must be tested to create an effective team, and new contractual arrangements must be evaluated to include the owner and designer in this team effort. The entire process requires an adequate ongoing training process to disseminate the results of such innovation and to create an environment that encourages innovation. This later point is essential as current policies within companies and outside regualtions tend to restrict and discourage such innovation.

CONCLUSION

Training is far too important an aspect of the human resources for a company to relegate it to an adhoc program. Those responsible for the development of this human resource must seek out training opportunities and encourage active participation by members of its organization. There need be no commitment for advancement on completion of a program, but recognition of satisfactory completion is important. Encouragement is often given in terms of compensating time while enrolled in formal educational activities, and often reimbursement of expenses is provided when satisfactory completion is achieved. This might extend to a policy where performance is recognized by complete reimbursement for the cost of an advanced degree after a period of 5 to 10 years with the company.

Top management must support the training, evaluation, and recognition of the outstanding performance of all personnel. The Merit Shop approach provides an effective method of reward for the craft labor forces, and the union movement should be well advised to adopt some of the innovations to preserve their position. The ability to classify craftsmen by actual obtained skill levels and pay them accordingly creates the motivation for training and yields benefit not only to the individual, but also to the employer.

The health of the construction industry is measured in terms of the skill level of management and craft labor. Other countries recognize this fact and are involved in extensive training programs and innovative processes that quite frankly are superior to those currently adopted by many U.S. firms. In some cases these training programs are supported by the governments involved and thereby create a subsidized competition; nevertheless, the fact is that the competition does exist, and if we are to maintain a viable industry we must be involved on a full-time basis in a strong training effort.

CHAPTER 15

FEDERAL FINANCING AND GOVERNMENTAL REGULATION

Franklin T. Matthias

Federal regulation has greatly expanded in the past few decades, imposing new demands and presenting increasingly serious complications to the management of construction projects. In this discussion a "construction project" is considered as a total major program from concept through planning, engineering, design, construction, and beneficial operation of a new facility. Even without these recent complications the requirements of successful project management are rigorous and exacting, touching, as they do, virtually every phase of community life. Regulation makes it tougher to bring major public and private projects through planned, orderly, and uninterrupted phases to completion and operation.

Federal financing of projects adds another dimension to the management functions of public projects through another level of regulation. The common practice of financing agencies is to impose controls and approval requirements on consultant selection, contract forms, construction contract terms and practices, contract awards, line budget items, system design and configuration; and to generate hiatuses between phases resulting from failure of timely approval. All contribute to the delay of projects, have debilitating effects on morale and productivity, and expose the project management to public and political criticism for failures over which it lacks unilateral control. A major element of this problem appears to be that the granting agencies believe their interest is best protected by requiring the expenditure of grant funds to follow federal procurement regulations, even though it is not direct federal procurement. The propensity of those agencies to insist on major participation in decisions of engineering and design can only be explained rationally by the questionable assumption that they have capabilities superior to those of the grantee and his management team of engineers, consultants, and administrators.

Initiation and orderly progress of construction projects are threatened by the growing participation of self-appointed or organized intervenors at any project stage. The influence of these intervenors is substantial in that many of the regulatory and funding agencies are sensitive to public demonstrations and highly vocal propagandizing of special interest groups, insignificant in numbers, but with the help of the press and other media, highly visible. Further, these actions and others may lead to legal suits that have resulted in extensive delay and final regulation by the courts.

This chapter is not intended to condemn all federal regulation per se, either by formally designated regulatory agencies or through the regulations imposed by financial agencies. Federal, state, and local regulations are necessary for the public interest and safety and to preserve the rights guaranteed the people of the United States by our constitution. They should not be so extensive that they impose a heavy burden on our economic community as they now do, in an amount roughly equivalent to the cost of our national government and a substantial percentage of our GNP.

This chapter relates the reported costs and effects of federal regulation generally on the economic community and more specifically on the construction industry. It suggests that the growing proliferation of government regulation on people and the economic community is counterproductive and debilitating to both. It suggests actions that can be taken by both the federal agencies and construction management that can mitigate the adverse effects of regulation.

It is not that regulation is bad, but that it is too much and is too pervasive. Taking medicine can aid in maintaining physical and mental health, but too much can be debilitating, possibly fatal. It appears that the personification of our government, Uncle Sam, is changing from the concept of an indulgent, tolerant uncle to that of a tyrannical grandfather who presumes to know best what is good for us and regulates us accordingly.

THE REGULATORY SCENE

Federal regulation of virtually all facets of our social, professional, industrial, economic, and personal activity has increased exponentially during the past several decades. It has become a largely nonproductive and inflationary burden equivalent to an extent to that of our national government budget. An editorial entitled "That Fourth Branch of Government" in the Novermber, 1976 issue of McGraw-Hill's *Construction Methods and Contracting* reported that in 1976 there were "11 departments, 44 agencies, and 1240 boards, committees and commissions of the federal government that employ an army of 100,000 regulators," It reported a "White House estimate that such regulation resulted in added costs to the nation in 1975 of about $130 billion." It states that in the first year, 1936, new regulations were printed in the *Federal Register*, they filled 2411 pages. In the 1970

Federal Register there were 20,036 pages, and in the 1976 publication there were 60,221 pages.

News and television reports on a 1979 state governor's conference stated the current annual cost to the nation of regulation was about $600 billion. It appears that this figure includes state and local regulatory costs that probably have increased with federal revenue sharing. An assumption of $500 billion seems to be reasonable as the toll of federal regulation in 1978. Some of these data are presented in figures 15-1 and 15-2. Relate these estimates to an estimated GNP in 1978 of $2107 billion and estimated federal expenditures in fiscal year (FY) 1979 of $493.4 billion. Total construction expenditures in FY 1979 were $212.8 billion (about 10% of the GNP) of which $165.5 billion was for private construction and $47.3 billion for public construction.

Regulatory actions most prominent in the national scene are oriented to environmental protection and augmentation, public and occupational safety and health, promotion of minority employment and development and use of minority companies by both public and private entities, banking and money supply and reporting on all kinds of business activity and employment. Federal government entities have an apparently insatiable appetite for statistical data. A practice of a federal entity is to require data reported in a format to best suit its need. Report requirements from several entities often call for the same type of content but with sufficiently different formats that special analyses must be done for each report. This may seem an innocuous practice, but businessmen complain that the time key administrative people spend on compliance is a substantial expense and diverts those key people from productive work. Multiplied by both the number of businesses and the number of federal entities involved, the cost can be significant to the national enocomy. A federal study of 1977 federal paperwork pegged its cost to the nation at $100 billion. And then there is

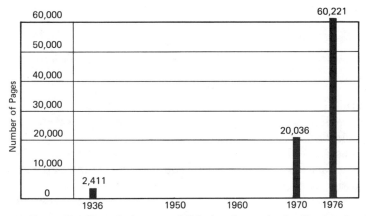

Figure 15-1 Pages of new regulations as published each year in the *Congressional Record*.

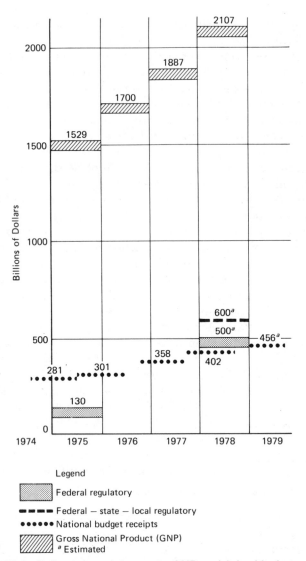

Figure 15-2 Estimated regulatory costs, GNP, and federal budget receipts.

the Internal Revenue Service. Figure 15-3 shows that the cost of complying with regulation from six agencies as experienced by 48 companies during 1977 was in excess of $2.6 billion.

The construction industry faces the same general burden of regulatory compliance faced by the rest of this country, plus some that are unique to the industry, particularly with respect to major projects. Efficiency of execution and cost effectiveness of major projects are achieved only through orderly progress through concept, planning, engineering, design, and construction phases into project operation. The most damaging regulatory ef-

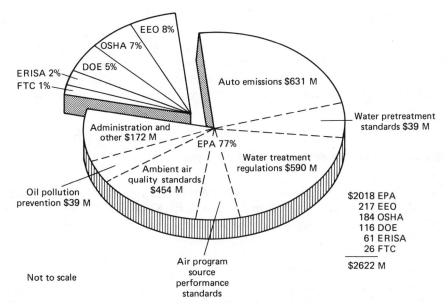

Figure 15-3 Incremental costs of regulations from six regulatory agencies to 48 companies. Civil Engineering-ASCE, September 1979

fects, whether from regulatory agencies or controls imposed by financing agencies, are delays in project progress. It appears that the estimates of total regulatory costs do not include significant construction costs incurred through added escalation, project delays, stopping and starting engineering and construction activity, loss of morale, reduced productivity, and other factors that increase cost and reduce cost effectiveness. It is difficult to find project controls by regulatory or funding agencies that help project management toward successful and efficient execution of projects; they usually erect roadblocks to project progress.

Many project delays occur because of regulatory sensitivity to pressures from environmental, labor, recreational, historical, minority, and other special interest groups. Effective delaying action by such groups, usually relatively small but vocal, has been aided by many laws and regulations, some through congressional action and some through rules promulgated by executive departments and agencies.

Another form of regulation develops through court actions at both federal and state levels. Class action and citizen complaint can be filed in court without responsibility. That is, aided by some members of the legal fraternity, who accept such cases on a contingent fee basis, complainants can initiate a suit, halt progress of a construction project, and prosecute the case with no financial exposure. Court judgments against the plaintiff often do not call for payment either of court costs or for the costs of project delay. Court judgments, if against the defendant, often call for additional construction or redirection of the project that can impose significant added costs. Federal, state, local, and private construction projects are all exposed to this hazard.

It appears likely that this high toll of regulation, a largely nonproductive national expense which is a significant percentage of the U.S. GNP, is a major cause of the high rates of construction cost escalation and general inflation which have been severe in the last decade and show no signs of abating.

PROJECT DELAYS DUE TO REGULATION

Project delay or redirection is the major adverse effect of federal regulation. A study, "Cost of Delays in Construction," by Enno Koehn, Fred Selling, Jeffrey Kuchar, and Randall Young was published in the September 1978 issue of the *Journal of the Construction Division Proceedings of the American Society of Civil Engineers*. The study rates principal reasons for delays in projects and evaluates their effects. The study method was to send questionnaires to the 500 leading engineering firms listed in the *Engineering News-Record* and the 532 consulting engineering firms of the state of Ohio. Significant responses totaled 214, representing over $30 billion of "work on the books," of which 117 were from the ENR 500 and 97 from the Ohio list, which averaged less than 10% of the total business volume of respondents.

The similarity of response from the ENR list (average high volume) and the Ohio engineers' list (average low volume) was striking. In brief summary the respondents by category answered as shown next.

To the question "Have construction delays due to governmental regulations occurred to the projects with which your organization is involved?" These were the ENR 500 answers: 56% substantially, 35% quite a bit, and 9% hardly at all.

Ohio engineers answered 47% substantially and 13% hardly at all.

To the question "Do you feel that government regulations that may cause construction delays apply to the type of work with which your company is involved?" These were the responses: ENR 500 answered 96% yes and 4% no. Ohio engineers answered 90% yes and 10% no.

To the question "Do you feel that construction delays due to governmental regulations benefit the general public, the contractor and the consultant?" response from both groups were close together, indicating that only about 10% of the delays were beneficial and about 90% did not benefit the general public, the contractor, or the consultant.

The duration of construction delays in months and resulting added costs were requested for actions of agencies or for other requirements in the following listing:

Environmental Protection Agency (EPA), approval process.

Court orders.

Public hearings, permits, or other paperwork.

Government-funding priorities.

Nuclear Regulatory Commission (NRC).

Other causes.

Weighted in terms of dollar volumes, the answers of the respondents indivated that for the ENR 500 delays totaled 36.6 months, with 47.2% of the project's cost attributable to the delays. The EPA- and NCR-imposed delays were more than half of the total delays.

For the Ohio engineers, delays totaled 29.4 months, with 27.7% of the project cost attributable to the delays. Delays imposed by EPA- and government-funding priorities accounted for well over half of the total delays with none attributable to NCR.

The authors of this report point out that both delays and costs reported "may be a bit inflated since a greater number of consultants who have experienced long delays may have returned the questionnaire than those who have experienced short or no delays. The results, however, are meaningful if the limitations in their development are recognized." While this study may not be quantitatively accurate as a picture of the adverse effect on project progress and efficiency, it does present appraisals by both the largest engineering firms and a representative group of smaller engineering firms. What does not appear to have been addressed in this study is the extent to which deficiencies in project management by owner and engineer contributed to delays and increased costs. Perhaps up to half of the delays and increased costs could have been avoided by enlightened vigorous management actions, but even half imposes a heavy toll on taxpayers and users of public projects and on consumers for private and public utility projects.

Horrible examples of regulatory agency-induced delays are plentiful; most prominent in these times are those related to nuclear energy projects. Heritage Foundation estimated that the cost of the Seabrook, New Hampshire, nuclear energy plant increased $419 million "due to flip-flops by federal regulators." It was reported in McGraw-Hill's *Business Week*, December 25, 1978, that San Diego Gas and Electric Co. had invested $96 million on its proposed Sun Desert nuclear project before it was canceled. The Sun Desert project organization could not submit reports required by NRC, EPA, and others fast enough to keep even; new reports required came faster than report sumittals could be completed.

At the other end of the scale a success story of coping with regulatory agencies was reported in McGraw-Hill's *Construction Contracting and Equipment*, July 1977. A major petroleum pipeline project in Alaska, through an area environmentally sensitive, was completed in 13 months after inception. The success was attributed to an enlightened and vigorous management effort. The principal regulatory and involved agencies were identified and participated in an interagency meeting at which the conceptual plan was presented and constructive suggestions to expedite approval processes were solicited. The short list of involved agencies grew to 42. Major interests, jurisdictions, and degrees of influence of each were identified, and the management campaign for approval was directed accordingly with outstanding success.

It is wrong to generalize conclusions based on either the horror stories or the success stories. However consideration of both lead to constructive approaches to the identification and solution of known and potential problems that arise in the drive for prompt and decisive action by regulatory agencies. Goaded by public outcry, demonstrations of special interest groups, and litigation cases, legislative bodies and executive departments both appear to respond by added regulations. Frequently, new rules are imposed while the project is in progress and sometimes with project effects approaching disaster proportions.

REGULATORY AGENCIES

Federal regulatory agencies most significant to construction are EPA, NRC, Occupational Safety and Health Administration (OSHA), the Federal Energy Regulatory Commission (FERC), DOE, the Department of Transportation (DOT), the Corps of Engineers (COE) the Department of Commerce (DOC), the Office of Federal Procurement Policy (OFPP), and the Federal Office of Contract Compliance (FOCC). Regulation by DOT is through its Federal Highway Administration (FHA), Urban Mass Transit Administration (UMTA), and Federal Aviation Administration (FAA). Regulation by DOC is through its Economic Development Administration (EDA). The Agency for International Development (AID) is under the Department of State (DOS); it funds foreign projects and exercises some regulation because of that function. Table 15-1 lists the principal regulatory and funding agencies significant to major construction projects.

The Corps of Engineers and the Water and Power Resource Service (Formerly the Bureau of Reclamation) are in a special category in that each funds projects through congressional appropriation for specific projects. Each normally performs the project planning, engineering, design, and construction supervision of construction by contract. Construction contractors must comply with all regulations for public construction. The Corps of Engineers has regulatory authority over projects that occupy airspace, water space, or underground space in areas of navigable waters.

Seven of the entities listed on Table 15-1 are shown as regulatory because their financing leads them to regulate projects in varying degrees.

Exclusive of officially established regulatory agencies, substantial regulation of project construction occurs through the action of unofficial organizations or groups such as the Sierra Club, Friends of the Earth, fish and game organizations, and others. They are special interests groups who profess dedication to the protection of the environment and the ecology and to the preservation of historic and aesthetic values, and the like. The influence of these groups is applied through legislative lobbying, by propaganda, public demonstrations, legal actions, and other means. Rarely do they engender

TABLE 15-1. Principal Regulatory and Funding Agencies Significant to Major Construction Projects

Entity		Regu-latory	Finan-cing	Notes
Environmental Protection Agency	EPA	*	*	
Nuclear Regulatory Commission	NRC	*		
Department of Labor	DOL	*		
Occupational Safety and Health Administration	OSHA	*		
Employment Standards Administration	ESA	*		
Equal Employment Opportunity Commission	EEOC	*		
Federal Energy Regulatory Commission	FERC	*		
Department of Transportation	DOT			
Federal Highway Administration	FHA	*	*	d
Urban Mass Transit Administration	UMTA	*	*	d
Federal Aviation Administration	FAA	*	*	d
Department of Energy	DOE	*	*	d
Department of Agriculture	DOA			
Rural Electrification Administration	REA	*	*	d
Soil Conservation Service	SCS	*	*	c
Department of Commerce	DOC			
Economic Development Administration	EDA	*	*	d, e
Corps of Engineers	COE	*	*	a, b
Water and Power Resource Service	WPRS		*	b
Office of Management and Budget	OMB	*		
Office of Federal Procurement Policy	OFPP	*		
Federal Office of Contract Compliance	FOCC	*		
National Aeronautical and Space Administration	NASA	*	*	
Department of State	DOS			
Agency for International Development	AID	*	*	d

[a]Jurisdiction under, in, on, or over navigable waters
[b]Projects funded by Congress—engineering and construction normally in house; construction by contract
[c]Projects normally small and handled in house
[d]Regulation through financing controls
[e]Former regulation of Minority Business Enterprise policy

support for a project; actions of these groups nearly always oppose construction projects. While they may not represent the will of the citizenry, such groups do exert substantial influence on Congress and regulatory agencies such as EPA and NRC through their vigorous assaults on construction projects and their readiness to initiate legal action to stop projects if other means fail.

Currently, within the regulatory agencies are organizational entities, each responsible for review and action relative to specific elements of the agency's overall responsibility. Virtually all final actions of a regulatory agency are dependent on the approval or concurrence of other government departments, agencies, commissions, administrations, and other entities. Many also require the approval or concurrence by the state or states in which the project is located. Private projects, such as nuclear and other energy-producing projects require acceptance of the Environment Impact Statement (EIS) by EPA, after which the agency with specific regulatory authority, such as the NRC or the FERC may issue a construction permit. For most other major private projects, acceptance by the EPA of the EIS permits construction to proceed provided state and local regulations are met. For public projects, construction usually can start after EPA acceptance of the EIS and after federal and local funding is available.

ENVIRONMENTAL PROTECTION AGENCY (EPA)

At the top of the hierarchy of federal regulatory bodies is the environmental Protection Agency (EPA). The congressional mandate under which it was created gives EPA a kind of omnipotent influence over virtually all human activities in this country, since they all impact on the total ecology. Environmental activists appear to have forgotten that people are part of the ecology and the needs of people deserve consideration, along with the needs of other flourishing or endangered biological systems. Both construction and operation are under the purview of the EPA with respect to environmental effects. All substantial construction projects—public, private, and those federally financed and managed by federal executive agencies—must be blessed by an EIS accepted by the EPA and, in addition, normally require positive approval or acceptance by other regulatory or involved agencies before construction can proceed.

The first steps toward an EIS acceptance is a complete description of a projects, the plan and schedule of construction, and identification of environmental impacts both beneficial and adverse. Although the public appears to believe that the regulatory mandate to EPA is limited to pollution control and abatement, EPA's jurisdiction is far more extensive, including public and employee safety, project disruption of business and personal activities, aesthetics, historical values, recreation, ecology, and other things that may be construed to be under the environmental umbrella. The environmental considerations are then identified, and an Environmental Impact Assessment (EIA) is prepared and usually reviewed by EPA at local and/or national levels. The EIA is then presented to the public through public hearings and to appropriate state and local political authorities. After incorporating input from the hearings and comments from state and local authorities, the EIS is prepared and submitted to EPA. The EIS is the formal document submitted to the EPA and for major projects is an impressive and expensive document that should be submitted early in the project engineering stage, since formal acceptance take several years. Spurred by environmental and conservation groups, the requirements of the EPA for the EIA, public hearings, and the EIS have increased at an exponential rate since they emerged from their embryonic state about a decade ago. They now impose a major roadblock to project initiation. An early and intimate working relationship between the owner-sponsor and senior EPA officials to identify all specific considerations to be analyzed and presented, together with vigorous actions to keep the EIS moving through the bureaucratic maze, might shorten acceptance time to a year or less. The risk of intervention by special interest groups would still exist. There is no way the owner-sponsor can insure protection against this risk but the risk may be mitigated by early discussion with the groups likely to be intervenors. Should be project configuration or design change materially the EIS would have to be amended or rewritten and resubmitted.

EPA is also a funding agency that provides grants for the major part of the cost of pollution protection projects of public agencies. With the grant, EPA imposes substantial control of the expenditures on the project and in the design and administration of the project. For some projects EPA has delegated limited authority to the state in regulation of expenditures, design, contract awards, and related administrative action. This procedure can result in more responsive action and timely decision on major actions, since many such actions can be taken by this more local level of administrative regulatory control. It has been said that the feeling of urgency for decisive action on construction problems is inversely proportional to the decider's distance from the jobsite. Construction industry leaders agree that delayed decisive action is the most critical adverse factor to project management.

The EPA regulatory procedure calls for a potentially long and complicated series of sequential actions on the EIS and supporting project reports and may be reiterative because some entity in the chain has objections to report content or to prior action along the chain. The project management may be requested to furnish more information, which may stop both the acceptance of approval process and project progress. Lack of local public and political support for the project, and active opposition, evidenced by special interest groups to which the regulatory agencies are sensitive, can compound delays and generate new requirements for the management team to meet. The wide range of EPA jurisdiction probably exposes it to attention by more kinds of special interest group pressure than any other regulatory agency. Because of radioactive and heat pollution potential it interacts with NRC in its regulation of the construction of nuclear energy plants and other nuclear facilities.

NUCLEAR REGULATORY COMMISSION (NRC)

The function of the Nuclear Regulatory Commission (NRC) is to protect employees and the public from hazards arising from the construction and operation of nuclear facilities. The principal nuclear facilities, other than for military purposes, are nuclear energy plants and facilities for nuclear fuel mining and processing, disposal of nuclear waste, laboratories, and others related to nuclear activity. Construction of nuclear plants is one of the most controversial issues of our time. The much-publicized possibility of a catastrophic accident that might injure masses of people and render a large area uninhabitable for a few thousand years is a specter that has terrorized a substantial percentage of our people. While the risk is considered extremely remote by most of the nuclear scientific community, there is no consensus that it could not happen, and even the remote possibility appears unacceptable to many people.

The lack of completely safe nuclear waste disposal facilities has added to the opposition. Open meetings, demonstrations, and other influences to convert the public into the opposition camp have been a major factor in imposing controls that have delayed the operation of finished nuclear plants and construction of new plants. The Three Mile Island experience generated further support to delaying action.

It is likely that no other major segment of our industry has ever been subjected to anything like the rigorous controls exercised by NRC over nuclear power. The resulting high cost and delays could have disastrous effects on our economy and life-style that have achieved their present statuses through the use of apparently abundant sources of energy. Currently, the major source of our energy is from fossil fuels, a limited world resource. The sources of energy currently perceived as available to us other than nuclear cannot come close to meeting future energy needs. Conservation of fossil fuels is a worldwide need.

To put it mildly, NRC is in an extremely difficult position. It is responsible for the regulation of an industry conceived to be capable of wreaking death and disaster in the areas it occupies, an industry that has a short history. It strives to safeguard people, the environment, and property by all available means, including requiring levels of quality of design, construction materials, and permanent materials and controls that are probably beyond precedent. As earlier mentioned, *Business Week* reported that Heritage Foundation estimated that the cost of the Seabrook plant in New Hampshire increased $419 million due to "flip-flops" in federal regulation. In this case significant regulatory changes and delays were attributable to EPA. A specific instance related to the cooling water system.

NRC regulation includes required acceptance or approval of nuclear en-

ergy plant sites, design of structures, control systems, safety and security
systems, quality of construction materials, construction procedures, construction workmanship, operating plans, operation personnel training, and
any other detail it wishes to control. Before a construction permit is issued
all special studies and reports ordered must be completed, changes ordered
in design must be made, the site approved, and EPA must have accepted
the EIS. Issuance of construction permits have taken several years during
which further changes are made and added reports ordered. The construction permit allows construction to start but does not stem the flow of new
reports required and design changes to be made that continues through
construction. Start of operation requires specific permits that also can take
long periods of time during which instructions for additions and changes
continue. While horrible examples can be found in many construction projects it appears that regulation has generated them at most nuclear power
projects planned or under construction during the past 10 years or so.

DEPARTMENT OF LABOR

Most important to the construction industry is the Occupational Safety
and Health administration (OSHA). The concept and mandate of OSHA
appear to have been born in the dangerous and unhealthy environment of
the coal mines of the West Virginia area. OSHA's regulation now encompasses virtually every human activity, except what occurs in private
homes. Its regulation of construction activity for the protection of the
health and safety of employees is pervasive; if there is any activity in
construction that is not identified in OSHA regulations, it is probable that
it was overlooked by the writers of those regulations.

Construction is, by its nature, a hazardous occupation. Workmen's compensation systems and state departments charged with industrial and construction safety did much to improve construction safety and health
through education and incentives long before the birth of OSHA. In underground work, the safety provisions developed by the Bureau of Mines were
generally accepted by contractors. State safety entities had authority for
punitive action to violators of their safety provisions, but it was not often
exercised. Construction contractors and engineers followed their precepts
and enjoyed the financial rewards that resulted from good safety performances. OSHA regulation is on top of and concurrent with the continued
workmen's compensation and state safety activities. OSHA regulations include no incentives but provide for punitive action for violators in the form
of fines and work stoppages.

OSHA's debut in regulation of the construction industry was not auspi-
cious. Its inspectors often lacked knowledge of construction and experience
in the types of construction they inspected. Construction is a high-risk
human activity and was immediately placed high on the priority list for
inspection. The OSHA inspectors entered construction sites whether or not
the employer gave them permission until a tough contractor refused them

entry and his right to do so was upheld by a Supreme Court ruling. Since then the inspectors can gain entry against the will of the employer only if armed with a search warrant. Receipt of a complaint that construction practices were unsafe by an employee of any category gave an OSHA official license to shut down the work until the claim could be investigated in detail. This was great for an employee with a grudge against his employer but was hardly appropriate in a free country. The policy does emerge in many segments of regulation and in law enforcement. It appears reprehensible as a national policy. The construction industry generally regards OSHA as oriented far more to inspection and citation than to education and prevention as the means to improve occupational health and safety. Many states maintain effective programs of safety training and accident and employee health protection and use the citation penalty procedure only when employers refuse collaboration. The imposition of OSHA regulation in such states is redundant and probably counterproductive.

The DOL works with the Department of Justice in enforcement of laws concerning labor and administration of wages and salaries. Within the DOL are the Employment Standards Administration (ESA), the Labor-Management Services Administration, and the Bureau of Labor Statistics. DOL works with the Department wages and salaries. It reviews EIS of construction projects, most of which deal with environmental effects on labor working conditions. While regulation is not extensive DOL demands for statistical information adds to the cost of construction project administration.

EQUAL EMPLOYMENT OPPORTUNITY COMMISSION (EEOC)

The objective of the Equal Employment Opportunity Commission (EEOC) appears to be the employment of persons without discrimination with respect to race, color, sex, religion, and age and persons physically handicapped. The regulation authority is fragmented and interfaces largely with the Department of Labor and to a lesser degree with all federal agencies that employ people. Enforcement in the private sector appears virtually impossible. The problem to the construction industry appears to arise from confusion about what is required for compliance. The regulations concerning use of minority employment and contractors are not specific, and many project delays have been experienced because of questionable allegations of noncompliance.

FEDERAL ENERGY REGULATORY COMMISSION (FERC)

Formerly the Federal Power Commission (FPC), the Federal Energy Regulatory Commission (FERC) has licensing authority over power projects, most of which are for public utilities. FERC's major impact on the construction industry is its review of design and its inspection of the construction of power projects. FERC and its predecessor, FPC, generally have had the respect of the construction industry through highly professional engineering orientation in the performance of their regulatory responsibilities. The rising tide of environmental pressures has widened the range of FERC's activities but does not appear to have impaired its professional approach. FERC participates in the program of dam safety inspection and repair, which is led by the Corps of Engineers.

DEPARTMENT OF COMMERCE (DOC)

The primary impact of the Department of Commerce's (DOC)regulatory role is its responsibilities with respect to Minority Business Enterprise (MBE) program. This regulatory function has been shared by other federal agencies involved in procurement of contract services for construction projects wholly or partly funded federally. MBE is the program that calls for participation of minority-owned and minority-managed companies in construction projects supported by federal funds. It is a major element in the affirmative action plan of contractors engaged in such projects. Recently, this regulatory function relative to Small Business Administration programs was assigned to the Office of Federal Procurement Policy (OFPP) and the Federal Office of Contract Compliance (FOCC), both agencies of the Office of Management and Budget (OMB). It appears likely that this regulatory assignment to OMB will be extended to all construction contracts supported by federal funds.

CORPS OF ENGINEERS

The Corps of Engineers (COE) has a unique position in the regulatory hierarchy. It is administered by the army, but with respect to its extensive civil responsibilities it functions as an independent agency. It has regulatory authority over navigable waters, including estuaries and offshore waters. Any construction or other activity in, under, or over navigable waters must have the approval of the Corps of Engineers. Supported directly by congressional appropriations, the Corps of Engineers builds dams and waterways for flood control and inland navigation, providing related benefits of hydroelectric power and water supply. It has a leadership role in the cooperative federal-states program of safety inspections and indicated corrective construction. It maintains navigation channels in U.S. harbors and constructs and maintains facilities for beach and shoreline erosion protection. Normally, it designs and manages its construction projects, which are constructed by contractors.

The construction industry respects the Corps of Engineers in both its regulatory and ownership roles for its professional approach.

OTHER AGENCIES

The current principal activities of the Department of Energy (DOE) relative to regulation do not impact significantly on the construction industry except as the managing entity for its own funded and sponsored projects.

DOE is more oriented to research and development in the energy generation field, although it may finance and construct demonstration projects. The Rural Electrification Administration (REA) and the Soil Conservation Services (SCS), both under the Department of Agriculture (DOA) fund construction projects and regulate through financing controls. Other agencies that regulate only through financing controls are shown in Table 15-1, and some are discussed next.

FINANCING AGENCIES

The principal funding agencies of the federal government for major construction are shown in Table 15-1 and include the Department of Transportation (DOT), with its Urban Mass Transit Administration (UMTA), Federal Highway Administration (FHA), and Federal Aviation Administration (FAA); the Department of Agriculture (DOA), with its Rural Electrification administration (REA); the department of Commerce (DOC), with its Economic Development Administration (EDA); the Environmental Protection Agency (EPA); the Department of Energy (DOE); the Corps of Engineers (COE); Water and Power Resource Service (WPRS) and the Department of State (DOS), through the Agency for International Development (AID).

Each of the agencies named, and others, finance public projects by grants or loans to city, county, district, and authority entities. The Corps of Engineers and the Water and Power Resource Service perform major construction projects authorized and funded by Congress. They maintain complete management control over their projects, normally by their own organizations. The Corps of Engineers have made grants to public agencies for flood control benefits incident to water storage projects but with no strings attached that influence construction management.

Funds are normally made available to the funding agencies through congressional or legislative authorizations and appropriations and usually these funds must be expended or committed within the fiscal year. Appropriations to a federal executive department may be specific for a project or for a class of projects to be allocated to specific projects at the discretion of that department. Authorizations and appropriations may include specific regulatory control provisions, but generally such provisions are promulgated by the appropriate executive department.

A notable exception to this procedure is the Highway Trust Fund administered by FHA into which gas tax funds are received directly and grants for highway construction are made to states by FHA under only general congressional mandate. Steps currently being taken could provide similar funding concepts to UMTA.

Procedures and regulations for grants and loans from appropriated funds are promulgated by the responsible federal executive depatment that usually has wide latitude in establishing financial and management controls on a grantee or loan recipient. In some cases, Congress imposes controls on specific appropriations. There is little consistency in the regulations of different executive entities in the financial and management controls imposed on project management.

EPA appears to be unique among federal financing agencies in that it regulates nearly everything and finances only public projects directed to pollution control and other environmental enhancement. In common with most federal financing agencies EPA's funding of capital construction projects is partial; state or local entities or both must provide the rest. Experimental, research, development, and demonstration projects are likely to receive full funding by such agencies as UMTA and DOE. Agencies such as UMTA and EPA frequently fund their parts of the cost of large projects for public transit and pollution control in project phases, starting with concept development. Successive phases that may be separately funded are project planning, preliminary engineering, and in-depth analysis of alternative systems at which point the "go" "no-go" decision is reached. A "go" decision leads to a capital grant covering design and construction. Federal appropriations frequently are separated between funds available for the preliminary phases and those available for capital grants, which dictates separate agreements between the funding agency and the grantee. The funding agency may authorize the preliminary phases separately, and the authorization process, normally starting only after completion of the preceding phase, can take months, interrupting the momentum of project progress and increasing the compounding escalation costs. Interruptions are debilitating to productivity and morale of the project management team and increase administrative costs.

Federal funding agencies tend to impose FPR provisions on expenditure of grant funds by the project management. These regulations apply to direct procurement and expenditure of funds by government agencies. It does not appear reasonable to impose these federal regulations to the use of grant funds that may not be consistent with the local and state regulations. Since basic requirements of financial grants are that a project be considered justified and project management be perceived as competent, a better approach would be to minimize detail control and depend on spot checks and monitoring to assure proper use of funds.

REGULATION THROUGH FINANCING

Generally, grant funds and local matching funds must be used concurrently in their specified ratios. The appropriate ratio of grant funds is usually withheld for local matching funds expended prior to officially authorizing the grant. UMTA, in its early years of operation, provided an avenue of relief through a "letter of no prejudice." Although reluctantly, UMTA has issued this letter, under special circumstances, which authorizes retroactive use of future grant funds matched to local funds expended for a project for which a grant is subsequently made. This device has been used to maintain project progress through the hiatus between completion of one phase and grant authorization for the next. Project management must take the lead in anticipating the problem early and taking vigorous management action to obtain such relief.

Establishing requirements for prior approval of a broad spectrum of project management actions is the common way for financing agencies to maintain varying degrees of control of projects. Such requirements effectively prevent the project management from the on-the-site prompt and decisive action essential to efficient performance. They generate nonproductive administrative costs and divert the attention of top management executives from their primary function. They rarely contribute to the success of the project. The requirements have adverse effects on the efficient conduct of the project, and it would appear that their effects are also adverse to the prime objective of the funding agency, which has to be the successful and economical completion and operation of the project.

Prior approval requirements, in addition to their inevitable delaying effects, gives the financing agency the opportunity to influence or dictate consultant selection, the form of consultant and construction contract, the award of contracts, working arrangements and negotiation with regulatory agencies, construction contract changes and claims, and many other actions for which project management carries prime responsibility. Requiring prior approval of budget line item adjustments and prohibition of overruns of any line item until approved sets up nearly impossible administrative tasks for the project management. Spending perhaps $50,000 to provide full justification and obtain approval for a contract adjustment of $5,000 or $10,000 is certainly counterproductive, and cases of this kind do occur under rigid imposed controls. These kinds of controls can extinguish the initiative and enthusiasm of the management team, and the frustrations are contagious in their effects on individuals in all levels of the organization.

It should be understood that no single agency imposes these described levels of control on any one project or exercises all the opportunities available for influencing or dictating management action. It is not unreasonable that a financing agency require approval of primary engineering consultants, major construction contracts, major procurement contracts, and similar major actions. Substantial changes in the overall project budget or in cash flow forecasts would be appropriately subject to approval. Beyond these, the project management team can only perform effectively if it is delegated authority for unilateral action. Reporting systems and intimate contact of a representative of the financing agency with the project provides the opportunity for effective monitoring of the project. Should irregularities develop, corrective action can be taken.

Tight control and pervasive influence on program management by funding agencies is rarely challenged by recipients of the funds because of the fear that such funds will be withheld. Evidence of unanimity of interest by the financing agency with the project management in completing a project, efficiently, economically, on time, and of good quality should dispel that fear. The construction management team can then develop intimate working relationships with the key members of the financing agency and explore together the needs of the agency and the project. Jointly, the agency and the project management can put together a program of control that will give the financing agency assurance that the controls and monitoring will serve their needs and give the project management the direct authority it needs.

For some years, UMTA has been seeking to achieve that balance of its control and project management authority that is most beneficial to the project. Through intimate working relationship with the Atlanta Rapid Transit program, monitoring has supplanted rigid controls to the apparent satisfaction of both parties. Contingency items have been incorporated into engineering, and the management team was given wide latitude of unilateral authority to make adjustment in line items in the budget and in construction contract changes within prescribed limits reasonable in relation to the project costs. Other changes from normal practices have been made. As an overall result the financing agency and the project management have achieved a partnership attitude.

POSITIVE CORRECTIVE ACTION—CONSTRUCTION MANAGEMENT

The project management team can do much to meet the regulatory problems head on at the inception of the project and avoid prolonged delays almost inevitable if positive early action is not taken. The management plan must incorporate an active program to accomplish that purpose as well as to manage the project itself. To a greater degree than managing the workings of the project, this part of the management program demands substantial activity and leadership by senior members of the management team who are recognized by the people in the regulatory chain as having high-level project authority. Those who will participate in the regulatory processes must be identified and partnership-oriented relationships developed between the leaders of those organizations and the project management team.

Although federal regulation is minimal during the early phases of a construction project, project management must anticipate specific regulatory actions early in the project and tailor its management program and project schedule to avoid project delays and interruptions that lack of timely regulatory decision can cause. Satisfaction of EPA requirements is usually a major work element. Preparation of the EIS should be accomplished during the planning and early engineering phase to allow schedule time and expediting effort to achieve an accepted EIS to clear the way for construction to start.

Ideally, the management team would organize an early meeting of such involved agencies to present the project concept and objectives and to determine, with the greatest possible specificity, what studies and information would be needed by each participant in the regulatory process to enable them to take prompt and decisive action. Open channels of communication should be established between the project management team and the regulatory participants to amplify and firm up specific needs and to obtain prompt response by the management team to further questions that might arise.

There is no magic formula that will guide a management team successfully through the existing maize of regulatory requirements and protect the project from delays caused by opposition and public demonstration of special interest groups, by class action and citizens suits against the project, by political opposition, or by other adverse actions over which the management lacks the muscle of unilateral authority. The potential problems must be anticipated and action taken to mitigate their effects.

The project management team should recognize that delay in regulatory acceptance or approval often develops from opposition to the project or to specific aspects of the project by individuals, citizen groups, special interest organizations, political entities, and others and generally originates in the project community area. Disgruntled individuals and special interest groups may take legal action against the project. Avowed friends of the project, individuals or groups, for reasons political or otherwise, can, and sometimes do, delay or block a public works project and continue to pose as an ardent supporter by the simple device of suggesting further study or specific modification of the program.

Counteracting these adverse influences must have a high-priority position in the project management program, requiring positive and continuous action. Public and political support is essential to the success of a public works project and is increasingly important to private projects because of the increasing public awareness and concern over potential adverse environmental and societal impacts. Through public meetings and the media, citizens and organized citizen groups should be kept informed of project plans and progress, invited to participate and comment on the program, and assured of attentive response by the project management team by communications. Giving the public the opportunity of comment and participation helps generate public support.

The project management team should take the lead in establishing working relationships with organized groups of such special interests as environmental, aesthetic, archaelogical and other societal orientation. Assurance that such groups' objectives were understood and that the project management team would work with such groups to solve project-related problems would tend to develop a sense of partnership that would make it difficult for them to make public complaints. Project management must be accessible to the people and must give careful consideration to individual or group problems; refusal to listen can make a minor problem become a major roadblock. Similar action should be taken with political entities, community planning organizations and agencies, and other groups whose interests may overlap and may even conflict with project objectives. These actions should minimize complaints reaching federal regulating and financing agencies that may be, and often are, extremely sensitive to them and are likely to overreact to the detriment of the project.

POSITIVE CORRECTIVE ACTION—FEDERAL REGULATION

Regulatory agencies should examine their regulations in collaboration with knowledgeable construction and construction management people and revise the regulations to permit simple and effective means of enforcement and compliance. The examinations should include review of the intent of the enabling legislation. Regulators should understand the great advantages in cost and time of a well-ordered, uninterrupted construction program and be conscious of the fact that the accomplishment of such means savings to the consumer and taxpaper, categories in which they are included. They should understand construction problems as well as the regualtions. They should delete regulations that appear unworkable or unreasonable and seek further legislation if necessary. They should measure performance by the degree of prevention of violation they can achieve rather than the number of punitive citations they issue.

Regulators should welcome and seek to establish close working relationships with construction management so that together they can solve problems before they become acute. They should realize the relative values of efficient construction as compared to the effects of enforcing the letter of the regulation. After all, regulations, if honestly written, are based on the writer's perception of the intent of enabling law; they are not law in themselves. Regulators should find ways to streamline their policies and procedures to reduce the burden on the construction industry and others as well as to expedite final action.

Periodically, the effectiveness of each regulatory agency should be appraised in terms of the regulations it promulgates and its performance and societal and economic value to and beneficial effects on the nation. These appraisals would be the basis of action to expand, contract, eliminate, or continue the agency or modify its operating methods and goals. It is disappointing that this action concept, called "sunset laws," has been floundering in legislative and executive circles of our government for an inordinate time without positive action.

In the absence of the stringent reforms suggested, there are still ways to improve the services rendered by a regulatory agency. The designation of a key senior official responsible for each major project in each primary regulatory agency with lateral access to each organizational entity within that agency and interacting agencies could greatly expedite review and decisive action. Clear definition of required content of submissions should be made available to project management to avoid redundancy and aid in covering all significant requirements. Except in cases of major importance, new requirements should not be applied retroactively when such action calls for added submission and delay in decision. Dedication of the regulatory agencies to project success and economy for the public good would lead to other improvements in procedure and execution.

The review process within each significant entity of such regulatory agencies as EPA and NRC should be carried on simultaneously and concurrently by those interacting agencies whose concurrence is a requirement of acceptance or approval. The comments, questions, and recommendations of each involved agency should be coordinated as soon as possible and the project management informed about what further studies or submissions are required. Should such requirements be extensive, there should be a meeting with the project management representative and representatives of each involved agency at which time all required action is described and explained. Compliance with the stated requirement should trigger a moratorium on any new demands on the construction management, except for matters of essential importance. Following approval or acceptance any further demands should be made only if timely enough to fit into orderly progression of the project without causing project delay or they are of such importance that they overbalance the penalties of delay. Communication lines and working relationships between the agency and the construction management should be maintained as long as the project's progress is vulnerable to regulatory action. The agency and project construction management should be alert to identify potential problems and settle them promptly.

Regulatory agencies should view demonstrations, public outcry, and related opposition in proper perspective and not overreact to the actions of relatively few people, however vocal they can be.

POSITIVE CORRECTIVE ACTION—FEDERAL FINANCING

Federal financing agencies have a different basis for regulatory type actions than do regulatory agencies. The mandate to regulatory agencies is to regulate. The mandate to financing agencies is to finance. Authority to make grants or loans for construction projects is based on congressional action that includes the appropriation of funds. The appropriations may be made for specific projects or for types of projects. For example, legislation authorizing funds for agencies like UMTA or EPA generally specify the type of projects they are to support and may specify percentages of total project cost that must be supported by funds from state or local sources. The agency can then unilaterally allocate funds to specific projects. Others, like the Corps of Engineers and the Water and Power Resource Service generally receive authorization of funds for specific projects. In most cases authorization for grant and loan funds for construction projects do not specify controls to be placed on the construction projects that they finance. Except for elements of controls that are law or governmental edict, these agencies can establish the detail controls on projects by unilateral action and participate in construction management to the extent they wish or feel necessary in the interest of the government and nation or for any other reason. Since they establish these controls they can also change them without reference to higher-executive or legislative authority. Incentives to empire building apperar to be less than for regulatory agencies whose mandate is continuous.

The preceding section discussed in some detail the changes construction management should promote to give itself the chance to execute projects efficiently and economically without jeopardy to the funding agency's mission and responsibilities. The agency's part is to accept the concept that their mission is to help the project through close working relationships, substitution of monitoring for advance approval, and close working rather than adversary relationships with the project management by key people of the agency who are sufficiently experienced in construction to understand construction problems and needs. Above all in importance is the dedication of the agency and its people to orderly progress and a successful project.

There are indications that some funding agencies appreciate the need for improvement and are taking steps toward implementation. Specifically, EPA and UMTA are taking steps to direct their controls to the benefit of the projects they finance. EPA provides incentives for its projects to use innovative concepts in engineering design and construction.

There should be no contest between benefical effects of maintaining project momentum and the delaying effects of bureaucratic inertia.

One of the "Quotable Quotes" from the December 1978 *Reader's* Digest is appropriate. "Most people would be glad to tend to their own business if the government would give it back."

SUMMARY

Federal regulation in increasing exponentially and has become a serious national problem currently exacting a toll on the national economy close to the national budget and is a significant percentage of our GNP. This largely nonproductive burden contributes to the frightening inflation we are experiencing. The construction industry, contributing about 10% of our GNP, shares the burden of direct regulation. In addition it incurs substantial costs arising from construction project delays induced by regulatory action or lack of action and to which the construction industry is intrinsically sensitive. For public projects, financed by federal loans or grants, another form of regulation generates nonproductive administrative and direct costs as a result of the project controls imposed by the financing agencies. This type of control has little or no basis in law; in nearly all cases, it is specified and administered unilaterally by the financial agencies.

This chapter identifies the principal regulatory and financing agencies significant to the construction industry. It suggests procedures for the owner-project management team to mitigate the adverse effects. It explains the need for regulatory and financing agencies to introspectively and by objective outside analyses appraise costs versus benefits, goals, and the compliance procedures of the regulations or imposed controls and carry out indicated reforms. It suggests positive ways to mitigate adverse effects of regulatory and financial controls within the mandates under which the agencies operate. In general, the federal agencies overreact to public demonstrations and other visible and vocal means by special interest groups who oppose projects but represent only a small percent of our citizenry. This overreaction should be eliminated.

Actions by some agencies are directed toward the mitigation of adverse effects. This offers promise for the future but is not of major significance in the overall solution of the national problem. Unless the legislative and executive branches of our government can manage and force the regulatory agencies to demonstrate that their work is worth doing and maintain strict accountability for their actions, it looks like regulation will be increasingly adverse to our national economy and our capacity for constructive accomplishment.

CHAPTER 16

ETHNIC MINORITIES
AND WOMEN*

Gerald L. Challenger
Audrey Barrie
Dennis F. Murphy

Few aspects of the construction industry can generate more passion and controversy than the principle of affirmative action to increase dramatically the paticipation of women and ethnic minorities in the construction force. The Public Works Employment Act of 1977 makes available $4 billion of federal subsidies for construction projects through local governments but requires that at least 10% of this work is awarded to ethnic minority companies, subcontractors, craftsmen, or suppliers. In 1967 the AGC challenged the constitutionality of the 10% requirement, and substantial litigation is in process.

This chapter presents three viewpoints regarding the position of disadvantaged groups in the construction industry:

- Ethnic minorities in construction.
- Women in construction.
- An objective analysis of discrimination in construction.

ETHNIC MINORITIES IN CONSTRUCTION*

To estimate where we are now and where we may be headed relative to the employment of minorities in the construction industry, it might be useful

---

*Some of the facts cited in the second and third sections of this chapter were obtained from articles published in the *Engineering News Record*. A list of specific articles is included in the bibliography.

*This section was prepared by Gerald L. Challenger, Manager, Equal Employment Opportunity, Kaiser Engineers, Inc., Oakland, California.

to briefly trace, in broad terms, an outline of past legal events applicable to problems of the employment of minorities in general.

To be specific, an inquiry into the history of minorities in construction would require a separate treatment of each ethnic group. However, the distinction would add little to the analysis. Therefore, we examine primarily the black American, since issues surrounding that group provide the most easily traceable documentation. Also, it must be noted that in the earlier stage of American history on employment, there is little value in attempting to isolate occurrences peculiar to the construction industry separate from national experiences of blacks in other industries.

LEGAL AND HISTORICAL BACKGROUND

To begin, let us first cover the efforts to resolve problems of discrimination in the United States. As we review the various attempts that have been made by legislation, executive order, or agreement to pursue equal employment, it becomes patently evident that large segments of society, our elected officials in particular, have perceived a serious need to correct practices of discrimination. As one reads, the question "Why?" must be asked.

The federal constitution in the due process clause of the Fifth Amendment and the due process and equal protection clauses of the Fourteenth Amendment have been interpreted to forbid invidious discrimination in government employment. Aspects of the early civil rights acts, in their recent interpretations, contributed to the current antidiscrimination doctrine in employment. The Civil Rights Act of 1964 created the Equal Employment Opportunity Commission (EEOC), which investigates allegations of discrimination. The Age Discrimination in Employment Act forbids discrimination against persons between ages 40 to 70 on the basis of age. The Equal Pay Act, part of the Fair Labor Standards Act, requires equal pay for equal work without regard to sex. The Vocational Rehabilitation Act of 1973 recognized the employment difficulties of the handicapped, just as the Vietnam era Veterans Readjustment Act of 1974 recognized the unique employment problems of our veterans. The Railway Labor Act and the National Labor Relations Act require labor organizations to represent all members of relevant bargaining units fairly without regard to race, religion, national origin, and sex. Several collective bargaining agreements now specifically forbid discrimination. Numerous states and local municipalities have enacted statutes and/or ordinances against discrimination. Efforts to counter discrimination in federal employment trace to 1933 in the Unemployment Relief Act. Specific attempts by presidents to stem discrimination in respect to employment were made by practically every president since Roosevelt. The notion of affirmative action to reverse the problems of employment discrimination was conceived in the final report of a committee headed by Vice President Nixon during the Eisenhower administration. Under Kennedy, nondiscrimination was meshed for the first time with affirmative action as an obligation of federal contractors. Since then, many citywide affirmative action plans have been established in relation to the construction industry.

DISCRIMINATION AND UPGRADING

Unquestionably, the reason for the foregoing history is because discrimination exists in many forms. One must wonder why our public officials, elected by majorities who can remove them, have enacted this amount of legislation over so many years. The first reason, of course, is that our system of government extends guarantees to its citizens that, through discrimination, are impeded. Second, an examination of the list of protective laws growing from that discrimination specifically covers person 40 to 70, women, minorities, the handicapped, Vietnam veterans, and a wealth of other groups embracing the entire population. For example, the Civil Rights Act of 1964 does not distinguish any race in its scope of application. A third and probably most pervasive reason in that discrimination has been recognized to be very costly. The impact of unemployment, welfare, subsidized training, plus much of federal, state, and local costs of government, and a large percentage of crime can be translated into huge dollar expenditures resulting from unlawful employment practices.

One historical study of black participation in U.S. employment reveals patterns of exclusion from various occupations and industries. The pattern of exclusion is consistent across industry lines in occupations requiring more training or education. This is borne out particularly when one examines statistics covering periods of full employment and labor shortage, when overall minority employment is at its height such as during wartime. Since, historically, high or full employment periods are typically conducive to gains in the employment status of minorities, the absence of meaningful numbers of blacks as skilled craftsmen in the construction industry suggests a persistent pattern of exclusion when compared to double-digit unemployment rates for blacks in the presence of affirmative action rules.

The use of blacks as strikebreakers in several industries during the early 1900s ultimately created antagonism against blacks by several unions. It is possible we are seeing today some vestiges of that antagonism in the construction industry. However, the more recent predominance of the open shop leads one to conclude that both union and management share in the responsibility equally at this time.

Writing in the *American Journal of Economics and Sociology*, January 1975 C. F. Peane notes that "while the assertion of unavailability of qualified blacks in often a subterfuge for not hiring blacks, a short supply can prevent increasing negro participation ratios." Based on events in the construction and other industries, however, it appears likely that this increase (the participation index for craftsmen between 1966 and 1970) resulted largely from upgrading experienced (black) workers who had previously acquired the skills necessary to move into craft positions."

ETHNIC MINORITIES AS INDIVIDUALS

W. B. Gould writing in *Black Enterprise*, October 1977, states, "The key to improving race relations is the opportunity for employment. A job changes a worker's hopes of improving his own environment."

As social beings, black Americans are no less interested nor capable of conforming to the social standards of this country than white Americans. In recent history, however, in fact, the period identified earlier in this chapter, blacks were subjected to segregated housing and inferior education, deprived access to public facilities, discriminated against in employment opportunities, and denied a sense of self-worth through failure to recognize positive contributions to American history—all personal values that mesh with American society. Is it possible for a minority race of people to uplift itself without government intervention in an environment where their color is used to pervasively against development? What legacy have the past practices of discrimination wrought, and, with a population upward of 25 million, how is the situation righted? Imagine a continuation of the pattern and try to estimate the legacy these practices implant for the future.

The riotous frustrations of the 1960s emerged primarily from a new breed of blacks. These blacks were men who were enraged and resentful about fighting a war in Korea, allegedly to preserve freedoms they were intentionally and routinely denied in this country exclusively because of their color. The riots, open conflicts over constitutional guarantees that seemed to protect all other American citizens (and historical form of protest throughout history), served to heighten awareness of the injustives.

Compromise and settlement are well tested legal concepts of making persons whole. On a massive scale, affirmative action is a process of compensating, through accelerated hiring, for the present effects of past discrimination. Interestingly, in large part, the beneficiary of these efforts is not typically a person who experienced the earlier discrimination. It is not easy to identify with the resentment of educated blacks who frequently are employed primarily because of their color even though fully qualified not to mention the resentment directed at them from those who object to affirmative action and let it be known. In the instance of the unskilled individual accepted for apprenticeship training, the opportunity for training and achieving a career tends to suppress feelings of injured pride at being selected for one's statistical impact on a goal and timetable. After all, having overcome the obstacle of restrictions for acceptance to a training program is only one of several probable hurdles ahead: obtaining a journeyman card if he's not in a union, becoming a union member affiliating with an auxiliary local for blacks, dealing with problems of seniority, and ultimately achieving a policy-making position within the union.

ACCOMPLISHMENTS AND PROBLEMS

In many sections of the country it is considered normal for blacks to occupy positions of leadership in the local unions for laborers, cement finishers, or teamsters. Often in years gone by there were separate black locals in the carpenters' unions and other trades in southern states.

The most significant exclusion of opportunities for blacks and other minorities has been in the metal trades. Up until very recently black electricians, plumbers, boilermakers, ironworkers, or sheet metal workers were almost nonexistent.

While this section deals predominatly with blacks as the focal point, the building trades have been equally oppressive to Hispanic workers in the Southwest, American Indians in many sections of the country, and Orientals in western areas.

The accomplishments of ethnic minorities in much of the construction industry are agonizingly slow and intimately tied to government-funded training or government-mandated affirmative action. Voluntary hometown plans have contributed little to the "success" side of the score sheet. In the final analysis, large-scale training is going to prove vital to any major victories for minorities.

Minority Firms

The black entrepreneur must be regarded as the very essence of minority development in the United States and the key to equal employment, if there is to be any solution to the problems and costs of discrimination discussed previously. Every culture that has attained significance in history has done so through its own pride and self-sufficiency. The entrepreneurs, working from within and using their own people and finances as resources, create the business opportunities on which the entire economic structure depends. As a culture prospers, it turns its concentration to education; as an investment in its future this scenario develops pride. The combination of pride, prosperity, and education can uplift the black community considerably. In doing so, there is a high probability that an educated and moderately affluent black candidate for employment will not require the efforts of affirmative action programs or equal employment opportunity law to compete fairly for available job openings.

This premise is not new. Federal commitments to minority business enterprises recognized that minority businesses must be provided an economic base from which to compete, plus some form of advantage to overcome the handicap imposed by documented discrimination. The advantage took the form of a 10% set-aside designed to safeguard the affirmative action objective. This method, enacted with the 1977 Public Works Employment Act, is not terribly unlike the goals and timetables used in employment. The objection seems to be the establishment of a specified quota. However, some effort should be made to recognize that the 10% feature, on balance, is far less costly than the nation's overall expense to date resulting from racial differences, and it is the nearest the country has come to a workable solution. Further, if the *Bakke* and *Weber* decisions can be regarded as an indication of the mood of the Supreme Court at this time, the quota or a near variation thereof will likely become a fact of life.

Many who recognize the objectives of Minority Business Enterprise (MBE) and oppose the principle do so primarily because they have personally been affected by the compliance process. The argument, of course, is constitutional in nature. Unfortunately, the same antagonism that is spawned in the employment aspect of affirmative action occurs in MBE. It is possible that antagonism must ultimately be the price of minority achievement. But it is also possible that a central ingredient of our economic success in this country has been overlooked by the government's authors of affirmative action, and therein may rest a solution. That factor is incentive, and it is preferably instituted on a graduated basis. The opportunity to win a federal contract through competitive bidding, with minimum and maximum profit incentives or performance bonuses for affirmative action accomplishments, could present the kind of challenge that American business would happily rise to meet (along with the prospect of appropriate sanctions and penalties for nonperformance of the contract).

Naturally, it would be necessary for certain impediments to be removed or modified that will enable minority contractors to compete. The problems of working capital at reasonable interest rates and the Catch-22 aspect of bonding can be overcome by inducements. However, the Davis-Bacon Act, which fixes a prevailing wage (usually the union wage) that all contractors must pay in federal work, is a serious obstacle to the employment of minorities and business opportunities in the construction industry. Possibly, the black caucus in the Congress, along with other minority groups, could join open shop contractors' associations in effective lobbying to repeal the law.

The Future

In a capsule, the future will probably show that domestic and worldwide political pressures will continue to influence U.S. policy and major court decisions regarding the treatment of minorities, females, the handicapped, and the aged. If these groups can begin to feel that their grievances are being satisfactorily corrected through positive mechanisms, the United States will take a major step toward equal employment and equal opportunity. The federal government will continue, for the next decade, to attack discriminatory loopholes in fair employment and minority business obstacles, with the same enthusiasm it now applies in the collection of taxes. This is because these areas are becoming lucrative opportunities for a growing number of lawyers. The combined effect of penalties for noncompliances, plus acceptance of the notion of incentives for greater compliance, will generate a far more positive racial atmosphere than exists today. But voluntary methods will probably not succeed.

The construction industry has seen its profits eroded by numerous forms of government intervention. This section has attempted to address the topic of minority involvement in the industry from the aspect of deriving a solution through reason, since statistics only demonstrate that a problem exists. The intent has been to convey that all indications point to continued and probably increased government intervention and costly lawsuits unless the industry comes to terms with its documented history and develops a self-monitored approach to compliance on private as well as public work.

WOMEN IN CONSTRUCTION*

Freud, father of modern analytical psychiatry, is reported to have once questioned in despair, "Women: What is it they want?" If Freud did not ask the question, today's contractors certainly do.

WOMEN IN THE CRAFT WORK FORCE

The civil rights acts, commonly called Title VII, enacted in 1964 and amended in 1972, prohibits discrimination because of ". . .race, sex creed. . ." Employment doors previously closed to women were suddenly open. The Department of Labor later mandated that certain quotas of women be hired on construction projects being run by contractors with approved status for government contracts.

The mandated quotas place union contractors in a Catch-22 position: they are forced to staff their craft jobs from the union hiring hall, which gives them no control over who is sent to the project, while at the same time, the government holds the contractor responsible for complying with the mandated quotas.

Unions, on the other hand, claim they are training the qualified women who apply for their apprenticeship programs but not enough qualified women are seeking union programs. Meanwhile, the women often claim they are discouraged by the unions from entering apprentice programs.

Contractors have perhaps a little more power than they admit. Where quotas are impossible to meet, a contractor need only prove intent to comply. For instance, if a woman applies to a jobsite for a job as an apprentice craftsperson, the contractor must refer her to the appropriate union. At the same time, the contractor is responsible for reporting her name and that of

*This section was prepared by Audrey Barrie, free-lance writer, Diablo, California.

the union under the contractor's established affirmative action program. The contractor has then proved his intent to comply, and it then becomes the union's responsibility to prove that the woman is receiving the requested training (or that she was not qualified to be admitted) or that its training program is full.

Another fact to consider is that the mandated hiring quotas and affirmative action programs apply only to firms employing more than 50 workers. A recent Department of Labor statistical study shows that 80% of those in today's job market are employed by small companies with 50 or fewer employees. This obscure fact clearly reveals that the majority of women are not receiving the benefits of affirmative action programs.

Yet the question remains: Where are the women? What with copious legislation and the excellent pay scale and fringes offered in the industry, women are clearly not yet heating a path to the crafts.

At least a portion of the explanation for the dearth of women in construction in surely found in our socialogical fabric, in the traditional role models of our young women entering the job market, in the way society perceives women and in the way women perceive themselves.

Except for the birth of "Rosie the Riveter" during World War II, it is a rarity to find a woman who was in the construction industry before the enactment of the civil rights legislation, so today's young women have no visible role model to encourage their entrance into the industry. Society continues to perceive women as protected, more delicate species incapable of doing "man's work." Because of this socialization, many women continue to limit themselves to employment deemed more traditional for women.

However, double-digit inflation is bound to play a major role in affecting a change of attitudes. Women today no longer work for pin money, or until they are married, or until a baby arrives, or for self-expression and satisfaction. They work today for the same major reason men work: money.

According to the Census Bureau, 10 years ago a scant 1 in 10 families was headed by a female wage earner. Today, that ratio has jumped to one in seven. The sheer weight of economics will force more women into higher-paying jobs.

Despite advances in the field of birth control, teenage pregnancy has risen dramatically. Children's Home Society of California says that 9 of 10 women who do not abort an unplanned, extramarital pregnancy keep their child to rear alone. These women are now effectively responsible for the support of two people, herself and her child. Drastic increases in the divorce rate also force more and more women into the role of wage-earning, head of household. At least partially due to economies and inflation, more than half of the married women in the United States are employed outside the home in career oriented positions.

In all likelihood, many sociologists feel this country has already seen the last generation of women who can afford to or will choose to be full-time wives and mothers.

College enrollment has also declined. As America becomes more leisure oriented and affluent, our youth has become less ambitious for accomplishment, prestige, posessions, and career advancement. Young women are beginning to realize that they can earn higher wages without investing four or more years in advanced education by seeking such previously male-dominated employment fields as telephone lineperson and installer. Sears Roebuck employs female technicians who service appliances in the home, and all of us are more frequently seeing female law enforcement officers and service station attendants. The construction industry cannot be far behind, but so well entrenched is the male figure in the professional, managerial, and crafts aspects of the industry that employment patterns are hard to change.

The United States is the only country that seems willing to spend millions on affirmative action programs while indulging in the luxury of wasting our female work force through the lack of education in job opportunities. Many men in hiring positions continue to insist that all facets of the industry is "man's work" and that women are an unneeded sexual stimulation, are too emotional, and are not strong enough.

Russia graduates more female engineers, architects, and physicians than men. Construction craftspeople are often female in China, Yogoslavia, and other Communist bloc countries. Israel's women woked side by side with their men in carving an agricultural and industrial economy from a barren desert, while simultaneously fighting several wars. It is only in the recent years since Israeli families have achieved a measure of affluence that women are permitted the luxury of being solely stay-at-home mothers or exclusively employed in traditional female fields.

Why waste the dollars spent on affirmative action? It seems more profitable to accept the reality and turn it into an advantage—educating and actively recruiting women who can fulfill the mandated quotas and also be productive workers.

Fortunately, some contractors are farsighted enough to see the practical value of female hard hats and are eager to abide by the spirit of Title VII. The motives of these contractors are not simply altruistic. In the February 8, 1979, issue of *Engineering News-Record*, several viewpoints are cited: William D. Parker, Personnel Director of C. C. Mangum Co., Raleigh, North Carolina, told a contractor's workshop panel, "I personally don't care it nobody hires women. I want them all. I can use all I can get." Among the advantages Parker cited was that women don't "hot rod" while operating heavy equipment. "That means that expensive equipment is down for repairs less frequently," he said. Another advantage is a decrease in sick leave. The average woman worker does not lay off work on Monday, and women do not tend to leave early on Friday.

Sherry M. Stevens, a construction supervisor with C&T Construction, Laurinburg, North Carolina, who also attended the workshop, agreed with Parker. "My warehouse is cleaned up. I have lost less materials and I have a better inventory than ever before. That's because of my women not my men."

Still another construction executive says his mind was changed about women in construction when he saw 90-pound women expertly operating huge cranes and other heavy equipment in Vietnam.

C. F. Kienast of Barrus Construction, Kingston, North Carolina, said his firm recruits and enrolls women for training as heavy equipment operators with excellent results.

Commenting on the requirement that by May 1979 companies receiving federal contracts in excess of $10,000 will be required to have a work force composed of at least 3.1% women, Henry C. West Jr., personnel director for Dickerson Construction Co., Monroe, North Carolina said: "Let's just say it gave us a kick in the southside. But don't fight it. Contractors are going to wake up to the fact that it is money in the bank."

Apparently, the workshop discussions turned a few heads. For example, J. Barry Weston of Crain and Denbo, Inc., Durham, North Carolina, went away saying, "Until I attended the workshop, I really didn't think women could do the job. But we're interested in getting good people and I think hiring women has potential."

Parker further reported to workshop attendees that his company actively recruits women, including paying home visits to women on welfare to encourage them to apply for high-paying construction jobs.

Perhaps the kind of workshop sponsored by the North Carolina contractors could serve as a model in other sections of the country to stimulate best efforts in an atmosphere of goodwill and "can do."

In another example of creative thinking, the Allied Construction Employers Association (ACEA) of Milwaukee established a training program to help make female hard hats a reality. ACEA sponsored a four-week orientation workshop for 300 women to provide an overview of the industry. The aim was to place 30 women in each of 10 specific tracks aimed at an apprentice job on a Milwaukee construction site. The program was promoted through local newspapers, radio, and television, with flyers to all vocational-technical schools and high schools in the metropolitan area. ACEA also contacted women's organizations to announce its program to the unemployed, underemployed, reentry women, and especially to single heads of households.

The total cost for the program was $259,110 or $863.70 per participant. Instruction was by established journeymen in the various trades. The program costs included fees for advertising, instruction, and text materials and payment of $2.90 per hour per student. The cost was underwritten by the ACEA, which also applied for funds from the Department of Labor.

WOMEN IN THE SALARIED WORK FORCE

Professional and white-collar women are perhaps making a bit faster progress. Women are beginning to appear in all the salaried functional tasks required in the construction industry, including accounting, purchasing, scheduling, estimating, engineering, personnel, and project management. Of all the minority engineers being graduated in the United States, women are the fastest growing group. However, even among the female engineers, not many are oriented to the construction industry.

Women as Salaried White-Collar Workers

Women in construction (WIC) is a growing support organization worthy of recognition for their efforts in educating women to job opportunities in the industry. WIC members are primarily white-collar workers employed directly by contractors. The members of this organization include clerical workers who are upwardly mobile and vitally interested in the industry, office managers, accountants, safety coordinators, cost accountants, and other management, support, and technical personnel employed by contractors.

WIC is a national organization with chapters in all 50 states and Canada. Chapters have also been chartered in England, Holland, and Germany. Membership is open to any woman directly employed by a construction, architectural, or engineering firm. WIC's objectives are to help qualify individuals for promotion, and educate the public, its own members, and employers as well as to recruit women into the industry. (Women belonging to a union are not accepted in WIC because of conflicts of interests that may occur at times of labor negotiations. WIC also feels that union members have their own support organization.)

Interestingly, the Seattle chapter is being sued by a man who was denied membership on the basis of sex.

WIC or National Association of Women in Construction , as the national organization is known, was founded in 1953. The organization is broadly committed to assisting women who have chosen to work in salaried positions in the construction field. It is currently working with the National Association of General Contractors to help set more realistic employment goals. The membership includes women of all races.

Dorothy Ericson, an officer of the national organization is Office Manager, Treasurer, and Safety Coordinator for the Homer J. Olsen Company in the San Francisco Bay Area. She has been in virtually every facet of the industry for more than 20 years and feels that all too often women are not actively encouraged by either unions or contractors to enter apprenticeship programs. "For too many years," she said, "you had to know someone in a union to be accepted for training."

Through NAWIC, Ericson and other members speak at high school career days and engage in other recruiting projects. NAWIC also awards scholarships to both males and females for studies pertaining to the construction industry. Scholarships are awarded through the National Merit Foundation and are paid according to grades received, with top grades receiving 100% tuition.

In 1975, after several years of study and evaluation, NAWIC began offering a four-year home study course toward a Certified Construction Associate degree. The comprehensive course was developed by Northeastern Louisiana State University in conjunction with NAWIC. Subjects covered include contract and labor negotiation, cost accounting, general accounting, job safety, law, legislation, office management, supervisory skill development, public relations, and much, much more. Periodic tests are given through local chapters of WIC. For more information on the home study program, contact the National Association of Women in Construction, 2800 W. Lancaster Avenue, Fort Worth, Texas 76107.

Together, WIC and NAWIC serve as an informal clearinghouse for job openings in construction. Many contractors feel that members are more professional and better qualified for their organizations than those recruited elsewhere. Also, members learn from other members when job openings occur in other construction companies that can lead to promotions for the career- and industry-oriented WIC member. One member pointed out that should she decide to spend a couple of years abroad, "...I'd just contact WIC in England, Holland or Germany to learn about job openings. Many of our members do that within the United States and experience little or no time lapse between jobs."

Monthly meetings are an education themselves. Industry executives, university professors, legislators, and union officials are just a sampling of recent guest speakers at a typical chapter meeting. The NAWIC also promotes national workshops and seminars on the construction industry. Urging female office support staff to join WIC would seem affirmative educational action for contractors and architects.

One major achievement of the Phoenix, Arizona, chapter is the publishing of a construction dictionary that defines the language of construction, technical terms, and other construction-oriented expressions. This excellent publication should be in every contractor's library.

Women as Professional Engineers

Perhaps the most influential organization serving to promote the interests of women in engineering positions is the Society of Women Engineers (SWE), a professional, nonprofit, educational service organization of graduate engineers and men and women with equivalent engineering experience.

The specific objectives of the society are as follows:

- To inform young women, their parents, counselors, and the general public of the qualifications and achievements of women engineers and the opportunities open to them.
- To assist women engineers in readying themselves for a return to active work after temporary retirement or leave of absence.
- To serve as a center of information on women in engineering.
- To encourage women engineers to obtain high levels of education and professional achievement.

The society was founded in 1949 when small groups of women engineers started meeting in New York City, Boston, Philadelphia, Pennsylvania, and Washington, D.C. It was incorporated in 1952. Headquartered in the United Engineering Center in New York City, the society joins many of the engineering societies representing specific disciplines: the Engineers' Joint Council, and the Engineers' Council for Professional Development.

In 1976 the society opened its ranks to men and all membership grades. Qualifications are the same for both sexes.

SWE sections are located in 23 areas of the United States, and student sections have been chartered in 92 colleges, universities, and other institutions located in 40 states and in Puerto Rico. The society has an international membership well over 5000 and about 60 corporate members, featuring many of the largest industrial, engineering, construction, and utility corporations in the United States.

The society administers several award, certificate, and scholarship programs designed to honor local sections and contributors to the advancement of women in the engineering profession by an individual, group, or a corporation. The "Society's Certificate of Merit" program honors high school girls who have demonstrated three years' excellence in mathematics and science. There are also several scholarships designed to assist women engineers in obtaining their baccalaureate degree.

PROBLEMS AND SOLUTIONS

The problems affecting women in the construction industry are numerous and complex. The solutions will come from the industry's most creative and resourceful managers.

Since the U.S. government is the largest letter of contracts in this country, it is therefore in the best position to force change. The government, however, has not been totally realistic in recognizing the physical requirements of some crafts or the problems in attracting women to untraditional craft jobs and has placed more pressure for hiring women on the contractors than on the unions where the pressure would perhaps produce results faster.

Every employment problem of every race and creed is magnified in the cause of women simply because one-half of every race and creed is composed of women. With that premise as a basis, it would appear worthwhile to look at some solutions that have aided ethnic minorities and try to alter them to aid women in entering the industry.

For instance, owners and contractors might recruit from their clerical, nonexempt personnel. It is standard practice to notify nonexempt personnel of promotion opportunities. Why not also let them know of craft and salaried training program opportunities?

Union leadership could more vigorously explore training opportunities within each craft that would be particularly well suited for women. It is also appropriate for both unions and employers to reexamine all job functions more realistically. Perhaps it is ideal for an electrician to be 6 feet tall and be able to lift a spool of cable weighing over 100 pounds. But if a manager were to follow an electrician around a job for a week and interview him closely, the manager would probably discover that the electrician rarely has need to use his 6 feet of height and probably has not lifted more than 25 pounds at one time all year. Does it not make sense then to rewrite job descriptions and physical requirements to reflect reality rather than adhere to an outdated ideal?

Another avenue to explore is a training "load-fund" or set-aside in each bid for the training and development of women. A given number of dollars or a small percentage of the overall cost could be identified as money to be spent training women in the crafts on each job. After the company has trained her, she could then be sent back to the union to be placed on other construction jobs. Obviously, the job would have to be of a long enough duration to make such training worthwhile. Not every craft could be covered on every job, but it does not seem unreasonable that a few women could be recruited and trained on each job. Perhaps the women could be recruited from the owners' or contractors' nonexempt staff. If given trainee status with wages and educational requirements similar to the apprentice programs, the emerging skills would benefit both the individual woman as well as the contractor.

The basis for change is education. To meet the mandates for government-sanctioned contractors education must be aggressive, broad, and rapid. Unions must disseminate information on training vigorously using television, newspapers, brochures to high schools, and any other means to attract women into the industry.

Managers must reeducate their own thinking and approach the hiring of women with less prejudice and more openness. Owners and contractors must abide by the spirit of the requirements and must search throughout their own organizations for jobs that can be performed by women and which would help the contractor meet his mandated quota.

Government agencies, so quick to mandate quotas and enact legislation, must examine the problems of implemantation and allow contractors and owners money and time for the recruiting and training of women.

Placing women in untraditional employment roles requires a virtual re-weaving of our social fabric. Such changes take time, time the construction industry does not have. It is incumbent on industry and union leaders to take dramatic, creative, aggressive action. These leaders must innovate, and when they do, the industry will benefit by including in the work force career-oriented women who will contribute to the overall efficiency and progress of the construction industry.

AN OBJECTIVE ANALYSIS OF DISCRIMINATION IN CONSTRUCTION*

The objective of this section is to pursue the idea of equal opportunity to see how it is affecting the construction industry today. Although an emphasis is placed on the Public Works Employment act of 1977, other minority quotas in construction are also discussed. Also, to insure objectivity, several points of view are presented.

CONTROVERSY AND LITIGATION

In August 1977, the Massachusetts Bay Transportation Authority (MBTA) decided to reject Perini Corporation's $18.2-million low bid for Boston's South Cove tunnel project. The reason for rejection was that "it [the bid] was not responsive to the contract because it did not meet the thirty percent minority goal." According to MBTA Chairman Robert R. Kiley, "If the bidder failed to comply with the provision, it is just as if he submitted a bid without listing a price for tunneling."

Perini disagreed with the ruling and has obtained a temporary restraining order preventing MBTA from awarding a $20.5-million contract to Peter Kiewit Sons' Company, the next lowest bidder. Perini claims that the minority provision was only a goal, not a mandatory contract requirement. It says that the firm searched extensively for qualified minority subcontractors, but could only obtain a 13% minority subcontractor participation.

Although the MBTA claims it rejected the bid in the public's best interest, Federal District Court Judge Frank H. Freedman issued the restraining order. Freedman holds the opinion that the bid was by $2.3 million the low one and thus "the taxpayers have to be given some consideration here."

The situation is no different across the country. David M. Schertler works as a resident engineer for Barrett and Associates (consulting engi-

---

*This section was condensed from the original paper entitled "Discrimination in Construction," prepared by Dennis F. Murphy while he was a graduate student in the construction management program Stanford University, California.

neering firm) on a sewage treatment plant in Covelo, California. The plant is part of a clean water grant that is 75% federally funded and is also 12.5% funded by the state of California. Schertler contends that much of his time is spent filling out standardized forms prescribed by the Department of Labor which assure that 10.5% of the work force is minority. The contractor must meet this 10.5% goal for the aggregate work force usezation or provide documentary evidence of good faith efforts.

According to an interview with Schertler, "The legislation of today is such that a good minority subcontractor is in the driver's seat. It seems that many contractors cannot find good minority subs and therefore they have to settle for inexperience. But, as long as the federal government is going to abide by these quotas, the contractors can afford to account for this inexperience by merely increasing their total bid. The irony of it all is that the final cost of these minority subs is being pushed back to you and me, the taxpayers. It should also be pointed out though, that it is certainly better to spend our tax money in this way, rather than use it for welfare and unemployment."

John Igoe, the Project Coordinator of the Yerba Buena Convention Center in San Francisco, also has a daily involvement with minority quotas. He explains in an interview: "The affirmative action programs can be a very good tool in a project if they are taken in a positive manner. They are really more than just a numbers game. There is a good transfer of technology from the big white majority firms to the smaller minority firms."

This is obviously what the federal government had in mind when it started the various programs. Unfortunately, a certain bitterness has evolved among the AGC with the recent 10% MBE goals of the Public Works Employment Act of 1977. President Jimmy Carter's Administration has made it very clear that it expects the general constractors and the surety companies to make an all-out effort to meet the goals written into Section 106 (F) (2) of this $4- billion law. It states:

> Except to the extent that the Secretary determines otherwise, no grant shall be made under this Act for any local public works project unless the applicant gives satisfactory assurance to the Secretary that at least 10 per centum of the amount of each grant shall be expended for minority business enterprises. For the purposes of this paragraph, the term "minority business enterprise" means a business at least 50 per centum of which is owned by minority group members or, in the case of a publicly owned business, at least 51 per centum of the stock of which is owned by minority group members. For the purpose of the preceding sentence, minority group members are citizens of the U.S. who are Negroes, Spanish-speaking, Orientals, Indians, Eskimos, and Aleuts.

If the contractors or sureties fail in this effort, the Carter Administration has given the grantee broad latitude to dispense with bidding procedures and bonding requirements in order to insure adequate minority-contract participation. According to Presidential Assistant Jack Watson, the objective of the MBE requirement is to "help minority businesses grow, become more self-sufficient, and competitive by assuring them a subtantial market for their goods and services."

ALTERNATIVE POSITIONS

The AGC has been against the MBE requirement from the start. At a midyear meeting in Atlanta, AGC concluded that "the ten percent MBE requirement runs afoul of the constitutional limitations of the Fifth Amendment prohibiting arbitrary and capricious classifications by discriminating against (white) contractors because of their race." The limitations are those that forbid the federal government from depriving any citizen of "life, liberty, or property without due process.", as stated in the constitution

Speaking on behalf of the MBE requirement, EDA General Counsel Walter G. Farr, Jr. explained that the law is "not a set-aside program, and it does not involve a quota." If a contractor feels that he cannot or will not use minority firms, then the attorney claims that "he does not have to bid!" But Farr added that the only consequence of a long-term lawsuit would be a costly hassle that could result in the cancellation of the public works projects altogether.

Objections to MBE requirements are generally stated as follows:

- In many cases there are only one or two bidders.
- In many cases awarding agencies are rejecting bids because of nonconformity to the minority requirements.
- In several instances, after the bidding process, the owners are negotiating with a contractor who probably fulfills the minority requirements.
- The taxpayer is being severely penalized, and the bidding process is in danger of destruction.

The destruction of competitive bidding was certainly not the initial goal of the public works law, but AGC now feels that it has become a consequence of that law. According to AGC as set forth in *Engineering News Record,* October 20, 1977, "Governmental concern more properly should be focused on providing training and assistance to all disadvantaged groups so that they will acquire the skills necessary to compete effectively." It also asserts that "the MBE requirement creates an internal inconsistency in the federal law—while one section requires a minority quota, another provision mandates that individuals will not be excluded from the projects on the grounds of race, color, sex or national origin,"

ATTEMPTS TO ADJUDICATE

As expected, the issue has now been brought to court. AGC chapters throughout the country have brought suits in federal courts hoping that the 10% requirement will be eased. The first ruling came out against the Construction Association of Western Pennsylvania (the local AGC chapter is a member). Judge Daniel P. Snyder upheld the constitutionality of the MBE requirement and turned down the contractors' request for a temporary restraining order. Stressing the fact that the program was implemented to provide temporary relief to Pittsburgh and other areas of high unemployment, Snyder said, "We have found a compelling interest that is served by the ten percent set-aside." The decision now enables the city and state governments to spend more than $20.7 million in federal public works quotas.

In its suit, the Construction Association, which represents heavy equipment contractors in 33 western Pennsylvania counties, labeled the MBE requirement a "quota system" that amounts to "invidious and unreasonable racial discrimination." But Snyder disagreed, saying, "We do not here decide broad principles of reverse discrimination, but hold only that in the area of a public works appropriations bill, limited of necessity in duration and scope, there is nothing unconstitutional in requiring a reasonable percentage of MBE participation."

As for the conflict of federal statutes, Snyder said that they (MBE requirements and antidiscrimination) have a common objective to assure equal opportunity and to remedy the lingering effects of discrimination. He also claimed that the court is not convinced that using race as a factor in awarding subcontracts creates such a conflict. The judge emphasized that because the public works program terminates at the end of 1978 there would be no danger that the 10% requirement "will become an entrenched entitlement for minority business."

Before the suit, black contractors in Pittsburgh, represented by Ernie Wright, pleaded that "it's the same old story. We [blacks] have trouble getting the bonding needed to bid on the jobs and as a result, they [white contractors] get 99 percent of the federal contracts." Then after the prominority decision, Wright proclaimed, "We thought the whole suit was unjustified in the first place. I think that ten percent is a very menial amount. . .if it were up to me, I'd make it 20 or 30 percent. This thing is going to be beneficial to the whole city."

The ruling was appealed to the Third Circuit Court of Appeals in Pittsburgh. But the final decision upheld the lower court ruling.

Only days after the prominority decision in Pittsburgh, a federal district court judge in Los Angeles made a pro-AGC decision in a similar lawsuit. Calling the minority system "invidious and unconstitutional." Judge A. Andrew Hauk granted a permanent injunction against the use of numerical minority quotas in all federal construction programs after December 31, 1977. He made it clear though that this applies only to future programs, not the current EDA allocations of $57 million to the Los Angeles area.

In his decision, Hauk said the legislative history of the public works act shows that its purpose is to create jobs for people who need them most, but "for the life of me," he added, "I cannot see how a quota system achieves that stated purpose." He went on to agree that minorities in general are hit the hardest by unemployement and that affirmative action programs are appropriate remedies, but that there are disadvantaged whites too. As an alternative, Hauk suggested that the contracts could be awarded on the basis of the economic status of an individual, giving favored treatment to any person who is unemployed or earned less than a specific amount of income within the last year.

When the Justice Department argued that the requirement was merely a goal set by Congress after previous requirements that contractors show "good faith" in hiring minorities proved ineffective, Hauk shot the theory down. "It's not a goal you are seeking, it's a quota you are demanding."

The judge completed his opinion by saying that "I have to keep in mind the tremendous harm I could cause if I tried to enjoin the four billion dollars already granted." Hence, the decision to halt the use of quotas only after December 31, 1977, was made.

AGC attorney Lawrence H. Kay felt that this Los Angeles ruling was a tremendous victory. But he also expressed disappointment that the court did not apply the injunction retroactively to work now in progress in the Los Angeles area.

Less than one month after the Los Angeles ruling, the federal court in Missoula, Montana, also held that the 10% MBE requirement discriminates against white contractos, but like the Los Angeles court, it refused to enjoin the current $4-billion program. Judge Russell E. Smith said that the operation of the program has harmed white contractors and will continue to do so. But he refused to issue a restraining order on the grounds that it would "frustrate the congressional policy to reduce unemployment." Smith, unlike Hauk of Los Angeles, refused to rule in the constitutional issues involved in the case. He felt that those issues would be clearer after the Supreme Court decided the *Bakke* case, where a white man (Bakke) was apparently not admitted to medical school because of increasing minority quotas.

Besides the settled decisions in Pittsburgh, Los Angeles, and Missoula, AGC chapters have also filed similar suits in Louisiana, Florida, Indiana, Pennsylvania, Wyoming, Rhole Island. According to AGC Assistant Executive Director John C. Ellis, the multiplicity of suits is designed to raise the same issues in the same manner in the maximum number of legal actions. Conflicting rulings will then mean that the issue will probably be settled in Supreme Court. Thus the multiple lawsuites will achieve "a high degree of uniformity in the ultimate issues presented (to the Supreme Court)."

It may be well to take a brief look at the similarity between the AGC litigation and the *Allan Bakke* case.

In a letter to the *New York Times*, Allan Bakke is quoted as follows:

> Applicants chosen to be our doctors should be those presenting the best qualifications, both academic and personal. Most are selected according to this

standard, but I am convinced that a significant fraction is judged by a separate criteria. I am referring to quotas, open or covert, for racial minorities. I
realize that the rationale for these quotas is that they attempt to atone for
past racial discrimination, but insisting on a new racial bias in favor of minorities is not a just situation.

This is the same general argument the AGC has with regard to the MBE
requirement.

In the opening argument of the *Bakke* case former Watergate prosecutor
Archibald Cox argued that openly favoring blacks and minorities in admission to professional schools is the only way to help make up for past generations of social and educational discrimination. Bakke's lawyer, Reynold
Colvin claimed, on the other hand, that his client had been the victim of a
quota, unconstitutional because it is based on race. Cox then argued that
the program was not a quota system. He went on to claim that the program is designed to achieve a desirable social goal—more minority doctors.

Without going into a great deal of detail, it is easy to see that the *Bakke*
case does indeed parallel the AGC case in many items. The similarity is
even more evident if you compare some of Chief Justice Warren Burger's
comments with those of Judge Hauk from Los Angeles. One in particular is
when Burger asked why the special admissions programs could not be
opened to economically "disadvantaged" applicants, regardless of race.
This is the same idea Hauk brought out while defending his decision in the
Los Angeles AGC versus the EDA lawsuit.

The Supreme Court in *University of California Regents v. Bakke* held
racial "quotas" invalid but refused to ban consideration of race in university admissions decisions. (Congressional Quarterly's *Guide to U. S. Supreme Court*, copyright 1979, page 56.) The court ruled 5–4 for Bakke and
he was admitted to medical school. The Court's close decision reflects the
country's devisiveness on the issue of racial quotas. AGC chapters throughout the country continue litigation concerning a mandated quota system of
awards to minority subcontractors mandating hiring quotas for women and
ethnic minorities.

ANALYSIS AND CONCLUSION

A review of initial cases and experience of contractors and others honestly
making a significant effort to comply with federal regulations strongly indicates that the federal government has become vulnerable to inefficiencies
brought about by not having the compliance machinery set up before the
inauguration of the programs. Certainly, there are valid arguments on both
sides of this controversial issue. Surely many of the bidders who have been
disqualified were not properly informed before they bid. This is what has
caused the tremendous mix-up that, in turn, has led to the lawsuits and to
the erosion of the competitive programs.

One the other hand, the idelogy behind the quotas in construction is, in fact, sensible. That is, if a desired end is an industry in which the individuals, unions, and companies involved represent proportionately Americans of every national origin, race, creed, and color, then the quotas are indeed reasonable. The fact is that we are far from this desired end, and, to achieve it, affirmative actions must be take. Opportunities to enter apprenticeship training program must be given to all Americans in order to constructively accomplish there goals.

Continous expensive litigation in this and future cases can be a serious mistake. An owner, private or public, has the right to determine how much money it will spend and how and with whom it will spend it. In trying to stall $4-billion worth of grants, the AGC could lose the chance at the money altogether. Currently, the rules of the business involve giving the minority a chance in the construction industry. Until this changes, AGC and other industry leaders would be better off if they would stop spending money on the lawsuits and start coming up with alternative plans. For now, implementing the quotas through proper apprenticeship and training are our only real answer to equal opportunity.

CHAPTER 17

RESEARCH AND DEVELOPMENT

Boyd C. Paulson, Jr.

For two decades inflation in construction has been nearly double that for the U. S. economy as a whole; productivity has stagnated; and owing to ignorance, inertia, and fear of liability consequences, the implementation of new technology in many cases appears even to have regressed. Although these problems transcend the whole engineering and construction industry, they have been particularly acute on large projects and in many cases have resulted in long delays and staggering cost escalations. These trends are continuing and now threaten to reduce the numbers and scope of future projects, projects long sought for the revitalization of urban centers, modernization of aging industrial facilities, and in general for the improvement of our quality of life.

Must the liability risks associated with innovation freeze construction technology at early-to-mid twentieth-century levels? Why must equivalent major construction works in the United States cost more than they do in other economically advanced countries? Is the engineering and construction industry right in placing primary blame on external regulators, labor unions, consumer activists, and lawyers for its problems? Or is a substantial share of the blame more deeply rooted in the industry's own institutional structure, organizational inertia and conservatism, shortsighted goals, lack of research, divisiveness, and fragmentation? If the latter is substantially the case, can programmatic research and development efforts or changes in government policies stimulate innovation, accelerate implementation of research, increase productivity, stabilize or even reduce costs, or otherwise provide the incentives to improve the industry's future?

This chapter, which is largely based on two recent policy studies aimed at assessing the potential role for research in construction, and upon four

407

ASCE construction journal articles,* provides some background that might lead to answers to some of these questions. The sections that follow first substantiate the declining economic state just mentioned, then examine current patterns of research in U. S. construction.

The situation in Japan is also examined because in that country research is an integral part of the industry and has contributed to Japan's rapid growth in world construction markets. Critical problem areas and their priorities are next considered. With this background, the final sections suggest ways in which a higher level of research might be established for the advancement of the construction industry in the United States.

STATE OF THE INDUSTRY

To appreciate the problems facing construction, and even to suggest where research might effectively bring about improvements, one must first understand the structure, institutions, traditions, and driving forces of the U. S. construction industry. These issues are dealt with subsequently.

INSTITUTIONAL OBSTACLES TO RESEARCH

In its share of the nation's GNP construction is the largest industry, but the majority of this industry's hundreds of thousands of participants are small businesses. The industry's firms are intensely competitive among themselves in the best tradition of the free enterprise system, yet compared to other industries its technological advances sometimes appear trivial.

Construction is very custom oriented; there is a strong feeling that if something is unique, it is better. Yet this also means that the industry has been slow to respond to the benefits of mass production. The industry's structure is specialized and layered, with complex interlocking interests and traditions. Its character makes it highly effective on practical or project matters, yet often ineffective on general or program matters.

Needless to say, research falls in the latter category of the less practical and more general and speculative. Accurate data are not available, but it is

---

*Fondahl, John W., and Boyd C. Paulson, Jr., Development of Research in the Construction of Transportation Facilities: A Study of Needs, Objectives, Resources, and Mechanisms for Implementation, U.S. Dept. of Transportation, Research and Special Programs Administration, Office of University Research, Washington, D.C., Report No. DOT/RSPA/DPB-50/79/ 12, August 1979; Paulson, Boyd C., Jr., Goals for Basic Research in Construction, Department of Civil Engineering, Stanford University, Stanford, California, July 1975; Paulson, Boyd C., Jr., "Goals for Education and Research in Construction," *Journal of the Construction Division*, ASCE, Vol. 102, No. CO3, Proc. Paper 12393, September 1976, pp. 479-495; and Paulson, Boyd C., Jr., "Designing to Reduce Construction Costs," *Journal of the Construction Division*, ASCE, Vol. 102, No. CO4, Proc. Paper 12600, December 1976, pp. 587-592.

generally assumed that only a small fraction of 1% of the industry's gross revenues is invested even in applied research let alone basic research. This is in strong contrast to industries such as electronics, where an estimated 15 to 20% of the revenues go into research and development. This, in turn, at least partially accounts for the quantum leaps the latter industry has taken in recent years. Even in a sector closely coupled to construction, the largest manufacturer of earthmoving equipment invests approximately 4% of its gross revenues in research and development.

It has been observed that the construction industry is almost completely incentive oriented. If there is little research and almost no basic research, it is likely that there is little incentive for investing in it. This probably results, in part, because advances in construction tend to result from innovations or "better ideas." Most of these cannot be protected either by secrecy or patents and thus disseminate rapidly through the industry. Thus there is little incentive for one firm to invest heavily in research that can soon be expected to equally benefit its competitors. If there is to be an increased research effort in construction, particularly a deliberate move into basic research, incentives will most likely have to be provided through nontraditional means.

ECONOMIC SITUATION

In recent decades, construction appears to have been declining relative to the economy as a whole. Figure 17-1, which normalizes the Composite Cost Index for Construction to a deflated U. S. economy, shows a 15-year inflation rate considerably higher than the national average. As a reference, the solid line in Figure 17-2 plots construction's percentage of the GNP on a dollar-for-dollar basis. At first glance, since there is only a slight downward

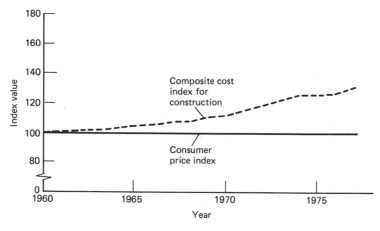

Figure 17-1   Variation of construction cost index from consumer price index.

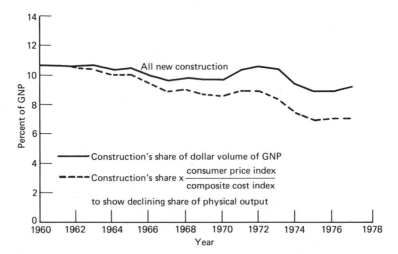

Figure 17-2 Construction's Declining Share of the GNP.

trend, if any, it would appear that the industry is holding its own. How-ever, if this curve is divided by the construction index shows in Figure 17-1, the Department of Commerce's Composite Cost Index for Construction, there is a definite and significant downward trend in the industry's *physical* share of the U. S. GNP, as shown by the dashed line in Figure 17-2. These graphs are but the tip of a large statistical iceberg lying in construction's path, and there is little evidence to indicate any change in the industry's course.

Another important economic characteristic of construction, especially as regards designers, constructors, and labor, is that its financial structure is similar to that of a service industry; thus the construction industry does not accumulate significant amounts of capital when compared to industries such as steel, transportation, oil, chemicals, and minerals. On the other hand, the service nature of construction makes it highly responsive to changes in market location and type of work. The industry can and routinely does survive in and respond to this environment year after year. In the words *survive* and *respond*, however, is another major clue to the industry's nature: it can do very little to shape or control the demand for its services. Furthermore, there is little coordination by owners or consumers of construction services to help smooth out radical fluctuations in market demand. The economy as a whole, and not just construction, suffers from this lack of coordination and its consequent waste of resources.

SLOW TECHNOLOGICAL ADVANCEMENT

Technologically, construction has advanced slowly compared to many other industries. Certainly, projects are bigger, and some are better; but relative to many others, construction remains in the early twentieth century. From a methods point of view, the main thing that really looks old-fashioned in old-time movies of Hoover Dam, the Empire State Building, or the Golden Gate Bridge is the movies themselves: they predate sound and color, and they flicker a lot.

Even to this day, most practitioners scoff at the need for research and development programs to bring about innovation in construction. Sentiments like "evolution, not revolution," and "do not be the first to try something new" are prevalent in engineering and construction conferences, publications, and marketing efforts. Even the barest hint that innovation carries with it some risk and liability for failure sends consultants and agency chiefs scurrying for shelter under tried and proven practices.

Construction practitioners are not alone, however, in their neglect of research. This peculiar blind spot also extends in large measure to government agencies, the academic research community, and consulting research organizations. This situation, however, does not appear to be a result of deliberate policies or neglect, but rather is a void that exists more from ignorance and lack of awareness on all sides. Indeed, it appears to be an inevitable by-product of the diverse and fragmented institutional structure of the construction industry and of its lack of built-in incentives for conducting its own research and development.

TRENDS AND CONSEQUENCES

With the limited amount of existing research, at present it appears that the discouraging trends indicated in figures 17-1 and 17-2 will continue. Regardless of the merits of individual research projects, their sum is insignificant compared to massive research efforts in rapidly advancing industries such as aerospace, electronics, and medicine; their gross impact in advancing the state of the art in construction has been inconsequential; thus we appear to be stuck with a "stable" and "mature" technology for implementing future construction projects.

CURRENT PATTERNS IN U.S. CONSTRUCTION RESEARCH

In the broad sense, research is an everyday activity in construction. Contractors are renowned for their ingenuity in developing solutions to specific problems. They modify or build new equipment, develop new exploratory methods, think up new construction procedures, and try out new applications for existing technology. The sophistication of this analysis, design, and development is frequently very high. In such innovation the contractors often work closely with specialized consultants, designers, equipment manufacturers, and materials suppliers. Indeed, in contrast to many industries, there is a remarkably free interchange of ideas and information between all these parties when problems arise. Very seldom, however, could these efforts be classified as basic or long-term research.

Traditionally, basic research is conducted in universities and in private and government research laboratories operated primarily for this purpose. It is generally assumed that because these institutions are several steps from the firing line they are in a better position to deal with long-term research. However, many people misinterpret this to mean that basic research conducted by such organizations is therefore less relevant. It should be emphasized that the nature and purpose of basic research is quite different from applied research and development. Each is important, and each has its appropriate role.

Where, then, should research be conducted? As mentioned, universities are one important source. Owing to their special significance, they are discussed in a separate section. For many reasons that have been given, construction contractors generally are neither motivated nor in a position to carry out research on a regular, programmatic basis. Nor are most architectural and engineering design firms. Nevertheless, these organizations should be deeply involved in advising and evaluating research efforts conducted elsewhere. Some larger manufacturers of materials and equipment have excellent laboratories that already do research related to construction. The Caterpillar Tractor Company's facility in Mossville, Illinois, is one example. Such laboratories, of course, are oriented primarily to the manufacturers' products, but they have broader potential. Government research laboratories include those operated by the National Bureau of Standards near Washington, D. C., the Navy Civil Engineering Laboratory at Port Hueneme, California, and the Army Corps of Engineers' Construction Engineering Research Laboratory in Champaign, Illinois. The latter, in particular, has placed considerable emphasis on research in the management of construction as well as on engineering aspects. Independent private sources include organizations such as the Portland Cement Association, the Battelle Memorial Institute, the Midwest Research Institute, SRI International, and the Electric Power Research Institute. All have capabilities for research in construction.

The determination of where particular research topics should be investigated depends on the nature of the research and on the capabilities of the organizations proposed to conduct it. Some research and some organizations are hardware oriented and depend on large sophisticated testing laboratories. Other research requires advanced computer facilities. Some may need the expertise of particular individuals in economics, the behavioral sciences, engineering, mathematics, business management, and so forth. It is beyond the scope of this chapter, however, to attempt to classify which types of research should be done where. One important source, however, does need further consideration. This source's role goes well beyond the actual quality and applications of its research output.

UNIVERSITY EDUCATION AND RESEARCH IN CONSTRUCTION

Since World War II, and especially in the last decade, numerous college and university programs have evolved that are aimed primarily at the construction industry. Suddenly, the construction process and its management—the logical culmination of the conceptual and design phases—have been recognized for what they are: integral parts of the total engineering and management process required to provide facilities. There are now dozens of four-year undergraduate programs; many are divisions within architecture, civil engineering, or architectural engineering. There are also a handful of graduate education and research programs; most are small, having anywhere from one to five full-time faculty members. Of these, most are identified with engineering departments in some of the most distinguished universities in the United States and abroad.

Although most are still fairly new, established graduate programs have already made significant progress in both research and education. Until a few decades ago there was very little university research and no coherent body of college-level coursework aimed specifically at construction. Many innovations that increasingly are taken for granted in the industry today either originated in or were considerably advanced through research efforts of these programs. Examples include time-lapse photography for operations analysis, computer simulation of field operations, behavioral science research into the workings of project management teams, computer-based information systems, studies of labor and industrial relations, and new methods and techniques for the planning, scheduling, and control of resources on projects.

On the education side, there are now many widely accepted courses that make up the core curricula of today's graduate and undergraduate programs. New courses continue to be introduced, and many of these will become standard subject matter in the future. There have by now been literally thousands of graduates from the established construction programs. Many have gone on to become managers on some of today's most challenging and successful projects. Others have advanced to top executive ranks in some of the largest and most reputable companies and in many smaller but innovative companies as well. Still others are found in government construction agencies, in large private consumers of construction services, and serve as faculty in construction programs in other universities.

It is especially important to recognize the indirect impact that university research has by its close relationship to the educational process. Of course, it is good when a given university research effort directly contributes to solving an existing problem. But in the long run, university research can have a greater impact through two influences it has on students. First, while research is in progress, student assistants have the opportunity to sharpen their minds and immediately apply their learning in doing research. Second, results of successful research efforts often find their way into courses that will be taken by other students, perhaps a decade or more in the future, who, in turn, will apply this new body of knowledge in their own careers. Universities are thus not only charged with developing new knowledge through research, but of passing that knowledge on to succeeding generations through education. It is in this interplay between research and education that universities can have their greatest impact.

RESEARCH IN THE JAPANESE CONSTRUCTION INDUSTRY*

This section outlines findings from a National Science Foundation-funded study of the role of in-house research in the technological advancement of the Japanese construction industry. The purpose of presenting these findings is threefold. First, they show how, in at least one part of the world, the construction industry can adopt the organized pattern of research and development found in the so-called high-technology industries and thus take the initiative and responsibility for its own technological development and advancement. Second, there are many aspects of the Japanese approach to research that could beneficially be applied in U.S. construction organizations, so a general understanding could be helpful toward this end. Third, since the Japanese are already taking limited steps toward bringing some of their advanced technologies to the U.S. urban construction marketplace, there could be increasing opportunities for U.S. and Japanese construction organizations to cooperate in accelerating this technological transfer. All sectors of the U.S. construction industry could thus benefit from a better understanding of construction research and development in Japan.

EVOLUTION OF CONSTRUCTION COMPANY RESEARCH LABORATORIES

From the beginning of its written history Japan has had a long and successful pattern of assimilating ideas from foreign lands, modifying and adapting them for its own needs, and advancing their development far beyond what the foreign originators had accomplished. These trends were accelerated in the Meiji restoration of 1867, at which time Japan turned abruptly from centuries of feudalism to emerge as a developing power among industrialized nations.

*Paulson, Boyd C., Jr., *Goals for Basic Research in Construction*, Technical Report No. 202, The Construction Institute, Department of Civil Engineering, Stanford University, Stanford, California, July 1975; and Paulson, Boyd C., Jr., John W. Fondahl, and Henry W. Parker, *Development of Research in the Construction of Transportation Facilities: A Study of Needs, Objectives, Resources, and Mechanisms for Implementation*, U.S. Department of Transportation, Report No. DOT/RSPD/DPB/50-77/14, Washington, D.D., September 1977.

The real beginnings of modern construction research and development patterns, however, came shortly after the end of World War II. For the first time in its history, Japan had been defeated and occupied by a foreign power. Two million of its people had been killed, and 40% of its urban area lay in waste from the bombings. Industry had been crushed. For what was left of the construction industry there was a massive rebuilding job ahead, and Japan desperately needed to advance its technology and procedures to incorporate the best of what was available in the world.

At that time, several of the largest engineering-construction companies established research institutes, although initially without laboratory facilities, largely for the purpose of studying Japan's reconstruction needs and for analyzing available technologies, domestic and foreign, that could most beneficially be assimilated and applied in the reconstruction effort. These institutes have since grown and become an integral part of the way of doing business in Japanese construction and have made significant contributions to the industry's strength in the domestic and international construction markets. Construction increased from a 15.6% share of the domestic GNP in 1960 to 20.7% in 1970. Japanese companies have been very competitive with their European and North American counterparts when working in the less-developed countries of SouthEast Asia, Africa, the Middle East, and South America, and now they are finding a market for their technologies in the advanced countries' home territories.

Today, about 25 of the largest engineering construction companies maintain laboratories specifically designated for construction research and development. Although 25 is small compared to the half million licensed contractors in Japan, the share of the market these firms have is disproportionally large compared to their 25 largest counterparts in North America. The influence of Japan's research permeates down through the half million firms, with the result that the overall state of construction technology in Japan is among the highest, if not the highest, in the world.

The laboratories' staffs range from two small ones having about 15 people, including 10 research engineers, through several in the 100 to 250 range, on up to the largest, which has over 300 people, including about 230 research engineers. Budgets range from about $500,000 annually to about $8,000,000 annually in direct laboratory staff and equipment costs. These numbers normally do *not* include research and development in other parts of the companies, such as development of new computer programs, advances that take place as part of regular engineering and design, or field-originated innovations to solve specific construction problems. The direct laboratory budgets range from about 0.3% to 1.0% of gross sales, although as a fraction of corporate capital investment the percentages are, of course, far higher. The physical facilities in the larger laboratories represent all construction-related engineering disciplines, and in scale they are often larger than those in the largest U.S. universities and government agencies.

INCENTIVES FOR RESEARCH

Although the research institutes began as a means to accelerate postwar reconstruction, today there is a mixture of incentives to keep the laboratories going. To some extent these relate to the status or favorable publicity that results from researcher publications about technological advances. This, in part, relates to recognition of research laboratories as part of the prequalification documentation needed to bid on major public works projects. There are also tax incentives.* But greater incentives result from the competitive technical edge given to a company by patenting and licensing technologies for more productive or economical or effective construction designs and procedures. New methods and ways of building different kinds of structures can also give an edge in marketing where clients themselves are moving into new areas. Underground LNG tanks are a recent example that has spurred intense research competition among the major contractors. The laboratories also serve to develop quantitative data to substantiate new designs to meet Japan's existing strict building codes and also to document claims for changed conditions and come up with economical solutions to field problems.

Perhaps the greatest incentives of all come from Japan's rigid physical and social constraints. The average vertical relief in this mountainous island country is several times the world average, and to compound matters the geology of these mountains is among the most difficult to be found anywhere, being laced with active faults, volcanic regions, widely varying rock types, and groundwater from the high annual precipitation. Frequent major earthquakes make seismic constraints among the most demanding in the world. Less than 20% of the land is suitable for agriculture, and what little flat land remains is increasingly yielding to urban development. With 110 million people living in a nation the size of California—or rather in what is left between the mountains—Japan is a notoriously crowded country. In short, "good" construction sites disappeared long ago, and new projects increasingly are sited in what most of the world would consider to be impossible geological conditions, or they are shoehorned in, at great expense, among existing urban structures. It is well known that with so many people living in such a small space, the impact of development on the environment has at times courted disaster. What is less well known, how-

*This section is based on findings of a six-month study in Japan conducted by the author under NSF Grant No. INT-77-12658. During this time, he was a Visiting Professor at the University of Tokyo and a guest of Ohbayashi-Gumi, Ltd., one of the world's largest engineering-construction firms. Also see: Paulson, Boyd C., Jr., "Research in Japanese Construction Industry," *Journal of the Construction Division,* ASCE, Proceedings Paper 15237, Vol. 106, No. CO1, March, 1980, pp. 1-16; and Paulson, Boyd C., Jr., *Transportation Construction in Japan,* Technical Report No. 240, The Construction Institute, Department of Civil Engineering, Stanford University, Stanford, Calif., August, 1979 (National Science Foundation Grant Int-77-12658, and U.S. Dept. of Transportation Contract OS-60150).

ever, is that the Japanese government, with a surprising degree of cooperation from industry, has imposed some of the world's strictest regulations to
preserve or restore the quality of air and water and to prevent noise, vibra-
tion, soil contamination, land settlement, and odors. Methods freely used
in the United States, such as organic chemical grouts, are no longer tolerated in Japan. To further complicate matters, fear of diversion to terrorists
is making it increasingly difficult to obtain explosives, thus removing another of the contractor's basic tools. Crowding and earlier displacements of
people have bred increasing social and political opposition to new construction and land acquisition; for their very survival, contractors must be good
neighbors, and every square meter made available for construction must be
used to maximum benefit for the community as well as for the project at
hand. Safety requirements and regulations are almost absolute. Since contractors incurring a serious accident can be removed from the prequalified
bidders' lists for months or years, thus seriously damaging or even ending a
business organization, safety procedures are designed to see to it that acci-
dents are avoided, even at great cost. Briefly stated, if North American and
European contractors wish to see what their own environmental and regulatory situation might be 10 or 20 years in the future, they need only go to
Japan.

What these contractors will also see, however, is a construction industry
that has learned to live with the constraints and that has taken a positive
attitude and approach in developing the technologies and business procedures to cope with the complex and growing demands of the late twentieth
century. While some American engineers are dreaming about using "underground space" to greater advantage in the future, the Japanese have been
doing so for years. The cities not only have the modern surface architecture
characteristic of twentieth century cities, but also consist of subterranean
honeycombs of transportation networks, shopping districts, and utility cor-
ridors. With over 1000 miles of tunnels traversing seemingly impenetrable
geologic conditions, the National Railways on some lines literally spend
more time underground than on the surface, even between cities. This
tunnel network will soon be augmented by the thirty-four-mile Seikan Un-
dersea Tunnel connecting the islands of Honshu and Hokkaido. Deep subway stations are constructed with almost negligible disruption to street-
level traffic and adjacent residential and commercial areas. In other sectors
of the industry, recently constructed steel mills, with annual production
capacities ranging from 6,000,000 to 16,000,000 tons, have skilled staffs
manning computer-controlled environmental monitoring centers, and they
run essentially pollution free. On completion of the Honshu and Shikoku
bridge system, 10 of the world's 20 longest bridges will be in Japan, including the longest, over the Akashi Straits, with a center span of 1780 meters.
Even the highest skyscrapers are constructed within fabric covers that block
most noise and dust emissions, and, needless to say, their designs are analyzed for seismic characteristics on the modern earthquake "shake-table"

simulators found in the construction company laboratories. This list could go on indefinitely and transcend all types of construction. What it boils down to, however, is that in the face of increasingly difficult constraints the Japanese construction industry is not only coping, but also responding positively to advance its technology. Although at the end of World War II its research institutes began by borrowing ideas around the world, Japan now has much to offer to the world construction industry.

TYPES OF CONSTRUCTION LABORATORY RESEARCH

From a technological viewpoint, the research covers all types of engineering that relate to construction. Typical facilities in the larger companies include fully equipped soil mechanics laboratories with minicomputers for control and monitoring of experiments; large-scale tension and compression machines, with massive reaction floors and abutment walls; large two-directional, computer-controlled shake-tables for earthquake simulation; minicomputer-controlled wind tunnels for bridge aerodynamics, smoke-stack diffusion tests, and microclimate analysis around models of urban building developments; large soundproof rooms for testing acoustic materials and designs for highway, railway, and industrial noise suppression as well as conventional architectural applications; cryogenic temperature apparatus for experimentation with structures for holding liquified natural gas and similar materials; solar energy systems for hot water, space heating and cooling as well as thermal analysis of various types of exterior materials for buildings; facilities for developing and testing electrical and mechanical systems, especially for building lighting and HVAC; materials laboratories for plain and reinforced concrete, masonry, soil grout compounds, et cetra; biochemical laboratories, with environmental control rooms, electron microscopes, mass spectrometers, and related equipment for both materials chemistry and environmental pollution control; and fire testing laboratories. One company even has a large hydraulics laboratory, complete with wave basin and dam and river modeling space.

The physical facilities are staffed by researchers selected from the best graduates of the top universities. Most have advanced degrees, including many with doctorates. They come from the scientific and engineering disciplines represented by the variety of facilities previously mentioned, and they engage in independent research and publication much like researchers in universities and in the advanced laboratories of the high-technology industries.

The types of research can also be classified according to its origin and purpose. Four categories typically found in the larger companies, together with the approximate percentage distribution from one of the companies, are as follows:

1. Problems that originate in the field but where the techni-   40–45%
cal expertise of the laboratory can help provide solutions in
time to help the project at hand.

2. Research studies originating with the researchers themselves, and conducted with management approval, which may or may not have short-run benefits.	40-45%
3. Research assigned as part of high-level corporate strategy, possibly for entering future markets.	5-10%
4. Research done for outside clients, often on a contractual basis.	5-10%

In the first category, the expertise of the researchers and the laboratory facilities are often applied in a manner analogous to consulting from a top-ranking expert in the field related to the problem, much like a nationally recognized soil mechanics professor might help contractors in the United States. Indeed, structural and geotechnical problems account for a major share of the research and development in this category. Frequently, the primary results apply only to the problem at hand, but, occasionally, with further research, a new method or potential item will result that is applicable categorically to many different projects. In almost all cases this is practical, applied research, although even here success is not always attainable.

In the second category one finds many of the more basic or fundamental kinds of research topics of the type funded by government agencies in American universities. The companies were often hard pressed to identify cases of applicable, profit-making results coming from this category; this makes it all the more significant that the companies allocate such a large portion of the effort in this area, indicating strong and open management support rather than clandestine "pet projects" conducted by researchers in their spare moments. The companies apparently recognize the indirect benefits from developing experience with technologies that may come together in some future application; from advancing the skills and expertise of the researchers themselves, giving them a deeper background to draw on for application in the other three categories; and from the open publications that not only add to the prestige of the company, but also advance the overall state of knowledge in scientific and engineering disciplines. They publish company journals of scientific research papers that are mailed to university, government, and public libraries. Also, some of this research, quite openly and acceptably, supports the thesis that helps an employee gain an advanced degree at a prestigious university. In general, in the United States one can find such attitudes among top managers in government research laboratories and in the scientific laboratories of large manufacturers of computers, communication equipment, chemicals, and others; but it would be unusual for a U.S. construction firm to even contemplate supporting this category of research within the company itself.

The third category, that directed from corporate policy or strategy, is smaller but very important. Recent examples have been spurred by the need to meet ever-growing regulatory constraints, such as developing quiet pile drivers and finding alternatives to organic grout compounds. Others are designed to give the company an edge in entering future or growing markets, such as advancing slurry-wall technology to 200-meter depths to capture a share of the domestic market for large underground oil storage tanks located near harbors.

The fourth category, contract research, is partially undertaken to maintain or build good relations with present or prospective clients for the companies' engineering and construction services. For example, a few years ago the gas companies wanted to develop technologies for underground LNG storage tanks to minimize the risk of earthquake-rupture in surface tanks as well as reduce the higher differential thermal stress on surface tanks. Several of the construction companies' research laboratories began to work on different kinds of problems related to underground tanks, including the creep of concrete at cryogenic temperatures, minimizing freezing and expansion stresses in the soils surrounding the tanks, et cetera. Extremely sophisticated laboratory equipment has been acquired for this research, but it is beginning to pay off.

MANAGEMENT SUPPORT AND GUIDANCE

Although the researchers enjoy considerable independence and freedom of choice in their research topics, by no means does the system allow them to become cloistered ivory-tower hermits who lose touch with the companies' primary business. In large measure this is satisfactory to both researchers and management and partially results from the high level of consciousness, support, and guidance top management devotes to the research institutes.

Support is most conspicuously evidenced in the fact that the laboratories are real and serious entities, often with the best physical facilities and large numbers of highly qualified researchers who are content working in a private, profit-making organization. The laboratories' annual budgets would represent a substantial share of corporate assets or profits, even though they do not at first appear large when compared to sales. One is also impressed, in speaking to top managers, that they are quite well informed and interested in the company's research activities and can generally quote many specific examples of successful research applications. A further degree of foresightedness is evidenced among the managers in companies that devote a significant share of their resources to more basic or fundamental topics, as was discussed in category 2 of the previous section.

Guidance is normally provided by one high-level policy committee, drawn from top managers in various company divisions, and also by technical committees in the major engineering disciplines that bring together researchers and experienced practitioners. Through a somewhat involved process, proposals and recommendations for desired research activities are submitted from various operating divisions of the company and also from the researchers themselves. Proposals of categories 3 and 4 also evolve from company policy meetings and requests from clients. These are considered by the various technical committees and may receive recommendations, endorsements, and revisions. The real priority and budget decisions, however, appear to be made in the policy committee, which might meet formally only twice a year. Prior to these meetings, however, there is considerable discussion that leads to some measure of consensus. The committee members also usually have a considerable amount of proposal priority and budget documentation to review prior to the meetings. The meetings, like the research function itself, are taken seriously, and this attitude prevails in the companies.

Research is thus an integral part of a large Japanese engineering-construction company. Project managers and engineers know the laboratory is available as a resource if they have problems, and the researchers themselves have relatively free access to the field for testing out new ideas. Even the clients, many of whom have their own construction research facilities (e.g., Ministry of Construction, Ministry of Transportation, the National Railway, steel companies), see nothing unusual in not only tolerating, but also cooperating with the contractors' research activities. In the first months of my investigation, I would often probe skeptically with questions looking for derogatory comments about ivory-tower researchers or the promotional or showcase laboratory that might be more of a prestige piece for marketing purposes. But the commitment was broadly rooted, and all that usually resulted from such questions was even more embarrassing questions in return about how the U. S. construction industry can continue to advance itself, and prevent further erosion of its competitive and leadership position, without its own systematic research and development efforts.

ASSESSMENT

The significance of all of this is that, given the proper economic and institutional climate, it is indeed possible for the private sector of the construction industry to support and benefit from a systematic research effort of the type one normally associates with capital-intensive manufacturing industries. Given that it is only a fairly recent development that has taken root and flourished in Japan, it could just be possible that the seeds for such institutions could be planted and successfully nurtured in other advanced industrialized countries, including the United States.

But in the United States there are many obstacles that would have to be overcome. In some sectors of industry there is a more intensely competitive climate that works against long-term investments. (In this regard, however, foreigners generally underestimate the degree of competition in Japan's domestic construction market; large companies especially are suffering from deliberate government policies to shift business to small and medium sized firms.) A major factor that is much more adverse in the United States is the deteriorating legal climate, especially its paralyzing effects on innovation and its associated risk. Contractual relationships in Japan are still based largely on trust and on promoting mutual cooperation toward a common objective. Then, of course, there are tax incentives and related government policies, but here it is worth pointing out that companies in other sectors of the U.S. economy still find it worthwhile to maintain research and development programs in spite of the supposedly less favorable tax situation. It is also just possible that Congress is beginning to reawaken to the relationship between research and development and America's economic strength.

The other incentives that drive Japanese research ought to operate just as well in the United States: creating new markets, solving practical field problems, offering corporate prestige, gaining a keener competitive edge, substantiating claims, and proving compliance with regulations. But for some reason these incentives have not taken hold. Perhaps by studying the evolution of construction research in Japan, a beginning can also be made in the United States.

CRITICAL PROBLEM AREAS

To be most effective, the limited resources available for construction research and development must be applied toward solving problems that most adversely impact productivity, drive up costs, and prolong schedules on construction projects. This section addresses problems in two principal areas: (1) Those involving interactions and functions of parties at the project and system level and (2) problems at the construction contract level. These areas also lead to comparison of system organizational structures and their relationship to decision making, responsibility, authority, and accountability.

In general, assessments reported here are based on (1) expert opinion and analysis, derived from a variety of techniques, such as surveys, interviews, and quantitative forms, from knowledgeable and respected individuals now involved in the administration, design, and construction of major projects; and (2) direct and indirect observation and studies of projects recently completed, now under construction, or planned. There are strong correlations between the various sources of information that indicate the problems and priorities identified here are ones urgently in need of solution.

Before proceeding, one concept needs further explanation to help keep the findings in perspective: the level of influence that decision makers (planners, designers, constructors) can have on the cost and performance as a project evolves from concept to reality.

LEVEL OF INFLUENCE*

Figure 17-3 illustrates several aspects of the level of influence concept. The lower portion simplifies the life of a project to a three-activity bar chart

*From Boyd C. Paulson, Jr., "Designing to Reduce Construction Costs," *Journal of the Construction Division*, ASCE, 102, CO4, December 1976, pp. 587–592. This figure also used as Figure 10-1 on page 154 of "Professional Construction Management, by Donald S. Barrie and Boyd C. Paulson. Jr., McGraw-Hill, New York, 1978.

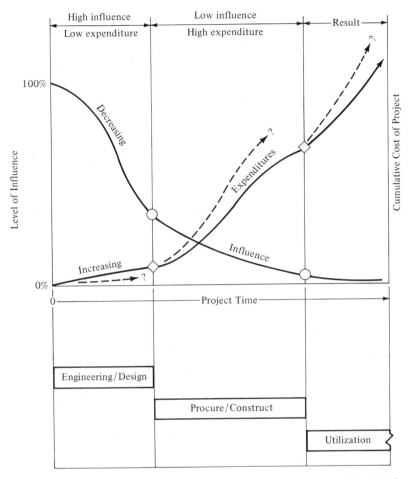

Figure 17-3 Level of influence on project cost. From Donald S. Barrie and Boyd C. Paulson, Jr., *Professional Construction Management*, McGraw-Hill, New York, 1978.

consisting of (1) planning and design, (2) procurement and construction, and (3) use or operation. The upper portion plots two main curves. the curve ascending to the right-hand ordinate tracks cumulative project expenditures. The curve descending from the left-hand ordinate shows the decreasing level of influence. The bar chart and both cruves are plotted against the same abscissa: project time.

The parts of the figure interrelate as follows: in the early phases of a project, that is, during feasibility studies, preliminary design, and even detail design, the relative expenditures are small compared to the project as a whole. Typically, engineering and design fees amount to well under 10% of total construction costs. Similarly, the capital costs invested by the time construction is completed often are but a small fraction of the operation and maintenance costs associated with the project's whole life cycle.

However, although actual expenditures during the early phases of a project are comparatively insignificant, the decisions and commitments made during that period have a much greater influence on what the expenditures later in the project will actually be.

CRITICAL COST FACTORS AND PRIORITIES AT THE SYSTEM LEVEL

This section describes a study undertaken for the purposes of (1) determining factors that have the greatest cost impact on a typical urban rapid transit project and (2) determining priorities for investigations to achieve improvement in these factors.

Potential for Improvements within the State of the Art

On the basis of in-depth interviews with, and detailed questionaires completed by experts in the field of transportation construction, the results in Figure 17-4 were obtained. Timeliness of decisions was ranked highest among controllable internal factors with respect to the potential for improvement within the existing framework of project techniques. Two other closely ranked variables were precontract preparations and organizational structure.

Of the external factors over which the owner, designer, and contractor have relatively little control, regulatory, environmental aspects ranked highest by a considerable margin. Among both internal and external factors, the variables with the least potential for improvement within the

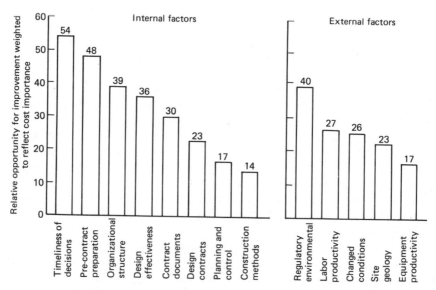

Figure 17-4   Improvement Opportunities Within the state of the art.

state of the art are construction methods, planning and control, and equipment productivity. These are areas that have received major research attention in the past, so the results may be an indication of the effectiveness
of such research funding.

Potential for Improvements beyond the State of the Art

Figure 17-5 averages responses for the forecasted potentials for improvement beyond the current state of the art. These improvements would be
achieved by research and development on new approaches and methods as
opposed to more effective implementation of presently available
procedures.

The highest ranked was design effectiveness. The brief description given
for this variable was the degree of standardization, cost effectiveness, constructability, and the need for change orders. Three other high-ranking
items were organizational structure, precontract preparation, and regulatory, environmental.

It should be noted that the forecast potential for improvement is not
inconsequential for any of the 13 items. On the other hand, it is clear that
certain factors are viewed as having considerably greater possibilities for
improvement through investigation and research into new approaches.

Priority Rankings

Conclusions for ranking with respect to the potential payoff for improvement within the state of the art are suggested by Figure 17-4. These indicate that those factors deserving greatest attention are the following:

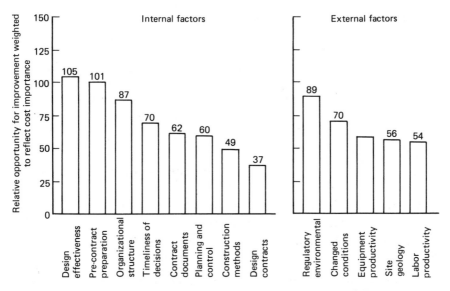

Figure 17-5   Improvement opportunities beyond the state of the art.

1. Timeliness of decisions.
2. Precontract preparations.
3. Regulatory, environmental.
4. Organizational structure.
5. Design effectiveness.

Conclusions for ranking with respect to the potential improvement beyond the current state of the art are suggested by Figure 17-5. These indicate that those factors deserving attention are the following:

1. Design effectiveness.
2. Precontract preparation.
3. Regulatory, environmental.
4. Organizational structure.
5. Timeliness of decisions (and also changed conditions).

PRODUCTIVITY ON THE CONTRACT WORKSITE

Although the principal limitations on construction productivity of a complex project are beyond the control of the construction contractor, there are technique and methods of job management that the contractor controls that do have significant effects on job costs. For this investigation productivity was considered in the qualitative sense in that it is a measure of how smoothly a job runs, of the lack of crises, the lack of wait-time, the lack of changes that affect work already done or work in progress, and the ability of the contractor to complete a job within budget and on schedule.

In comparing good contracts (profitable, smooth running, relatively crisis free) with marginal contracts and in comparing more preductive managers with those who are ordinary, one does not find differences that could be classified as breakthroughs in either ideas of concepts. Rather one finds that productive managers generally have been able to make effective use of the human resources available, have been able to develop a team of people who care about and work hard on the problem, and have put into consistent use many of the good management techniques available to everyone.

There is some consensus that the following items are very important for productive jobs:

1. Effective and open communications and interaction with all elements of the jobsite.
2. Iterative and detailed advanced planning to develop optimum solutions and determine risks and problems of each task.
3. Measures that develop motivation in employees, including timely recognition for good productivity and other desired behavior.

An important area of research that could build on problem areas identified here would be a more detailed study to actually quantify the kinds of savings that can be realized through better jobsite management and control.

IMPLICATIONS OF PROJECT ORGANIZATIONAL STRUCTURES

Although this chapter started out with its main focus on interactions during the actual construction phase of a project, it is clear that little can be gained without looking at the overall organizational context in which such construction projects take place. As has been shown, the die has been largely cast by the time construction begins, and some of the major problems impacting construction costs and schedules have their roots in the overall organizational framework.

Project Organizations

In a typical major public works construction project, some of the key parties include (1) the owner, normally a state or local public agency; (2) planners, designers, and design consultants who sometimes are within the agency and sometimes are obtained by contract; (3) construction contractors, owners' inspectors, suppliers, subcontractors, crafts, regulators, and others involved in physical construction; (4) operations and maintenance organizations, normally a part of the public agency; and (5) the users or consumers of the project's function or service who normally also pay the bill through taxes, fares, utility rates, or tolls. The interactions between these parties are shown at a conceptual level in Figure 17-6. In large projects, these relationships can become much more complex.

Lessons

It is not possible accurately to quantify the dollar effect on total project costs of a type of organization, nor is it possible to justify one organization over another by an initial cursory look. Unfortunately, there is too little

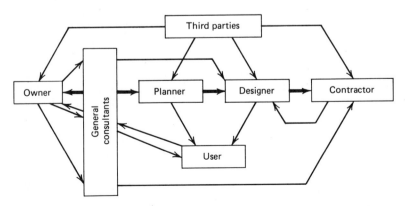

Figure 17-6 Interactions between key parties involved in a major project.

positive learning and transfer from one organization to another; indeed, many newer organizations contain what in effect are negative reactions to avoid perceived mistakes of their predecessors. There is too little actual research to determine which features should be adopted and which discarded; too often it is just a personal conviction of one or a few key individuals.

The problem is that far too little is known about how to build and operate effective organizations for the management of large projects, and at present the industry is groping for solutions that are much more complex than is generally realized. Many of the highest-priority problem areas identified in figures 17-4 and 17-5 were a consequence of this fact. One of the most productive investments of research funds could thus be into studies of major projects to determine what does and does not work and what guidelines could be offered for the organization and administration of future large projects.

INCREASING CONSTRUCTION RESEARCH

Increasing construction research first requires a better understanding in the industry of how research takes place, from concept to implementation. Then comes futher development of institutions and sources of financing to make such research possible. Each of these is discussed in this section.

CONCEPT DEVELOPMENT DIAGRAM*

The concept development diagram in Figure 17-7 helps visualize the process by which new ideas and concepts develop and are implemented (or rejected) by the industry. Stages of development reflected in the diagram include the following:

1. *Concept Formulated*   In low use in industry, little research has been performed; little knowledge is available about the concept.

2. *Concept Researched*   In low use in industry, concept has not yet been widely accepted; however, adequate research has been performed, and adequate knowledge of the ideas has been established.

3. *Concept Innovation*   In high use in industry, concept has been widely accepted, but little formal research has been performed on the idea. Industry acceptance occurred through innovation, word of mouth, and other lines of communication.

4. *Concept Researched and Accepted*   In high use in industry, concept is in general use; adequate research has been performed on the idea. Industry

*The content of this subsection was developed by James Kopplin, a 1976–1977 graduate student at Stanford University, California.

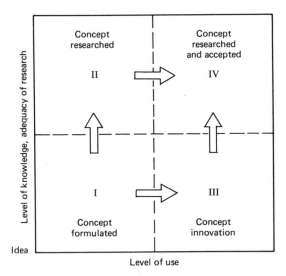

Figure 17-7   Development paths.

acceptance occurred through innovation, word of mouth, and other lines of communication.

The two basic development paths shown in Figure 17-7 are (*a*) from stage I to stage IV via stage II; or (*b*) from stage I to stage IV via stage III. Of course, not all ideas will be developed all the way to stage IV, and some drop out in various stages of the development process (i.e., idea found not feasible; concept in wide use without extensive formal research; difficulty in implementing idea into wide use by the industry, etc.).

To help visualize the process of concept development further, a reason for development or driving force will be introduced. The driving force in the vertical direction, to promote more research, could be thought of as the *potential* for cost savings or cost effectiveness. The driving force in the horizontal direction, increasing acceptance in the industry, could be *actual* cost effectiveness.

Placing filters and barriers on the diagram, as shown in Figure 17-8, helps demonstrate that there normally is not an unobstructed path for the development of an idea from concept to implementation. Example types of filters and barries include (1) Research filter (generally, only those ideas expected to be highly cost effective will be studied further in great depth); (2) risk of innovation barrier (the degree of risk for firms in starting the implemention of a concept before sufficient research has been performed to demonstrate its effectiveness); (3) technology transfer barrier (problems of awareness, communications, and approvals in getting ideas into general practice once they have been researched to a level of knowledge adequate for implementation).

INCENTIVES FOR FUNDING

As mentioned earlier, the fragmented, intensely competitive nature of construction makes it difficult to undertake industry-wide programmatic efforts such as a significant venture into research. Furthermore, construction is similar to a service industry and thus does not accumulate significant amounts of capital when compared to industries such as steel, transportation, and minerals. One sees this in comparative financial surveys such as the "Fortune 500," where, although several of construction's largest firms are listed each year on the basis of sales (cumulative annual contract awards or revenues in construction), and sometimes on the basis of profits, few, if any, are anywhere near the "top 500" on the basis of assets. Hence if a firm cannot preserve the fruits of its research innovations in the form of new processes or more efficient capital facilities, it has less incentive to invest in research. For these and other reasons, it is unlikely that the construction industry itself, whether as individual firms or in its trade associations, could invest in research on the scale found in capital-and-technology–intensive industries. A possible, but as yet largely untapped exception in this picture, is the wage-based industry advancement funds available in some areas.

Nevertheless, there are major financial incentives for investing not only in applied research in construction, but also in basic research. These days one too often hears of large projects with cost escalations measured not just in millions of dollars, but in billions. The cumulative effect of cost escalations on smaller projects is undoubtedly even greater. American ingenuity and know-how is still effectively coping with most technological problems

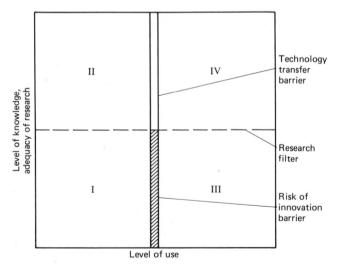

Figure 17-8   Filters and barriers.

in construction, but management and administration are too frequently inadequate in the face of larger, more complex projects, and growing demands for accountability to external organizations. If investments in research could overcome some of these difficulties and begin to pare down these billion-dollar cost increases, someone ought to benefit. It has been suggested that the consumers of construction services, in both government and private industry, ultimately should be willing to make such investments, since they and their customers will be the primary beneficiaries. Once recognized, however, there is still a quantum leap to be taken to develop effective institutions to support such research in a coordinated and productive fashion.

When thinking of government funding, it is interesting to note similarities between construction and agriculture. Both account for a very large segment of the GNP, and both are composed primarily of small businesses. Given free rein, the competitors in each are inclined to drive one another down to a marginal subsistence level. Each has also become increasingly subject to direct and indirect governmental intervention, whether through fiscal policy, regulatory agencies, special purpose legislation, or whatever. In agriculture, however, it is worth recognizing the far-reaching effects of one aspect of governmental influence, the Land Grant College Act of 1862. This, of course, is the legislation behind the numerous university-based state agricultural experiment stations. These have admirably served the cause doing research on a very high level, yet have remained conscious of the main purpose of their research: transfer to and application by farmers in their respective states and communities. For better or worse, the so-called "green revolution" is in a very great way the product of the legislation that led to agricultural experiment stations in the United States. Although times have changed and the industries certainly do have fundamental differences, similar approaches might provide corresponding advances in construction.

Given that construction is often considered the backbone of the American free enterprise system, it would seem appropriate that it avoid overdependence on and control by government, even in the support of research. In the private sector, it has been suggested that an organization such as the Business Roundtable could provide leadership in establishing a coordinated program for funding basic research in construction. Already, this organization and its predecessor, the Construction Users Anti-inflation Roundtable, have performed a highly visible role in construction. It is worth pointing out, however, that efforts involving mutual cooperation of American businesses must carefully heed restrictions imposed by antitrust legislation. Nevertheless, there is considerable potential for construction research in private industry if it can seize the initiative for its establishment and guidance. Certainly, there is much to be learned from the Japanese in this area.

Since little exists at present, specific efforts must be made to develop both the sources of funds and the organizations for evaluating proposals and administering research in construction. This chapter, however, must stop short at simply suggesting general possibilities such as those given previously. It would be worthwhile for organizations such as the Business Roundtable, NCIC, the National Institute of Building Sciences, AGC, NCA, and others to pursue this subject further.

CONCLUSION

Clearly, there are tremendous problems in costs, schedules, and productivity in the construction industry; these are tough, complex problems that are challenging some of the best professionals in the business. There will be no simple solutions; no panaceas will evolve through research. But a well-structured program of research, guided by knowledgeable and experienced people, that concentrates its finite resources on problems which are indeed of highest priority, can at least start overcoming some of the obstacles that unnecessarily drive up costs and cause delays on construction projects.

How will this all come about? The implementation of this program may be threatened by a chronic obstacle. There is a real lack of high-level leadership in the construction industry and in the professional and governmental organizations associated with it. Certainly, there are excellent managers, even true leaders, at the project and corporate levels, in some of the industry's professional and trade associations, and in the labor unions. But there are scores of these organizations even at the national level and thousands of top-notch companies, most of which are simultaneously clamoring for the things that suit their own interests best. When trying to speak to Congress or to the public at large, the voices of these organizations and companies are thus lost as waves breaking on the shore; each has its brief moment but is then drowned out by the others.

A half century ago, plans were being laid for Hoover Dam, the Golden Gate Bridge, the Empire State Building, and other structures that in their time marked quantum leaps forward in scale and complexity. Although it now sounds like a quaint anachronism, these structures were indeed considered among the man-made wonders of the world, and they provided inspiration and hope for a depression-ravaged public wondering whether the world could ever be put right again. The creators of these structures too, although not exactly household words today, were in their time well known and were respected for their courage, vision, and leadership. We still have the names of Roebling, Eads, Savage, and Strauss; these men and their contemporaries had to be men of courage and leadership to pursue their project dreams for the 20 or more years it took to gain approval and to overcome the numerous and powerful critics who said it could not be done. However, one can categorically state that there is no way the Golden Gate Bridge would have been constructed if Strauss had had to cope with today's fail-safe, lawsuit-prone climate, where failure or even the risk of failure is a sin punishable by multimillion-dollar damage assessments or even prison sentences.

In times past, leadership also involved risks; someone with a concept that could potentially be of great benefit to others still had to stick his neck out. It takes courage to innovate and persist with an idea until it achieves success. But too often today, when conformity and anonymity are cherished virtues, innovation and leadership appear to some cynics to mean foolhardy.

Nevertheless, there must be individuals and organizations willing to accept leadership responsibilities if the concepts contained in this chapter are ever to be of real value. Some of this leadership must come from individuals in congress who appreciate that there can be better ways to build construction projects in the future. Leadership must come from within government agencies and private owner groups to put meaningful policies and programs into action and from the research community to respond to the tough problems that have been identified. There must be leadership within local agencies, engineering consulting firms, and construction contractors, who ultimately are responsible for implementing the new methods that must be accepted if there is to be any progress. Leadership involves a high degree of tolerance, which is contrary to the fail-safe mind, because real progress inevitably involves setbacks, and there will be failures en route to a better way.

What are the alternatives? What are the consequences of freezing technology and procedures at a level that involves no risk? The facts were stated clearly enough in figures 17-1 and 17-2; just project the deteriorating trends documented there, and it is evident that the future holds only higher costs, longer delays, and lower productivity. These, in turn, mean that there will be fewer projects of a smaller scope, fewer cities that can plan modern public works facilities for a better future, higher taxes for less service, and a quality of life that is far less than it could be.

CHAPTER 18

HOPE AND GUIDANCE FOR THE FUTURE

Donald S. Barrie

The construction industry of today is often divided with substantial internal turmoil as the various contractors, unions, regulators, owners, industry associations, suppliers, politicians, and other factions endeavor to further their individual goals in an ever-changing domestic, national, and world environment. Yet individuals in construction as well as in all other industries continue to aspire to a higher quality of work life, and in the United States the traditional work ethic has fallen by the wayside in the wake of the increasing affluence of the work force. Yet in the final analysis the individual pride and skill that have been characteristic of the American construction worker, engineer, specialist, or manager still remain important to the individuals involved. The successful contractor, design firm, owner, intervenor, or government of the future will recognize this innate pride of craftsmanship and accomplishment and will structure the projects of the future to enable all the individual participants to achieve a pride of individual performance and growth while collectively advancing the goals of the company, industry, and nation.

Today's construction specialist has learned how to solve any functional or technical problems. Yet the overall integration of these individual solutions into a successful project or overall industry solution has failed to retain past productivity and individual pride of accomplishment under the changing conditions of today's regulated environement. Yet outstanding management teams still achieve remarkable results on finite-sized projects where individual motivation and pride are apparent at all organizational levels. For the first time in the United States purely technological advances both in larger and more productive machinery and in increasingly sophisticated planning and control systems have failed to show a corresponding increase in productivity and, in fact, have often proved counter-productive at the intermediate and large-project level.

Truly the hope for the future is management performance. Yet it must be a people-oriented management that is (1) sufficiently technically accomplished to recognize and encourage performance of all the required functional skills; (2) capable of structuring project organization and individual tasks which will benefit the individual, the group, and the enterprise; and (3) broad and skilled enough to obtain the overview necessary to supply leadership toward the achievement of practical goals in a changing and dynamic environment. At the same time the management must be equally tough minded in defining and preserving the overall integrity of the industry and the company for mutual benefit in the face of numerous nonproductive shortcuts that may prove beneficial to individual participants or owners to the overall detriment of the industry, the company, and, inevitably, the country.

The challenges of the 1980s are tremendous. Yet the largely untapped ability of the work force to solve individual problems has never held greater potential. This last chapter explores some of the ways that may prove helpful in the quest to achieve ever-increasing productivity, along with an increase in both worker satisfaction and performance without which the deterioration of our industry as we know it is inevitable.

OWNER INFLUENCES

In the long run what is good for the overall industry is good for the owner, although an individual owner's short-term project objectives may prove counterproductive to the overall industry. Progressive owners may help benefit themselves and the industry in several ways as presented next.

STRUCTURING THE OVERALL PROJECT

Future top owner-managers must become skilled in recognizing the overall organizational approaches that are most beneficial and appropriate for a particular project. Design-construct, design-manage, the fixed price contract, the cost plus general contract, CM, or the owner-management organization all have advantages and disadvantages when applied to a particular project, in a particular location, for a particular owner. Yet the choice that may preclude or enhance chances for a successful project may be made initially by nonindustry-oriented owner executives based on the hard sell, tradition, whim, or minimum managerial expenditures.

How can an owner choose the best method for a new project? Most owners do not have the benefit of many years of experience in construction management in order to acquire the mature judgment and industry knowledge that must be applied if major projects are to be initially organized in the most productive manner. Many major projects completed during the

1970s were initially organized in a manner dictated by the owner or by nonconstruction executives in a way that many knowledgeable industry professionals knew could never achieve performance comparable to expectations or in line with historical standards.

One of the most powerful ways in which owners can help both themselves and the overall industry is to try to structure the projects insofar as possible so that the marketplace determines the price and the inefficient or marginal participants are squeezed out of business, while the efficient producers are able to make a fair profit through exercise of their organizational skills and ingenuity.

Residential and Housing Construction

The housing industry has been quick to respond to supply and demand, interest rates, and the ever-increasing affluence of the homeowner. Periodically, inefficient and marginal operators fail during periods of business contraction, and even successful firms have difficulty in making reasonable profits. Yet in the inevitable expansion that has followed such shakeouts, the best-managed companies have prospered and have substantially increased profits while producing a quality product. In many ways the majority of developers and contractors are in reality acting as owners who are building for resale, and properly structured developments and individual undertakings will continue to be successful while improperly structured projects will result in failures during cyclical shakeouts characteristic of the industry.

Building and Institutional Construction

In the building, institutional, and commercial fields the owner has a wide choice of overall structure to use. The correct choice of single fixed price, negotiated general contract, CM, or design-construct will largely be a function of the individual owner's needs, the state of the economy, the qualification of the individual companies, and the sophistication of the owner. Hopefully, competitive fixed price bids on finished plans and specifications will continue to perform a substantial share of work in this area, suplemented by the other options tailored to achieve individual owner objectives. Contractors who can compete effectively in fixed price, negotiated cost reimbursable, and CM should find a considerable advantage over their colleagues who restrict their abilitites to compete to a single option.

Industrial Construction

In the industrial field, minimizing the time of construction and familiarity with process knowledge will continue to influence major owners. A trend with owners requiring design-constructors to take substantially more risk began to emerge during the latter stages of the construction boom of the late 1970s. If industrial owners continue to require fixed prices or incentive fee contracts for design-construct industrial projects and if the leading firms do, in fact, engage in price competition for as yet undesigned major projects, a substantial shakeout of the industry can be expected. Perhaps the firms that will emerge as industrial leaders in the next decade will have learned how to compete profitably as pure contractor and construction manager under competitive conditions, and as pure architect-engineer or designer in straight design competition. Then by using the same competitive skills on design-construct, accompanied by the managerial and humanistic skills now receiving recognition, they may be in the position to both outsell and outperform their competition who may choose to take lump sum design-construct risks without a cost effective design and construction staff or who will restrict their efforts to performing only cost plus contracts in a maturing economy.

Heavy Engineering construction

Heavy construction owners have almost always been able to obtain a firm price for their projects under the traditional unit price contract favored by the public nature of the major projects. The decline of major traditional new projects, such as dams, tunnels, highways, and other massive works in the lower 48 states, will be accompanied by a massive increase in the maintenance and upgrading of the highways, bridges, and other facilities that we already have. This change will include complying with increasing safety requirements for dams, tunnels, and other facilities.

Foreign work, as well as work in Canada, Alaska, and Mexico, will offer major opportunities largely using present-industry methods but with the owner or governement accepting the risks of the unknown as economic and political risks will continue to increase in a changing world. The emergence of the international joint venture will combine technologically advanced contractors or design-constructors from one country and businesswise local partners from another. Familiarity with national and local conditions will assist the achievement of organizational, technical, and businesslike implementation methods and may help to provide an answer to increasing productivity, while minimizing risks in order to better cope with public owners' traditional competitive requirements on increasingly complex projects. CM will begin to be applied to more traditional heavy construction projects both to spread the risk and achieve some of the advantages of phased construction or fast track, and heavy construction companies operating worldwide will increase their design capabilities.

The Superprojects

Superprojects with super risks will continue to offer the greatest challenge to the industry. The fixed price incentives may prove least productive in a climate of continual change and regulatory bureaucracy that will continue throughout the massive undertaking. Possible in this area the cost plus an award fee orientation or an other financial incentive plan structured to encompass the entire project and all the participants, including the craftsmen, supervisors, designers, technicians, and managers at all levels will prove more effective. Perhaps a more qualitative human-oriented evaluation of performance at all levels may have more success than the guaranteed maximum price, target man-hour concept, or other reward programs geared to finite objectives in an ever-changing fluid environment that have largely proved ineffective.

At the time of this writing it is fashionable to predict the demise of nuclear fission as a viable source of energy in the future. On the other hand the Moslem world is in ferment, and dependence on foreign fossil fuel is clearly very hazardous and at best is only a short-term solution. In spite of all the problems, failures, hazards, and economic overruns associated with the nuclear power industry, the following summary of overall economics of fuel costs* indicates that we must find a way to develop nuclear power in a better and more acceptable manner or face substantial major adjustments in our way or life.

	Total cost/kwh		Fuel cost/kwh	
	1978	1977	1978	1977
Nuclear plant	1.5¢	1.5¢	0.3¢	0.3¢
Oil fired plant	4.0¢	3.9¢	2.4¢	2.3¢
Coal fired plant	2.3¢	2.0¢	1.3¢	1.1¢

One important lesson has been learned from the superprojects, whether they were built cost plus, fixed price, CM, or design-construction. None of the traditional methods have shown satisfactory performance when numerous changes and revisions have been interposed on the on-site work. Manager, craftsmen, designers, and even the regulators have all suffered a frustration, helplessness, and loss of sense of purpose that is evident in the productivity studies which show individual functional performance for measurable items of about one-third of that possible on well-run, more finite projects. The superproject owner of the future must find a way to eliminate or greatly minimize the continual changes that have been apparent in major schedule and cost overruns commensurate with the loss of efficiencies at all functional levels. Maybe we can actually speed completion and minimize cost overruns by taking several years to thoroughly plan the overall project and thoroughly detail the work one year or more ahead of actual construction. Possibly, the future owner who eliminates the frustration due to constant change will find that not only are overruns smaller but that the actual overall design-construction period may be significantly shortened as well.

OPEN SHOP

Owners are increasingly giving consideration to open shop projects in areas that heretofore have been traditionally building trades oriented. Many of

*Handy Facts and Figures, Atomic Industrial Forum, Inc., April 1979.

the major owners are aggressively choosing to affirmatively select open shop contractors, and in other areas this trend has motivated concessions to established practice on the part of the building trades. The growth of the ABC's merit shop program is accelerating the trend by supplying specialty contractors, competition, manpower training, and management assistance to open shop contractors. AGC's open shop component is growing each year, and many more contractors are structuring their companies to be able to go double breasted and compete in both closed and open shop projects.

As the trend toward open shop continues, more and more resources will be available, and the owner will be able to select from the full range of organizational methods available with the assurance of substantial competition among industry contractors.

OWNER-BUILDERS AND OWNER-MANAGERS

Looking backward the promise of the owner-builder has largely been unfulfilled, and few major owners today believe that they can perform construction work with their own in-house forces in a manner that is economically sound; yet many owners believe that they can be their own manager. Many superprojects currently feature either an integrated organization with the owner's top management in important positions or a duplicate team of owner-manager employees to oversee the construction manager, designer, or general contractor. Since the owner has the money, he makes the rules, and there will always be several firms that will supply managers and technical personnel to work under the owner's overall direction.

The business of the large industrial or utility project owner is not construction. The initial performances of the integrated owner-led protect team or the duplicate owner management organization are not sufficiently promising to predict that overall management by nonconstruction personnel in a noncompetitive cost reimbursable environment will prove economically viable in the future any more than it has in the past. Yet the construction industry must improve performance, or the trend toward owner management will continue.

CONTRACTOR INFLUENCES

Individual contractors must assess both the short term and the long term if they are to survive in the future's rapidly changing construction environment. No one can predict the future, but the successful contractor will recognize that the industry must achieve performance with increasing productivity if individual companies are to continue to prosper and grow. Each of the basic divisions of the industry will be faced with new problems. Inside each of these divisions the very large contractor will have different problems from those of very small. Yet both contractors will share several common problems for which common solutions may help industrywide. Similarly, each of the divisions will have problems peculiar to that division, but overall each segment will face problems common to other divisions. Each of the individual contributors has reviewed the present state of the art, pointing out problems and potential solutions. This section and the remaining portion of this chapter endeavors to discuss these and other possible directions that can aid performance in all components of the overall construction industry and are of interest to each.

THE MANAGEMENT GAP

In the past construction managerial and supervisory personnel developed from promotion of successful individuals who had many years of solid job-site experience in supervising the building trades. A technical education was not necessary, but the understanding of craft skills and the individual viewpoint of the workers and their relationship with the unions was essential if performance were to be achieved. And in the "good old days" performance was usually a prerequisite for promotion.

The successful manager and supervisor at all levels of the business came up through the functional route, knew his subordinates jobs, and generally demanded "a day's work for a day's pay" as a matter of pride in keeping with industry practice. This spirit of pride in performance was personified in the traditional general and specialty contractor through the individuals who were responsible for the company performance. As owners began to demand shorter design-construct periods and as inflation and interest rates began to reach double-digit figures, management technology became fashionable in the industry. CPM became fashionable, and projects were planned in a highly theoretical program designed to allow construction to proceed simultaneously with design. Suddenly, engineers and technicians were developing overall programs for managing the work. Construction Management offered the opportunity to avoid cost plus while still achieving substantial time savings while preserving the fixed price concept using several lump sum bid packages in a phased or fast track construction program.

Suddenly, a new breed of manager began to be apparent. He was the individual with an engineering education, who could comprehend the critical path diagram, and who could communicate with the new computerized management methods that developed during the management boom; yet he took for granted without really understanding the on-site functional craft skills that represented the foundation of the industry. The old-time "construction stiff" could not survive the managerial entry requirements in the critical path age developed during the management boom. Yet the engineers and technicians supported by the computer have not been able with all their sophisticated controls to manage and effectively control the performance at the crew level that was paramount and largely taken for granted during the development of the construction industry in the United States.

Neither the old-line craftsman who ultimately prospered to develop his own construction company through dedication, hard work, and luck nor the highly educated construction engineer of today skilled in the use of integrated cost and progress control systems and in the development of sophisticated computer-controlled programs has proved effective in realizing by themselves the potential of the management boom.

Tomorrow's successful companies will recognize that it takes both skills, supplemented by managerial and humanistic knowledge. One successful construction mangement program initiated in the early 1970s with a compound growth rate of over 20% per year recruits its budding young managers from bachelor's and master's degree recipients at several major universities specializing in a construction program at the graduate level. Yet this company prefers candidates who have worked summers on construction projects to help finance their way through school. Craftsmen are preferred, but other on-the-job experience is acceptable. Other potential managers are chosen where possible from those who have both educational qualifications and craft experience. Coupled with this program is a similar outlook that identifies outstanding craft supervisors with growth capacity who are given increasingly challenging management responsibilities, along with an opportunity to learn management and motivational skills.

The companies of the future that obtain or groom managers who are able to talk and understand the language of the skilled craftsman, the language of the engineer, and the language of the manager will prove to be the survivors in an era of increasing challenge to all main industry participants to acquire the overall management viewpoint necessary to cope with an ever-changing and increasingly complex construction environment.

THE CONTRACTORS THEMSELVES

Today's contractors obviously have the greatest incentive of any industry group to improve their performance through better management, enlightened leadership, and developing a mutually beneficial rapport with the work force. Some of the items that could help both the contractors and the industry to achieve improved performance are reviewed next.

Housing and Residential Contractors

Prefabrication and shop fabrication have proved successful in the mobile home area. The trend toward multiple dwellings such as semidetached houses, condominiums, and town houses may offer a renewed opportunity for prefabrication and shop fabrication in the home building industry. The importance of energy conservation will also serve to introduce additional sophistication and opportunities for prefabrication. With more multiple dwellings, the economies of scale and increased productivity due to prefabrication may well offer a dramatic opportunity to reduce unit dwelling costs for the innovative contractor. However, this trend will require considerably more capital, management skills, and business knowledge that has not been posessed by the numerous small contractors operating in the residential market for single homes. Therefore, the sucessful future mass marketing firm will have to adopt many of the managerial skills as well as technical and control requirements common to those who will be successful in other branches of the industry. The successful firms in the future will retain their functional skills now required to construct single-family dwellings but will improve productivity and customer value through manufacturing methods that will minimize the on-site labor requirements while achieving economies of scale and application of value engineering principles for the prefabricated components.

The young couples of the future will not be denied an opportunity for their own home. However, the future family will probably share common walls, facilities, and grounds with their neighbors in innovative ways that will preserve their privacy, minimize land usage per individual, and be designed to take advantage of mass-production techniques.

The traditional stick built home will continue to survive in the custom home market, in smaller multiple residence developments, and in outlying areas. Maintenance, restoration, and remodeling in the suburbs and the central city, along with subcontracting roles on larger developments should provide ample opportunity for the large number of individual entrepreneurs and small businessmen and minority-owned businesses in the future marketplance.

Building, Institutional, and Commercial Construction

This traditional sector of the industry should continue to offer significant oportunities to the small businessman, the craftsman entrepreneur, and to the moderate-sized general and specialty contractor. The traditional architect-designed, competitive bid single general contract will continue to be a major force sharing billing on the larger projects with a professional construction management, owner developer, or CM approach. Architects, general contractors, design-constructors, and pure construction managers will compete for future work, and the most innovative and productive firms will prosper. The survival of the fittest will continue to weed out those individuals and firms unable to prepare realistic bids and schedules and perform accordingly in a largely fixed price environment.

With the exception of some of the very largest projects the traditional functional approach has proved very effective, and overly sophisticated management tools have neither really been needed nor have they been adopted by the most successful firms. The fact that these functional and

individual skills have not been equally successful on superprojects in no
way minimizes their effectiveness in the majority of work performed in this
category.

Regional firms will perform essentially all the work within their area.
And even national firms operating in this sector will probably find that
regional affiliates or subcontractors who are thoroughly similiar with the
local environment will be necessary for suvival in a largely price competitive atmosphere.

Industrial Construction

This section of the industry will continue to show wide variation between
the productivity obtained on smaller- or medium-sized, well planned projects and the superprojects. The preponderance of work will continue to be
performed by the design-constructor acting as design-manager using local
or the regional contractors to perform the actual work, although significant
overall amounts will be performed by regional contractors under the traditional single contract or multiple contract CM approach. Perhaps the problems of the major design-construction companies in achieving overall project productivity that approaches that attainable by the regional contractor
on moderate-sized work is the greatest challenge to the future design-construction companies. The future survivors will be the companies that can
best meet this challenge so that the superproject performance records will
bear some reasonable resemblance to the original program.

The successful design-constructor of the future must develop broad
guage managers. He must also find the way to encourage individual motivation through recognition and growth so that each level of the operation is
able to achieve a pride of performance in individual and group accomplishment that is still prevalent in the well-run traditional project in the building, institutional, commercial, or light or medium industrial project.

The most successful design-constructors of the future will be judged
more for their performance than from their promises. The matrix organization will be adopted by the progressive firms that will combine the functional skills of the traditional general and specialty contractor approach
with the team project orientation now favored by most of the major design-constructor firms. Figure 18-1 shows alternatives of managerial power
distribution for individual project and overall functional authority. The
pure functional approach has proved ineffective on the superproject. However, the task force approach has been equally ineffective. A balanced matrix organization that preserves a balance of power will be difficult to install
and maintain but could prove extremely rewarding for the industry leaders
who have the courage to review and understand the present and past problems of the superproject.

Perhaps the most promising overall organizational structure for tomorrow's most profitable design-constructors in the *Engineering News-Record's* top 400 will combine the functional skills with project responsibility

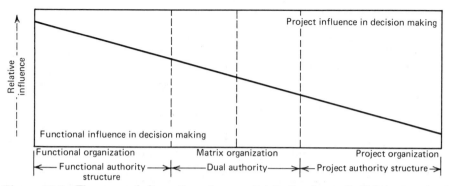

Figure 18-1   The range of alternatives of power distribution for project versus functional authority. Reprinted from *Project Management Quarterly*, Vol. X, No. 2, June 1979.

in a manner shown in Figure 18-2. A separate construction division will compete with contractors for construction and CM projects on a competitively bid and negotiated basis. A separate design division will compete in a similar manner for architectural-engineering services and straight design services with other engineers and designers. The ability to compete successfully in these functional skills will insure the continuing quality and competitiveness of both the design and construction services as judged by the impartial marketplace and the bottom line. The project management division will be responsible for the sales and management of turnkey projects that will be the firm's primary business. It will be able to set up task forces on major projects that will still benefit from the functional knowledge of the overall firm in setting up, planning, and staffing new projects. It can choose between a functional, line and staff, or matrix organization at the individual job level and develop broad gauge managers at every level who have an appreciation and respect for the functional skills necessary for a successful project. The top managers can become people-oriented individuals with a major emphasis on interrelated communications at every level of the work force from craftsman to the client's management. Such an organization, with appropriate leadership at the top, would be organizationally capable of welding together the promises of the management boom and the increasingly humanistic or people-oriented approach to productivity now beginning to show promising results. Such a union while preserving the functional skills could truly represent the management performance that must replace the promises if major industrial projects and a sizable share of the construction industry are to continue productive growth under changing and demanding conditions not subject to prior determination.

Heavy Engineering Construction

The future for heavy construction companies will continue to be heavily influenced by the functional skills and the ability to predict costs in an

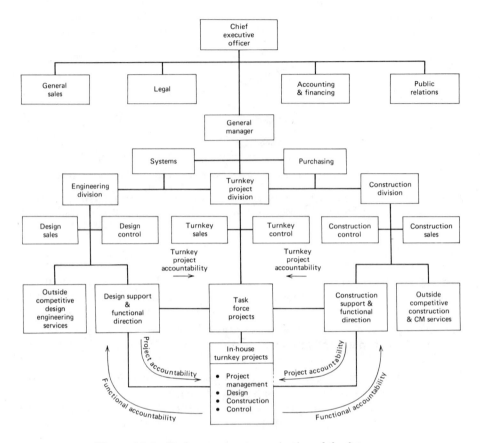

Figure 18-2   Design-construct organization of the future.

ever-changing environment. The successful large companies of the future will broaden their role to include design services and even turnkey operations as the market for large projects continues to be available in the remote areas of North America and South America and in the developing countries. This merging of the rolls of design and construction will produce more negotiated contracts in view of the major financial risks that must largely be assumed at the governmental level.

A people-oriented approach featuring communications, understanding, and respect between managers at all levels of the work force will be increasingly important to the heavy construction companies as major work continues to be found overseas in remote regions of the developing countries. The dual accomplishments of the individual engineer as set forth in *The Ugly American** who completed needed technological improvements within the cultural and normal working practices of the developing country must be achieved on a project and company level if American companies are to

*Lederer, Wm. J. and Eugene Burdick, Norton, 1958.

succeed and prosper in an increasingly hostile environment found in the rapidly developing countries.

For the heavy construction industry to continue to grow, it is, of course, necessary for the individual companies to grow and prosper. The successful firms will find a better way to solve the individual employee problems of relocating, often to a different culture. Government tax policies inhibiting overseas growth must be replaced by more far-seeing policies designed to place American companies on a par with their foreign and multinational competition. Continuing employment and opportuntiy for all employees to achieve promotion and recognition within the company will become important as benefits such as health and accident insurance, life insurance, retirement benefits, and opportunities for vocational and management training become more significant to the individual with each passing year. Perhaps our heavy construction industry will approach the Japanese system where most individuals expect to work long years or even for a lifetime for a single company and are able to maintain a climate of progressive and high internal morale throughout the working years.

Many of the organizational and managerial requirements of the heavy construction company of the future will parallel the discussion on super-projects in the industrial sector. In the past many major companies operated both in the heavy construction sector and the industrial area. In the future on major overseas projects it is anticipated that the line between heavy engineering construction and industrial construction, especially on overseas projects, will become less distinct and the two divisions will tend to merge with like objectives and managerial requirements if future success is achieved in terms beneficial to the United States, to the foreign country involved, to the companies associated in the project, and most of all to the individuals associated with the project who must benefit if the overall industry is to survive.

THE WORK FORCE

The work force includes the craft workers, the foremen, and superintendents; the draftsmen, designers, and discipline engineer; the specialists, including estimators, schedulers, and control engineers; the support group, including legal, procurement, labor relations, public relations, accounting, and other staff members; and the managers at every level who hold the key to future industry growth and prosperity in their ability to put together all the individual disciplines and tasks necessary to complete projects in a productive manner.

THE SKILLED CRAFTSMAN

At present the craft unions are clearly on the downgrade. With the changing economic pattern in the United States, coupled with the retirement of

George Meany in 1979, the influence of the building trades in overall AFL-CIO policies will deteriorate and lobbying effectiveness will become more oriented to the manufacturing, services, and government employee areas. Open shop and its principal spokesman Merit Shop continues to capture a larger share of the available market annually.

Yet history has a way of repeating itself. There were many advantages of the craft unions to the individual, the contractor, and the overall industry. As the open shop sector expands and as the traditional craft unions lose much of their power, it appears that many of the individual needs that led to unionization will be unfulfilled and open shop may find the emergence of ferment and discontent when meaningful competition with union craft organizations for available skilled manpower is minimized or eliminated.

In the more distant future the emergency of an industrial type union organization for construction seems to offer considerable promise. Apprentice programs could be structured to train basic skills, while advancement by all members of the work force would be possible through the acquisition of all the traditional craft skills. Thus a journeyman qualified to perform basic skills of both an electrician and a pipe fitter, for example, could be paid more money and given more responsibility through the supervision of several helpers and trainees of various levels. In fact, the old District 50 Construction Union developed by the United Mineworkers in the 1950s showed considerable promise before internal union problems handicapped its further constructive development. With such an industrial type union, both open shop and unions could serve to act as a check and balance on each other without recourse to many of the archaic and counterproductive traditions that persist in many craft union relationships long after the need for their solidarity has passed.

MATERIAL AND EQUIPMENT SUPPLIERS

One of the major interface problems between the suppliers and the contractor is the quality of the product and the actual delivery compared to quoted delivery. Both manufacturing and construction companies have remarkably similar problems with the work force at all levels that have resulted in deteriorating quality and performance in the final construction product. Automation on the assembly line has reached its peak in the manufacturing industries. Yet the final product in too many cases does not reflect the pride of the craftsman to the extent that minor flaws within the control of the worker are remedied before major problems occur. The ability of pure technology to further automate the manufacturing process without regard to the quality of work life for the worker has become suspect. In this regard both construction and the manufacturing industries share a common problem. Possibly, some of the programs and studies and actual experiments on the quality of work life now being pioneered in a manufacturing environment could have similar application in construction if successful.

ARCHITECTS, ENGINEERS, AND TECHNICIANS

As in the many other branches of the industry, the designers are becoming more fragmented and less knowledgeable about actual construction practice and economy. A designer or draftsman may never visit a construction job and may not have any practical guidance to create a design that is functional, economical, and socially acceptable.

Traditional value engineering, with its review of a completed design, has been ineffective in the commercial sector, in part, due to the time delays associated with redesign and the resentment of criticism on the part of the designer by outsiders. In past decades design for economy of materials and design to basic rules of thumb were cost effective. However, in today's unsettled climate methods effective in one part of the country or the world are counterproductive in other areas.

The successful designer of the future will learn how to benefit from construction cost knowledge at the conceptual stage in an organized manner within the professional guidelines of the profession. Both engineering and construction management and professionals will benefit from setting joint economic goals in project design and working together to achieve success in a way that benefits each.

Yet in another context many leaders are questioning the ability of efficient design to solve what are essentially social problems involving human relationships. Eugene S. Ferguson is quoted in an article "Have Engineers Gone Too Far" in the *Chicago Tribune*: "When an engineering project goes sour from a social standpoint, the trouble is often in the engineer's absorption in the technical aspects of the project and his forgetting or misjudging the human dimensions.

"Yet it is precisely these human aspects that have become of concern. Instead of massive, centrally controlled systems, some of us are now calling for simpler solutions on a human scale. We want to see more solutions that fit the problems.

"Social problems can have social solutions, which usually require discussion and compromise. Unless we insist upon this, we can expect technological solutions to all problems because they are easiest to devise."

CONSTRUCTION MANAGEMENT

Construction management in the future must bridge the widening gap between all the complex interfaces present on a construction project. The designer, lawyer, accountant, schedular, estimator, owner, subcontractor, craftsman, intervenor, regulator, and many others are all necessary for technological solutions to particular problems and for initial plans and programs to enable the manager to control the project. Yet the summation of individual incremental solutions or programs will not by itself create an effective overall plan or program for the project. Each discipline impinges on others, and the effective final plan is often a compromise between individual components to permit an overall combination into an effective program that will achieve the overall project objectives (performance) rather than achieve individual optimization of individual parts.

The ability to perform in the foregoing manner will separate the successful managers of the future from their more traditional associates. The future of the construction industry in the United States is truly in the hands of the managers. Yet the managers must forge together overall projects that can achieve the social solution and preserve the economic and technological excellence which has characterized the industry and which will contribute to the pride of performance and quality of work life for each individual or group of individuals associated with the program.

OTHER INFLUENCES

Remaining influences on the future direction of the construction industry include legal and contractual considerations, federal financing and government regulations, owner and employer organizations, research and development, women and ethnic minorities, and education and training. These influences are discussed next.

LEGAL AND CONTRACTUAL CONSIDERATIONS

Legal and contractual requirement continue to proliferate. In fact, the terms and conditions and regulatory requirements associated with many bid packages today often occupy more space than the technical information necessary to prepare the proposal. A medium-sized city of 10 years ago could print all its laws in a single volume. Today, it may require 10 volumes.

In opening areas of the world such as China no formal legal system exists. It will be obviously impossible to inflict our legal system on the Chinese. Yet some basis for international dealings must be preserved in developing the legal and administrative requirements for contracts and for an administrative team to manage them and to adjudicate differences of opinion.

The future dealings with developing countries without an entrenched and codified legal system offer an outstanding opportunity to simplify legal and contractual considerations in an equitable manner that could have significant benefit toward fostering a similar movement in our own country.

FEDERAL FINANCING AND GOVERNMENT REGULATIONS

Governmental regulations continue to make it difficult or impossible to bring major public and private projects through planned, orderly, and uninterrupted phases to completion and operation. Federal financing on ma-

jor projects is dictating methods requiring bureaucratic red tape that
threatens to destroy productivity in the very areas which need the most
improvement. In the case of NRC, the average nuclear power plant since
inception has exceeded initial estimates by 300% due largely to ever-increasing regulatory technical and administrative requirements throughout
the construction period. Perception of this trend by major utilities appears
to threaten the viability of future nuclear plants irrespective of operating
and social consequences developed from the Three Mile Island accident.

All areas of American life, including the construction industry, are being
constrained by big government. Government financing brings government
control by bureacrats and adds a new constraint on major projects that is
largely outside the control of the industry. A way must be found to achieve
the social responsibilities and environmental objectives that led to the creation of the government regulators without the counterproductive red tape
and administrative regulations which have proved counterproductive on
most major projects. Perhaps the very survival of the United States depends on our reversing the trend toward increasing government control
and regulation over all walks of life that has clearly failed the performance
test.

Policemen and firemen strike for higher wages. The Bart mass transit
workers in San Francisco stage sit-in, vandalize trains,and strike in order to
achieve their wage objectives, and our largest city is paralysed by the 11-
day New York transit strike.

This area of concern does not appear to have a technical or engineering
solution. Yet a social solution equitable to all must be developed or the
future of all industries and continual social progress in the United States
appears to be prejudiced. Perhaps some new incentives for industry self-
regulation could prove effective.

Owner and Employer Organizations

Perhaps a way in which the construction industry can help is to use the
existing format of owner and employer associations in an effort to help
minimize federal control through promoting and fostering achievement of
social and regulatory objectives through internal industry control. Yet to
be effective these associations must eliminate the fear of antitrust viola-
tions and the internal strife and fragmentation that have prevented them
from acting as an effective lobbying or leadership force which must be
achieved if the governmental dominance is to be reversed.

RESEARCH AND DEVELOPMENT

Inflation in construction has been substantially in excess of the U.S. economy as a whole. Productivity has stagnated on the larger projects, and the

implementation of innovative solutions have been severely handicapped by liability risks and governmental regulations. It appears that technology by itself will not reverse these discouraging trends.

What we need is broad gauge leadership at all levels of the industry, but especially in the associated professional and governmental organizations. We need to recognize the real underlying social and economic problems and to develop positive industry programs to eliminate detrimental factors of regulation, declining productivity, and constraints affecting workable solutions that seem to be outside industry control.

Perhaps the fundamental research problem is: How can the industry organize to recapture control over its own destiny while adopting the social and environmental objectives of the federal government; how can we develop a program to achieve the social and environmental objectives of all the people of the United States and at the same time regain the opportunity to enhance our individual, company, and industry productive future.

Women and Ethnic Minorities

Simple mandating of the use of minority workers, including women, in the work force has been important in the achievement or near achievement of social goals fundamental to the Constitution of the United States. The challenge of the future will be to continue to further these goals, but at a program of accomplishment designed to actually increase productivity. We must achieve the social objectives that our way of life requires. Yet if we can achieve these objectives in a way that actually boosts productivity, we will have created even more opportunities for further social gains to the overall betterment of the entire country.

EDUCATION AND TRAINING

Education and training for the future must continue to enhance and develop the functional and technological skills necessary for any construction project. Yet increasingly we need to develop managers who can communicate between skills in order to tie the functional disciplines into an effective whole. We need to teach human skills so that the needs of the individual are met in a climate that also benefits the company and the industry. Pure technology and engineering skill and management have failed to achieve the social and environmental objectives of today's society. Similarly, the humanistic approaches of the social scientist, the intervenor, and the regulator have failed to be either cost or socially effective as evidenced by the deteriorating productivity and unrest in the work force.

Future managers in the construction industry must be sufficiently educated in functional skills to be able to communicate with the work force. They must be equally knowledgeable regarding social and environmental objectives and the reasons behind their desirability. They must have a belief in the individual and a desire to understand that individual's objectives and company objectives must be complimentary in a way which will be of benefit to both as well as to the industry. Equipped with all the foregoing skills, the future manager must understand management practices and techniques that will assist him in his overall task.

CONCLUSION

This book, like all others about the construction industry, is largely about technology and the state of the art in the functional management of construction projects. These methods have worked well for finite-sized and traditional projects in the past. Increasing, size, complexity, overlapping of design and construction, continual change, introduction of outside regulation, and other constraints will continue to handicap the construction project of the future. Successful construction managers must develop humanistic skills and organizational capabilities so that all members of the construction industry can be helped to cope successfully with the everyday problems of interaction which are best handled at their individual level.

As in the everyday construction world the presentation of appropriate managerial behavior in this book has lagged behind the technical development of management systems and individual functional controls. It is not surprising that managers, engineers, and technicians in the construction industry are reluctant to deal with the vagaries of motivation. The traditional builder has been a master of the concrete and the tangible and has great difficulty in dealing realistically and effectively with such intangibles. Yet managers who are unable to deal effectively with people are the primary cause of inefficiencies in the present-day construction environment. Competent and enthusiastic leaders are the dynamic force which will determine the success of any organization in the fluid atmosphere that is destined in the future.

Figure 18-3 illustrates a total system for managing by objectives, offering an opportunity to turn problems into benefits at any organizational level. Figure 18-4 illustrates a cyber-climate for results featuring organizational development.

Perhaps the major challenge of the future is to find a more effective use of human resources in industry. "The manager of the future will be unable to focus his attention narrowly on productivity. He will be expected to espouse purposes that are rooted in philosophy. He will be required to give specific attention to interpersonal relationships, not only between managers and subordinates but among managers themselves. His practice, while guided by management principles, will be saturated by human understanding. His art will reflect a dedication to duty and a perception of the way his

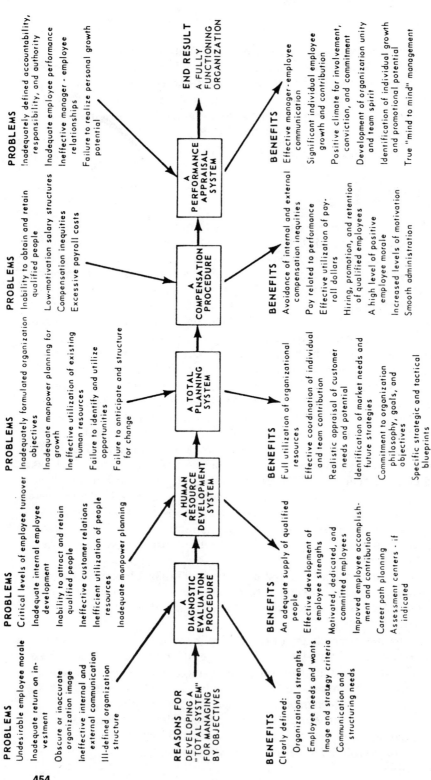

Figure 18-3 Organizational developments, a total system for managing by objectives. From Joe D. Batten, *Tough-Minded Management*, American Management Association, AMACOM, New York, 1978.

454

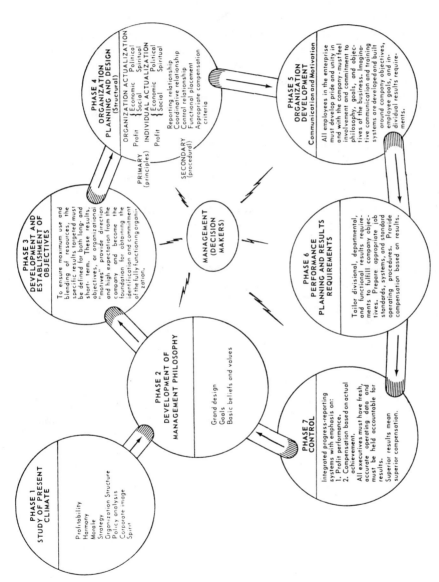

Figure 18-4 The cyber-climate for results (organizational developments). From Joe D. Batten, *Tough-Minded Management*, American Management Association, AMACOM, New York, 1978.

personal efforts should be expended. Both the manager and his team will be concerned about bridging the gap between capabilities and responsibilities. The manager of tomorrow will be increasingly concerned about his ability to satisfy the multifarious demands that inevitably fall upon those who manage."*

In reality this concentration on motivation and human values is nothing new in the construction industry. Men like Henry Kaiser, Steve Bechtel, Guy Atkinson, Henry Morrison, Lou Perini, Pete Kiewit, and others turned such values into the creation of solid organizations that delivered top performance in the heavy-growth years of our country. The personal dynamic leadership of these men stamped an imprint in their surviving companies that often still remains.

Yet in tomorrow's climate, the man at the top cannot stimulate and motivate the overall organization except through his managers at every level from foreman to company president. The successful organization of the future will put it all together with tough-minded, results-oriented managers who realize that people can both help themselves and their organization for mutual gain. Such an organization, equipped with all the technical concepts and tools developed in the management booms will be successful in any future environment, and the time for management performance will have arrived.†

---

*This paragraph as well as several ideas expressed in this section is from *Manager for Tomorrow*, published by the New American Library, New York, 1967, Pg. 19
†The concept of tough minded management as well as additional thoughts set forth in this chapter is from Joe D. Batten, Tough-Minded Management, AMACON, New York, 1978

BIBLIOGRAPHY

CHAPTER 1

Barrie, Donald S. and Boyd C. Paulson, Jr., *Professional Construction Management*, McGraw-Hill New York, 1978.

Drucker, Peter F., *Management*, Harper and Row, New York, 1974.

CHAPTER 2

Barrie, Donald S. and Boyd C. Paulson, Jr., *Professional Construction Management*, McGraw-Hill, New York, 1978.

Drucker, Peter F., *Management*, Harper and Rowe, New York, 1974.

Keener, Donald F., *Managerial Functions, Responsibilities, and the Team Approach from Effective Project Management Techniques*, American Society of Civil Engineers, New York, 1973.

Kettle, Kenath A., *Project Delivery Systems for Construction Projects*, Journal of the Construction Division, ASCE, Vol. 102, No. CO4, December 1976.

CHAPTER 3

Barrie, Donald S. and Boyd C. Paulson, Jr., *Professional Construction Management*, McGraw-Hill, New York, 1978.

Kaiser Builder, *Foothill Electric Corporation*, summer 1979, Kaiser Engineers, Inc., Oakland, California.

Professional Managers Guide, Fourth Edition, Louis A. Allen Associates, Inc., 1969.

Project Management Institute, *State of the Art Series*, Northern California Chapter, San Francisco, 1978.

CHAPTER 4

Borcherding, John D., *Improving Productivity in Industrial Construction*, Journal of the Construction Division, ASCE, Vol. 102, No. CO4, December 1976.

Cherry, Mike, *On High Steel*, Ballantine, New York, 1974.

Cockshaw, Peter A., *Employers Must Regain their Right to Manage before Productivity can Improve*, Plant Facilities, November/December 1977.

Planning, Engineering, and Constructing the Super Projects, Proceedings of the Engineering Foundation Research Conference, Pacific Grove, California, ASCE, New York, 1978.

CHAPTER 5

Cost Study Standard Quality Single Family Residence, Appraisal Department, Bank of America, San Francisco, California.

Mayer, Martin, *The Builders*, W. W. Norton, New York, 1978.

McGowan, Thomas F., *Building and Marketing Energy Conserving Homes*, Preprint 3607, ASCE Convention, Atlanta, Georgia, October 1979.

The Downturn in the Housing Industry is More Real Than Has Been Perceived, Los Angeles Times, March 4, 1979.

CHAPTER 6

Architects Handbook of Professional Practice, The American Institute of Architects, 1735 New York Avenue, N.W., Washington, D.D. 20006.

Building Construction Contracting Methods, The Associated General Contractors of America, 1957 E Street, N.W., Washington, D.C. 20006.

CM for the General Contractor—A Guide Manual for Construction Management, The Associated General Contractors of America, 1957 E Street, N.W., Washington, D.C. 20006.

GSA System for Construction Management, General Services Administration, 18th and F Streets, N.W., Washington, D.C. 20405.

Handbook of Construction Techniques, McGraw-Hill Construction Contracting, 1221 Avenue of the Americas, New York, New York 10020.

Using Construction Management for Public and Institutional Facilities, Public Technology Inc., 1140 Connecticut Avenue, N.W., Washington, D.C. 20036.

CHAPTER 7

Barrie, Donald S. and Boyd C. Paulson, Jr., *Professional Construction Management*, McGraw-Hill, New York, 1978.

Burch, Gilbert, *A Time for Reckoning for the Building Unions*, Fortune, June 4, 1979.

Planning, Engineering and Constructing the Super Projects, Proceedings of the Engineering Foundation Research Conference, Pacific Grove, California, ASCE, New York, 1978.

Sider, Don, *The Big Boondoggle at Lordstown*, Fortune, September 1969, New York.

CHAPTER 8

Frein, Joseph P., Editor, *Handbook of Construction Management and Organization*, Second Edition, Van Nostrand Reinhold, New York, 1980.

Parker, Albert D., *Planning and Estimating Underground Construction*, McGraw-Hill, New York, 1970.

Parker, Albert D., *Planning and Estimating Dam Construction*, McGraw-Hill, New York, 1972.

Stubbs, Frank W., Jr., *Handbook or Heavy Construction*, McGraw-Hill, New York.

CHAPTER 9

Compressed Air: 100 Years of Industrial Progress, Air Comments, Vol. II, No. 4, December 1973.

Jantid, Ingvar, *The Swedish Method,* reprint from DAEDALUS, 1963 Transactions of the Swedish Museum of Science and Technology, Stockholm.

Probing the Future, Engineering News-Record, Centennial issue, April 30, 1974.

CHAPTER 10

Aldridge, Wayne, Business Representative of United Brotherhood of Carpenters and Joiners of America, *Interview*, July 1979.

A Study on Unions' Influence on Management's Rights, Unpublished Report, Department of Architectural Engineering, University of Texas at Austin, 1979.

Blum, Albert A., *A History of the American Labor Movement*, American Historical Association, Washington, D.C. 1972.

Burch, Gilbert, *A Time of Reckoning for the Building Unions*, Fortune, June 1979.

Clough, Richard H., *Construction Contracting*, 3rd Edition, Wiley, New York, 1975.

Constitution and Laws of the United Brotherhood of Carpenters and Joiners of America, January 1979.

Construction Craft Jurisdiction Agreements, The Bureau of National Affairs, Inc., Washington, D.C.

Crittenden, Ann, *Jane Fonda chooses Working Woman's Pay as her Next Campaign*, New York Times News Service, July 22, 1979.

Estey, Marten, *The Union's Structure, Development, and Management 2nd Edition*, Harcourt Brace Jovanovich, New York, 1976.

Falcone, Nicholas S., *Labor Law*, Wiley, New York, 1962.

Female Hiring Goals Elusive, Engineering News Record, June 7, 1979.

Flanagan, Robert, *American Unions Face 1980*, Stanford, California, 1979.

GAO Blasts *Minority Hiring*, Engineering News Record, March 29, 1979.

Grimm, C. T., *Estimating Masonry Wall and Column Costs*, Journal of the Construction Division, ASCE, Vol. 103, No. CO4, December 1977.

Joyce, John T., *Non-Union Construction--Wave of the Future, or Numbers Game?*, Excerpts from Seminar of Brick-layers and Allied Craftsmen, July 1977.

Nelson, Larry, President of Nelson Construction Company, Austin, Texas, *Interview*, July 1979.

Northrup, Herbert R., and Howard G. Foster, *Open Shop Construction*, The University of Pennsylvania, 1975.

Supreme Court Upholds Affirmative Action, Engineering News Record, July 5, 1979.

The Labor Story, Texas AFL-CIO, Austin, Texas, 1977.

This is the AFL-CIO, Publication No. 20, American Federation of Labor and Congress of Industrial Organizations, Washington, D.C., March 1978.

This is the Texas AFL-CIO, Texas AFL-CIO, Austin, Texas, 1979.

Turner Says Media Trample Unions, Engineering News Record, June 7, 1979, McGraw-Hill, New York, 1979.

Willenbrook, Jack H., *The Effect of Contractual and Non-Contractual Practices on Productivity*, Power Plant Construction -- Education and Research Needs, Chapter 8, Keynote address 1, Pennsylvania State University, University Park, Pa., June 1977.

CHAPTER II

Bourdon, C., and R. E. Levitt, *Union and Open Shop Construction*, Lexington Books, Lexington, Mass., 1980.

Mooney, B., *Builders for Progress*, McGraw-Hill, New York, 1965.

Steffens, J.L., *The Shame of the Cities*, McClure Phillips, New York, 1905.

CHAPTER 12

Borcherding, J., *Improving Productivity in Industrial Construction by Effective Management of Human Resources*, Project Management Institute Proceedings, Montreal, Quebec, Canada, 1976, pp. 87-98.

Bourdon, C. C., and R. E. Levitt, *A Comparison of Wages and Labor Management Practices in Union and Non-Union Construction*, M.I.T. Research Report No. R78-10, Massachusetts Institute of Technology, Cambridge, Mass., June 1, 1978.

Burch, Gilbert, *A Time of Reckoning for the Building Unions*, Fortune, June 4, 1979.

Levitt, R. E., *Union vs. Non-Union Construction in the U.S*, Journal of the Construction Division, ASCE, December 1979, Proc. Paper No. 15020.

Levitt, R. E., and C. C. Bourdon, *Cost Impacts of Prevailing Wage Laws in Construction*, Journal of the Construction Division, ASCE, Vol. 105, No. CO4, Proc. Paper 15019, December 1979, pp. 281-288.

Logcher, R. and W. Collins, *Management Impacts on Labor Productivity*, Journal of the Construction Division, ASCE, Vol. 104, No. CO4, Proc. Paper 114235, December 1978, pp. 447–461.

Mills, D. Q., *The Labor Force and Industrial Relations*, Contractor's Management Handbook, J. O'Brien and R. Zilly, eds., McGraw-Hill, New York, 1971.

Northrup, Herbert R., *Open Shop Construction: A Formidable Force in the Market Place*, Merit Shop Contractor, May 1978.

Tremmer, John P., *Merit Shop Construction . . . Significant Developments*, Merit Shop Contractor, March 1978.

Trends in Open shop Construction, Contractors Mutual Association, December 1975.

CHAPTER 13
Abbett, Robert W., *Engineering Contracts and Specifications*, Fourth Edition, Wiley, New York, 1963, 461 pp.

Acret, James, *Architects and Engineers: Their Professional Responsibilities*, McGraw-Hill, San Francisco, 1977, 499 pp.

Barrie, Donald S. and Boyd C. Paulson, Jr., *Professional Construction Management*, McGraw-Hill, New York, 1978, 453 pp.

Clough, Richard H., *Construction Contracting*, Wiley, New York, 1960, 382 pp.

Dib, Albert, *Forms and Agreements for Architects, Engineers and Contractors*, New York, Clark Boardman and Co., 1976 (looseleaf).

Dunham, Clarence W., Robert D. Young, Joseph T. Bockrath, *Contracts, Specifications, and Law for Engineers*, 3rd ed., McGraw-Hill, New York, 1979, 369 pp.

Engineering News-Record and Conference and Exposition Management Co., Inc., *Construction Claims and Disputes: How to profitably Complete the Job*, Conference, New York and Los Angeles, Engineering News-Record, 1979, 369 pp.

Legal Briefs for Architects, Engineers and Contractors, McGraw-Hill, New York, 1977.

National Academy of Sciences, *Better Contracting for Underground Construction*, Washington D.C., National Technical Information Service, U.S. Department of Commerce, 1974, 143 pp.

U. S. Energy Research and Development Administration: U.S. Army Corps of Engineers Middle East Division, *Corps of Engineers Project Management Overview*, by Capt. Stephen L. Osborn, Construction Earned Value Seminar, Gaithersburg, Md., 1977, 54 pp.

CHAPTER 14
ABC (Associated Builders and Contractors), *PACE- Profits and Advancement Through Construction Education*.

AGC (Associated General Contractors), *Construction Sepervisors Training Program*.

Master Agreement, AGC (Operating Engineers of Northern California), *Apprenticeship Pay Rates*.

University Curriculum:

University of Florida Baccalaureate in Construction.

University of California—Berkeley Civil Engineering Baccalaureate with emphasis in construction.

University of California—Berkeley Civil Engineering Masters in Construction.

San Francisco State University—Extension Masters in Construction.

CHAPTER 15

Catalog of Federal Domestic Assistance, Office of Management and Budget, Washington, D.C. 20503.

Carter, Jimmy, *President's Report on the Economy*, 1979.

Cutting Red Tape on Atlanta Subway Job, Civil Engineering, ASCE, April 1978.

Finally—Feds Set Minority Ground Rules, Construction Contracting, McGraw-Hill and Company, July 1979.

GAO Eyes Slow Rapid Transit Grants, Engineering News Record, August 24, 1978.

Halmos, Eurgene E. Jr., *Government Paper Work Drowns Construction Industry*, The Military Engineers, March-April 1978.

Jacobus, William W., *Lopping Off the Long Lead Times*, Construction Contracting and Equipment, McGraw-Hill, July 1977.

Jacobus, William W., *That Fourth Branch of Government*, Editorial, Construction Methods & Equipment, June 29, 1978.

Koehn, Enno, Fred Selling, Jeffrey Kuchar and Randall Young, Ohio Northern University, *Cost of Delays in Construction*, The Journal of the Construction Division, American Society of Civil Engineers, September 1978.

Seabrook Cooling System Approved Again, Engineering News-Record, August 10, 1978.

Subway Cost High, Construction Contracting, September 1978.

Tatum, C. B., *Managing Nuclear Construction - An Experience Survery*, ASCE Preprint No. 317 9, ASCE Spring Convention 1978, Pittsburgh, Pa., ASCE News, October 1978.

CHAPTER 16

AGC Locals Tear Into Set-Asides, Engineering News-Record, September 29, 1977.

AGC to Challenge Minority Contracting Goals, Engineering News-Record, September 29, 1977.

Bakke—Man Behind Emotional Dispute, San Francisco Chronicle, October 13, 1977.

Black Workers in White Unions - The Discrimination Labor Doesn't Talk About, W. B. Gould, Black Enterprise, October 1977.

Carter Wants 10% Minority Business Requirement Met, Engineering News-Record, September 1, 1977.

Contractors Praise Women Hardhats, Engineering News-Record, February 8, 1979.

Davis-Bacon Needs a Decent Burial, G. Fowler, Nation's Business, March 1979.

High Cout's Historic Day -- Bakke Case Arguments, San Francisco Chronicle, October 13, 1977.

Hiring Goals Set for Women, Minorities, Engineering News-Record, August 25, 1977.

Labor Relations and Social Problems, R. N. Covington, J. G. Getman, J. E. Jones, Bureau of National Affairs, Washington, D.C., 1976.

Minority Contractors Seek a 10% Set-Aside, Engineering News-Record, August 18, 1977.

Negro Occupation - Employment Participation in American Industry, C. F. Peake, American Journal of Economics and Sociology, January 1975.

Public Works Minority Suit Filed, Engineering News-Record, September 29, 1977.

Racial Quota Dispute May Delay Federal Jobs Plan, Palo Alto Times, October 31, 1977.

Southerners Do Battle Against Minority Quotas, Daily Pacific Builder, October 13, 1977.

Suits Challenge Validity of Minority Quotas, Engineering News-Record, October 20, 1977.

The Bakke Minority Admissions Case: A Step Backwards or Healing a Wound, The Daily Californian, October 12, 1977.

The Snags in Trying to Get Minorities Hired, Business Week, December 1973.

U.S. Judge Rules Against Quotas in Construction, Palo Alto Times, November 1, 1977

CHAPTER 17

Barrie, Donald S., and Boyd C. Paulson, Jr., *Professional Construction Management,* McGraw-Hill, New York, 1978.

Fondahl, John W., Boyd C. Paulson, Jr., and Henry W. Parker, *Reducing Costs in Urban Transportation Construction,* Journal of the Construction Division, ASCE, Vol. 105, No. CO1, Proc. Paper 14406, March 1979, pp. 51–63.

Fondahl, John W., and Boyd C. Paulson, Jr., *Development of Research in the Construction of Transportation Facilities: A Study of Needs, Objectives, Resources, and Mechanics for Implementation,* U.S. Department of Transportation, Research and Special Programs Administration, Office of University Research, Report No. DOT/RSPA/DPB-50/79/12, Washington, D.C., August 1979.

Paulson, Boyd C., Jr., *Goals for Basic Research in Construction,* Technical report No. 202, The Construction Institute, Department of Civil Engineering, Stanford University, Stanford, Ca., July 1975.

Paulson Boyd C., Jr., *Goals for Education and Research in Construction,* Journal of the Construction Division, ASCE, Vol. 102, No. CO3, Proc. Paper 12393, September 1976, pp. 479–495.

Paulson, Boyd C., Jr., Research in Japanese Construction Industry, *Journal of the Construction Division,* ASCE, Vol. 106, No. CO1, Proc. Paper 15237, March 1980, pp. 1–16.

Paulson, Boyd C., Jr., John W. Fondahl and Henry W. Parker, *Development of Research in the Construction of Transportation Facilities: A Study of Needs, Objectives, Resources, and Mechanisms for Implementation,* U.S. Department of Transportation, Report No. DOT/RSPD/DPD/ 50-77/14, Washington, D.C., September 1977.

Paulson, Boyd C., Jr., *Transportation Construction in Japan,* Technical Report No. 240, Construction Institute, Stanford University, Stanford, California, 1980.

CHAPTER 18

Batten, Joseph D., *Tough Minded Management,* Third Edition, AMACOM, American Management Associates, New York, 1978.

Drucker, Peter E., *Management,* Harper and Row, New York, 1974.

Harvard Business Review on Management, Harper and Row, New York, 1975.

Lederer, Wm. J. and Eugene Burdick, *The Ugly American* Norton, 1958.

Managers for Tomorrow, Staff of Rohrer, Nibler and Replogle, New American Library, New York, 1978.

McCarthy, John J., *Why Managers Fail,* Mcgraw-Hill, New York, 1978.

Professional Managers Guide, Fourth Edition, Louis A. Allen Associates, Inc. 1969.

Probing the Future, Engineering News-Record Centennial Issue, April 30, 1974.

INDEX

465

Department of Housing and Urban
Development (HUD), U.S., 280,
287, 297, 298
Department of Labor, U.S., 290, 373,
374, 391, 392, 394
Department of Transportaiton (DOT),
U.S., 264, 368, 376
Design-construct (Design-build), 6,
25-28, 141, 142, 143, 148, 151,
155, 163, 164, 165, 171, 172,
178, 179, 182, 303-306, 342,
436, 439, 443, 446. *See also*
Contract(s)
Design-manage, 141, 142, 143, 151,
153, 163-165, 171, 172, 306,
307, 436. *See also* Contract(s)
Developers, 6, 31, 42, 82, 88, 89,
437, 443
Drucker, Peter F., 3, 168

Education and training, 15-16, 335-
359, 452
craft labor training, 336-340
management training, 340-352
problems impacting training, 352-
358
Employer and owner associations,
12, 13, 14, 68, 69, 253-277,
451
history of, 254-266
Energy-conserving homes, 89-90
Engineer, *see* Architect-Engineer
Engineering News-Record, 25, 266,
269, 324, 366, 367, 385, 393,
444
Environmental Protection Agency
(EPA), 73, 366, 367, 368, 370-
372, 377, 378, 382, 383
Equal Employment Opportunity
Commission (EEOC), 374, 386
Estimates:
basic types, 45, 50
bid type, 187, 188, 189
conceptual, 45, 49, 106-110, 135,
138, 140
cost and comparison to estimate
report, 45, 58, 59, 151, 161
residential cost study, 84
Ethnic minorities and women, 17,
385-405, 452
minorities in construction, 385-391
objective analysis of discrimination,
399-405

women in construction, 391-399

Federal Energy Regulatory Commission, 374
Federal Financing and Governmental
Regulation, 16, 86, 87, 97, 100,
101, 361-384, 450, 451
financing agencies, 376-379
positive corrective action, 379-383
project delays due to regulation,
366-368
regulatory agencies, 368-376
regulatory scene, 362-366
Federal Mine Safety and Health
Administration (MSHA), 16
Federal Trade Commission, 73
Financial and construction feasibility,
123, 124
Fluor Corporation, 269

General contractor, 6, 10, 21, 22, 23,
24, 25, 86-88, 92-103, 118-123,
155, 160-162, 173-180, 200-201,
266, 267, 294, 302-303, 313,
314, 324, 326, 436, 437, 439,
442, 443, 445, 446, 447
General Electric Corporation, 166
General management concepts, 31-
38, 435, 436. *See also* Construction projects management concepts
General Services Administration, 31
Governmental regulation, *see* Federal
financing and governmental
regulation
Graham, Dugan, 214
Guarantees, 326-330

Heavy engineering construction, 9,
11, 12, 42, 173-201, 438, 445
contract form, alternate, 180-182
current problems in construction
management, 197-201
contractors staff, 198-199
disputes, 200
labor relations, 199-200
engineer, 182-183
extent of unionization, 238
labor, 183-184
management and organizational
practices and problems, 173-180
managing project, 184-197
bids or proposals, 184-187